Advanced Game Design with HTML5 and JavaScript

Rex van der Spuy

Apress®

Advanced Game Design with HTML5 and JavaScript

ISBN-13 (pbk): 978-1-4842-5800-1

ISBN-13 (electronic): 978-1-4842-5801-8

Managing Director: Welmoed Spahr
Lead Editor: Ben Renow-Clarke
Technical Reviewers: Gaetan Renaudeau and Tom Barker
Editorial Board: Steve Anglin, Mark Beckner, Ewan Buckingham, Gary Cornell, Louise Corrigan,
    Jim DeWolf, Jonathan Gennick, Robert Hutchinson, Michelle Lowman, James Markham,
    Matthew Moodie, Jeff Olson, Jeffrey Pepper, Douglas Pundick, Ben Renow-Clarke,
    Dominic Shakeshaft, Gwenan Spearing, Matt Wade, Steve Weiss
Coordinating Editor: Christine Ricketts
Copy Editor: James A. Compton
Compositor: SPi Global
Indexer: SPi Global
Artist: SPi Global

Distributed to the book trade worldwide by Springer Science+Business Media New York, 233 Spring Street, 6th Floor, New York, NY 10013. Phone 1-800-SPRINGER, fax (201) 348-4505, e-mail orders-ny@springer-sbm.com, or visit www.springeronline.com. Apress Media, LLC is a California LLC and the sole member (owner) is Springer Science + Business Media Finance Inc (SSBM Finance Inc). SSBM Finance Inc is a Delaware corporation.

For information on translations, please e-mail rights@apress.com, or visit www.apress.com.

Apress and friends of ED books may be purchased in bulk for academic, corporate, or promotional use. eBook versions and licenses are also available for most titles. For more information, reference our Special Bulk Sales–eBook Licensing web page at www.apress.com/bulk-sales.

Any source code or other supplementary material referenced by the author in this text is available to readers at www.apress.com. For detailed information about how to locate your book's source code, go to www.apress.com/source-code/.

Contents at a Glance

Contents

About the Author

Rex van der Spuy is a leading expert on video game design and interactive graphics, and he is the author of the popular Foundation and Advanced series of books about how to make video games. Rex has designed games and done interactive interface programming with Agency Interactive (Dallas), Scottish Power (Edinburgh), DC Interact (London), Draught Associates (London), and the Bank of Montreal (Canada). He's also built game engines and interactive interfaces for museum installations for PixelProject (Cape Town, South Africa), and built "Ga," the world's smallest full-featured 2D game engine. He created and taught advanced courses in game design for many years at the Canadian School of India (Bangalore, India). The highlight of his career was programming video games on the Annapurna glacier at 4,500 meters (which, to his delight, was 1,000 meters higher than the maximum permissible operating altitude of his laptop).

About the Technical Reviewers

Gaëtan Renaudeau (aka @greweb) is a web enthusiast studying toward a master's degree in computer science in France. Since 2009, he has worked as a web architect for a web startup company called Zenexity, based in Paris, where he builds web applications, web services, and mobile applications. He enjoys being involved both in front-end (JavaScript, HTML5, CSS3) and server-side (Play framework mainly) development.

For fun you'll find him trying to push the limits of the Web forward, making web experiments, libraries, applications, and games, such as "Drone Tank Arena," his recent WebGL (3D) game made in seven days for the 7DFPS contest. His work is frequently published at `http://greweb.fr/`.

Gaëtan's current hobbies are practicing archery and learning Chinese.

Tom Barker has been a software engineer since the 90s, focusing on the full stack of web development. Currently he is Director of Software Development & Engineering at Comcast, an Adjunct Professor at Philadelphia University, a husband, a father, an amateur power lifter and armchair philosopher. He is obsessed with elegant software solutions, continual improvement, refining process, data analysis, and visualization.

Acknowledgments

All illustrations were created by the author, except the following:

- The game graphics for Treasure Hunter were designed by Lanea Zimmerman from the Tiny 16 tileset: `opengameart.org/content/tiny-16-basic`. Thanks, Lanea!

- For the game Flappy Fairy, the scrolling cloud background was created by the author Downdate (`opengameart.org/content/cartoony-sky`) and the green block by the author GameArtForg (`opengameart.org/content/blocks-set-01`).

- In Chapter 8, the walking elf character was based on graphics designed by Wulax (`opengameart.org/content/lpc-medieval-fantasy-character-sprites`) and forest background graphics were based on tiles designed by Leonard Pabin (`opengameart.org/content/whispers-of-avalon-grassland-tileset`).

Thanks to Sami ur Rahman Qazi for a suggested improvement on how the `gotoAndStop` method handles texture atlas frames of differing sizes in Chapter 4.

And, as always, thanks to the superhuman efforts of Ben Renow-Clarke and Christine Ricketts for the seemingly impossible feat of pulling this whole book together and making it such a fun project to work on.

Introduction

How do you make a video game? This book will show you everything you need to know. You'll learn how to make all kinds of 2D action games by building your own development tools, from scratch, using low-level open-source technologies. All you need is this book, a text editor, a web browser and any old computer. No libraries, no frameworks, no game engines, no black-box mystery code, and no expensive proprietary software or licenses. And you'll be able to publish your games cross-platform to the desktop, mobile devices, and the Web. As you'll soon see, by writing just few hundred lines of code, you'll be well on your way to developing any 2D video game you can imagine.

Sound like fun? It's the best fun there is! Here's what you'll learn:

- New JavaScript tips and tricks, including some that arrived with ES6 (Chapter 1).

- How to draw graphics on the screen and use those graphics to create reusable game components (Chapters 2 and 4).

- How to create a **scene graph** (a parent-child hierarchy for game objects) for maximum flexibility in creating game scenes (Chapter 4).

- How to efficiently load images, sounds, fonts, and other game assets (Chapter 3) and build a loading progress bar (Chapter 11).

- How to animate objects with physics (Chapter 5), and how to created detailed game characters using keyframe animation (Chapter 8).

- Everything you need to know about collision detection (Chapter 7), including the video game designer's "secret black art": vector math (Appendix A).

- Saving and loading game data, running a game in full screen mode (Chapter 1), and scaling a game to any window size (Chapter 11.)

- What is the separating axis theorem (SAT) and why is it useful for games? Find out in Appendix A!

- How to create buttons, add mouse, touch and keyboard interactivity to your games, and learn how to create a drag-and-drop system for game objects (Chapter 6).

- How to add special effects to your games: easy parallax scrolling, particle effects (Chapter 8), and screen shaking (Chapter 11).

- How to play and control sound files and how to generate synthesized sound effects dynamically from pure code (Chapter 9).

- How to build a tweening system and make game objects follow fixed curved paths (Chapter 10).

- How to put all these pieces together to make your own game engine so that you can build games in the quickest, easiest, and most fun way (Chapter 11).

- And you'll learn lots of the most modern coding and game development practices along the way.

This book is a self-contained, classical education in making video games and a compendium of all the important techniques you'll need to know to flourish as a game designer. If you were alone on a desert island with only a solar-powered laptop, a pile of coconuts, and this book, you'd have everything you need to recreate the entire history of 2D video games from Spacewar! to Flappy Bird.

Things You Need to Know

To make the best use of this book you need to have a moderate degree of programming literacy. You should be able to glance at a block of code in whatever programming language you're most familiar with and have a general idea of how it works. You don't need to think of yourself as a "programmer" or some kind of expert. You just need to be able to fumble your way through programming problems with a reasonable degree of confidence. If you enjoy programming, you'll love this book.

The programming code in this book is written in JavaScript. JavaScript belongs to the C family of languages (C, C++, C#, Objective-C, Java, and AS3.0) so if you know any of those languages, you'll be able to use JavaScript with ease. And even if you've never used JavaScript before, Chapter 1 gives you a quick primer.

Have you never done any programming before? Then start with this book's predecessor, *Foundation Game Design with HTML5 and JavaScript*. It will teach you how to program, while you're learning how to make games, and cover everything you need to know to start using this book.

Have you read *Foundation Game Design with HTML5 and JavaScript*? If so, you're well prepared. If you think you might have forgotten a bit, or need a refresher before you start, relax! I've written this book in a very sneaky way. It covers all the basics, from scratch, and squeezes in all the advanced, interesting new stuff all along the way. So, if you've forgotten something, like how to make and render a sprite, don't worry: it's all in here and packed with loads of clever new tricks. Where the Foundation book was all about learning how to program and how to do things in the most *understandable* way, this Advanced book is all about doing things in the *best* and *most exciting* ways. I've written this to be a completely comprehensive book about making games that will reintroduce you to our beloved art form with enlightening and eye-opening new ways of doing things.

How to Read This Book

This is a storybook. You can read it in bed, or on the beach. Just as you would with *Jane Eyre* or *The Lord of the Rings*, start at Chapter 1 and work your way through to the end. Each chapter builds on the techniques and concepts of the previous chapter. But if there are specific techniques you want to know about right away, just jump in at any spot—you should be still be OK.

The only part that's different is Appendix A: "Vectors for Movement and Collision Detection." You can read it at any time. Appendix A is a deep exploration of vector math concepts which are generally relevant to all the other chapters in the book—but also optional. If you want to know all about vectors before you start Chapter 1, go ahead and read the Appendix first. But if you're not really that interested, or just want to keep it for future reference, you can skip it completely.

The Source Code

Most of the content in this book is actually not *in* this book. You'll find it in the source code files that accompany each chapter. You can download the source code from this book's product page at www.apress.com, or at this book's GitHub repository:

https://github.com/kittykatattack/agd

Yes, there's a lot of source code! In fact, there's so much that most of the printed examples in this book only highlight the most significant, vital parts. You're a good enough programmer to understand how those parts fit into the bigger picture. But if you have any doubts, open up the complete working source code and take a look.

All the code in this book is written in pure JavaScript and HTML. It doesn't use any abstraction layers like CoffeeScript, TypeScript, or JQuery.

This book was written during a time when many of the best features of HTML5 for game developers were still experimental and required "vendor prefixes" to work properly on all platforms. I'll mention in the text if it's likely that you'll need to use them, but I'll try to keep them out of the printed code in this book. (For maximum compatibility I've kept them in the source code, but usually tidied them away in a JS polyfill file.) Hopefully, you're reading this book in a happy, future time when these vestigial tails of HTML5's evolution have disappeared. But until then, here are the most common vendor prefixes in current use:

Vendor	CSS Prefix	JavaScript Prefix
Microsoft	-ms-	ms
Mozilla	-moz-	moz
Opera	-o-	o
Chrome, Safari	-webkit-	webkit

▩ **Tip** Writing cross-platform CSS can be particularly difficult, because there are often discrepancies between vendors about how CSS properties are defined. You can make CSS fun again by using a good preprocessor like Sass, and use its Compass extension to create all the vendor-specific code for you automatically.

Also, make sure that you run all the source code in a webserver. Many JavaScript and HTML5 features that we'll be using in this book, like XHR, will only work inside a webserver. A nice cross-platform way to do this is to install Node, which is a marvelous pure JavaScript server. Visit nodejs.org and follow the instructions to install it on your platform. Then install a great little helper utility that runs on top of it, called http-server: (github.com/nodeapps/http-server). It's a fast, mini-webserver that you can run with one line of code. Use the command line to CD to the root directory of your project and type

http-server

Then open any web browser to

http://localhost:8080/

If you have a file in your project directory called `index.html`, you'll see it displayed automatically. If not, just add the name of any other HTML file in your project root.

If you're using a modern code editor like Brackets, Atom, Light Table, or Sublime Text, many of these will launch a webserver for you automatically when you preview an HTML file. Check the documentation of the editor you're using. If you're using a text editor like Vim or Emacs with Unix, you could use `watch` or `fswatch` (for Mac OSX) with `make` to run tasks when files have changed, and then use browser extensions like `tincr` (Chrome) or `Auto Reload` (Firefox) to refresh the browser automatically. There are countless configurations, so experiment a bit and find a workflow that you're comfortable with.

CHAPTER 1

■ ■ ■

Level Up!

This first chapter of *Advanced Game Design with HTML5 and JavaScript* is a fast-paced, jam-packed, stuff-your-face buffet of cool, interesting, new, practical and sometimes delightfully mind-bending techniques that you can start using with your game projects right away. Everything you need to know to take your development skills to the next level is right here in this chapter:

- Sparkling new JavaScript tricks, including everything you need to make games with ES6

- Using configuration objects

- JavaScript's getters and setters

- Promises

- Using classes and composition to make new objects from old ones

- Organizing your projects with modules

- Reading and writing JSON files with XHR

- Displaying full-screen games

- Distributing games with iFrames and minified source code

You can think of this chapter as the modern game developer's boot camp for all the essential skills you need to know to start making games with HTML5 and JavaScript.

You'll be able to apply all of these techniques to your game projects immediately, and they're the core skills that the rest of the chapters of this book are based on. If you've read *Foundation Game Design with HTML5 and JavaScript*, this is a bit like the "secret last chapter" of that book. But if you haven't read that book, and you like to learn things quickly by example, this chapter is a blitzkrieg-style introduction to JavaScript and HTML5, from the ground up.

This chapter is very different from the others in this book in that it's a kind of quick-start start reference guide. Read as much or as little as you need to, in whatever order, and then just jump ahead to Chapter 2 whenever you feel ready.

Some New JavaScript Tricks

This book is written using the latest version of JavaScript, known as ES6 (ECMAScript 6). If you're new to JavaScript, you'll find the language easy to learn because it follows the paradigms of most modern programming languages. If you already know JavaScript, but you learned it before about 2015, then you're in for a surprise. ES6 is almost like a whole new language. But the good news is that it's a nicer, simpler, and friendlier version of JavaScript than the one you know. And, best of all, it's easy to learn, so you'll be able to use it fluently by the time you're done reading this chapter.

In this first section of the chapter, I'm going to introduce all the important concepts you should know about how the language works. You'll learn the most important new features of ES6, and some helpful features of the previous version of JavaScript, ES5, that you might not have been aware of.

▓ **Note**   If you want to write your code in ES6, but still have it work on older platforms, you can use a **transpiler** like Babel or Traceur, which converts as it compiles, in this case from ES6 down to ES5. I recommend you do this. The little extra work it takes to transpile your code is more than made up for by the mental overhead you save by using ES6.

Variables: `let`, `const`, and `var`

Use the keyword let to create a variable:

```
let anyValue = 4;
```

The let keyword gives the variable **block scope**. That means the variable can't be seen outside the pair of curly braces that it's defined in. Here's an example:

```
let say = "hello";
let outer = "An outer variable";

if (say === "hello") {
  let say = "goodbye";

  console.log(say);
  //Displays: "goodbye"

  console.log(outer);
  //Displays: "An outer variable"

  let inner = "An inner variable";
  console.log(inner);
  //Displays: "An inner variable"
}

console.log(say);
//Displays: "hello"

console.log(inner);
//Displays: ReferenceError: inner is not defined
```

A variable defined outside the if statement can be seen inside the if statement. But any variables defined inside the if statement can't be seen outside it. That's what block scope is. The if statement's curly braces define the block in which the variable is visible.

In this example you can see that there are two variables called say. Because they were defined in different blocks, they're different variables. Changing the one inside the if statement doesn't change the one outside the if statement.

You can also create variables using var and const:

- var: This gives the variable **function scope**. That means the variable will be visible anywhere inside a function, even outside the block in which it was created.

- const: This creates a variable that can't change its value. If you try to change its value, you'll get an error. This is helpful if your code depends on a value not being changed by accident. const variables also have block scope.

In almost every case, however, you should just use let. It protects you against making all sorts of little mistakes in your code that can sometimes result in nail-biting debugging sessions.

Variables are your most important JavaScript building block, and you use them with functions to build programs.

Functions

Use functions to run and define blocks of code, to perform calculations, and to return values. JavaScript has two types of functions: **function declarations** and **function expressions**.

In JavaScript you define a **function declaration** this way:

```
function saySomething(value) {
  console.log(value);
}
```

Function declarations are loaded at **compile time**. That means your program knows about them before any other code in your program is run. Even if you define a function right at the end of your program, a function declaration will be loaded in advance before the code at the beginning of your program runs. That lets you call the function before you define it, as in this example:

```
saySomething("Hello from a function statement");
```

//Displays: "Hello from a function statement"

```
function saySomething(value) {
  console.log(value);
}
```

JavaScript also has **function expressions**. You create them using a **fat arrow**, like this:

```
let saySomething = (value) => {
  console.log(value)
};
```

The => symbol represents an arrow pointing to the right, like this: ➔. It's visually saying "use the value in the parenthesis to do some work in the next block of code that I'm pointing to."

You define function expressions in the same way you define a variable, by using let (or var). Each one also needs a semicolon after its closing brace. Unlike a function declaration, a function expression must be defined before you use it, like this:

```
let saySomething = (value) => {
  console.log(value)
};

saySomething("Hello from a function statement");
```

3

That's because function expressions are read at **run-time**. The code reads them in the same order, from top to bottom, that it reads the rest of the code. If you try to call a function expression before it has been defined, you'll get an error.

If you want to write a function that returns a value, use a return statement, like the following:

```
let square = (x) => {
  return x * x;
};

console.log(square(4));
```

//Displays: 16

As a convenience, you can leave out the curly braces, the parentheses around parameters, and the return keyword if your function is just one line of code with one parameter:

```
let square = x => x * x;

console.log(square(4));
```

//Displays: 16

This is a neat, compact and readable way to write functions.

■ **Note**   A nice feature of arrow functions is that they make the scope inside a function the same as the scope outside it. This solves a big problem called **binding** that plagued earlier versions of JavaScript. Briefly, a whole class of quirks you had to work around are no longer issues. (For example, you no longer need to use the old var self = this; trick.) There are a few extreme circumstances where binding is still an issue, but I'll explain those in full when we encounter them.

You can write a function expression without using a fat arrow, as follows:

```
let saySomething = function(value) {
  console.log(value)
};
```

This will work the same way as the previous examples, with one important difference: the function's scope is local to that function, not the surrounding code. That means the value of "this" will be undefined. Here an example that illustrates this difference:

```
let globalScope = () => console.log(this);

globalScope();
```

//Displays: Window...

```
let localScope = function(){
  console.log(this);
};
```

```
localScope();
```

//Displays: undefined

This difference is subtle but important. In most cases I recommend that you use a fat arrow to create a function expression because it's usually more convenient for code inside a function to share the same scope as the code outside of the function. But in some rare situations it's important to isolate the function's scope from the surrounding scope, and I'll introduce those situations when we encounter them.

■ **Note**　If you're using ES5, you'll need to force a function expression to use local scope by adding "use strict" as the function's first line.

```
var localScope = function(){
  "use strict";
  console.log(this);
};
```

The "use strict" statement tells the JavaScript compiler to use ES5's strict mode, which, among other features, locks the function to local scope.

Now that you've got the hang of variables and functions, let's look at how to store and manipulate them using arrays.

Getting Loopy with Arrays

One of the things you do most often as a game designer is loop through arrays. Does the following code look familiar?

```
let planets = ["jupiter", "venus", "saturn", "mars"];
for (let i = 0; i < planets.length; i++) {
  planet = planets[i];
  console.log(planet);
}
```

It displays the name of each planet in the console:

```
jupiter
venus
saturn
mars
```

This is a classic bit of code, which gets a nice update with ES6. Because the i loop index counter is defined using let, it is local to the for loop. That means you can reuse the variable name i in as many other loops as you like, and their values won't conflict.

Our dear old for loop still has its place in JavaScript, and often it's still the best tool for the job. But with ES6 (and ES5) you have some convenient new methods for looping through arrays that can help make your code a lot more readable.

■ **Note**   for loops tend to be highly optimized by JavaScript engines like V8 and SpiderMonkey, and so they are still the safest bet for games where you may be looping through thousands of objects each frame. In this book I'll highlight when it's generally safe to use one of the newer loop methods, and when you should probably play it safe with a for loop. If you're curious about the relative performance differences between different loop methods on the platform you're using, visit jsperf.com and run a few test cases.

Using forEach

ES5 introduced an array function called forEach that specializes in looping through arrays. It makes the use of a loop index counter optional. It also invokes a **callback function** to do its work. (You'll see how callback functions work ahead.) That means you can reuse the same code to transform other arrays if you need to. Here's how to use forEach to display the names of four planets:

```
let planets = ["jupiter", "venus", "saturn", "mars"];

planets.forEach(displayElements);

function displayElements(element) {
  console.log(element);
}
```

The result of this is exactly the same as our first example: the console displays each of the planet names in order.

You can see that forEach's argument is the function called displayElements:

```
planets.forEach(displayElements);
```

This means that the array should send each of its four elements to the displayElements function, one at a time. displayElements is what's known as a **callback function**. It's a function that's being "called back" by another function to do some extra work. It's as if forEach is saying, "Hey! displayElements, come and help me display these planet names!"

The displayElements function has one parameter, which represents the current element that it's processing:

```
function displayElements(element) {
  console.log(element);
}
```

The first time the loop runs, the value of element will be jupiter. The second time, it will be venus, and so on.

The loop will run as many times as there are elements in the array. You don't need a loop counter variable, like i, to keep track of it.

The other advantage is that you can reuse the displayElements function with another array if you want to. Here's how to use it to display the contents of a second array, called mountains:

```
let planets = ["jupiter", "venus", "saturn", "mars"];
let mountains = ["everest", "k2", "kanchanjunga", "lhotse"];

planets.forEach(displayElements);
mountains.forEach(displayElements);

function displayElements(element) {
  console.log(element);
}
```

This will now display all the planets and all the mountains. We only need to write the displayElements function once, and it works perfectly with both arrays.

What about the index counter variable, our dear old friend, i? We can access it by using a second, optional parameter in the callback function. Here's how:

```
let planets = ["jupiter", "venus", "saturn", "mars"];

planets.forEach(displayElements);

function displayElements(element, i) {
  console.log(i + ": " + element);
}
```

Here's the result:

```
0: jupiter
1: venus
2: saturn
3: mars
```

forEach and the other array methods we'll look at ahead also let you use a third optional parameter in the callback function. It's a reference to the array itself. Here's an example:

```
function displayElements (element, i, array) {
  console.log(array.toString());
}
```

This will display the calling array, which in this example would be:

```
jupiter, venus, saturn, mars
```

In most cases you'll probably only need to use a loop once, and not need to separate the forEach method from the callback function. In that case, you can use forEach with an **anonymous callback function**, like this:

```
let planets = ["jupiter", "venus", "saturn", "mars"];

planets.forEach((planet) => {
  console.log(planet);
});
```

It's **anonymous** because the arrow function that does the work doesn't have a name. Applying what you've just learned about formatting ES6 functions, you can write the whole thing very succinctly and readably as follows:

```
planets.forEach(planet => console.log(planet));
```

This simple format will replace most of your for loops when you're working with arrays.

Using a for of Loop

As an alternative to forEach, you can use a for of loop. It lets you easily loop over the values of an array, like this:

```
for (let planet of planets) {
  console.log(planet);
}
```

//Displays: "jupiter", "venus", "saturn", "mars"

A for of loop can be used to create an **array comprehension**. This is a feature that lets you create an array by dynamically processing another array. Here's an example of how to process a list of numbers into another array that stores the squares of those numbers:

```
let numbers = [1, 2, 3, 4, 5];
let squared = [for (x of numbers) x * x];

console.log(squared);
```

//Displays: [1, 4, 9, 16, 25]

Notice that you don't need to use the loop's curly braces. Array comprehensions provide a conveniently compact syntax to use for writing mathematical expressions.

Looping through Objects

JavaScript has many methods that make it just as easy to loop through objects as it is to loop through arrays. If you want to find all the properties of an object, you can use a method called Object.keys(). It returns an array of all object properties as strings. (An object's "key" is its property name.) Here's how to use it:

```
Object.keys(anyObject);
```

This code represents an array of strings that contains all of anyObject's property names.

Here's a practical example of how to use object keys. Imagine that you're making an adventure game, using room objects. Your room objects maintain the state of a room in the game, as well as what the room contains:

```
let room = {
  door: "open",
  light: "on",
  contents: ["carpet", "mouse", "katana"]
};
```

You can see that the room has three properties. You can view these properties as an array of strings with this syntax:

```
console.log(Object.keys(room));
```

Here's what this displays:

```
["door", "light", "contents"]
```

That's interesting, but not useful—yet. Object.keys becomes really useful when you combine it with forEach:

```
Object.keys(room).forEach(key => {
  let value = room[key];
  console.log("key: " + key + ", value: " + value);
});
```

That code will display the following:

```
key: door, value: open
key: light, value: on
key: contents, value: carpet,mouse,katana
```

You can access the property name by key and the property value with value. It will now be really easy to apply any game logic that you need to the room, its state, or its contents.

▓ **Note**   Remember, if you ever need to check whether an object contains a property, use `hasOwnProperty()`, like this:

```
if(room.hasOwnProperty("light")) { ... }
```

If you prefer, you can use a `for of` loop to do the same thing:

```
let roomProperties = Object.keys(room);
for (let key of roomProperties) {
  let value = room[key];
  console.log("key: " + key + ", value: " + value);
}
```

The output is exactly the same as the first example.

But there's another way to do this! We can use a good old-fashioned `for in` loop, which has been part of JavaScript since version 1. Here's how to use it to produce the same output as the previous examples:

```
for(let key in room) {
  let value = room[key];
  console.log("key: " + key + ", value: " + value);
}
```

There are two important things to be aware of if you use a `for in` loop. First, it doesn't loop through the object's keys in any specific order. So if the order is important to you, be aware that you can't rely on it. Second, it will loop through keys that belong both to the object and to its **prototype** (see "Making Objects" later in this chapter for more about object prototypes.) If you need to guarantee that only the object's own properties are being accessed, you must test for that with the object's `hasOwnProperty` method in an additional `if` statement.

```
for(let key in room) {
  if (room.hasOwnProperty(key) {
    let value = room[key];
    console.log("key: " + key + ", value: " + value);
  }
}
```

Neither of these features might be a problem, depending on the object you're loop through and what you want to achieve. But if you want to play it safe, the combination of `Object.keys` and `forEach` is a little more reliable.

Looping through Only Some Array Elements

You might only want to loop through an array until you find one element that you're looking for. When you've found it, the loop should stop checking further. You can do this with a method called `some`. The `some` method will check all the elements in the array until the callback function returns `true`. As soon as `true` is returned, it quits.

Here's an array that lists five musical instruments.

```
let instruments = ["guitar", "piano", "tabla", "ocarina", "tabla"];
```

Do you see that tabla is listed twice? That will help illustrate how the some method works. Now let's use the method to find out if it can find the tabla in this array:

```
instruments.some(find);

function find(instrument) {
  if (instrument === "tabla") {
    console.log("Tabla found!");
    return true;
  } else {
    console.log("No tabla found...");
    return false;
  }
}
```

When this is run, some loops through the array and quits when it finds the first tabla. It quits because the function has returned true. Here's what this bit of code will display in the console:

```
No tabla found...
No tabla found...
Tabla found!
```

It stops as soon as it gets the first true value, and doesn't continue checking. It finds the first tabla element but quits before it finds the second one. This achieves the same effect as using a for loop with a break statement.

You can use some with an anonymous callback, just as you can with forEach. Also, the false condition is optional. That means you can make all this code a lot more compact, this way:

```
let instruments = ["guitar", "piano", "tabla", "ocarina", "tabla"];

let found = instruments.some(instrument => {
  if (instrument === "tabla") {
    return true;
  }
});

if (found) {
  console.log("tabla found!");
}
```

Or, you could write it even more compactly:

```
let found = instruments.some(instrument => instrument === "tabla");
if (found) console.log("tabla found!");
```

The some method can be really useful if you want to find out whether any of the elements in an array pass a certain test. For example, you can use it to check whether any values in an array are greater than 100:

```
let numbers = [11, 43, 9, 112, 64, 15];

let tooBig = numbers.some((number) => {
  //Return true if a number is greater than 100
  return number > 100;
});

console.log(tooBig);
```

This code will display true in the console. Here's a more compact version that does the same thing:

```
let tooBig = numbers.some(number => number > 100);
```

Because the loop contains only one parameter and one statement, you can leave out the parentheses and curly braces. Also, return is implied, so you can leave that out as well.

There's another array method, called every, that's the exact inverse of some; it quits the loop when the function returns false. Use every instead of some if you think quitting on a false value better matches the logic you're testing for.

■ **Note** Remember, if you ever just need to check whether an array contains an element, use indexOf, this way:

```
if (instruments.indexOf("tabla") !== -1) {//Tabla found!}
```

Or you can use findIndex, which you'll learn about in the next section.

Finding Array Elements

The array's some method is actually a feature of ES5, so it's been part of JavaScript for a while. ES6 has a newer array method called find that finds only a specific element in an array. It uses the same syntax as some, but it returns the full value of the element, not just true or false. Here's how to use find:

```
let instruments = ["guitar", "piano", "tabla", "ocarina", "tabla"];

let found = instruments.find(x => x === "tabla");

console.log(found);
```

//Displays: tabla

Just like some, the find method quits and returns true on the first element that matches the condition. If the condition can't be met, find returns undefined.

If you need to know the array index number of an element, use `findIndex`:

```
let index = instruments.findIndex(x => x === "tabla");

console.log(index);
```

//Displays: 2

These are two helpful new methods you can use that make working with arrays a lot more fun. But there are many more!

Mapping an Old Array to a New Array

Sometimes it's useful to make a new array based on the elements in another array. JavaScript lets you do this with a method called `map`. Here's an example of how `map` is used to create a new, improved array of words based on an existing array.

```
let words = ["fun", "boring", "exciting"];

let betterWords = words.map(improveGrammar);

function improveGrammar(word) {
  return word + "ish";
}

console.log(betterWords);
```

This displays the following:

```
funish, boringish, excitingish
```

The `map` method uses the `words` array to create a new array called `betterWords`, which looks like this:

```
["funish", "boringish", "excitingish"]
```

Vastly improved, as I'm sure you can see! The `map` method uses the same syntax as the `some` method, so you can use any of the syntax permutations you saw in the previous section. Here's an ultra-compact way of using `map` that achieves the same result as the preceding code:

```
let betterWords = words.map(x => x + "ish");
```

Smooth!

Using the map method isn't the only way to achieve this result. You can do the same thing using a `for of` loop in an array comprehension:

```
let betterWords = [for (word of words) word + "ish"];
```

The result is exactly the same. The difference is purely stylistic, so use whichever style you prefer.

Filtering Elements from an Array

Use the `filter` method if you want to cut out certain elements of an array. For example, maybe you have a list of numbers and want to copy all the numbers greater than 100 into a new array. You can use the `filter` method to do that, as follows:

```
let numbers = [11, 43, 9, 112, 64, 312, 92];

let bigNumbers = numbers.filter(findBigNumbers);

function findBigNumbers (number) {
  return number > 100;
}

console.log(bigNumbers);
```

You'll now have a new array, called `bigNumbers` that looks like this:

```
[112, 312]
```

Here's the array comprehension version that does the same thing:

```
bigNumbers = [for (number of numbers) if (number > 100) number];
```

The `filter` method has another extremely helpful use—it can easily cut elements out of an array. This is similar to using the array `splice` method, but it results in much simpler code.

The trick to doing this is to assign the new filtered array *back into the original array*. The next example will make this clearer. Here's how to cut out all the numbers greater than 100 from an array:

```
let numbers = [11, 43, 9, 112, 64, 312, 92];

numbers = numbers.filter(x => x < 100);

console.log(numbers);
```

Here's the resulting numbers array. All the numbers greater than 100 have been removed:

```
11,43,9,64,92
```

Did you notice how the filtered numbers array is being copied back into itself?

numbers = numbers.`filter(x => x < 100);`

Sneaky!

Here's the array comprehension version:

```
numbers = [for (number of numbers) if (number < 100) number];
```

What's the advantage to using these techniques over using a `for` loop and `splice` to cut elements out of an array? You don't have to loop backward or manually decrement the loop counter variable by 1 to compensate for the removed element. But don't worry; the technique of removing elements from an array with an old-fashioned `for` loop and `splice` still has its place, as you'll see when you learn about collision detection in Chapter 7.

Reducing Array Elements to a Single Value

The reduce method lets you take all the elements in an array and turn them into one value. For example, you might have some numbers in an array and want to know what their total is. You can do that as follows:

```
let numbers = [73, 19, 2, 144, 43, 7];

let total = numbers.reduce(addNumbersTogether);

function addNumbersTogether(a, b) {
  return a + b;
}

console.log(total);
```

This displays

288

Here's the compact version:

```
total = numbers.reduce((a, b) => a + b);
```

The reduce method works by looping through each element and adding it to its neighbor on the right. In this example, a is the first element and b is the next element. It continues to do this for all the elements in the array until it has reduced everything down to a single value.

reduce has a second optional parameter: the initial value to start with. Here's how you could start at an initial value of 100 in the example we just looked at:

```
total = numbers.reduce((a, b) => a + b, 100);
```

total will now be 388.

There are some surprising uses for reduce. Have you ever had a 2D array that you wished you could flatten into a 1D array? This is easy to accomplish with reduce. Here's how:

```
let numbers2D = [[73, 19],[2, 144],[43, 7]];

let numbers1D = numbers2D.reduce(flattenArray);

function flattenArray(a, b) {
  return a.concat(b);
}

console.log(numbers1D);
```

The numbers1D array that you end up with looks like this:

```
[73, 19, 2, 144, 43, 7]
```

reduce loops through the array from right to left. If you need to loop through the array starting from the end, use reduce's sister method, reduceRight.

You've now got lots of useful new ways of working with elements in arrays. But what if you have some values in an array that you'd like to quickly assign to variables?

Making Variables from Arrays with Destructuring

Imagine that you've got three variables and want to give them initial values. Here's the plain-vanilla way of doing that:

```
let age = 16,
    height = 170,
    grade = 10;
```

A feature called **destructuring** lets you do this in a different way. Destructuring unpacks the values of an array and automatically copies them to variables. Here's how:

```
let statistics = [16, 170, 10];
let [age, height, grade] = statistics;
```

You now have three new variables: age has the value 16, height has the value 170, and grade has the value 10. You can display these using a **template string**, like this:

```
console.log(`Age: ${age} Height: ${height} Grade: ${grade}`);
```

This displays

```
Age: 16 Height: 170 Grade: 10
```

A template string is a way of combining text with variables. It's a replacement for the old JavaScript way of concatenating strings by using plus sign characters. To make a template string, surround the string in **back tick characters** and insert a variable in curly braces, preceded by a dollar sign. Here's the format to use:

```
`This is a template string that displays a ${variableName}`
```

▨ **Note**   Be careful; a back tick character is not a single quotation mark! You might find it on your keyboard sharing the same key as the tilde character: ~

Template strings can span more than one line, and you can also use expressions in place of variables if you want to.

Destructuring can also be used to swap the values of two variables very efficiently. Here's how:

```
let x = 120,
    y = 12;
```

//Swap the values:

```
[x, y] = [y, x];
```

```
console.log(`x: ${x} y: ${y}`);
```

//Displays: x: 12 y: 120

In previous versions of JavaScript you couldn't do this without a third, temporary variable.

Destructuring works for objects as well. Here's how to capture an object's property values as individual variables.

```
let position = {x: 120, y: 12};
let {x, y} = position;
```

You now have two new variables, called x and y. The value of x is 120 and the value of y is 12. You can test this with console.log:

```
console.log(`X: ${x}`);
console.log(`Y: ${y}`);
```

This displays

```
X: 120
Y: 12
```

You can see that destructuring is a convenient way to extract values from arrays and objects. ES6 has some convenient features for working with functions as well.

Function Arguments

ES6 gives you three new flexible ways of assigning function arguments. You can give functions **default** values in the parameters, as shown here:

```
function display(name = "rose", color = "red") {
  console.log(`Name: ${name}, Color: ${color}`);
}

display();
```
//Displays: Name: rose, Color: red

```
display("balloon");
```
//Displays: Name: balloon, Color: red

```
display("computer", "beige");
```
//Displays: Name: computer, Color: beige

Alternatively, you can send any number of arguments to a function and then tell the function to read those arguments as an array. Just add three dots ... (known as the **spread operator**) in front of one of the function's parameters. That parameter will then contain the arguments as an array. It's easiest to understand this with a working example:

```
function displayColors(...colorArray) {
  for (let color of colorArray) console.log(`Color: ${color}`);
}

displayColors("red", "green", "blue")
```

This displays

```
Color: red
Color: green
Color: blue
```

You can also reverse this process. You can use an array as an argument, and tell the function to convert the array values into individual arguments:

```
function displayNumbers(x, y, z) {
  console.log(`X: ${x}, Y: ${y} Z: ${z}`);
}

displayNumbers(...[12, 30, 10]);
```

//Displays: X: 12, Y: 30 Z: 10

These three ways of getting information into functions give you a great deal of flexibility, and you can combine them in dozens of different ways to get yourself out of some tricky corners. But let's look at another, more low-tech way of initializing a function that you might prefer.

Initializing a Function with a Configuration Object

In JavaScript you can initialize a function with any value: numbers, strings, other functions, or object literals. If you initialize the function with a single object literal, you can use the object's property values to configure the function. This is called a **configuration object**, and although it's not a new feature of JavaScript, it's a style of initializing functions that's widely used and useful to know about.

Let's get back to basics for a moment. Here's an example of a simple function that displays three arguments: the name of a sprite, its *x* position, and its *y* position.

```
display("spaceship", 312, 112);

function display(name, x, y) {
  console.log(`name: ${name}, x: ${x}, y: ${y}`);
}
```

Here's what it displays:

```
name: spaceship, x: 312, y: 112
```

Nothing special! You've probably written hundred of functions just like this. It works just fine, but there's one small problem with it. It's not a technical problem, it's a human problem: **readability**. When you're working on a big project with possibly dozens of functions that are similar to this, you might completely forget what this function is supposed to do.

```
display("spaceship", 312, 112);
```

Huh? What is "spaceship" and what do those two numbers refer to? There's no way to tell just by glancing at the function call. You'd have to track down the function definition to remind yourself what those arguments refer to, and the order in which you have to include them.

You can fix both problems using a very helpful technique called a function **configuration object**. Instead of sending multiple arguments to a function, *just send one object*. That single object can contain as many properties as you need to initialize the function. Let's rewrite the previous code with a configuration object so you can see how it works.

In the function's argument, supply an object:

```
displayClearly({name: "spaceship", x: 312, y: 112});
```

Do you see the curly braces surrounding the object? The object has three properties: name, x, and y. The values of those properties are the values that you want to send to the function definition to do its work. This has made the code suddenly much more readable, because it's clear what these values refer to.

You then need to create a function that accepts a single object as parameter. The parameter name in this example is config, but you can give it any name you like:

```
function displayClearly(config) {
  console.log(`name: ${config.name}, x: ${config.x}, y: ${config.y}`);
}
```

Now instead of using the parameter values, the function uses the config object's properties. The result is exactly the same as the previous example, but the code is much more readable. In addition, you're no longer limited to supplying three arguments to the function in any strict order. You can use as many or as few properties as you like. You can also set up the function to assign default values if you leave out any that it might depend on.

You'll see many examples of how to use a configuration object in this book. So far in this chapter we've covered variables, arrays, and functions, so now let's take a closer look JavaScript's object literals.

Getters and Setters

JavaScript object literals have features called **getters** and **setters** that give you fine control over what happens when an object's property values change. A simple example will show you how they work.

Imagine you've got a JavaScript cookie jar. You want to be able to take cookies from the jar and fill the jar up when it's empty. You can create a simple cookie jar object literal to do this:

```
let jar = {
  cookies: 10
};
```

You can now change the number of cookies in the jar with this code:

```
jar.cookies = 8;
jar.cookies = 2;
```

But there's a small problem. The jar shouldn't be able to hold more than ten cookies or fewer than zero cookies. In our current model there's nothing stopping you from filling it with 100 cookies, or assigning a negative number of cookies:

```
jar.cookies = 100;
jar.cookies = -50;
```

We need to be able to keep the range of cookies between 0 and 10. We'll solve this problem in two steps.

The first step is to change the numbers of cookies using *intermediary methods* called **get** and **set**. Here's how they work:

```
let jar = {
  numberOfCookies: 10,
  get cookies() {
    return this.numberOfCookies;
  },
  set cookies(value) {
    this.numberOfCookies = value;
  }
};
```

■ **Note**   Notice that, unlike ordinary object properties, object methods don't use a colon (:) to assign their values.

We've now got a get method called cookies, and a set method, also called cookies. If you want to find out how many cookies are in the jar, use the get method, like this:

```
jar.cookies;
```

This will give you the value of numberOfCookies, which is 10.

It looks like you're reading a property called cookies on the jar object, but you aren't. You're actually calling the get method called cookies. It's a method that looks and behaves like a property.

You can change the number of cookies in the jar like this:

```
jar.cookies = 7;
```

Again, it looks like you're changing a property value, but, again, you aren't. You're calling the set method called cookies.

So far, this is interesting, but the example seems pretty useless. Where the technique becomes helpful is that we now have a convenient way of intercepting a request to read or change a property value. That means we can check to see if the request is valid before we return or change the value.

The next example will clarify this. Remember that our jar doesn't have room for more than 10 cookies. We also shouldn't be allowed to assign a negative number of cookies. Now that we have get and set methods set up, these constraints are easy to implement. The new code is highlighted here:

```
let jar = {
  numberOfCookies: 10,
  get cookies() {
    return this.numberOfCookies;
  },
```

```
  set cookies(value) {
    if (value >= 0 && value <= 10) {
      this.numberOfCookies = value;
    } else {
      throw new Error("Please use a number between 0 and 10");
    }
  }
};
```

Now if you set `cookies` to any number between 0 and 10, it will work just fine:

```
jar.cookies = 3;
```

But if you assign a number less than zero or greater than 10, as with either of these two statements:

```
jar.cookies = 11;
jar.cookies = -2;
```

You'll get this error in the console:

```
Please use a number between 0 and 10
```

As you can see in the preceding code, the `set` method validates the value before assigning it to `numberOfCookies`.

Getters and setters are a very convenient way to use methods that look and behave just like ordinary properties. They can give your code a lot of expressive power. However, use them with caution! In this example they have a focused, limited use: they're only affecting one property, `numberOfCookies`, in a predictable way. But there's nothing stopping you from creating a getter or setter that changes multiple properties on an object at the same time in exotic ways. What if `jar.cookies` didn't just change the `numberOfCookies`, but also updated a score, changed some sprite colors, and also ordered you pizza online? If you don't use getters and setters with care, they can create complex effects that ripple through your code and result in unpredictable bugs that might be very difficult to track down.

Preventing Changes to Properties with `Object.defineProperty`

You might have noticed a small problem with the last example. We were able to limit the number of cookies in the jar by using a getter and setter, but what's to prevent us from simply changing `numberOfCookies` directly, like this?

```
jar.numberOfCookies = 100;
```

Absolutely nothing! If you were writing a complex game in which assigning an invalid number to a property like this could cause your game to freeze or crash, you might want to ensure that this can't happen. ES5 has a method called `Object.defineProperty` which prevents property values from being changed directly like this.

There are two kinds of properties you create with Object.defineProperty. The first is called a **data descriptor**. It's just an ordinary property that you can make writeable or not. Here's how you can use it to create a nonwriteable property called cookies in our jar object:

```
//1. Create a jar object
let jar = {};
```

```
//2. Use Object.defineProperty to create a property called
//cookies in the jar object. Set its value and other properties
//that determine how it can be viewed or changed
```

```
Object.defineProperty(jar, "cookies", {
  value: 10,
  writeable: false,
  enumerable: true,
  configurable: true
});
```

This creates a cookies property in the jar object. (Do you see how it does this using a configuration object?) You can access it this way:

```
jar.cookies
```

Its value is 10. However, because its writeable property is set to false, you can't change it. If you try to change it, you'll get an error message:

```
jar.cookies = 120;
Uncaught TypeError: Cannot assign to read only property 'cookies' of #<Object>
```

jar.cookies has two other properties: enumerable and configurable. If enumerable is true, it means that the cookies property will show up if you use Object.keys to get an array of the jar's properties. If configurable is true, it means that you can change all these properties later; they're not locked down permanently. Setting configurable to true also lets you delete the property from the object if you think you might need to. The writeable, enumerable and configurable properties all default to false unless you explicitly set them to true.

This capability is really powerful. If your game depends on a constant value that should never be changed, deleted, or even accessed, you've now got a way to ensure that.

Object.defineProperty lets you create another kind of property, called an **accessor descriptor**. This is a property that uses a getter and setter to change its value. Here's how to create a cookies property in the jar object with a value that you can change:

```
//1. Create a jar object
let jar = {};
```

```
//2. Use Object.defineProperty to create a property called
//cookies in the jar object. Create a getter and setter so
//that its value can be changed
```

```
Object.defineProperty(jar, "cookies", {
  get() {
    return this.value;
  },
```

```
  set(newValue) {
    this.value = newValue;
  },
  enumerable: true,
  configurable: true
});
```

//3. Give the new property an initial value
```
jar.cookies = 10;
```

The jar now has a cookies property that we can change. It's a got simple getter and setter that can read and write any value you give it. To make this more useful, let's limit the value that you can assign it to a number between 0 and 10. Here's how:

```
Object.defineProperty(jar, "cookies", {
  get() {
    return this.value;
  },
  set(newValue) {
    if (newValue >= 0 && newValue <= 10) {
      this.value = newValue;
    } else {
      throw new Error("Please use a number between 0 and 10");
    }
  },
  enumerable: true,
  configurable: true
});
```

You're now prevented from assigning a number less than 0 or greater than 10. If you try the following:

```
jar.cookies = 25;
```

you'll receive this error message:

```
Please use a number between 0 and 10
```

What's nice about using `Object.defineProperty` to create a getter and setter like this is that we only have one property that can be accessed and changed: `jar.cookies`. There's no way to sneak around the limit by trying to change `jar.numberOfCookies`—that property doesn't exist.

You can define many properties on an object at the same time using a related method called `Object.defineProperties`. Here's a jar object with two properties: `cookies` and `lid`:

```
var jar = {};
Object.defineProperties(jar, {
  "cookies": {
    value: 10,
    writable: true,
    enumerable: true,
    configurable: true
  },
```

```
  "lid": {
    value: "closed",
    writable: false,
    enumerable: true,
    configurable: true
  }
});
```

Just follow this format for as many properties as you need.

There are two more things you should know about Object.defineProperty:

- You can't mix the data descriptor style (the first example) with the accessor descriptor style (the second example). The property that you create with Object.defineProperty has to be either one or the other.

- You can use Object.defineProperty to redefine properties of existing objects, at any time. Object.defineProperty is a reasonably advanced feature of JavaScript that you will probably rarely use in your day-to-day game development. However, it's indispensable if you're building a JavaScript framework or toolset, like a game engine, and you'll see it used in many examples in this book.

Object literals are one of the most important building blocks in a JavaScript program. But before we go any further, let's step back and take a deeper look at how object literals work.

Creating Objects

As simple as they may seem, JavaScript objects hold some surprising hidden complexities. In this section you're going to learn some new and interesting things about objects that will help you use them with greater skill in your games. We'll go on a grand tour from objects to function closures, and we'll end with an introduction to classes.

But first, let's get back to basics. What do we already know about objects?

In JavaScript you create an object like way:

```
let bird = {
  legs: 2,
  eyes: 2,
  speak() {
    console.log("Chirp!");
  }
};
```

■ **Note**   If you've used previous versions of JavaScript, notice that ES6 gives you a streamlined way to write object methods. You no longer need a colon and the function keyword.

Then use dot notation to access the object's properties and methods, as shown here:

```
bird.eyes
```

This equals 2.

Here's how to make the bird speak:

```
bird.speak();
```

This will display

```
Chirp!
```

If you decide to add a new property to the bird, you can do that at any time, with this syntax:

```
bird.canFly = true;
```

The bird now has a new `canFly` property that's been added to it dynamically.

You can also access or change an object's property using array literal notation, like this:

```
bird["eyes"]
```

This notation is the same as using `bird.eyes` and it gives you the same value: 2. Array literal notation highlights the fact that objects are really just arrays that use strings instead of index numbers to access elements. (This type of array is known as **associative**.) Any information that you can store in an array, you can also store in an object, with the convenience of being able to access each bit of information with a name.

Use array literal notation if you want to create properties on objects by using functions or inside loops. For example, here's a function that lets you add a new property on the `bird` object called `wings`:

```
makeNewProperty(bird, "wings", 2);

function makeNewProperty(object, propertyName, value) {
  object[propertyName] = value;
}
```

The `bird` now has a `wings` property with the value 2 that you can access or change like this:

```
bird.wings
```

You'll soon see how we're going to use this feature as a building block for making complex objects.

If you've created an object you like, you can use it to make related objects that are similar. Let's find out how to do that next.

Making Objects from Other Objects

It can often be really useful to create a general object as a template and then make more related objects based on that template. This lets you assign default properties to the template, and all the objects that you make from it can use those properties. In JavaScript there are two important ways to create objects as templates:

- **Composition:** You can create new objects by combining properties from other objects.

- **Classes:** These are functions that return new, customized objects.

■ **Note**   You can also create new objects using **pure prototypal inheritance** with Object.create. I recommend that you don't use this feature unless you're really careful with what you're doing. The problem is that it is often difficult to know which properties belong to the object and which belong to its prototype. See the chapter's source files for detailed working examples of making objects with Object.create and some of the pitfalls you need to be careful of.

Let's start with composition!

Composition

So how does composition work? Just wrap an object in a function, and make the function return that object. Easy!

Here's a simple example. Imagine that you want to create different animals, like cats, birds, and mice. These animals all share similar properties: legs, eyes, and an ability to make sounds. So it makes sense to start with a general animal object as a template, and then use that template as a base to create specific animals.

Here's how you can do that using composition. Create a function called animal. The animal function returns an object that contains properties that could be used by many different kinds of animals.

```
function animal() {
  return {
    legs: 4,
    eyes: 2,
    say: "Huh?",
    speak () {
      console.log(this.say);
    }
  };
}
```

You can now call animal to make specific animals. Here's how to use it to make a cat:

```
var cat = animal();
```

The cat object now has all the properties and methods of the object that animal returned. You can test this by making the cat speak:

```
cat.speak();
```

This displays

```
Huh?
```

That's correct, but it's not what cats usually say. Let's customize the cat's say property, and then call the speak method again:

```
cat.say = "Meow!";
cat.speak();
```

Here's what you'll see displayed in the console:

```
Meow!
```

It works! We customized the say property, but we used the original object's existing speak method:

```
speak() {
  console.log(this.say);
}
```

This is really useful if you're making lots of objects that share similar traits, like animals. It means you don't have to keep creating the same properties over and over again for each new object you make. You just need to make one template object and use its built-in default properties.

For example, here's how easy it is to make a bird and customize it.

```
let bird = animal();
bird.say = "Chirp!";
bird.speak();
```

This displays

```
Chirp!
```

The bird has the same speak method as the original template object, so it can just use that speak method instead of having to create its own from scratch. The bird's own say property, however, has been customized.

By using a function to return an object, we're creating a completely fresh, new object whenever the function is called. We're also taking advantage of a powerful JavaScript feature called **function closure**, which has all kinds of useful and unexpected benefits. You'll find out exactly what closure is and why it's useful in the next section.

Understanding Closure

Let's look at a slightly more complex example where we'll make our animals speak using a list of random words. This will show how you can run some initialization tasks before you create each new object, and also help you understand what function closure is.

In this next example we're going to make our animal object speak a random word. Choosing random numbers is such a common task in games that it's convenient to use a helper function to do it. Here's a useful function called random that will return a random integer within a minimum and maximum range:

```
function random(min, max) {
  return Math.floor(Math.random() * (max - min + 1)) + min;
}
```

To use it, just call the function with the minimum and maximum random values that you want it to choose from. Here's how to create a random number between 1 and 10:

```
random(1, 10)
```

Now let's use this function to create an animal that says a word at random when its speak method is called:

```
function animal() {

  //Declare the variables we'll use in this function
  let newObject, words;

  //A helper function to return a random integer within a minimum and maximum range
  function random(min, max) {
    return Math.floor(Math.random() * (max - min + 1)) + min;
  }

  //The animal's vocabulary
  words = ["Food!", "Sleep!", "Video games!"];

  //A `speak` function that chooses random words
  function speak() {
    let say = words[random(0, 2)];
    console.log(say);
  }

  //Create a `newObject` and add the `speak` function to it
  newObject= {};
  newObject.speak = speak;

  //Return the `newObject`
  return newObject;
}
```

Now let's use this code to create an animal and make it speak:

```
let cat = animal();
cat.speak();
```

This randomly displays "Food!", "Sleep!" or "Video games!" The perfect life!

Here's something really interesting about what's happening. The cat object has only one property: speak. That's because when the newObject object was created, the only property that was attached to it was the speak function:

```
newObject = {};
newObject.speak = speak;
return newObject;
```

But each time the speak method is called, it's quietly using these two other things inside the animal function:

```
words
random
```

The cat object doesn't have access to the words array or the random function and can't change them. All it knows about is its own speak method. The speak method is **public**, and all those other hidden variables and functions are **private**.

The code works this way thanks to the feature of JavaScript functions called **closure**. It means you can use functions to create complex objects and selectively decide which features should be publicly accessible.

This general style of writing JavaScript code like this is sometimes called the **module pattern**. Are you beginning to understand composition now?

Configuring Objects

You'll probably want to initialize your objects with custom properties or values when you create them. You can do that by initializing the animal function with a configuration object. Then copy all the properties from the configuration object onto the new object before you return it. The returned object will contain all of the template's default properties, in addition to any properties or values you set in the configuration object.

That's the idea, but it's much easier to understand with a working example. Let's imagine we want to make a cat and set its say property to "Meow!" We also want to give it a new custom property called fur. Add these properties as a configuration object when you call animal:

```
let cat = animal({
  say: "Meow",
  fur: "black"
});
```

The animal function then takes the config object as a parameter. It creates the newObject template and then copies the config object's properties onto it:

```
function animal(config) {

  //Create the `newObject` template
  var newObject = {
    legs: 4,
    eyes: 2,
    say: "Huh?",
    speak() {
      console.log(this.say);
    }
  };

  //Copy the config object's properties onto the `newObject`.
  //They will override the default properties
  Object.assign(newObject, config);

  //Return the `newObject`
  return newObject;
}
```

The config object contains all the property names and values that we want the new object to have. After the newObject is created, the code uses Object.assign to copy all the properties of the config object onto the newObject:

```
Object.assign(newObject, config);
```

Remember that the cat's config object contains two properties: fur and say. fur is added to the newObject as a new property, and say replaces the newObject's own say property.

What will happen now if we make the cat speak?

```
cat.speak();
```

The console displays:

```
Meow!
```

"Meow!" is the custom say property we provided in the config object. We can confirm all of the cat's properties with the help of Object.keys(), like this:

```
console.log(Object.keys(cat))
```

This displays

```
["legs", "eyes", "say", "speak", "fur"]
```

You can see that it includes all the default properties, the customized say property, and the cat's unique fur property.

What we've actually done is combine two objects, config and newObject, to make a new object: cat. We can take this idea one intriguing step further.

Mixing and Matching Objects

When you start to get the hang of composing objects like this, you'll soon realize that you can make new objects by combining the properties of other objects. In this next example let's use Object.assign to create a cyborg by combining a robot with a human. Haven't you always wanted to do that?

First, let's create two functions that return our robot and human objects:

```
function robot() {
  return {
    skill: "vaporizing death ray"
  };
}

function human() {
  return {
    hobby: "bake cookies"
  };
}
```

Next, we're going to create a cyborg function that combines these two objects into a new one:

```
function cyborg() {

  //Make a `newObject` and add the robot's and human's properties to it
  let newObject = {};
  Object.assign(newObject, robot());
  Object.assign(newObject, human());

  //Create a `speak` function
  //`this` will refer to whatever object this function is attached to
  function speak() {
    console.log("I like to " + this.hobby + " using a " + this.skill);
  }

  //Attach the `speak` function to the `newObject`
  //(Adding the function like this ensures that `this` points to `newObject`)
  newObject.speak = speak;

  //Return the `newObject`
  return newObject;
}
```

Now let's create a cyborg and make it speak:

```
let zxlorb = cyborg();
zxlorb.speak();
```

Here's what it says:

```
I like to bake cookies using a vaporizing death ray
```

Charming! Remember to invite me to the party.

You can see that the newObject contains both the robot's skill and the human's hobby. When it speaks, it uses both of them:

```
function speak() {
  console.log("I like to " + this.hobby + " using a " + this.skill);
}
```

The identifier this will refer to whatever object the function is attached to. This next line attaches it to the newObject:

```
newObject.speak = speak;
```

This means that this.hobby and this.skill in the function will be interpreted as newObject.hobby and newObject.skill.

This general technique of composing new objects from other objects is sometimes called the **mixin pattern**. There are many variations on it.

Now that you know to use a function to create and return an object, let's look at one of the most common and useful ways to do this.

Classes

A special feature of JavaScript is that functions are also objects. To clearly understand how this works and why it's important, let's start with a simple function that returns an object:

```
function animal() {
  let newObject = {};
  newObject.eyes = 2;
  newObject.feet = 4;
  return newObject;
}

let cat = animal();

console.log(cat.eyes);
//Displays: 2
```

This should look familiar, because it's exactly the same pattern we've been using to create objects over the last few pages.

Now let's change this so that the function returns itself as an object. To do that, remove the newObject, get rid of the return statement, and attach the object properties to this:

```
function Animal() {
  this.eyes = 2;
  this.feet = 4;
}
```

this refers to "this function object." Also notice that the A in Animal is capitalized. This is a naming convention that tells you that the function returns itself as an object.

You can now use the new keyword to make new objects with Animal as the prototype. Here's how:

```
let bird = new Animal();

console.log(bird.eyes);
//Displays: 2

bird.legs = 2;

console.log(bird.legs);
//Displays: 2
```

The new keyword triggers the function to return itself as an object.

If you want to give the Animal a method, attach the method to a special property called prototype, like this:

```
Animal.prototype.speak = () => {
  console.log("Huh?");
};
```

Any objects made from `Animal` can now use the speak method, with this syntax:

```
bird.speak();
//Displays: "Huh?"
```

Creating objects like this is extremely useful, but it's also a little awkward. To make this whole process a lot more streamlined, you can use a JavaScript ES6 **class**. A class is just a function that returns itself as an object but includes a whole bunch of extra conveniences. The best way to understand how a class works is to see it in action. Here's a class called `Animal` that does just what you think it should:

```
class Animal {
  constructor() {
    this.legs = 4;
    this.eyes = 2;
    this.say = "Huh?"
  }
  speak() {
    console.log(this.say);
  }
}
```

Create a new instance of the `Animal` class like this:

```
let cat = new Animal();
```

You now have a new `cat` object that works just like all the previous cats in this chapter. You can use, change, or add methods and properties just as you would with any other object.

You can see that the `Animal` class has a special method called `constructor`. Any code you put inside the constructor method runs automatically whenever you create a new object from the class. You can pass it any custom arguments that your new objects might need to initialize themselves. Here's a simplified `Animal` class that lets you customize the `legs` property when you create a new object:

```
class Animal {
  constructor(legs) {
    this.legs = legs;
  }
}

let bird = new Animal(2);

console.log(bird.legs);
//Displays: 2
```

The `bird` passes 2 as the argument of the class, and that value is copied into the `legs` property by the class's `constructor` method.

33

You can also initialize a class with a configuration object. This is really convenient because you can then set lots of custom properties at one time. Here's how to use a configuration object to create a mouse. First, set up the Animal class to accept an object called config as the constructor's argument:

```
class Animal {
  constructor(config) {

    //Set the default properties
    this.legs = 4;
    this.eyes = 2;
    this.say = "Huh?"

    //Use the `config` object's properties
    Object.assign(this, config);
  }
  speak() {
    console.log(this.say);
  }
}
```

When the constructor runs, it first sets the class's default properties and then uses Object.assign to add the config object's properties. If the config object has properties that are the same as those of the class, then the config property values will be used. If the config object contains new properties, they'll be added to the object that the class returns.

Next, use the Animal class to create a new object, like this:

```
let mouse = new Animal({
  say: "Squeak!",
  tail: "curly"
});
```

Notice that the argument is a single object with two properties: say and tail. The mouse object is customizing the say property and adding a new property called tail. It doesn't change eyes or legs, so those remain the same as the default properties in the Animal class.

To confirm that this is working the way you'd expect, make the mouse say something and display its properties:

```
mouse.speak();
//Displays: Squeak!

console.log(Object.keys(mouse));
//Displays: ["legs", "eyes", "say", "tail"]
```

Thanks to classes, you've now got a powerful, easy, and flexible way to make new objects.

▨ **Note**   Remember, just think of a class as a specialized function that returns an object. That means you can also use a class to compose objects using the mixin pattern, and also use closure to hide internal variables that you don't want the rest of the program to access.

Inheritance

A convenient feature of classes is that they make it easy to set up an **inheritance** pattern. Inheritance is a way of establishing a parent class with general properties, and then using that parent to create child classes that implement more specific features. If you use inheritance wisely, you can achieve complex results with minimal code.

To set up a basic inheritance chain, first create a general class with properties and methods that could apply to many different types of objects of a similar kind. Here's a general Monster class that has some general monster-like properties:

```
class Monster {
  constructor(hitPoints, scariness) {
    this.name = "Monster";
    this.hitPoints = hitPoints;
    this.scariness = scariness;
  }
  speak() {
    console.log(
      `I'm a ${this.scariness}
      scary ${this.name}
      with ${this.hitPoints} hit points`
    );
  }
  attack(skill) {
    console.log(`The ${this.name} attacks with ${skill}!`);
  }
}
```

This class is known as the **parent** or **super** class. You can now make a specific monster based on this class by **extending** it. Here's a Dragon class that extends the Monster class:

```
class Dragon extends Monster {
  constructor(hitPoints, scariness, weapon) {

    //call the parent class's constructor with `super`
    super(hitPoints, scariness);
    this.name = "Dragon";
    this.weapon = weapon;
  }
  breatheFire () {
    //Call the parent class's `attack` method
    super.attack(`flaming ${this.weapon}`);
  }
}
```

This Dragon class is a **child** of the Monster class. The Dragon has inherited all the properties of the Monster, but it also includes its own custom ones. It can call methods on the Monster class with the keyword super. Now let's create a new Dragon object and make it speak:

```
let fluffy = new Dragon(10, "somewhat", "furballs");
fluffy.speak();
```

35

This displays

```
I'm a somewhat scary Dragon with 10 hit points
```

You can see that the speak method is in the Monster class, but it's using the Dragon class's properties. What happens when we make fluffy breathe fire?

```
fluffy.breatheFire();
```

This displays:

```
The Dragon attacks with flaming furballs!
```

It's using fluffy's custom furball weapon, along with the Dragon's name and breathFire method, and then sending all of that to the Monster's attack method. I've intentionally made this a little overly complex to help you see how all these bits and pieces can interact. Check the code again and see if you can puzzle through how it all fits together!

The inheritance pattern is sort of the "evil twin sister" of the mixin pattern we looked at when discussing composition. Between inheritance and mixins, you have a great set of tools to make all kinds of objects from bits and pieces of other objects.

■ **Note**   Why is inheritance the evil twin? Because with great power comes great danger. She will tempt you into building fragile chains of dependencies in which a class inherits from a class, which inherits from a class, which inherits from a class, which inherits from a... you get the picture! Don't do it! It's a fairy ring from which you will only emerge 100 years later without any hair left. If you have an inheritance chain more than two levels deep, take a step back and ask yourself if you can possibly achieve what you need using composition. Fluffy the Dragon has shown you how ridiculously easy, and extremely fun, it is to create deeply unnecessary complexity with no trouble at all. Building objects using composition usually leads to more stable systems. That's because it encourages you to build systems where all the component parts are visible at one time. Whereas inheritance tends to be a house of cards, composition is like your bedroom floor: all your toys are just lying there. But if you can use inheritance with care and skill, and you understand the possible risks, go for it. Inheritance lets you get a lot done with very little code.

With classes under our belt, we've now covered all the most important component pieces that go into writing JavaScript programs. But how can you organize small bits of code into big applications?

Modules

JavaScript lets you build complex games and applications from different parts using **modules**. Modules are self-contained bits of code that are isolated from the global scope and other modules. If you want a module to share a property or method with another module, add the export keyword in front of whatever you want the module to share. Other modules can then import those properties and methods if they want to use them. Anything in the module that isn't exported can't be seen or used by any other module, making it essentially private to that module. Let's look at some simple examples that illustrate how modules work.

The most important thing you need to know is that a module is any file with a `.js` extension. It's no more complex than that.

However, you can also define a module inside an HTML file with a `<script>` tag with the type set to `module`:

```
<script type="module">
  //This is the module
</script>
```

You can add a name property if you want to give the module a name:

```
<script type="module" name="nameOfTheModule">
```

This lets you import the module by name into other modules, if you need to.

To load a module that's in a JS file from an HTML landing page, set the `<script>` tag's `src` property, like this:

```
 <script type="module" src="main.js">
```

■ **Note** HTML5 also includes a `<module>` tag to replace the `<script>` tag. The spec for the `<module>` tag was not final at the time of publication, but you should use it if it's available to you.

You can also define a block of code as a module inside a JS file with this syntax:

```
module "theModuleName" {
  //Write the module code here
}
```

You only need to do this if you want to use more than one module in the same file. However, I recommend you just keep things simple and use only one module per file.

■ **Note** You'll find working examples of all the code ahead in the `modules` folder in the chapter's source files. Use it as a sandbox to practice playing around with modules.

Module Basics

Here's a simple example of a module, called firstModule. It's just an ordinary JS file called firstModule.js, with one line of code:

```
//firstModule.js
export let hello = "Hello from the firstModule!";
```

The keyword export means that the hello variable can be used by another module. Now let's use this hello variable in another module, called main. This new module is an ordinary JS file called main.js, which is in the same directory as firstModule. Here's how to import the hello variable from firstModule into main.

```
//main.js
import {hello} from "firstModule";
console.log(hello);
```

This displays

```
Hello from the firstModule!
```

You can see that the import keyword is used to import the property from another module, using this syntax:

```
import {exportedProperty} from "moduleName"
```

The module name is the same as the JavaScript file name, but *without the* .js *extension* (it's implied that it's a JavaScript file.) You can load modules from different directories by including their file path in their name, as shown here:

```
import {exportedProperty} from "path/to/modules/moduleName"
```

JavaScript's module system is very flexible in the ways it lets you import and export properties, so let's take a look at some of the most useful techniques.

Importing a Property as a Different Name

If you don't like the name of the property you're importing from a module, you can change it, with this syntax:

```
import {oldName as newName} from "moduleName";
```

This lets you assign any name to the imported property that you like or that happens to be convenient. It also lets you resolve conflicts between two modules that might be exporting properties that have the same name.

For example, imagine that you've got two modules, firstModule and secondModule. Both modules export a property with the same name: hello.

```
//firstModule.js
export let hello = "Hello from the firstModule!";
```

```
//secondModule.js
export let hello = "Hello from the secondModule!";
```

When the `main` module imports these, it can change the name of the `secondModule`'s `hello` property to anotherHello.

//main.js
```
import {hello} from "firstModule";
import {hello as anotherHello} from "secondModule";

console.log(hello);
console.log(anotherHello);
```

This displays

```
Hello from the firstModule!
Hello from the secondModule!
```

These imported properties are **mutable**, which means they can be changed (mutated). Thus you can change the value of anotherHello after you've imported it, like this:

```
helloTwo = "Huh?"
```

Module Export and Import Options

If you don't want to add export in front of every property to be exported, you can export all your properties in a batch, like this:

//thirdModule.js
```
export {color, shape};

let color = "red",
    shape = "circle";
```

This is convenient because it declutters your code and lets you keep all your export decisions in one spot. It doesn't matter where you put the export statement, so I suggest you put it right at the beginning of the module so that it's easy to find. (export statements are read at *compile time*, just like function declarations, so they'll be read before the rest of the code in the module runs.)

■ **Note** You can also change the exported names:

```
export {color as hue, shape as form};
```

Here's how to import multiple properties from a module:

//main.js
```
import {color, shape} from "thirdModule";
```

You can also import an entire module as an object. The following module stores *x*, *y*, and *z* position values. It exports *x* and *y*, but not *z*:

//fourthModule.js
```
export {x, y};

let x = 10,
    y = 20,
    z = 30;
```

You can then import the whole thing by defining it as a module with the object name position:

//main.js
```
module position from "fourthModule";
console.log(`x: ${position.x}, y: ${position.y}, z: ${position.z}`);
```

This displays

```
x: 10, y: 20, z: undefined
```

Only properties that you've explicitly exported are visible, which is why *z* is "undefined." This is a great way to set module properties as public or private selectively.

This new position object is read-only (**immutable**), so you can't change its *x* and *y* properties directly. If you want to change them, copy them into new variables that are local to the current module.

Module Default Exports

If you have a module that exports only one property, you can make that property the default export. This technique is especially useful if you have a big class that you want to use as a module. Here's a file called Animal.js that has one class for creating animals:

//Animal.js
```
export default class {
  constructor() {
    this.legs = 4;
    this.eyes = 2;
    this.say = "Huh?";
  }
  speak() {
    console.log(this.say);
  }
}
```

Notice that you don't have to give default class a name. Here's how to import it into the main module:

//main.js
```
import Animal from "Animal";

var cat = new Animal();
cat.say = "Meow!";
cat.speak();
```

You can give the class any name you like when you import it; the class name doesn't have to match the module's file name.

Re-exporting Modules

Did you import properties into a module that you want to re-export into another module? You can re-export all of a module's properties, with this syntax:

```
//main.js
export * from "fourthModule";
```

Or selectively export properties, like this:

```
export {x, y} from "fourthModule";
```

Modules and Code Architecture

As you can see, you have a rich variety of ways to load and use modules. JavaScript's module system doesn't prescribe a fixed methodology or best-practice way of using them. It's been designed to be simple to use and think about. Just come up with your own creative system for using modules that feels right based on your personal coding style. You'll see many examples of strategies you can use to organize your code for games in this book.

JavaScript's module system also has a Loader API, which gives you a fine level of control over how modules should load. It lets you conditionally load modules, precompile modules that might be written in other languages like CoffeeScript or TypeScript, and import code built with other module systems like Browserify, RequireJS, or AMD. It's a bit beyond the scope of this book to go into that, so for more details, visit the Module Loader API spec at `wiki.ecmascript.org`.

One feature of the Loader API that you'll want to use regularly, however, is the `System.baseURL` property. It sets a directory that should be used to import modules, like this:

```
System.baseURL = "path/to/modules/";
```

The `baseURL` can be anywhere on your local computer system or an HTTP address on the Internet.

If you have a module that just runs once to perform some kind of initialization tasks, and you don't need to reference by name, you can import and run it with this syntax:

```
import "initializer";
```

Make sure the script is inside an immediate function so that it runs automatically as soon as it loads, like this:

```
//initializer.js
(() => {
  //This code will run as soon as the module loads
})();
```

■ **Note**   If you need to load AMD modules, CommonJS modules, or global scripts into your project, you can use a universal module loader called SystemJS (`github.com/systemjs/systemjs.`) It figures out what kind of module you're trying to load and also automatically fixes any global namespace conflicts.

Working with External Data

In this next section we're going to look at the basics of loading and saving game data. This is an area that can become quite complex, and could, in fact, fill an entire book on its own. Here I'll just show you the most important fundamental techniques you need know to get started quickly, and then point you to some of the many exciting resources you can use to take these skills further.

Loading Data with JSON and XHR

JSON (Java Script Object Notation) is a universal format for structuring data that's cross-platform and language-independent. It's the most widely used modern format for exchanging data between computer systems. It's easy to read, easy to write, and, as you'll soon see, you already know how to use it. XHR (XMLHttpRequest) is a technology used for reading data into and out of programs, and to send data between servers and client computers. In this first example you're going to learn how to use JSON and XHR to read a data file into a game.

Imagine that you're creating a text adventure game. Adventure games use a lot of data, so you've decided it makes sense to keep all that data in a separate file, which you'll load into your main program when it starts up. That way you can easily update your game by changing the easy-to-read data file, and you won't have to touch your messy source code. Your adventure game has many rooms, all of which have their own properties. Each room has an ID number, a description, a list of the things it contains, a list of exits, and a light that can be on or off. Let's create a data file to describe these rooms.

First, create a new text file called `rooms.json`. Then start adding rooms in the JSON format. Here are the first two rooms of your game:

```
{
  "closet": {
    "id": 0,
    "description": "A dark coat closet.",
    "light": {
      "on": false
    },
    "contents": [],
    "exits": ["east"]
  },
  "livingRoom": {
    "id": 1,
    "description": "A living room in an old, rambling house.",
    "light": {
      "on": true
    },
    "contents": ["fireplace", "sofa", "dagger"],
    "exits": ["west", "north", "south"]
  }
}
```

This is your JSON data file. Look familiar? It sure does! It's essentially just a JavaScript object literal. The only difference is that the property names are surrounded by quotation marks. Values can be strings, numbers, arrays, Boolean (true/false) values, nested objects, or null. JSON objects can't contain any JavaScript logic; they're only able to store data. That's really all there is to it; if you understand the basics of JavaScript objects, you understand JSON.

■ **Note** If a JSON property doesn't have a value, set to it to null.

But although it looks like a JavaScript object, it's not a JavaScript object just yet. The next step is to load it into your program with XHR, and then convert it to a real JavaScript object that you can use with your game. Here's how to do that:

```
//Create an empty object to hold the JSON data
let rooms = {};

//Create a new xhr object
let xhr = new XMLHttpRequest();

//Use xhr to load the JSON file
xhr.open("GET", "rooms.json", true);

//Tell xhr that it's a text file
xhr.responseType = 'text';

//Create an `onload` callback function that
//will handle the file loading

xhr.onload = event => {

  //Check to make sure the file has loaded properly.
  //`200` means that the load was successful
  if (xhr.status === 200) {

    //Copy the JSON file into the `rooms` object
    rooms = JSON.parse(xhr.responseText);
    console.log("JSON data loaded");

    //Now you can use this data to view the library contents
    console.log(rooms.livingRoom.contents);

    //Check whether the closet's light is on
    if (rooms.closet.light.on === false) {
      console.log("The closet light is off");
    }
  }
};

//Send the request to load the file
xhr.send();
```

You've now got a JavaScript object called rooms that contains all the data from the JSON file, and that behaves just like any other ordinary object. For example, you could find out the contents of the livingRoom with the following code:

```
rooms.livingRoom.contents
```

The result is an array that looks like this:

```
["fireplace", "sofa", "dagger"]
```

You can now use it or modify it the same way you would any other array. If you want to find out if the closet light is off, you could check with a statement like this:

```
if (rooms.closet.light.on === false) {
  console.log("The closet light is off");
}
```

Using a JSON file like this is a great way to initialize your game and create a clean separation between game data and logic. (You'll learn more about how important it is to do that in Chapter 2.) Now let's take a look at how all this new code works.

How XHR Loads the JSON file

Although XHR can be a complex technology, you'll mostly be using it in a limited way to read files into your game, as we've done here. In this example, we're loading a JSON file, which is just plain text. You can use this same well-trodden procedure for loading any other kind of plain text files into your game.

■ **Note**   XHR can also be used for reading and writing binary files. Binary files, lovingly known as **blobs** (Binary Large OBjectS), are files that store nontext data, like images and sounds.

The first step is to create a new, empty JavaScript object to store the incoming JSON file, and a new XHR object to help load it:

```
let rooms = {};
let xhr = new XMLHttpRequest();
```

The xhr object then initializes a request to load a file with the open method:

```
xhr.open("GET", "rooms.json", true);
```

"GET" is the HTTP transfer system it will use, "rooms.json" is the file you want to load, and true means that we want to use a callback function to handle the file loading. Using a callback handler is important, because it means that our game can continue performing other tasks while it's waiting for the file to load. (This is called **asynchronous** file loading, and it's one of JavaScript's samurai super-powers.) As soon the file has been loaded, the callback handler will run, and we can then do something useful with that file.

onload is an event that's called when the file has loaded. When status is 200, you know that the file has been successfully loaded into the program:

```
xhr.onload = event => {
  if (xhr.status === 200) {
    rooms = JSON.parse(xhr.responseText);
  }
};
```

The loaded JSON text file is stored in the xhr object's responseText property. JSON.parse converts the JSON data into an ordinary JavaScript object called rooms.

The last bit of code you need is the send request that actually starts the process of loading the file:

```
xhr.send();
```

This is all you need to know to get started using JSON or text files in your games, but you'll see many more examples of how to use XHR to load data files of all kinds throughout the rest of this book.

▓ **Note** What about XML? If you know what XML is, and wonder why there's almost no mention of it in this book, that's because it's largely been replaced as a universal data format by JSON. JSON is a simpler, better format for data that's as easy for humans to read and write as it is for computers. And if you're wondering whether XMLHttpRequest has anything to do with XML, it doesn't. It was a technology that came of age when XML was all the rage, and, although you can certainly use it to load XML files, that's not its primary use anymore. If you ever do need to use XML data with your games, load the XML file in the same way as a JSON file, but replace responseText with responseXML. That will let you access the data in an XML tree-like structure.

We'll be using XHR a lot in this book to load all kinds of data into our games.

Saving Game Data with localStorage

Now that we've loaded some data, how do we save it? In this section you'll learn how to store and retrieve data with localStorage. It's a great technology for single-player games that don't require more than about 5 MB of saved data. Don't be fooled by its apparent simplicity—it might be all you need for many kinds of games, and it works as well for web-based games as it does for mobile apps.

Here's how to save some data to localStorage:

```
let anyNumber = 34;
localStorage.setItem("data", anyNumber);
```

setItem saves a property in localStorage called data which has the value of 34. This is called a **key/value pair**, and it's stored like this:

```
"data" : "34"
```

setItem converts all values to strings. See that "34"? It used to be a number, but now it's a string. This is important—more on it ahead!

This key/value pair is now saved in the browser or HTML5 app permanently. If the user quits the app or closes the browser, that data will still be there when they come back, as long as they're accessing it through the same domain as their first visit. That means you can resume a game just by reloading this localStorage data.

■ **Note** If you need to remove some data from local storage, use localStorage.removeItem("keyName"). To clear all the data in one shot, use localStorage.clear().

Now that's it's been saved, here's how you can retrieve it:

```
let loadedData = localStorage.getItem("data");
```

loadedData now has the value "34". Yes, it's still a string! So use parseInt to convert it back to a number, like this:

```
loadedData = parseInt(loadedData);
```

loadedData is now a normal number again: 34.

■ **Note** This general process of storing an object as data is called **serializing**. Reconstructing an object from data is called **deserializing**.

This is how to set and get one item of data in localStorage. But it's likely that in most of your games you'll have quite a few variables that you'll want to store at the same time. For example, you might want to store the player's name, score, and current level. The best way to deal with this is to organize all the data that you want to save into a single object. Here's an example.

```
let gameData = {
  playerName: "Rex",
  levelCompleted: 5,
  score: 84,
  items: ["hat", "umbrella", "katana"]
};
```

You can now save the entire gameData object as a single value.

But there's a catch! Remember that localStorage converts all values into strings. So if we store this object as-is, it will turn all the property names and values into one big string of data, which will make it really difficult to use when we reload it. Fortunately, we can work around that by saving the object in JSON data format and then reconverting it back into a normal object when we load it.

To convert an object into JSON format, use `JSON.stringify`:

```
let gameDataJSON = JSON.stringify(gameData);
```

Then use `localStorage` to save this new JSON version of the object:

```
localStorage.setItem("gameData", gameDataJSON);
```

Now when you retrieve this data, use `JSON.parse` to convert it back into a normal object:

```
loadedData = localStorage.getItem("gameData");
let data = JSON.parse(loadedData);
```

`loadedData` is now an object that contains all of the values you saved. For example, if you want to access the player's array of items, you can do that with this syntax:

```
data.items
```

This will give you the following array:

```
["hat", "umbrella", "katana"]
```

`data` is an ordinary object full of saved data that you can use in your game however you like.

■ **Note**   To simplify this, consider using a wrapper like store.js that takes care of all these details for you. (github.com/marcuswestin/store.js). For more flexibility, take a look at the LocalForage.js library.

More Options for Loading and Saving Game Data

If you want to share game data, store or process it on a server, let multiple users modify it, or be able to access the local file system, you're going to need to use some other technologies. Here's a quick rundown of the universe of options that you should gradually begin to explore.

- The HTML5 File API. Lets you load, edit, create, and save files, including images. Until this API stabilizes, consider using the open-source FileSaver.js library.

- If you're looking for more complex ways to structure local storage data, take a look at the HTML5 FileSystem API (which, confusingly, is completely different from the File API.) It lets you simulate a file system inside local storage. The IndexedDB API is another alternative; it lets you structure, read, and write your data like a conventional database. If you need a cross-platform database that can sync with a server, consider the excellent open-source PouchDB. These options are probably all better suited for data-heavy apps than for games, but you should know that they're out there.

- You can use XHR to send data to a NodeJS web server. The server can then write that data file to the file system or process it in many other ways. NodeJS is a fundamental technology, and you'll find it fun and easy to learn. You can write server scripts in pure JavaScript, so you don't need to learn PHP, Perl, Ruby, or other traditional server-side languages.

- Hey, it's the 21st Century now! If you want to make a real-time multiplayer game, you don't need to configure your own web server or write a single line of back-end code anymore. There are numerous cloud services and app-creation tools that will do this for you. Let them! New ones pop up like mushrooms every day, but, at the time of writing, these were some of the best-established: Parse, Firebase, Backendless, Hoodie, Meteor, Deployd, Nodejitsu, Amazon S3, and remoteStorage. The best of these will let you add multiplayer features to your game within minutes. Some, like Hoodie and Meteor, are free and open source, but others, like Parse and Firebase, are closed-source and commercial. So you'll need to decide whether the convenience of a commercial service is worth being locked into their technology. Considering the amount of work and expertise it would take you to write a multiplayer game server from scratch, it very well might be.

Watch this space! Data storage and sharing is a rapidly changing and volatile field, so keep your eye out for new developments in emerging and current technologies.

Using Promises

Promises are a new feature of JavaScript ES6. They let you sequence tasks in order. Promises don't have a direct application to games, but they are a really neat feature that you'll surely want to use and will probably find some creative uses for.

Let's find out how to use them to display a message once each second. First, create a wait function that uses setTimeout to let you count milliseconds. The wait function will return a Promise object when setTimeout is finished counting:

```
function wait(duration = 0) {
  return new Promise(resolve => setTimeout(resolve, duration));
}
```

Promise has one argument, which is a function with a parameter, called resolve, that is actually a special function built into the Promise object. Whenever the task is finished, call resolve to tell the Promise that the task is done. In this example, resolve will be called when setTimeout is finished counting:

```
setTimeout(resolve, duration);
```

You can now use this wait function to chain a series of tasks together. Use a special function called then to chain each task to the next one. Here's how to display a new message once every second:

```
wait(1000)
  .then(() => console.log("One"))
  .then(() => wait(1000))
  .then(() => console.log("Two"))
  .then(() => wait(1000))
  .then(() => console.log("Three"));
```

After waiting 1000 milliseconds, the code displays "One", "Two" and "Three" in order, with a 1 second delay between them. Without promises, you'd need to set up a complex tangle of if statements to achieve the same result. You now have a very readable and sensible way to sequence a series of tasks.

To help you better understand how promises work, let's look at them from another angle. You could optionally write the wait function like this:

```
function wait(duration = 0) {
  let timer = resolve => {
    setTimeout(resolve, duration);
  }
  let promise = new Promise(timer);
  return promise;
}
```

It does the same thing as the first version, but all the component pieces are little more clearly exposed. You can see that the promise object sets the timer function as its argument:

```
let promise = new Promise(timer);
```

The timer function needs an argument called resolve to make the promise happy:

```
let timer = resolve => {//...
```

setTimeout then calls resolve when it's finished counting milliseconds:

```
setTimeout(resolve, duration);
```

That fulfills the promise, so the wait function can return it:

```
return promise;
```

This is a slightly new way of thinking about sequencing JavaScript events; but, with a bit practice, you'll enjoy using promises.

▓ **Note**   For an insightful approach to structuring games using promises, see Gaëtan Renaudeau's article "Promisify your Games," at http://greweb.me/2014/01/promisify-your-games/.

In this example, resolve is being run as a callback by setTimeout. But you can call resolve when anything important happens in your game, like this:

```
if (theAlienMothershipCrashed) {
  resolve();
}
```

You can also give resolve an argument:

```
resolve("The task is finished");
```

You can now access that argument's information it in the then function, with like syntax:

```
task().then(result => console.log(result));
```

This will display "The task is finished" in the console.

■ **Note** Promises also have a second, optional parameter called `reject`. Its syntax is as follows:

```
return new Promise((resolve, reject) => {
  if (taskFails) {
   reject(new Error("Oh no, the task failed!"));
  }
});
```

Use `reject` if you want to know if a task has failed to complete.

We've now covered most of the essential JavaScript features you need to know to make the best use of this book. But before we finish this chapter, let's look at a few important techniques you can use to package and polish your finished games.

Playing Games Full-Screen

By using HTML5's Fullscreen API you can make browser-based games that fill the entire screen. It's a powerful effect that can make even the simplest games feel really immersive. There are a few little quirks you need to navigate to make sure that your full-screen game looks the same on all platforms, but in this next section we'll look at how to set this up so that your games will look great.

You'll get the best full-screen effect if you design your game with height and width dimensions that match one of these two aspect ratios:

- 16:9. This is the classic wide-screen ratio, and it looks great on a wide range of mobile devices, TVs and computer monitors. Any resolutions between 1136 × 640 and 2048 × 1152 work well on modern hardware.

- 4:3. This the classic "old TV" ratio, and it is widely used by many devices. The range of resolutions for modern hardware is between 1024 × 768 and 4096 × 3072.

The API will only let you enter full-screen mode if the user clicks something in your game, such as a button or a DOM element, like the canvas. You can accommodate this by adding a "play" button to your game that both launches full-screen mode and starts the game. You should also make sure your games have a button that lets players exit full-screen mode. In the following examples, I'll show you how to make an element become full screen, and then how to make a button that lets you toggle full-screen mode on and off.

■ **Note** The Fullscreen API was still very much experimental at the time of writing, so if it's still unstable when you're reading this, consider using a wrapper like screenfull.js to smooth out all the bumps (github.com/sindresorhus/screenfull.js).

Using the Fullscreen API

In the source files you'll find a program called fullScreen.html. It loads an image that you can click on to display full-screen. There are two images you can use for testing this effect. One is 1136 × 640 (16:9) and the other is 1024 × 768 (4:3) (You'll find these in the images folder as ratio_16x9.png and ratio_4x3.png). Figure 1-1 shows what these images look like in the browser before they're clicked, and what they look like on my 16:10 laptop screen when they enter full-screen mode. It also shows the code you need with the CSS :full-screen pseudo-selector to achieve different alignments.

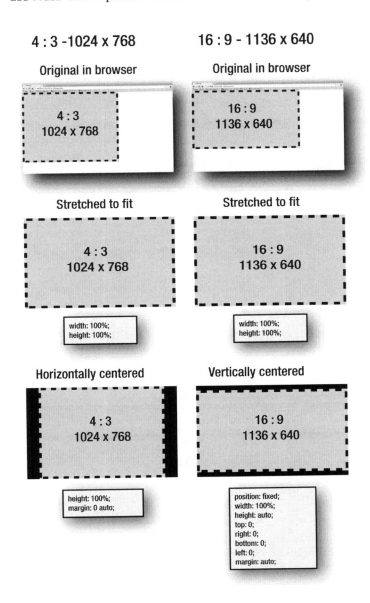

Figure 1-1. *Make an element full-screen*

The most reliable cross-platform way to align a full-screen element is to wrap it in a containing `<div>`, like this:

```
<div id="stage">
  <img src="images/ratio_16x9.png">
</div>
```

Then use `requestFullscreen` on the parent tag to make the browser enter full-screen mode when it's clicked:

```
let stage = document.querySelector("#stage");

stage.addEventListener("mousedown", event => {
  stage.requestFullscreen();
}, false);
```

You'll need some CSS to make sure the contained image aligns properly. First, clear any default margins or paddings:

```
* {
  margin: 0;
  padding: 0;
}
```

Then give the containing `<div>` a height, width, and optional background color:

```
#stage {
  width: 100%;
  height: 100%;
  background-color: black;
}
```

Also make sure that the image is a block element; otherwise it won't align properly:

```
img {
  display: block;
}
```

You can now use the `:fullscreen` pseudo-selector to define what the image should look like when it enters full-screen mode. Because it's actually the containing `stage` tag that's being made full-screen, you use `:fullscreen` on the `stage` element and target its containing `img` tag, like this:

```
#stage:fullscreen img {
  /* align the containing image tag here */
}
```

Now you need to decide how you want to align the image. Here's how to stretch its height and width to fill the entire screen:

```
#stage:fullscreen img {
  width: 100%;
  height: 100%;
}
```

This will distort the image if its aspect ratio doesn't exactly match the screen's. To prevent this, you can instead expand the image to its maximum height or width, and then center it vertically or horizontally. (Refer back to Figure 1-1 to see the effects these next bits of CSS have on the alignment of the full-screen image.)

4:3 games look good when they're centered horizontally:

```
#stage:fullscreen img {
  height: 100%;
  margin: 0 auto;
}
```

16:9 games look good centered vertically. This bit of CSS creates that classic *letterbox* look:

```
#stage:fullscreen img {
  position: fixed;
  width: 100%;
  height: auto;
  top: 0;
  right: 0;
  bottom: 0;
  left: 0;
  margin: auto;
}
```

To exit full-screen mode on web a browser, users will need to press the Esc key. Will they know or remember to do this? You should never assume that, so always add a button to your game that lets users exit full-screen mode. You'll learn how to do this next.

Creating a Full-Screen Toggle Button

You can create a toggle button that launches and closes full-screen mode whenever it's clicked. Figure 1-2 shows an example of a full-screen button with two states, which change automatically depending on the current screen mode. You'll find a full working example in the source files.

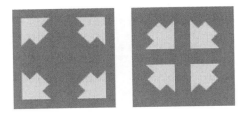

Figure 1-2. The two states of a full-screen toggle button

These states will be represented by two images: makeBig.png and makeSmall.png. To make a button, add a `<div>` tag with the ID **button** inside the containing **stage**.

```
<div id="stage">
  <img src="images/ratio_16x9.png">
  <div id="button"></div>
</div>
```

Add some CSS to set its size and position, and give it a background image that implies "Click to launch full screen."

```
#button {
    position: absolute;
    right: 4%;
    top: 6%;
    width: 96px;
    height: 96px;
    background-image: url(images/makeBig.png);
    cursor: pointer;
}
```

Then add the CSS for its fullscreen state. Reposition the button if you need to, and change the background image to its second state: "Click to exit full screen":

```
#stage:fullscreen #button{
    background-image: url(images/makeSmall.png);
    right: 4%;
    top: 10%;
}
```

Add a **mousedown** listener to the button. Then check to see if there are any elements currently displayed at full screen. If there aren't, make the stage full screen. If full-screen mode is currently active, exit it.

```
let button = document.querySelector("#button");
button.addEventListener(
  "mousedown",
  event => {

    //Is there any element that's currently full screen?
    if (!document.fullscreenElement) {

      //If not, make the stage full screen
      stage.requestFullscreen();
    } else {

      //If there is, exit full screen mode
      document.exitFullscreen();
    }
  },
  false
);
```

This bit of code works by checking `document.fullscreenElement`. It can hold the value of one element that's displayed full-screen. If `fullscreenElement` is `null`, it means there's nothing being displayed full-screen, so you can go ahead and launch it. But if it's not `null`, then full-screen mode must currently be running. In that case, exit the mode using `document.exitFullscreen()`.

■ **Note**   Rather than making your game take over the user's entire screen, it's can be less intrusive just to make the game scale to the maxium available size of the browser window. You'll learn how to do this in Chapter 11.

Minifying Your JS Source Code

Most of your games will probably end up needing a great many dependent JavaScript files. Before you deploy your game, you should combine all these files together into one file, and **minify** it. Here's how:

1. **Concatenate** your code: Copy all your JS files into one single, huge, file that contains all your code. You should add the code in the same order that your `<script>` tags load it.

2. **Minify** your code: When you minify your code, it becomes compressed and optimized. Whitespaces, linebreaks, and comments are removed, and the variable and function names are shortened. Some minifiers will even rewrite your code to inject slight micro-optimizations. The minified code isn't meant to be human-readable or editable, but it's easier for computers to read. You can think of your minified code as a JavaScript binary or blob file. Not only will it load faster, but it will probably run faster too.

Now, instead of launching your game with a dozen dependent `.js` files, your game will just need one single `.min.js` file.

There are many minifiers to choose from, including these: Google's Closure Compiler, UglifyJS, and YUI Compressor, among others. You'll find many online tools to help you use them, and minification-on-save is a common feature in code editors like Sublime Text, Brackets, Atom, and Light Table. Services like Grunt, Gulp, and Yeoman will also do this for you, and you can set file watchers that will concatenate and compress files for you automatically when they change.

Here's the "cave-man-style" Unix command-line way to concatenate and minify your code using UglifyJS:

1. Download and install UglifyJS from `github.com/mishoo/Uglify`. You can either do this using git's `clone` command or install it with node's npm package manager.

2. Navigate to the directory that contains the JavaScript files you want to minify. Use the built-in Unix application called cat to combine all your separate JavaScript files into one big file (concatenate them). Then use the pipe command to send the concatenated file to UglifyJS to be minified:

```
cat file1.js file2.js file3.js file4.js | uglifyjs -o finishedFile.min.js
```

You now have a new file called `finishedFile.min.js` that includes all the code from the other three files, in the order that you listed them.

Why is the tool called Uglify? Just take a look at the minified code it produces to find out!

Using iFrames to Distribute Your Games on the Web

You can use an **iFrame** to run your HTML5 game seamlessly inside any web page. This is a great way to distribute your game over the web that doesn't require users to access or install your source code. Just drop an iFrame that embeds your game into any existing web page.

Here's how to use an iFrame:

1. First make sure that your game is aligned to the exact-top-left corner of an HTML page. It shouldn't have any padding, margins, or borders.

2. Host this HTML page on the Internet somewhere.

3. Use an `<iframe>` tag in any other web page where you want your game to be played. Link to your game and give it the exact same `width` and `height` as your original game. Add a `seamless` attribute and set `allowfullscreen` to `"true"`. The HTML looks like this:

```
<iframe
  src="sourcePage.html"
  seamless
  width="640"
  height="480"
  allowfullscreen="true"
></iframe>
```

The `seamless` attribute removes borders and scrollbars from the iFrame. Setting `allowfullscreen` to `"true"` means that your game's full-screen mode will still work even though it's running through the iFrame. That's pretty amazing, because it means you can distribute and embed your game on any other web site, and as soon a player clicks the full-screen button, they're completely immersed in your game world. iFrames are completely **sandboxed**, which means your JS scripts and CSS won't conflict with the code running on the hosting page, and vice-versa.

This iFrame has now become your finished game. One tag, no files, and no dependencies; it just works. Email it, share it, embed it—you're done! (You'll find a working example of how to use an iFrame to embed another page, including using full-screen mode, in the iFrames folder in the chapter's source files.)

Setting Focus to the iFrame

A small problem that you might encounter when using iFrames is that your game may not have **focus** until content inside the iFrame is clicked. Focus determines which part of the browser window is aware of mouse, touch, or keyboard events. This behavior is browser-specific but, to be safe, you should just assume that your iFrame game won't have focus until the user clicks or touches it. The best way of dealing with this is to require users to start the game with a start button or launch it with a full-screen button. This forces users to click or touch the content before the game starts, and that action will give the iFrame content the focus it needs.

If you want to ensure that the iFrame content gets focus automatically, there's a little trick you can use. Use `setTimeout` to focus the iFrame's `contentWindow` after a delay of 300 milliseconds:

```
setTimeout(setFocus, 300);

function setFocus() {
  let frame = document.querySelector("iframe");
  frame.contentWindow.focus();
}
```

The `contentWindow` is the window object on the iFrame, and calling the `focus` method sets the browser's focus to that content. 300 milliseconds is enough time to allow the iFrame's JS script to load, and that ensures that iFrame is properly instantiated before `focus` is called.

Summary

This chapter is the modern game developer's boot camp for all the essential skills you need in order to start building games with HTML5 and JavaScript from scratch. We've covered everything from new JavaScript ES6 toys and fun coding tricks to JSON, XHR, and deployment strategies, and we've even had some out-of-body experiences with objects, classes, and prototypes. These are all the little goodies that you'll need to know to start building games in the chapters to come.

■ ■ ■

CHAPTER 2

The Canvas Drawing API

The Canvas Drawing API is the HTML5 game designer's best friend. It's easy to use, powerful, available on all platforms, and really fast. Not only that, but learning the Canvas Drawing API gives you an excellent introduction to low-level graphics programming that you'll be able to apply to a wide range of different game design technologies. As a core technology for learning the art of HTML5 game design, it's the best place to start.

■ **Note**   What is an API? It stands for Application Programming Interface. It's just a code library of functions and objects that helps you perform a specific set of tasks, like drawing shapes.

In this chapter you're going to get a quick crash course on drawing lines, shapes, images, and text on the canvas so that you can start using them to make components for your games. We'll look at all the basic ways to make and modify lines and shapes.

Setting Up the Canvas

Before you can start drawing, you need a surface to draw on. Here's how to use JavaScript to create a canvas HTML element and a drawing context.

```
let canvas = document.createElement("canvas");
canvas.setAttribute("width", "256");
canvas.setAttribute("height", "256");
canvas.style.border = "1px dashed black";
document.body.appendChild(canvas);
let ctx = canvas.getContext("2d");
```

What does that code do? It creates a `<canvas>` HTML tag in the body of the HTML document in which looks like this:

```
<canvas id="canvas" width="256" height="256" style="border:1px dashed #000000;"></canvas>
```

You can think of the **canvas** tag as a frame that contains a drawing surface. The width and height of the canvas that this code creates is 256px, and it has a dashed border 1 pixel wide around it.

The actual drawing is done on the canvas's drawing **context**. You can think of the context as a kind of programmable drawing surface that sits inside the canvas frame. The context is represented as **ctx** in this code:

```
let ctx = canvas.getContext("2d");
```

You're now all set up to start drawing lines and shapes.

■ **Note**   You'll notice that most of the image width and height sizes in this book are powers of two, such as 32, 64, 128, and 256. That's because graphics processors have historically handled images in powers-of-two sizes very efficiently: it's the same format in which binary graphics data is stored in computer memory. You'll find that if you keep your game images to a power-of-two size, they'll fit neatly inside most computer and device screens.

Drawing Lines

Let's start with the simplest graphic element: a line. Here's how to draw a line from the top-left corner of our canvas (0, 0) to its middle point (128, 128). The line is black and 3 pixels wide:

```
//1. Set the line style options
ctx.strokeStyle = "black";
ctx.lineWidth = 3;

//2. Draw the line
ctx.beginPath();
ctx.moveTo(0, 0);
ctx.lineTo(128, 128);
ctx.stroke();
```

Figure 2-1 shows what this code creates.

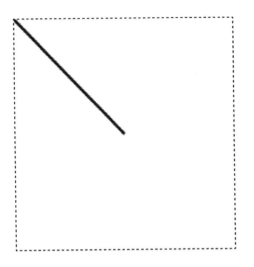

Figure 2-1. *Draw a line on the canvas*

Here's how it works. First, we set the line style options. strokeStyle lets you set the color of the line, which can be any RGB, Hexadecimal, or predefined CSS string color name, like "black".

```
ctx.strokeStyle = "black";
```

Then give it a lineWidth, in pixels. Here's how to assign a line width of 3 pixels:

```
ctx.lineWidth = 3;
```

Now that you've got the line options set, you can start drawing the path with the beginPath method. This is just a way to say "We're going to start drawing the line now!"

```
ctx.beginPath();
```

Set the line's starting *x, y* position with moveTo. 0, 0 is the top-left corner of the canvas. (The *x* and *y* values at the top-left corner are both zero.)

```
ctx.moveTo(0, 0);
```

Then use lineTo to define where you want the line to end. In this case, it will end at an *x, y* position of 128, which is in the middle of the canvas. (Remember, our canvas is 256 by 256 pixels.)

```
ctx.lineTo(128, 128);
```

When you're finished drawing the shape, you can optionally use closePath to automatically connect the last point to the first point in the path.

```
ctx.closePath();
```

Finally, we need to make the line visible, using the `stroke` method. This applies the line color and thickness options that we set earlier, so we can see the line on the canvas:

```
ctx.stroke();
```

These are all the basics you need to know to start using the drawing API. You'll see next how we can connect lines together to form shapes and fill the shapes with color.

Line Caps

You have fine control over what the end of lines look like. The `lineCap` property has three options you can use: `"square"`, `"round"`, and `"butt"`. (Note that the quotes are literal.) You can apply any of these styles with the following syntax:

```
ctx.lineCap = "round";
```

(This line has to come before we call the `ctx.stroke()` method.)

Figure 2-2 shows the effect of these styles. You'll need a line with a fairly thick `lineWidth` to see these differences in your lines.

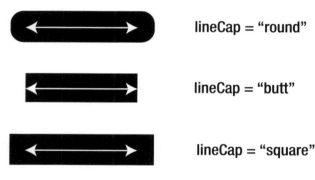

lineCap = "round"

lineCap = "butt"

lineCap = "square"

Figure 2-2. *Line cap styles*

Connecting Lines to Create Shapes

You can join lines together to form shapes, and fill those shapes with color. Use the context's `fillStyle` property to define the color that you want to fill the shape with. Here's an example showing how to set the `fillStyle` to a transparent gray RGBA color:

```
ctx.fillStyle = "rgba(128, 128, 128, 0.5)";
```

The color is a string that describes the color in RGBA, Hexadecimal, or HLSA format. It can also be any of the 140 color words, like "blue" or "red," that are part of the HTML/CSS specification.

After you've drawn the outline of the shape using lines, use the context's `fill` method to fill the shape with the `fillStyle` color:

```
ctx.fill();
```

Here's how to draw a triangle in the center of the canvas and give it a transparent gray fill color. Figure 2-3 shows what you'll see, along with the moveTo and lineTo commands used to create it.

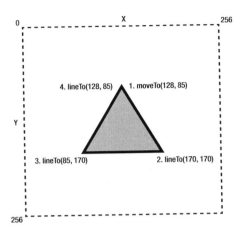

Figure 2-3. *Draw a triangle*

```
//Set the line and fill style options
ctx.strokeStyle = "black";
ctx.lineWidth = 3;
ctx.fillStyle = "rgba(128, 128, 128, 0.5)";
```

```
//Connect lines together to form a triangle in the center of the canvas
ctx.beginPath();
ctx.moveTo(128, 85);
ctx.lineTo(170, 170);
ctx.lineTo(85, 170);
ctx.lineTo(128, 85);
ctx.fill();
ctx.stroke();
```

Drawing Complex Shapes

If your shape is complex, you can define it as a 2D array of points and use a loop to connect those points together. Here's a 2D array of *x, y* point coordinates that forms the same triangle as in the previous example:

```
let triangle = [
  [128, 85],
  [170, 170],
  [85, 170]
];
```

Next, define a function that loops through these points and connects them using moveTo and lineTo. We can keep the code as simple as possible by starting at the last point, and connect the points clockwise from there:

```
function drawPath(shape) {

  //Start drawing from the last point
  let lastPoint = shape.length - 1;
  ctx.moveTo(
    shape[lastPoint][0],
    shape[lastPoint][1]
  );

  //Use a loop to plot each point
  shape.forEach(point => {
    ctx.lineTo(point[0], point[1]);
  });
}
```

You can now use this drawPath function to draw the shape, like this:

```
ctx.beginPath();
drawPath(triangle);
ctx.stroke();
ctx.fill();
```

You can use this technique to make complex shapes with any number of points.

Line Joins

You can style the way lines connect with other lines. Use the lineJoin property to do this. You can set it with any of the following options: "round", "mitre", or "bevel" (again, the quotes are literal). Here's the format to use:

```
ctx.lineJoin = "round";
```

Figure 2-4 shows the effect of these styles.

lineJoin = "round"

lineJoin = "mitre"

lineJoin = "bevel"

Figure 2-4. *Line join styles*

Drawing Squares and Rectangles

Use the rect method to create a rectangle quickly. It has the following format:

```
rect(x, y, width, height)
```

Here's how to make a rectangle with an *x* position of 50, a *y* position of 49, a width of 70, and a height of 90:

```
ctx.rect(50, 40, 70, 90);
```

Set the line and fill style options to draw the rectangle shown in Figure 2-5.

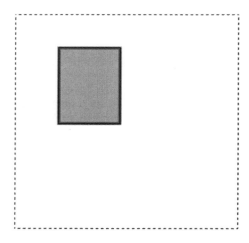

Figure 2-5. *Draw a rectangle*

```
//Set the line and fill style options
ctx.strokeStyle = "black";
ctx.lineWidth = 3;
ctx.fillStyle = "rgba(128, 128, 128, 0.5)";

//Draw the rectangle
ctx.beginPath();
ctx.rect(50, 40, 70, 90);
ctx.stroke();
ctx.fill();
```

Figure 2-6 illustrates how the size and position values are used to draw the rectangle.

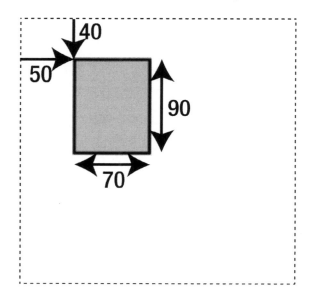

Figure 2-6. *The x, y positions and the width and height of the rectangle*

Alternatively, you can draw a rectangle using the shortcut `strokeRect` and `fillRect` methods. Here's how to use them to draw the rectangle shown in Figure 2-7.

```
ctx.strokeStyle = "black";
ctx.lineWidth = 3;
ctx.fillStyle = "rgba(128, 128, 128, 0.5)";
ctx.strokeRect(110, 170, 100, 50);
ctx.fillRect(110, 170, 100, 50);
```

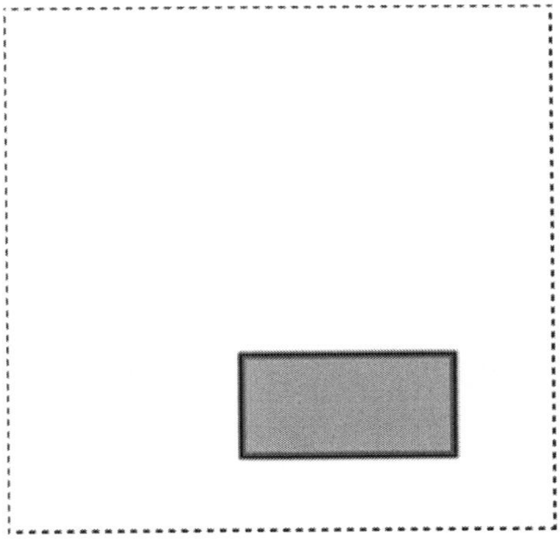

Figure 2-7. Use `strokeRect` and `fillRect` to draw a rectangle

Gradients

You can create two types of gradients: **linear** or **radial**.

To create a linear gradient, use the `createLinearGradient` method. It takes four arguments. The first two arguments are the *x, y* coordinates of the point on the canvas where the gradient should start. The second two arguments are the *x, y* coordinates of the gradient's end point.

```
let gradient = ctx.createLinearGradient(startX, startY, endX, endY);
```

This defines a line on the canvas that the gradient should follow.

Next, you need to add **color stops.** These are the colors that the gradient will blend together to create a smooth transition of tones. The `addColorStop` method does this blending using two arguments. The first is the position on the gradient where the color should start. This can be any number between 0 (the start position) and 1 (the end position). The second argument is the color (which is a string in RGBA, Hexadecimal, or HLSA format, or one of the 140 HTML color words).

Here's how to add two color stops at the very start and the very end for a gradient that transitions from white to black.

```
gradient.addColorStop(0, "white");
gradient.addColorStop(1, "black");
```

(If you wanted to add a third color between these two, you could use any number between 0 and 1. A value of 0.5 would place the third color halfway between 0 and 1.)

Finally, apply the gradient to the context's `fillStyle` to be able to use it to fill shapes:

```
ctx.fillStyle = gradient;
```

Here's an example of a gradient that fills a square. The gradient starts at the square's top-left corner and ends at its bottom-right corner. Figure 2-8 shows what this code produces.

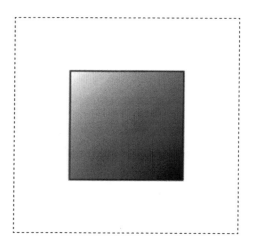

Figure 2-8. *Fill a shape with a linear gradient*

```
//Set the line style options
ctx.strokeStyle = "black";
ctx.lineWidth = 3;

//Create a linear gradient
let gradient = ctx.createLinearGradient(64, 64, 192, 192);
gradient.addColorStop(0, "white");
gradient.addColorStop(1, "black");
ctx.fillStyle = gradient;

//Draw the rectangle
ctx.beginPath();
ctx.rect(64, 64, 128, 128);
ctx.stroke();
ctx.fill();
```

In this example I made the gradient slightly bigger than the square, just to soften the effect slightly:

```
ctx.createLinearGradient(64, 64, 192, 192)
```

Only the first three quarters of the area of the gradient that fall inside the rectangle will be visible.

To create a radial gradient, use the `createRadialGradient` method. It takes six arguments: the first three are the position of the gradient's starting circle and its size, and the last three are the position of the gradient's ending circle and its size.

```
let gradient = ctx.createRadialGradient(x, y, startCircleSize, x, y, endCircleSize);
```

The start and end circles usually have the same position; only their sizes will be different.

You can add color stops and apply the gradient to the canvas `fillStyle` in exactly the same way you do with a linear gradient. Here's how to fill the square with a radial gradient:

```
let gradient = ctx.createRadialGradient(128, 128, 10, 128, 128, 96);
```

The gradient's *x* and *y* positions of 128 match the center point of the square in the canvas. Figure 2-9 shows the result.

Figure 2-9. *A radial gradient*

Drawing Circles and Arcs

Use the arc method to draw a circle. Here are the arguments to use:

```
arc(centerX, centerY, circleRadius, startAngle, endAngle, false)
```

The center *x, y* coordinates are the point on the canvas that determines the circle's center point. The `circleRadius` is a number, in pixels, that determines the circle's radius (half its width). The `startAngle` and `endAngle` are numbers in radians that determine how complete the circle is. For a full circle, use a `startAngle` of 0 and an `endAngle` of 6.28 (2 * `Math.PI`). (The `startAngle`'s 0 position is at the circle's 3 o'clock position.) The last argument, `false`, indicates that the circle should be drawn clockwise from the `startAngle`.

Here's how to draw a full circle with a radius of 64 pixels in the center of the canvas:

```
ctx.arc(128, 128, 64, 0, 2*Math.PI, false)
```

Figure 2-10 shows a circle with a gradient fill, which you can create with the code that follows.

Figure 2-10. *Draw a circle with a gradient*

//Set the line style options
```
ctx.strokeStyle = "black";
ctx.lineWidth = 3;
```

//Create a radial gradient
```
let gradient = ctx.createRadialGradient(96, 96, 12, 128, 128, 96);
gradient.addColorStop(0, "white");
gradient.addColorStop(1, "black");
ctx.fillStyle = gradient;
```

//Draw the circle
```
ctx.beginPath();
ctx.arc(128, 128, 64, 0, 2*Math.PI, false);
ctx.stroke();
ctx.fill();
```

■ **Note**   Radians are a unit of measurement for circles that is a bit easier to work with, mathematically, than degrees. 1 radian is the measurement you get when you take the radius and wrap it around the edge of the circle. 3.14 radians equal half a circle, which, very conveniently, equals PI (3.14). A full circle is 6.28 radians (PI * 2). There are about 57.3 degrees in one radian, and if you ever need to convert degrees to radians, or radians to degrees, use these formulas:

radians = degrees * (Math.PI / 180)

degrees = radians * (180 / Math.PI)

You can use the same arc method to easily draw an arc (an incomplete circle). Just use a startAngle greater than 0 and an endAngle less than 6.28 (2 * Math.PI). Here's some code that draws an arc from 3.14 to 5 radians, as shown in Figure 2-11.

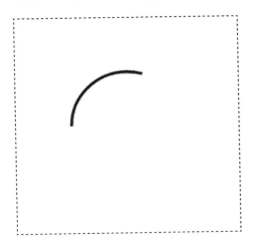

Figure 2-11. *Draw an arc*

```
ctx.strokeStyle = "black";
ctx.lineWidth = 3;
ctx.beginPath();
ctx.arc(128, 128, 64, 3.14, 5, false)
ctx.stroke();
```

If you need to shape your curved line, the Canvas Drawing API has some advanced options, which we'll look at next.

Drawing Curved Lines

There are two types of curved lines you can draw: **quadratic curves** and **Bezier curves**.

To draw a quadratic curve, use the quadraticCurveTo method. The following code produces the curve you can see in Figure 2-12.

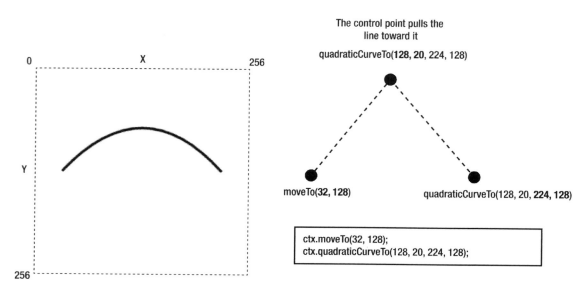

Figure 2-12. *A quadratic curve*

```
ctx.moveTo(32, 128);
ctx.quadraticCurveTo(128, 20, 224, 128);
```

The code alone is confusing, but it's easy to understand with the help of the diagram. The first thing you need to do is use moveTo to define the starting point of the line, near the left-center edge of the canvas:

```
ctx.moveTo(32, 128);
```

Then use the quadraticCurveTo method to define the curve. The first two arguments define what's known as the **control point**. You can think of the control point as a kind of invisible gravity point that pulls the line toward it. In this example, the control point is near the center top of the canvas, at an *x* position of 128 and a *y* position of 20, which I've highlighted here:

```
ctx.quadraticCurveTo(128, 20, 224, 128);
```

The last two arguments are the line's end point, near the right-center edge of the canvas:

```
ctx.quadraticCurveTo(128, 20, 224, 128);
```

Can you see in Figure 2-12 how these points work together to create the curve?
Bezier curves are similar but add a second control point:

```
bezierCurveTo(control1X, control1Y, control2X, control2Y, endX, endY);
```

Again, it's really difficult to understand how this works until you see a clear example. Figure 2-13 shows a Bezier curve and the four points used to create it. Here's the code that produces that curve:

```
ctx.moveTo(32, 128);
ctx.bezierCurveTo(32, 20, 224, 20, 224, 128);
```

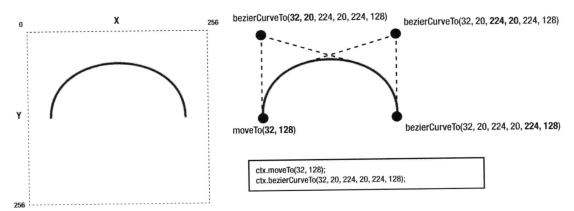

Figure 2-13. *A Bezier curve*

Compare the code with the diagram, and try making a few of your own curves until you get a feel for how quadratic and Bezier curves work. If you close the lines so that they start and end at the same point, you'll produce a shape that you can fill with a color or gradient.

Shadows

You can add drop shadows to any line or shape with the shadowColor, shadowOffsetX, shadowOffsetY, and shadowBlur properties. Figure 2-14 shows a circle with a light gray, slightly blurred drop shadow. Here's the code that produced it:

```
ctx.shadowColor = "rgba(128, 128, 128, 0.9)";
ctx.shadowOffsetX = 10;
ctx.shadowOffsetY = 10;
ctx.shadowBlur = 10;
```

Figure 2-14. *Add a shadow*

The shadowColor can be any RGBA (as in this example), HSLA, hexadecimal, or CSS color string name. Giving shadows a transparent alpha color (in this case 0.9) makes them look more realistic when they overlay another object. shadowOffsetX and shadowOffsetY determine by how many pixels the shadow is offset from the shape. shadowBlur is the number of pixels by which the shadow should be blurred, to produce a diffuse light effect. Play around with these values until you find a combination that produces an effect you like. Drop shadows like this will work with any shape, line, or text.

Rotation

The Canvas Drawing API doesn't have any built-in method to rotate individual shapes. Instead, you have to rotate the whole canvas, draw the shape onto that rotated state, and then rotate the whole canvas back again. You also have to shift the drawing context's coordinate space. Its *x, y* 0,0 point is usually the canvas's very top-left corner, and you need to reposition it to the shape's center point.

At first, this seems like it's a crazy, bad feature of the Canvas Drawing API. Actually, it's one of the best features. As you'll see in Chapter 4, it allows you to create very useful nested parent-child relationships between shapes with minimal code. But it does require a bit of a conceptual leap at first to understand what's going on. So let's find out how canvas rotation works.

The following code draws a rotated square, which is illustrated in Figure 2-15. I'll walk you through exactly how it works after the code listing.

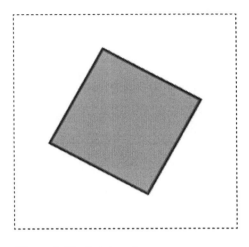

Figure 2-15. *Rotate a shape*

```
//Set the line and fill style options
ctx.strokeStyle = "black";
ctx.lineWidth = 3;
ctx.fillStyle = "rgba(128, 128, 128, 0.5)";

//Save the current state of the drawing context before it's rotated
ctx.save();

//Shift the drawing context's 0,0 point from the canvas's top left
//corner to the center of the canvas. This will be the
//square's center point
ctx.translate(128, 128);

//Rotate the drawing context's coordinate system 0.5 radians
ctx.rotate(0.5);

//Draw the square from -64 x and -64 y. That will mean its center
//point will be at exactly 0, which is also the center of the
//context's coordinate system
ctx.beginPath();
ctx.rect(-64, -64, 128, 128);
ctx.stroke();
ctx.fill();

//Restore the drawing context to
//its original position and rotation
ctx.restore();
```

Here's how all this works. The first thing we need to do is save the drawing context's current state:

```
ctx.save();
```

This is important, because we're going to move and rotate the entire context. The save method lets us remember its original state so that we can restore it after we've finished drawing the rotated square.

Next, the translate method shifts the context's coordinate space so that position 0,0 is at the same point on the canvas as the center of the square that we're going to draw. The center of the square will have an *x* position of 128 and a *y* position of 128, to place it at the very center of the canvas.

```
ctx.translate(128, 128);
```

This means that instead of the context's 0,0 position being the top-left corner of the canvas, the 0,0 position has been shifted 128 pixels to the right and 128 pixels down. This will be the square's center point. Figure 2-16 shows how this coordinate space has been shifted. If we don't do this, the square won't appear to rotate around its center. Instead, it will appear to rotate around the canvas's top-left corner. Figure 2-16 shows the invisible but important effect that this bit of code has on the context's coordinate position.

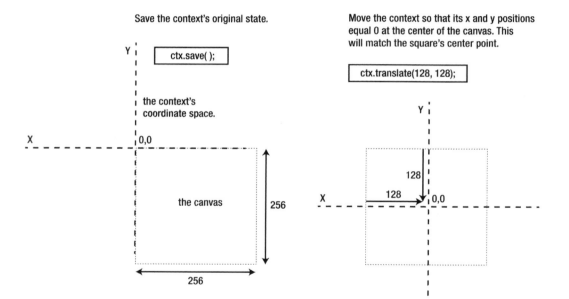

Figure 2-16. *Move the context's coordinate space to the center of the canvas*

Next, the context's entire coordinate space is rotated by 0.5 radians (28.6 degrees) clockwise, as shown in Figure 2-17.

```
ctx.rotate(0.5);
```

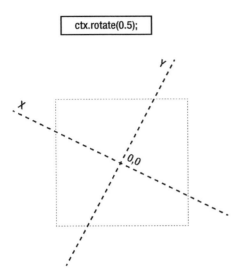

Figure 2-17. *Rotate the context*

The next step is to draw the rectangle *around* the context's center point. This means you have to offset the rectangle by negative half its width, and half its height. The square is 128 pixels wide and high, so its *x*, *y* positions both need to be –64.

```
ctx.beginPath();
ctx.rect(-64, -64, 128, 128);
ctx.stroke();
ctx.fill();
```

This is confusing, so take a look at Figure 2-18 to clarify what's happening. You can see that after the rectangle has been drawn, its center point falls on the context's 0,0 point. And because the context has been rotated, the square also appears to be rotated.

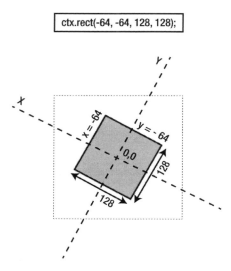

Figure 2-18. *Draw the square so that it's centered over the context's rotated center point*

Finally, we have to restore the context to the state it was in before it was moved and rotated:

```
ctx.restore();
```

This lets us add more lines or shapes after this point, and they won't be rotated. Figure 2-19 shows what this final restored state looks like.

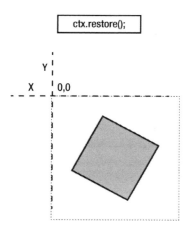

Figure 2-19. *Restore the canvas's state to normal after the rotation*

Even though the context's position and rotation have been restored, the square remains in the same place where it was drawn.

This whole process of saving the context's state, moving it, rotating it, drawing the shape onto it, and restoring it occurs in a fraction of a millisecond. It's really fast and you'll never see it happen. But you must follow this same procedure, step by step, for each line or shape that you want to rotate. It's tedious to do manually like this, but in Chapter 4 you'll learn how to automate the process with a custom shape sprite and render function that will do it all for you.

Scale

The canvas context's `scale` method lets you easily scale the shape's width and height along the *x/y* axis:

```
ctx.scale(scaleX, scaleY)
```

`scaleX` and `scaleY` values between 0 and 1 will scale the shape between 0 and 100% of its original size. That means if you set `scaleX` and `scaleY` to 0.5, the shape will be scaled to 50% of its size.

```
ctx.scale(0.5, 0.5)
```

Setting those values to 2 will scale the shape to 200% of its original size:

```
ctx.scale(2, 2)
```

Finally, `scaleX` and `scaleY` values of 1 will set the shape to its original scale.

Figure 2-20 shows the effect these scale values have on the rotated rectangle from the previous example.

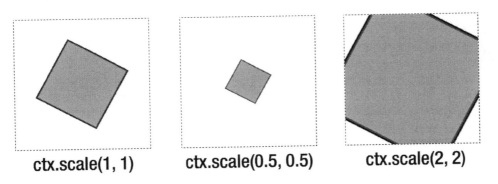

Figure 2-20. *Scale a shape relative to its size*

Just as with rotation, it's not actually the shape that's scaled, but the *entire canvas context*. The amount by which the context is scaled is relative to the width and height of the line, shape, or image that it's currently drawing. So just as you do with rotation, you need to insert the `scale` method between a pair of `save` and `restore` methods so that the context will return to its original scale for the next thing it needs to draw. Although this might seem like a clunky way to do things at first, in Chapter 4 you'll see how it lets us easily create a complex nested sprite hierarchy using very little code.

Making Things Transparent

There are two ways of making canvas elements transparent. The first, which you've seen in earlier examples, is to use RGBA or HSLA colors and set the alpha value (the last number in the arguments) to a number less than 1. (**Alpha** is the graphic design term for transparency.) The second way is to use the canvas context's globalAlpha property. globalAlpha is similar to rotate in that it affects the entire canvas. That means to apply transparency to only one shape, you need to sandwich globalAlpha between save and restore, as in this example:

```
ctx.save();
ctx.globalAlpha = 0.5;

//...Draw your line or shape...

ctx.restore();
```

globalAlpha takes a number between 0 (completely transparent) and 1 (completely opaque). Figure 2-21 shows a square and circle that have been made semitransparent using globalAlpha. Following the figure is the code that does this.

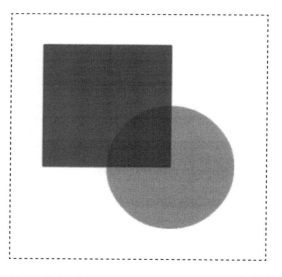

Figure 2-21. *Make shapes transparent with* globalAlpha

```
//Set the fill style options
ctx.fillStyle = "black";

//Draw the rectangle
ctx.save();
ctx.beginPath();
ctx.globalAlpha = 0.6;
```

```
ctx.rect(32, 32, 128, 128);
ctx.fill();
ctx.restore();

//Draw the circle
ctx.save();
ctx.beginPath();
ctx.globalAlpha = 0.3;
ctx.arc(160, 160, 64, 0, Math.PI * 2, false)
ctx.fill();
ctx.restore();
```

Using Blend Modes

The canvas context has a `globalCompositeOperation` property that lets you assign a **blend mode** to the canvas. The blend mode determines how the colors of two intersecting shapes or images should be combined. There are 16 blend modes to choose from, and they have the same effect as the same blend modes in image editing software like Photoshop. Depending on the blend mode you use and the colors of the shapes or images, the effect can be anything from a subtle transparency to a dramatic color inversion.

Here's how to use `globalCompositeOperation` to set the blend mode to "`multiply`":

```
ctx.globalCompositeOperation = "multiply";
```

Multiply is a contrast effect which uses a formula to multiply the values of overlapping colors to produce a new color. Figure 2-22 illustrates the effect this has with a blue circle overlapping a red square.

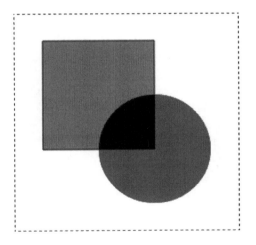

Figure 2-22. *Use blend modes to combine the colors of overlapping images*

Here's the code that creates this effect:

```
//Set the blend mode
ctx.globalCompositeOperation = "multiply";

//Draw the rectangle
ctx.save();
ctx.fillStyle = "red";
ctx.beginPath();
ctx.rect(32, 32, 128, 128);
ctx.fill();
ctx.restore();

//Draw the circle
ctx.save();
ctx.fillStyle = "blue";
ctx.beginPath();
ctx.arc(160, 160, 64, 0, Math.PI*2, false)
ctx.fill();
ctx.restore();
```

Here's a full list of the blend modes you can use, and the effect each produces:

- **No blending**: "normal"
- **Contrast**: "soft-light", "hard-light", "overlay"
- **Lighten**: "lighten", "color-dodge", "screen"
- **Darken**: "darken", "color-burn", "multiply"
- **Color inversion**: "difference", "exclusion"
- **Complex blending**: "hue", "saturation", "color", "luminosity"

The best way to appreciate the effects is to open your favorite image editor, and observe the effect these blend modes have on two overlapping images. The effect will be the same using the Canvas Drawing API. For much more detail on how these blend modes work, the W3C's surprisingly readable specification is a great place to start: dev.w3.org/fxtf/compositing-1.

Compositing Effects

The globalCompositeOperation method also gives you detailed control over how overlapping shapes should be combined. There are twelve **Porter-Duff operations** you can apply to shapes; they cover all possible ways that two shapes can be combined.

■ **Note**   The Porter-Duff operations are named after Thomas Porter and Tom Duff, who developed them while working on visual effects for the *Star Wars* films.

You apply the Porter-Duff operations in the same way you apply blend modes:

```
ctx.globalCompositeOperation = "source-over";
```

Figure 2-23 illustrates the effects of these operations, and the table that follows (Table 2-1) is a brief description of what each one does.

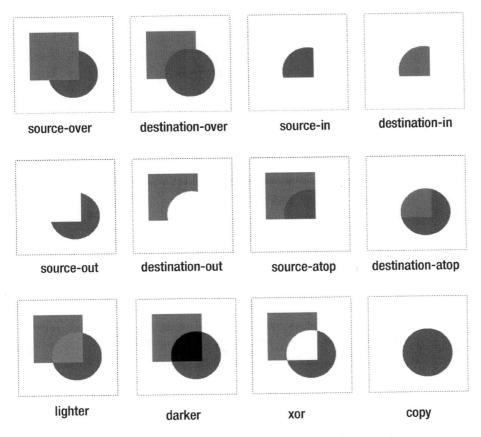

Figure 2-23. Use composite operations to merge and mask overlapping shapes

Table 2-1. *Canvas compositing effects*

Composite operation	What it does
"source-over"	Draws the first shape in front of the second shape.
"destination-over"	Draws the second shape in front of the first shape.
"source-in"	Draws the second shape only on the section of the canvas where the two shapes overlap.
"destination-in"	Draws the first shape only on the section of the canvas where the two shapes overlap.
"source-out"	Draws the second shape where it doesn't overlap the first shape.
"destination-out"	Draws the first shape where it doesn't overlap the second shape.
"source-atop"	Draws the second shape only where it overlaps the first shape.
"destination-atop"	Draws the first shape only where it overlaps the second shape.
"lighter"	Blends the overlapping shape colors together into a lighter shade.
"darker"	Blends the overlapping shape colors together into a darker shade.
"xor"	Makes the overlapping region transparent.
"copy"	Draws only the second shape.

So far in this chapter we've just been working with shapes, but you can apply all of these techniques just as easily to images. We'll do that next.

Filling Shapes with Images

You can fill a shape with an image using the createPattern method. Figure 2-24 shows how an image of a cat has been used to fill a square.

Figure 2-24. *Fill a shape with an image*

This is done by drawing a square with the rect method and then using an image pattern as the fillStyle. The border is optional; if you don't use a stroke style, there won't be a border around the image. Also, if you want the top-left corner of the image to match up with the top-left corner of the shape, you need to offset the canvas to match the shape's *x, y* position. This is the same trick that we used in the previous example, but it's a bit simpler because we're not rotating anything. I'll explain how this works ahead. Here's the code that produces this effect:

```
//Load an image
let catImage = new Image();
catImage.addEventListener("load", loadHandler, false);
catImage.src = "images/cat.png";

//The loadHandler is called when the image has loaded
function loadHandler() {

  //Set the line style options
  ctx.strokeStyle = "black";
  ctx.lineWidth = 3;

  //Draw the rectangle
  ctx.beginPath();
  ctx.rect(64, 64, 128, 128);

  //Set the pattern to the image, and the fillStyle to the pattern
  let pattern = ctx.createPattern(catImage, "no-repeat");
  ctx.fillStyle = pattern;

  //Offset the canvas to match the rectangle's x and y position,
  //then start the image fill from that point
  ctx.save();
  ctx.translate(64, 64);
  ctx.stroke();
  ctx.fill();
  ctx.restore();
}
```

When the image is loaded, the code draws and positions the rectangle on the canvas, as you've seen in previous examples:

```
ctx.beginPath();
ctx.rect(64, 64, 128, 128);
```

It then uses the createPattern method to turn the loaded image into a shape image pattern. That pattern is stored in a variable called pattern, and then assigned to the fillStyle:

```
let pattern = ctx.createPattern(catImage, "no-repeat");
ctx.fillStyle = pattern;
```

In this example the pattern is set to "no-repeat". If you wanted a shape with a textured pattern effect, you could use a smaller image, and make it repeat across the shape's area. In addition to "no-repeat", there are three other options you can use: "repeat" blankets the surface of the shape with unbroken repeating images of the pattern, and "repeat-x" and "repeat-y" just repeat the image along one axis.

In this example I wanted the top-left corner of the cat image to be aligned exactly with that of the rectangle. To achieve this, I needed to offset the canvas with the translate method before setting the fillStyle. The amount of offset matches the *x*, *y* position of the rectangle (64 by 64 pixels):

```
ctx.save();
ctx.translate(64, 64);
ctx.stroke();
ctx.fill();
ctx.restore();
```

The save and restore methods are used to reset the canvas back to its original position after the shape is filled with the image. If you don't do this, the image will be drawn from the canvas's top-left corner at position 0, 0, not the shape's top-left corner at 64, 64.

Drawing an Image

If you just want to display an image on the canvas, the context's drawImage method is an easy way to do that. After the image has loaded, use ctx.drawImage to define the image name, its *x* position, and its *y* position:

```
ctx.drawImage(imageObject, xPosition, yPosition);
```

Here's how to preload an image of a cat and use drawImage to display it centered in the canvas. Figure 2-25 shows the result.

```
//Load an image
let catImage = new Image();
catImage.addEventListener("load", loadHandler, false);
catImage.src = "images/cat.png";

//The loadHandler is called when the image has loaded
function loadHandler() {
  ctx.drawImage(catImage, 64, 64);
}
```

Figure 2-25. *Draw an image onto the canvas*

Using drawImage like this is quick and easy. But for most game projects you'll want to use a slightly more flexible way to display game images, which we'll come to in a minute. First, a quick detour into masking.

Masking an Image

A **mask** is like a window frame. Any images under the mask will be visible only inside the mask's area. Parts of the image that go beyond the mask's area won't be displayed outside the frame. You can turn any shape into a mask by using the clip method.

Figure 2-26 shows our cat image masked by a circle shape.

Figure 2-26. *Use the clip method to turn a shape into a mask*

To create a mask, draw a shape and then use the clip method instead of stroke or fill. Anything in the image or shape drawn after clip will be masked. Here's the code that produced the image in Figure 2-26:

```
//Draw the circle as a mask
ctx.beginPath();
ctx.arc(128, 128, 64, 0, Math.PI * 2, false);
ctx.clip();

//Draw the image
ctx.drawImage(catImage, 64, 64);
```

You can mask shapes just as easily as you can mask images.

Blitting an Image onto the Canvas

It can be very useful to display only part of an image on the canvas. This capability is important for making games because it means you can store all your game characters and objects in single image file, called a **tileset** or **sprite sheet**. You then construct your game world by selectively displaying and positioning on the canvas only those parts of the tileset that you need. This is a really fast and resource-efficient way to render game graphics, called **blitting**.

In this next example we're going to take a tileset with many game characters and objects, and display only one of those objects: a rocket ship. Figure 2-27 shows the tileset that we're going to load, and the single rocket ship that we're going to display on the canvas.

tileset.png   The canvas

Figure 2-27. *Copy part of an image file onto the canvas*

The code uses the drawImage method to accomplish this. drawImage needs to know the origin *x* and *y* positions of the section of the tileset we want to display, as well as its height and width. It then needs to know the destination *x*, *y*, width, and height values to draw the image on the canvas.

```
//Load the tileset image
let tileset = new Image();
tileset.addEventListener("load", loadHandler, false);
tileset.src = "images/tileset.png";
```

```
//The loadHandler is called when the image has loaded
function loadHandler() {
  ctx.drawImage(
    tileset,        //The image file
    192, 128,       //The source x and y position
    64, 64,         //The source height and width
    96, 96,         //The destination x and y position
    64, 64          //The destination height and width
  );
}
```

The tileset.png image file is 384 by 384 pixels. The image of the rocket ship is 192 pixels to the right and 128 pixels down. This is its *x*, *y* source position. Its width and height are both 64 pixels, so those are its source width and height values. The rocket ship is drawn onto the canvas at an *x*, *y* position of 96, using its same width and height values (64). These are its destination values. Figure 2-28 shows how this code works by selecting the correct section of the tileset and displaying it on the canvas.

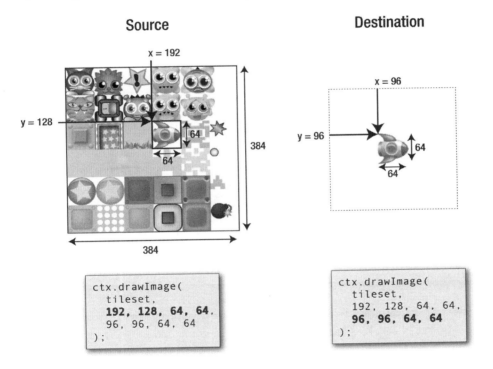

Figure 2-28. *How blitting works*

If you're new to blitting, play around with some of these numbers in the working example in the source files, and you'll quickly see how easy it is to display the images you want, in whatever size and location, anywhere on the canvas.

■ **Note**   The word "blit" comes from "bit-block transfer," which is an early computer graphics term for this technique.

We've covered lines, shapes, and images, so let's now take a look the final piece of the canvas puzzle: text.

Text

The Canvas Drawing API has few useful properties and methods to help you plot text. The next example shows how you can use them to display the words "Hello world!" in bold, red letters, centered in the middle of the canvas. Figure 2-29 shows what the following code produces.

Figure 2-29.   *Display text on the canvas*

```
//Create a text string defines the content you want to display
let content = "Hello World!";

//Assign the font to the canvas context.
//The first value is the font size, followed by the names of the
//font families that should be tried:
//1st choice, fall-back font, and system font fall-back
ctx.font = "24px 'Rockwell Extra Bold', 'Futura', sans-serif";

//Set the font color to red
ctx.fillStyle = "red";
```

```
//Figure out the width and height of the text
let width = ctx.measureText(content).width,
    height = ctx.measureText("M").width;
```

```
//Set the text's x/y registration point to its top left corner
ctx.textBaseline = "top";
```

```
//Use `fillText` to Draw the text in the center of the canvas
ctx.fillText(
    content,                              //The text string
    canvas.width / 2 - width / 2,         //The x position
    canvas.height / 2 - height / 2        //The y position
);
```

Let's find out how this works.

The canvas context's font property lets you define the font size and family using this format:

```
ctx.font = "24px 'Rockwell Extra Bold', 'Futura', sans-serif";
```

The first font family name, Rockwell Extra Bold, is the primary font that should be used. If it's not available for some reason, the font property will fall back on Futura. If Futura isn't available either, the good old system font sans-serif will be used.

■ **Note**   In this example I've used some reliable web-safe fonts that are found on all modern web browsers. (You can find a list of web-safe fonts at cssfontstack.com.) In Chapter 3 you'll learn how to preload a custom font from a file using the CSS @font-face rule.

You can use the measureText method to figure out the width of the text, in pixels, like this:

```
width = ctx.measureText(content).width
```

You need to do this *after* the font style has been assigned so that the text is measured correctly based on the size of the letters for that particular font and point size.

The measureText method doesn't have a matching *height* property to tell you the height of the text in pixels. Instead, you can use this very reliable and widely used hack to figure it out: measure the width of an uppercase M:

```
height = ctx.measureText("M").width
```

Amazingly, this perfectly matches the pixel height of text for most fonts.

You also need to define a **text baseline**, which tells the context where the text's x, y 0 point should be. To define the x/y point at the text's top-left corner, set textBaseline to "top":

```
ctx.textBaseline = "top";
```

Setting the top-left corner as the text's x, y registration point keeps coordinates for text consistent with our coordinates for circles, rectangles, and images.

Other values you could assign to textBaseline besides "top" are "hanging", "middle", "alphabetic", "ideographic", and "bottom". These are more options than you'll probably ever need, but Figure 2-30 illustrates how each affects the alignment of text.

Figure 2-30. *Text baseline options*

fillText is used to draw the string content at a specific x/y position. If you know the width and height of the text, you can use fillText to center the text in the canvas, as follows:

```
ctx.fillText(
  content,                        //The text string
  canvas.width / 2 - width / 2,   //The x position
  canvas.height / 2 - height / 2  //The y position
);
```

These are the most important techniques you need to know for displaying text on the canvas.

Summary

You now know the basics of drawing lines and shapes with the Canvas Drawing API. The Canvas Drawing API is one of the most useful and flexible tools a game designer needs to know. It has a simple elegance that allows you to create a lot of complexity with minimal code. Modern JavaScript runtime systems (like web browsers) hardware-accelerate canvas drawing calls with the GPU, so you'll find that that, even in comparison with WebGL, canvas drawing is plenty fast enough for most 2D action games.

The drawing API is fairly low-level, which means that that you need to build some helper functions and objects if you want to create lots of shapes quickly and easily to use in games. But before we learn how to do that, let's first find out how to efficiently load images, fonts, data files and other useful assets into our games.

CHAPTER 3

■ ■ ■

Working with Game Assets

A game's **assets** are all the font, sound, data, and image files that it uses. In this chapter you'll learn how to implement a clear strategy for loading and managing assets so that they're easy to use in your game code. You'll learn how to create an `assets` object that stores references to all your game assets, and also how to create a preloader that loads assets and initializes your game when everything is ready.

Games usually use a lot of images, and managing all those images can often be a big headache if you're not smart about how you handle them. But fear not! Game designers have a secret weapon for working with images: the **texture atlas**. In the second half of this chapter you'll learn all about what a texture atlas is and how you can use it to help manage game images in a fun and efficient way.

The *assets* Object

In this chapter we're going to build a utility object called `assets` that will be a central storehouse for all the game's assets: images, sounds, fonts, ordinary JSON data, and JSON data that represents a texture atlas. Before exploring how the `assets` object works, let's see how you'll be able to use it in your finished programs.

The `assets` object has a `load` method that accepts one argument: an array of filename strings. List all the names of the file you want to load, with their complete path, in the array. The `load` method returns a `Promise` when all the assets have loaded, so you can then call a `setup` function to initialize your game when everything is ready. Here's how you might use the `assets.load` method to load an image, font, and JSON file, and then run a setup function:

```
assets.load([
  "images/cat.png",
  "fonts/puzzler.otf",
  "json/data.json"
]).then(() => setup());

function setup() {
  //Initialize the game
}
```

The setup function will run only after all the assets have loaded. You'll then be able to access any asset, such as the set of images, anywhere in your main game program, with this syntax:

```
let anyImage = assets["images/cat.png"];
```

You'll only need to build this asset loader once, and you can then use it in any game project. It's also designed to be easily customizable so that you can use it to load any kind of file your game might need.

■ **Note**   In this chapter you'll learn how to configure the asset loader so that it's also ready for loading sound files. But we're not actually going write the code that loads sounds until Chapter 9, where we'll fill in those details as we discuss the WebAudio API.

Let's look at the all code that makes this work.

Building the *assets* Object

The assets object looks complex at first, but as you'll soon see it's just a collection of individual components that all follow the same pattern. Here's the entire code listing that you can use as a reference. Don't worry about understanding all of it now; I'll walk you through how it works in the pages ahead, including how it interprets a JSON texture atlas:

```
export let assets = {

  //Properties to help track the assets being loaded
  toLoad: 0,
  loaded: 0,

  //File extensions for different types of assets
  imageExtensions: ["png", "jpg", "gif"],
  fontExtensions: ["ttf", "otf", "ttc", "woff"],
  jsonExtensions: ["json"],
  audioExtensions: ["mp3", "ogg", "wav", "webm"],

  //The `load` method creates and loads all the assets. Use it like this:
  //`assets.load(["images/anyImage.png", "fonts/anyFont.otf"]);`
  load(sources) {

    //The `load` method will return a Promise when everything has loaded
    return new Promise(resolve => {

      //The `loadHandler` counts the number of assets loaded, compares
      //it to the total number of assets that need to be loaded, and
      //resolves the Promise when everything has loaded
      let loadHandler = () => {
        this.loaded += 1;
        console.log(this.loaded);

        //Check whether everything has loaded
        if (this.toLoad === this.loaded) {
```

```
    //Reset `toLoad` and `loaded` to `0` so you can use them
    //to load more assets later if you need to
    this.toLoad = 0;
    this.loaded = 0;
    console.log("Assets finished loading");

    //Resolve the promise
    resolve();
  }
};

//Display a console message to confirm that the assets are
//being loaded
console.log("Loading assets...");

//Find the number of files that need to be loaded
this.toLoad = sources.length;

//Loop through all the source filenames and find out how
//they should be interpreted
sources.forEach(source => {

  //Find the file extension of the asset
  let extension = source.split(".").pop();

  //Load images that have file extensions that match
  //the imageExtensions array
  if (this.imageExtensions.indexOf(extension) !== -1) {
    this.loadImage(source, loadHandler);
  }

  //Load fonts
  else if (this.fontExtensions.indexOf(extension) !== -1) {
    this.loadFont(source, loadHandler);
  }

  //Load JSON files
  else if (this.jsonExtensions.indexOf(extension) !== -1) {
    this.loadJson(source, loadHandler);
  }

  //Load audio files
  else if (this.audioExtensions.indexOf(extension) !== -1) {
    this.loadSound(source, loadHandler);

  //Display a message if a file type isn't recognized
  else {
    console.log("File type not recognized: " + source);
  }
  });
 });
},
```

```
loadImage(source, loadHandler) {

  //Create a new image and call the `loadHandler` when the image
  //file has loaded
  let image = new Image();
  image.addEventListener("load", loadHandler, false);

  //Assign the image as a property of the `assets` object so
  //you can access it like this: `assets["path/imageName.png"]`
  this[source] = image;

  //Set the image's `src` property to start loading the image
  image.src = source;
},

loadFont(source, loadHandler) {

  //Use the font's filename as the `fontFamily` name
  let fontFamily = source.split("/").pop().split(".")[0];

  //Append an `@afont-face` style rule to the head of the HTML document
  let newStyle = document.createElement("style");
  let fontFace
    = "@font-face {font-family: '" + fontFamily + "'; src: url('" + source + "');}";
  newStyle.appendChild(document.createTextNode(fontFace));
  document.head.appendChild(newStyle);

  //Tell the `loadHandler` we're loading a font
  loadHandler();
},

loadJson(source, loadHandler) {
  //Create a new `xhr` object and an object to store the file
  let xhr = new XMLHttpRequest();

  //Use xhr to load the JSON file
  xhr.open("GET", source, true);

  //Tell xhr that it's a text file
  xhr.responseType = "text";

  //Create an `onload` callback function that
  //will handle the file loading
  xhr.onload = event => {

    //Check to make sure the file has loaded properly
    if (xhr.status === 200) {

      //Convert the JSON data file into an ordinary object
      let file = JSON.parse(xhr.responseText);
```

```
    //Get the filename
    file.name = source;

    //Assign the file as a property of the assets object so
    //you can access it like this: `assets["file.json"]`
    this[file.name] = file;

    //Texture atlas support:
    //If the JSON file has a `frames` property then
    //it's in Texture Packer format
    if (file.frames) {

      //Create the tileset frames
      this.createTilesetFrames(file, source, loadHandler);
    } else {

      //Alert the load handler that the file has loaded
      loadHandler();
    }
  }
};

  //Send the request to load the file
  xhr.send();
},

createTilesetFrames(file, source, loadHandler) {

  //Get the tileset image's file path
  let baseUrl = source.replace(/[^\/]*$/, "");

  //Use the `baseUrl` and `image` name property from the JSON
  //file's `meta` object to construct the full image source path
  let imageSource = baseUrl + file.meta.image;

  //The image's load handler
  let imageLoadHandler = () => {

    //Assign the image as a property of the `assets` object so
    //you can access it like this:
    //`assets["images/imageName.png"]`
    this[imageSource] = image;

    //Loop through all the frames
    Object.keys(file.frames).forEach(frame => {

      //The `frame` object contains all the size and position
      //data for each sub-image.
      //Add the frame data to the asset object so that you
      //can access it later like this: `assets["frameName.png"]`
      this[frame] = file.frames[frame];
```

```
      //Get a reference to the source so that it will be easy for
      //us to access it later
      this[frame].source = image;
    });

    //Alert the load handler that the file has loaded
    loadHandler();
  };

  //Load the tileset image
  let image = new Image();
  image.addEventListener("load", imageLoadHandler, false);
  image.src = imageSource;
},

loadSound(source, loadHandler) {
  console.log("loadSound called - see Chapter 10 for details");
}
};
```

You'll find this code in the library/utilities folder in the book's source files. You can import and use it in your game code as an ES6 module like this:

```
import {assets} from "../library/utilities";
```

Now let's find out exactly how this works.

Initializing the Loading Process

When you want to load some files into your game, send an array of file source paths to the assets object's load method:

```
assets.load(["images/tileset.png", "fonts/puzzler.otf"]);
```

The load method first uses the array's length to figure out how many assets it should load, and copies the result into the toLoad property.

```
load(sources) {
  //...
  this.toLoad = sources.length;
```

It now knows how many assets you want to load.

All the code within the assets.load method is wrapped inside a Promise:

```
load(sources) {
  return new Promise(resolve => {
    //... all of the load function's code is here...
  });
}
```

Each time an asset is loaded, the `loadHandler` is called. It adds 1 to the `loaded` property. If the number of assets loaded matches the number of assets to load, the promise is resolved:

```
let loadHandler = () => {
  this.loaded += 1;
  console.log(this.loaded);

  //Check whether everything has loaded
  if (this.toLoad === this.loaded) {

    //Reset `toLoad` and `loaded` to `0` so you can use them
    //to load more assets later if you need to
    this.toLoad = 0;
    this.loaded = 0;
    console.log("Assets finished loading");

    //Resolve the promise
    resolve();
  }
};
```

But before the `loadHandler` is called, the code needs to figure out what kinds of assets you want to load. It does this by first looping through each file source path from the `sources` array:

```
sources.forEach(source => {
  let extension = source.split(".").pop();
```

The `forEach` method loops through each source, and finds its file extension. How does it do that?

First, `split` converts the source string into a new array. It does this by splitting the string at each dot (.) character. Thus every section of the string that's delineated by a dot will be turned into an array element and copied into the new array:

```
source.split('.')
```

For example, let's imagine that our original string looks like this:

```
"images/tileset.png"
```

The `split` method scans the string for the dot. It copies everything on the left side of the dot into an array element, and everything on the right into another array element. This means that the source string is now in an array that looks like this:

```
["images/tileset", "png"]
```

We're halfway there. We're only really interested in the file extension name, `"png"`. It's the last element in the array. How can we access it? Using the pop method:

```
source.split('.').pop()
```

This line "pops out" the last element in the array, which—very conveniently—is the file extension name. When all this is finished, the variable called extension now has the value "png". But how does the code know that png is an image file?

The assets object has four arrays that store all the file extensions for each file type:

```
imageExtensions: ["png", "jpg", "gif"],
fontExtensions: ["ttf", "otf", "ttc", "woff"],
jsonExtensions: ["json"],
audioExtensions: ["mp3", "ogg", "wav", "webm"],
```

We can use these arrays to figure out what kind of thing "png" is. Use the array's indexOf method to help you do this.

```
if (this.imageExtensions.indexOf(extension) !== -1) {
  this.loadImage(source, loadHandler);
}
```

If indexOf can't match "png" to a value in the imageExtensions array, it will return -1, which means "not found." Any number higher than -1 means that a match was found, so the "png" must be a type of image.

■ **Note**   Alternatively, you can use JavaScript ES6's find method to help you do this.

Loading Images

If extension refers to an image, the loadImage function runs:

```
loadImage(source, loadHandler) {

  //Create a new image and call the `loadHandler` when the image
  //file has loaded
  let image = new Image();
  image.addEventListener("load", loadHandler, false);

  //Assign the image as a property of this `assets` object
  this[source] = image;

  //Set the image's `src` property to start loading the image
  image.src = source;
},
```

The first thing loadImage does is create a new Image object and set the image's loadHandler:

```
let image = new Image();
image.addEventListener("load", loadHandler, false);
```

When the image has finished loading, it will call the `loadHandler` on the `assets` object. (Remember that each time the `loadHandler` runs, it adds 1 to the value of `loaded`. When all the assets have finished loading, the `Promise` is resolved and all the loading is finished.)

The next step is to store this `Image` object in the `asset` object itself, and to be able to reference it by its file and path name. How can we do that?

Here's a bit of programming voodoo that you'll find very interesting. Remember that if we want to access an image in our main program, we should be able to write some code that looks like this:

```
assets["images/tileset.png"]
```

How can we set this up?

Create a property on the `assets` object that references the image and has the same name as the image file. Here's how:

```
this[source] = image;
```

You can now access any images you load, with this syntax:

```
assets["images/rocket.png"]
assets["images/cat.png"]
assets["images/star.png"]
```

This syntax is easy to read and write, and it has saved us from having to add a separate search function to the `assets` object.

The final step is to start loading the image by setting its `src` property:

```
image.src = source;
```

We're now done with images, but what about the other file types?

Loading Fonts

Fonts pose a particular problem because, unlike images, there's no built-in HTML5 API to force them to load. The best you can do is link to the font file that you want to use with the help of the CSS `@font-face` rule. Here's how:

```
@font-face {
  font-family: "fontFamilyName";
  src: url("fonts/fontFile.ttf");
}
```

But this code doesn't actually load the font; it just tells the browser where to find it. All browsers will only download the fonts when they're used on the page, and never before. This means that anyone playing your game might see a brief flash of unstyled text before the font is loaded. And unfortunately, at the time of writing, there's no new HTML5 spec on the horizon to help solve this. (But if you're reading this in some happy, future time far after the publication date of this book, double-check! The HTML5 spec might include this by now.)

If you don't think this is going to be a problem, then don't worry about preloading fonts and just use `@font-face`. Case closed!

But if you want more control, use an open-source font loader. All the preloaders work in the same way. They create some invisible HTML text, style it, and use some programming sleight-of-hand to figure out when the font file has been loaded. A good option for a font preloader is the open-source project font.js (github.com/Pomax/Font.js). It's a lightweight, battle-hardened script that lets you load fonts using the same syntax you use to load images. To use font.js, download it and include it in your game with a script tag:

```
<script src="Font.js"></script>
```

You can then load your font like this:

```
let anyFont = new Font();
anyFont.src = "fonts/fileName.ttf";
anyFont.onload = function () {
  console.log("font loaded");
}
```

The syntax is just like loading an image. If that works for you, go for it! But in the DIY spirit of this book, we're not going to go that route. Instead, we'll use a little trick that should work for most of your font-loading needs for games, without requiring a third-party script.

If the assets.load method detects that we're trying to load a file with a font extension ("ttf", "otf", "ttc", or "woff"), it calls the loadFont method, which simply writes and appends an @font-face rule into the HTML document:

```
loadFont(source, loadHandler) {

  //Use the font's filename as the `fontFamily` name. This code captures
  //the font file's name without the extension or file path
  let fontFamily = source.split("/").pop().split(".")[0];

  //Append an `@afont-face` style rule to the head of the HTML document
  let newStyle = document.createElement("style");
  let fontFace
    = "@font-face {font-family: '" + fontFamily + "'; src: url('" + source + "');}";
  newStyle.appendChild(document.createTextNode(fontFace));
  document.head.appendChild(newStyle);

  //Tell the loadHandler we're loading a font
  loadHandler();
},
```

The first thing loadFont does is find the name of the font inside the full source path:

```
let fontFamily = source.split("/").pop().split(".")[0];
```

I know, this code looks like scribbles on an asylum wall! But, hey, we're supposed to be grown-ups—we can take it! All it does is extract the letters after the last slash (/) and before the last dot (.) character. For example, let's say your font source path looks like this:

```
"fonts/puzzler.otf"
```

fontFamily now has this value:

`"puzzler"`

Everything before the / and after the . is gone.

The next thing the code does is write an @font-face rule into the HTML page's <head> section:

```
let newStyle = document.createElement("style");
let fontFace
  = "@font-face {font-family: '" + fontFamily + "'; src: url('" + source + "');}";
newStyle.appendChild(document.createTextNode(fontFace));
document.head.appendChild(newStyle);
```

If you were using a font called `puzzler.otf`, these lines would write the following HTML and CSS code:

```
<style>
  @font-face {
    font-family: 'puzzler';
    src: url('fonts/puzzler.otf');
  }
</style>
```

As I mentioned earlier, this code won't actually load the font file; it just tells the browser where to look for the font when it's requested by an HTML element or the canvas. But as you'll see in the next chapter, this is rarely a problem for games. Because games are rendered in a continuous loop, any custom fonts you use will usually be requested continuously each frame. That means they should be loaded and rendered by the time the rest of your assets load, and you probably won't see a flash of unstyled text in most cases.

■ **Note** If you're not requesting custom fonts in a loop, the font file almost certainly won't load. In that case, make your life easier and use font.js or an equivalent font preloader.

Just as with the code that loaded the image, the last thing the loadFont method does is call the loadHandler:

`loadHandler();`

This registers that the font has been loaded and, if it's the last asset to load, resolves the load method's promise.

Now that you know how to load images and fonts, let's find out how to load JSON data files.

Loading JSON Files

In Chapter 1 you learned how to use XHR to load and parse JSON files. If the assets.load method detects that you're trying to load a JSON file, it uses most of that same code, as-is, to load the file.

```
loadJson(source, loadHandler) {

  //Create a new XHR object
  let xhr = new XMLHttpRequest();
  xhr.open("GET", source, true);
  xhr.responseType = "text";

  xhr.onload = event => {
    if (xhr.status === 200) {
      let file = JSON.parse(xhr.responseText);
      file.name = source;
      this[file.name] = file;

      //If the JSON file has a `frames` property then
      //it's in Texture Packer format
      if (file.frames) {
        this.createTilesetFrames(file, source, loadHandler);
      } else {
        loadHandler();
      }
    }
  };

  //Send the request to load the file
  xhr.send();
},
```

After the JSON file has been loaded and parsed successfully, the code adds a reference to it on the assets object:

```
file.name = source;
this[file.name] = file;
```

That means we can get a reference to the JSON object later in our application code, like this:

```
assets["json/data.json"]
```

The loadJson function also does one additional thing. It checks to see if the JSON file has a property called frames. If it does, then the JSON file must be a texture atlas, and the function calls the createTilesetFrames method:

```
if (file.frames) {
  this.createTilesetFrames(file, source, loadHandler);
} else {
  loadHandler();
}
```

What is a texture atlas, and what does createTilesetFrames do? Let's find out!

Using a Texture Atlas

If you're working on a big, complex game, you'll want a fast and efficient way to work with images. A **texture atlas** can help you do this. A texture atlas actually consists of two separate files that are closely related:

- A single PNG tileset image file that contains all the images you want to use in your game
- A JSON file that describes the size and position of those subimages in the tileset

To use a texture atlas, you'll typically load the JSON file into your game, and use the data it contains to automatically create individual objects for each of the subimages it defines. Each of those objects contains the x, y, width, height, and name of the subimage, and you can use that information to blit the images from the tileset to the canvas.

Using a texture atlas is a big time saver. You can arrange the tileset's subimages in any order, and the JSON file will keep track of their sizes and positions for you. This is really convenient because it means the sizes and positions of the subimages aren't hard-coded into your game program. If you make changes to the tileset, like adding images, resizing them, or removing them, just republish the JSON file and your game will use that updated data to display the images correctly. If you're going to make anything bigger than a very small game, you'll definitely want to use a texture atlas.

The de facto standard for tileset JSON data is the format that is output by a popular software tool called Texture Packer. Even if you don't use Texture Packer, similar tools like Shoebox output JSON files in the same format. Let's find out how to use it to make a texture atlas with Texture Packer, and how to load it into a game program.

▓ **Note** Texture Packer's "Essential" license is free, and you can download it at www.codeandweb.com.

Creating the Texture Atlas

Open Texture Packer and choose the {JS} configuration option. Drag your game images into its workspace. You can also point it to any folder that contains your images. Texture Packer will automatically arrange the images into a single tileset image and give them names that match their original image names. It will give them a 2-pixel padding by default. Figure 3-1 shows a tileset made from three images.

Figure 3-1. *Use Texture Packer to create a texture atlas*

When you're done, make sure the Data Format is set to JSON (Hash) and click the Publish button. Choose a filename and location, and save the published files. You'll end up with a PNG file and a JSON file. In this example, my filenames are `animals.json` and `animals.png`. To make your life easier, just keep both files in your project's images folder. (Think of the JSON file as extra metadata for the image file).

The JSON file describes the name, size, and position of each image in the tileset. Here's the complete JSON data that describes the tileset:

```
{"frames": {

"cat.png":
{
  "frame": {"x":2,"y":2,"w":128,"h":128},
  "rotated": false,
  "trimmed": false,
  "spriteSourceSize": {"x":0,"y":0,"w":128,"h":128},
  "sourceSize": {"w":128,"h":128},
  "pivot": {"x":0.5,"y":0.5}
},
"hedgehog.png":
{
  "frame": {"x":132,"y":2,"w":128,"h":128},
  "rotated": false,
  "trimmed": false,
  "spriteSourceSize": {"x":0,"y":0,"w":128,"h":128},
  "sourceSize": {"w":128,"h":128},
  "pivot": {"x":0.5,"y":0.5}
},
```

```
"tiger.png":
{
  "frame": {"x":262,"y":2,"w":128,"h":128},
  "rotated": false,
  "trimmed": false,
  "spriteSourceSize": {"x":0,"y":0,"w":128,"h":128},
  "sourceSize": {"w":128,"h":128},
  "pivot": {"x":0.5,"y":0.5}
}},
"meta": {
  "app": "http://www.codeandweb.com/texturepacker",
  "version": "1.0",
  "image": "animals.png",
  "format": "RGBA8888",
  "size": {"w":392,"h":132},
  "scale": "1",
  "smartupdate": "$TexturePacker:SmartUpdate:
    a196e3e7dc7344bb1ddfbbb9ed914f90:
    06a75246a1a4b65f2beacae47a5e81d7:
    b00d48b51f56eb7c81e25100fcce2828$"
}
}
```

You can see that the file contains three main objects, named "cat.png", "hedgehog.png", and "tiger.png". Each of these subimages is called a **frame**, and its first set of properties describes the location of the subimage on the tileset. There's also an object called "meta", which tells you the name and size of the image these frames belong to, in addition to some other information.

■ **Note**   Among the many advantages to using software like Texture Packer to build a texture atlas is that it adds 2 pixels of padding around each image by default. This is important to prevent the possibility of **texture bleed**, an effect that happens when the edge of an adjacent image on the tileset appears next to a sprite. This happens because of the way that your system's renderer (the GPU or CPU) decides how to round fractional pixels values. Should it round them up or down? This choice will be different for each renderer. Adding a 1- or 2-pixel padding around images on a tileset makes all images display consistently.

Loading the Texture Atlas

Now that we've got this information, how can we load it into our game code? You'll notice that the very first property in the JSON file is called "frames":

```
{"frames": {
```

When the `assets.load` method has loaded any JSON file, it checks the file's first property. If that happens to be `"frames"`, then you know that you're loading a file in Texture Packer format, and you can interpret it using the `createTilesetFrames` method:

```
if (file.frames) {
  this.createTilesetFrames(file, source, loadHandler);
} else {
  loadHandler();
}
```

What does `createTilesetFrames` do? It loops though all the frame objects in the JSON file and adds them to the `assets` so that you can access them in your code later. It also loads the tileset image file:

```
createTilesetFrames(file, source, loadHandler) {

  //Get the tileset image's file path
  let baseUrl = source.replace(/[^\/]*$/, "");

  //Use the `baseUrl` and `image` name property from the JSON
  //file's `meta` object to construct the full image source path
  let imageSource = baseUrl + file.meta.image;


  //The image's load handler
  let imageLoadHandler = () => {

    //Assign the image as a property of the `assets` object so
    //you can access it like this:
    //`assets["images/imageName.png"]`
    this[imageSource] = image;

    //Loop through all the frames
    Object.keys(file.frames).forEach(frame => {

      //The `frame` object contains all the size and position
      //data for each subimage.
      //Add the frame data to the asset object so that you
      //can access it later like this: `assets["frameName.png"]`
      this[frame] = file.frames[frame];

      //Get a reference to the source so that it will be easy for
      //you to access it later
      this[frame].source = image;
    });

  //Alert the load handler that the file has loaded
  loadHandler();
  };
```

```
//Load the tileset image
let image = new Image();
image.addEventListener("load", imageLoadHandler, false);
image.src = imageSource;
}
```

The code first figures out what the tileset image's file path is. Because the JSON file and PNG file are stored in the same folder, they'll both have the same path name. That means you can find the image's base file path by extracting everything in the source string except the image name. The first part of createTilesetFrames uses regular expressions along with the replace method to find the filename and replace it with an empty string:

```
let baseUrl = source.replace(/[^\/]*$/, "");
```

If the source string is "images/animals.json", then baseUrl will now have the value "images/".

■ **Note**   In the source string syntax, [^\/] refers to any character that isn't a slash. The * that follows it matches any number of characters, and the $ refers to the end of the string. This means that the regular expression will match any characters at the end of the string that aren't slashes. To learn more about regular expressions, my favorite resource is "Learn Regular Expressions in About 55 Minutes" at http:qntm.org/files/re/re.html.

Now that we know the file path to the tileset image, we can use the meta.image property in the JSON file to construct the full image source:

```
let imageSource = baseUrl + file.meta.image;
```

And now that we have a reference to the image source, we can load it the same way we load any other image and call the imageLoadHandler when we're done:

```
let image = new Image();
image.addEventListener("load", imageLoadHandler, false);
image.src = imageSource;
```

The imageLoadHandler loops through each of the frame objects in the JSON file and stores references to them in the assets object.:

```
let imageLoadHandler = () => {
  this[imageSource] = image;
  Object.keys(file.frames).forEach(frame => {
    this[frame] = file.frames[frame];
    this[frame].source = image;
  });
  loadHandler();
};
```

Each frame object also gets a reference to the tileset it belongs to in a property called source. That will make it easy for us to associate the frame with its tileset later in our game code. When that's all done, the code calls the assets.load method's loadHandler to inform the asset object that the JSON file and its associated PNG file have loaded.

Loading and Using the Texture Atlas in Your Game Code

So what does all this get us in the end?

It means that you can load a texture atlas into your game code with this syntax:

```
assets.load([
  "images/animals.json"
]).then(() => setup());
```

You can then access the JSON object and PNG image file like this:

```
assets["images/animals.json"]
assets["images/animals.png"]
```

And you can access each individual frame in the JSON file like this:

```
assets["cat.png"]
assets["tiger.png"]
assets["hedgehog.png"]
```

Those are the frame objects that contain the size and position information of each subimage. You can now use that information to extract the subimages from the tileset image, and blit them to the canvas.

And how do we do that? That's what the next chapter is all about!

Summary

You've now got all the skills you need to load and manage images, fonts, and texture atlases in your game. We've created a useful assets object that stores all of your game assets in an easy-to-use format. You've also learned how to build a fairly complex mini-application that uses Promises to notify your program when its work is complete.

This is just a starting point; you can customize the assets object in any way you need to for the specific needs of your games. If you need to load other kinds of file types, like video, just add the file extensions to the extensions array and write your own custom load function to manage loading. In Chapter 9 we'll revisit the assets object and learn how to customize it to load sound files compatible with the WebAudio API.

In Chapter 2 you learned how to draw and display basic graphics for your games with the canvas, and in this chapter you learned how to load external files. In the next chapter you'll learn how to put these two skills together and use them to build reusable game components called sprites.

CHAPTER 4

■ ■ ■

Making Sprites and a Scene Graph

The game designer's fundamental building block is the **sprite**. A sprite is any image, shape, or text that you move, animate, or interact with on the screen. In this chapter you'll learn how to make sprites from scratch, and then, in the chapters that follow, you'll learn how to move them, make them interactive, add some collision detection, and use them to build a game.

An important feature of the sprite system that we're going to build is that you'll be able to compose sprites together to make compound objects and game scenes. Each sprite will have its own local coordinate system, so that if you move, scale, or rotate a sprite, any nested child sprites that it contains will move, scale, or rotate along with it. This is a feature called a **scene graph**: a hierarchy of nested sprites. As you'll see, it's an easy feature to implement and gives you a great deal of flexibility to make complex display systems for games.

By the end of this chapter you'll have a simple and powerful way to display shapes, images, lines, and text that will form the most important building block for making games.

■ **Note** In this chapter we're going to build a sprite display system closely modeled on the classic Flash API, but with a few new twists. The Flash API is the foundation for most modern 2D sprite rendering systems, including Starling, Sparrow, CreateJS and Pixi, so if you've ever wondered how those APIs work their magic under the hood, this chapter will show you.

What Are Sprites?

In Chapter 2 you learned how to make basic shapes and lines using the Canvas Drawing API. This API is described as a **low-level** API. That means you have a lot of control over very small details of the code, to customize it to a fine degree in any way you like. That's good, but the drawback is that it takes a lot of code to create something very simple. For example, if you want to draw a rectangle, rotate it, and give it a bit of transparency, you have to write 13 lines of code, like this:

```
ctx.strokeStyle = "black";
ctx.lineWidth = 3;
ctx.fillStyle = "rgba(128, 128, 128, 1)";
ctx.save();
ctx.globalAlpha = 0.5;
ctx.translate(128, 128);
ctx.rotate(0.5);
ctx.beginPath();
```

```
ctx.rect(-64, -64, 128, 128);
ctx.closePath();
ctx.stroke();
ctx.fill();
ctx.restore();
```

It took 13 laborious lines of code, just to make a simple rectangle? And what's worse is that you have to repeat these 13 lines of code for every rectangle you make. Forget about building a game like that!

There's a better way! You can solve this problem by employing an important programming skill called **abstraction**. Abstraction is a strategy for hiding all the messy details of your code so that you're only working with the big, important ideas. So instead of having to write 13 lines of tedious low-level code, you might only have to write two lines of **high-level** code. Here's how you could possibly abstract those 13 lines into 2 lines:

```
let box = rectangle();
render(canvas);
```

Much more readable, isn't it? How can you do this?

■ **Note**   What's the difference between low-level and high-level code? Low-level code tends to be a list of instructions that tell the computer how to do something. High-level code tends to be list of instructions describing *what* to do. Writing a good game program is about maintaining a healthy balance between low-level and high-level code. You need to understand and access the low-level code to fix things when they go wrong. But you want to do your creative work with as much high-level code as is practical so that you're not burdened by a distracting tangle of low-level details. Figuring out the perfect high-level/low-level balance takes practice, and it will be different for each project.

The first task is to look carefully at the low-level code and try to figure out if you can organize it into different jobs. Here are the two main jobs that our rectangle code is doing:

1. **Describing the rectangle**: Its height, width, position, rotation, and transparency.

2. **Rendering the rectangle**: Displaying the rectangle on the canvas.

In our current 13 lines of code, these two jobs are all jumbled together in one big mess. This is what programmers call **spaghetti code**. We need to untangle all the strands of spaghetti so that we can sort them into sensible and reusable components. In most game projects, you'll have three strands of spaghetti that you need to untangle: the game **information**, the game **logic**, and the game **rendering** system.

Game developers have a great way of keeping the threads separate by making components called **sprites**. In the next few sections you'll learn how to make a game sprite and, in the process, learn how to untangle spaghetti code of any kind.

Abstraction is going to be our guiding principle for the rest of this chapter, and you'll see how we use it to solve some complex problems so that we can start making games quickly.

Making a Rectangle Sprite

Let's start with a really small and simple example so that you can get a broad overview of how a basic sprite system works. We're going to build a minimalist sprite that just displays a rectangle. You'll be able to define the shape, size, color, and position of the rectangle, and make as many copies of it as you like.

The children Array

First, create an array to hold all the sprites you're going to make:

```
let children = [];
```

Every time you make a new sprite, you'll push it into this `children` array. As you'll see, this will make it easy for you to render the sprites efficiently.

Why is this array called `children`? Think of your main game as a big container. Every time you create a sprite it will exist inside this big container. The container is the **parent**, and everything inside the container is a **child** of that parent. You'll see in later steps how we're going to extend this concept to build a convenient parent-child hierarchy for all our sprites.

The rectangle Sprite

The next task is to write a function that creates and returns an abstracted rectangle sprite. The function should accept all the sprite's parameters that you want to control in your game code: size, position, and color. You should also be able to set its alpha, rotation, scale, and visibility. Because you might want to move the rectangle sprite, we're also going to add vx and vy properties that represent the sprite's velocity. (You'll learn all about velocity and how vx and vy work in Chapter 5.) The sprite object also should have its own internal render function that describes how the Canvas Drawing API should draw the rectangle. The last thing the rectangle function will do is push the sprite into the `children` array so that we can access it later. Here's the complete `rectangle` function that does all this:

```
let rectangle = function(
  //Define the function's parameters with their default values
  width = 32,
  height = 32,
  fillStyle = "gray",
  strokeStyle = "none",
  lineWidth = 0,
  x = 0,
  y = 0
) {

  //Create an object called `o` (the lowercase letter "o")
  //that is going to be returned by this
  //function. Assign the function's arguments to it
  let o = {width, height, fillStyle, strokeStyle, lineWidth, x, y};

  //Add optional rotation, alpha, visible, and scale properties
  o.rotation = 0;
  o.alpha = 1;
  o.visible = true;
  o.scaleX = 1;
  o.scaleY = 1;

  //Add `vx` and `vy` (velocity) variables that will help us move the sprite
  o.vx = 0;
  o.vy = 0;
```

```
//Add a `render` method that explains how to draw the sprite
o.render = ctx => {
  ctx.strokeStyle = o.strokeStyle;
  ctx.lineWidth = o.lineWidth;
  ctx.fillStyle = o.fillStyle;
  ctx.beginPath();
  ctx.rect(-o.width / 2, -o.height / 2, o.width, o.height);
  if (o.strokeStyle !== "none") ctx.stroke();
  ctx.fill();
};

//Push the sprite object into the `children` array
children.push(o);

//Return the object
return o;
};
```

Most of that code is self-explanatory, but there's one new thing you probably haven't seen before. The function uses ES6's object literal shorthand to conveniently assign the function arguments into the object that the function returns:

```
let o = {width, height, fillStyle, strokeStyle, lineWidth, x, y};
```

In ES6, if an object's property name is the same as its value, you don't need to specify the value. So the previous statement is the equivalent of writing this:

```
let o = {
  width: width,
  height: height,
  fillStyle: fillStyle,
  strokeStyle: strokeStyle,
  lineWidth: lineWidth,
  x: x,
  y: y
};
```

The code just creates an object that has properties whose names have the same values as the function's argument values.

There's also an alternative way to write this code using Object.assign, which might be better in many circumstances:

```
let o = {};
Object.assign(
  o,
  {width, height, fillStyle, strokeStyle, lineWidth, x, y}
);
```

The advantage of using Object.assign is that it creates completely new properties and values on the object, instead of just pointer references to an existing object.

The render Function

Now that you have a function that creates sprites, you need a global render function to display them. The job of the render function is to loop through all the objects in the children array and use each sprite's own internal render function to draw the shape on the canvas. The function will only draw the sprite if it is visible, and it will set the canvas's properties to match the sprite's properties. Here's the code:

```
function render(canvas, ctx) {

  //Clear the canvas
  ctx.clearRect(0, 0, canvas.width, canvas.height);

  //Loop through each sprite object in the `children` array
  children.forEach(sprite => {
     displaySprite(sprite);
  });

  function displaySprite(sprite) {

    //Display a sprite if it's visible
    if (sprite.visible) {

      //Save the canvas's present state
      ctx.save();

      //Shift the canvas to the sprite's position
      ctx.translate(
        sprite.x + sprite.width / 2,
        sprite.y + sprite.height /2
      );

      //Set the sprite's `rotation`, `alpha` and `scale`
      ctx.rotate(sprite.rotation);
      ctx.globalAlpha = sprite.alpha;
      ctx.scale(sprite.scaleX, sprite.scaleY);

      //Use the sprite's own `render` method to draw the sprite
      sprite.render(ctx);

      //Restore the canvas to its previous state
      ctx.restore();
    }
  }
}
```

We now have everything in place to make some sprites. Let's do it!

Making Sprites

Here's some code that uses our new `rectangle` and `render` functions to make and display three rectangle sprites, each with different property values. Figure 4-1 shows what this code produces. The `rectangle` constructor arguments represent width, height, fill color, stroke (outline) color, outline width, *x* position, and *y* position. You can also set the sprites' `alpha`, `scaleX`, `scaleY`, `rotation`, and `visible` properties.

Figure 4-1. *Three rectangle sprites*

```
let blueBox = rectangle(64, 64, "blue", "none", 0, 32, 32);
blueBox.rotation = 0.2;

let redBox = rectangle(64, 64, "red", "black", 4, 160, 100);
redBox.alpha = 0.5;
redBox.scaleY = 2;

let greenBox = rectangle(64, 64, "yellowGreen", "black", 2, 50, 150);
greenBox.scaleX = 0.5;
greenBox.rotation = 0.8;

//Render the sprites
render(canvas, ctx);
```

You can use this same format to make as many rectangles as you like, and customize their sizes, positions, and colors however you like. You might be surprised to learn that we've just unlocked the most important door to making games with HTML5 and JavaScript. Even if you don't go much further than making these basic rectangle sprites, you'll be able to use the techniques in the rest of the book to start making games. But, we can do much better!

Building a Scene Graph

The next step is to create a system where you can **nest** a sprite inside another sprite. A nested sprite is a **child** of its **parent** container sprite. Whenever the parent sprite changes its scale, position, rotation, or alpha transparency, the child sprite should match that change. The child sprite also has its own local coordinate system inside the parent sprite. This system is called a **scene graph**, and it's the foundation for making game scenes and for creating complex sprites out of different components. Figure 4-2 illustrates a basic child-parent sprite relationship.

Figure 4-2. *A nested parent-child sprite hierarchy*

It takes a bit of planning to create a scene graph. First, your sprites need these new properties:

- **children**: An array that stores references to all the child sprites the sprite contains.

- **parent**: A reference to this sprite's parent.

- **gx** and **gx**: The sprite's *global x* and *y* coordinates, relative to the canvas.

- **x** and **y**: The sprite's *local* coordinates, relative to its parent.

- **layer**: A number that refers to the sprite's depth layer. You can make sprites appear above or below other sprites by changing their depth layers.

Sprites also need two new methods to help you manage their parent-child relationships:

- **addChild**: Lets you add a sprite as child to the parent sprite. addChild just pushes a sprite into the parent's children array.

- **removeChild**: Lets you remove a child sprite from this parent sprite.

In addition, you need a root container object that acts as the parent for all the top-level sprites in the game:

- **stage**: The stage is an object at position 0,0 that's the same width and height as the canvas. It has a children array that contains all the top-level sprites in the game. When you render your sprites, you'll do so by looping through the stage's children array.

And finally, you need a new render function that loops though the all the child sprites in the stage object and then recursively loops through all the children of those children. Let's take a look at the new code we need to implement all this.

117

Creating Nestable Rectangle Sprites

With all these new features, the code for our rectangle sprite looks like the following.

```
let rectangle = function(
  width = 32, height = 32,
  fillStyle = "gray", strokeStyle = "none", lineWidth = 0,
  x = 0, y = 0
) {

  //Create an object called `o` that is going to be returned by this
  //function. Assign the function's arguments to it
  let o = {width, height, fillStyle, strokeStyle, lineWidth, x, y};

  //Create a "private" `_layer` property. (Private properties are prefixed
  //by an underscore character.)
  o._layer = 0;

  //The sprite's width and height
  o.width = width;
  o.height = height

  //Add optional rotation, alpha, visible and scale properties
  o.rotation = 0;
  o.alpha = 1;
  o.visible = true;
  o.scaleX = 1;
  o.scaleY = 1;

  //Add `vx` and `vy` (velocity) variables that will help us move
  //the sprite in later chapters
  o.vx = 0;
  o.vy = 0;

  //Create a `children` array on the sprite that will contain all the
  //child sprites
  o.children = [];

  //The sprite's `parent` property
  o.parent = undefined;

  //The `addChild` method lets you add sprites to this container
  o.addChild = sprite => {

    //Remove the sprite from its current parent, if it has one and
    //the parent isn't already this object
    if (sprite.parent) {
      sprite.parent.removeChild(sprite);
    }
```

```
  //Make this object the sprite's parent and
  //add it to this object's `children` array
  sprite.parent = o;
  o.children.push(sprite);
};


//The `removeChild` method lets you remove a sprite from its
//parent container
o.removeChild = sprite => {
  if(sprite.parent === o) {
    o.children.splice(o.children.indexOf(sprite), 1);
  } else {
    throw new Error(sprite + "is not a child of " + o);
  }
};


//Add a `render` method that explains how to draw the sprite
o.render = ctx => {
  ctx.strokeStyle = o.strokeStyle;
  ctx.lineWidth = o.lineWidth;
  ctx.fillStyle = o.fillStyle;
  ctx.beginPath();
  ctx.rect(-o.width / 2, -o.height / 2, o.width, o.height);
  if (o.strokeStyle !== "none") ctx.stroke();
  ctx.fill();
};


//Getters and setters for the sprite's internal properties
Object.defineProperties(o, {

  //The sprite's global x and y position
  gx: {
    get() {
      if (o.parent) {

        //The sprite's global x position is a combination of
        //its local x value and its parent's global x value
        return o.x + o.parent.gx;
      } else {
        return o.x;
      }
    },
    enumerable: true, configurable: true
  },
```

```
    gy: {
      get() {
        if (o.parent) {
          return o.y + o.parent.gy;
        } else {
          return o.y;
        }
      },
      enumerable: true, configurable: true
    },

    //The sprite's depth layer. Every sprite and group has its depth layer
    //set to `0` (zero) when it's first created. If you want to force a
    //sprite to appear above another sprite, set its `layer` to a
    //higher number
    layer: {
      get() {
        return o._layer;
      },
      set(value) {
        o._layer = value;
        if (o.parent) {

          //Sort the sprite's parent's `children` array so that sprites with a
          //higher `layer` value are moved to the end of the array
          o.parent.children.sort((a, b) => a.layer - b.layer);
        }
      },
      enumerable: true, configurable: true
    }
  });

  //Add the object as a child of the stage
  if (stage) stage.addChild(o);

  //Return the object
  return o;
};
```

A new feature of this code is that it uses a **private** property called _layer:

```
o._layer = 0;
```

By convention, private properties are always prefixed by an underscore character. The underscore indicates that you shouldn't change the property directly in your main game code, but only access or change it through a getter/setter. That's because the object might need to validate a value or do some calculation before it can return the value. On our rectangle sprite, you can see that the layer getter/setter acts as interface for the private _layer value. (You'll learn exactly how _layer works to change the sprite's depth layer in the pages ahead.)

The rectangle sprite also has a getter/setter for the sprite's gx and gy properties. Those tell you the sprite's global position, relative to the canvas's top-left corner. The sprite's global position is just its local position plus its parent's global position.

The Stage and the Canvas

We need to create an object called `stage` that acts as the root parent for all the sprites. In this example the stage is just a simple object with some important properties we will need to display its child sprites.

```
let stage = {
  x: 0,
  y: 0,
  gx: 0,
  gy: 0,
  alpha: 1,
  width: canvas.width,
  height: canvas.height,
  parent: undefined,

  //Give the stage `addChild` and `removeChild` methods
  children: [],

  addChild(sprite) {
    this.children.push(sprite);
    sprite.parent = this;
  },

  removeChild(sprite) {
    this.children.splice(this.children.indexOf(sprite), 1);
  }
};
```

Creating a canvas element and drawing context is such a common task that it's valuable to have a reusable function that does it for you. Here's the makeCanvas function, which creates the canvas element, adds it to the HTML document, and creates the drawing context:

```
function makeCanvas(
  width = 256, height = 256,
  border = "1px dashed black",
  backgroundColor = "white"
) {

  //Make the canvas element and add it to the DOM
  let canvas = document.createElement("canvas");
  canvas.width = width;
  canvas.height = height;
  canvas.style.border = border;
  canvas.style.backgroundColor = backgroundColor;
  document.body.appendChild(canvas);

  //Create the context as a property of the canvas
  canvas.ctx = canvas.getContext("2d");

  //Return the canvas
  return canvas;
}
```

121

Here's how to use makeCanvas to create a new canvas element that's 512 × 512 pixels:

```
let canvas = makeCanvas(512, 512);
```

As a convenience, makeCanvas creates the drawing context as a property of the canvas, so that you can access it like this:

```
canvas.ctx
```

Now let's find out how to render sprites on the canvas.

The New render Function

The render function first loops through all the sprites in the stage object's children array. If a sprite's visible property is true, the function displays the sprite using the same code we used earlier in the chapter. After the sprite is displayed, the code checks whether the sprite has any children of its own. If it does, the code repositions the drawing context to the parent sprite's top-left corner and draws the child sprites with recursive calls to the displaySprite function.

```
function render(canvas) {

  //Get a reference to the drawing context
  let ctx = canvas.ctx;

  //Clear the canvas
  ctx.clearRect(0, 0, canvas.width, canvas.height);

  //Loop through each sprite object in the stage's `children` array
  stage.children.forEach(sprite => {
    displaySprite(sprite);
  });

  function displaySprite(sprite) {

    //Display a sprite if it's visible
    if (sprite.visible) {

      //Save the canvas's present state
      ctx.save();

      //Shift the canvas to the center of the sprite's position
      ctx.translate(
        sprite.x + (sprite.width / 2),
        sprite.y + (sprite.height / 2)
      );

      //Set the sprite's `rotation`, `alpha`, and `scale`
      ctx.rotate(sprite.rotation);
      ctx.globalAlpha = sprite.alpha * sprite.parent.alpha;
      ctx.scale(sprite.scaleX, sprite.scaleY);
```

```
    //Use the sprite's own `render` method to draw the sprite
    sprite.render(ctx);

    //If the sprite contains child sprites in its
    //`children` array, display them by recursively calling this very same
    //`displaySprite` function again
    if (sprite.children && sprite.children.length > 0) {

      //Reset the context back to the parent sprite's top-left corner
      ctx.translate(-sprite.width / 2, -sprite.height / 2);

      //Loop through the parent sprite's children
      sprite.children.forEach(child => {

        //display the child
        displaySprite(child);
      });
    }

    //Restore the canvas to its previous state
    ctx.restore();
  }
 }
}
```

A new feature of this code is that the sprite's alpha transparency is set to be relative to its parent's alpha:

```
ctx.globalAlpha = sprite.alpha * sprite.parent.alpha;
```

So if a child has an alpha of 0.5 and its parent also has an alpha of 0.5, the child will be rendered with an alpha of 0.25. This technique makes transparency for nested objects behave the way you think it should naturally: if you change the transparency of the parent, the child's transparency will adapt proportionately.

The key to making the whole scene graph work is this if statement at the end of the render function:

```
if (sprite.children && sprite.children.length > 0) {
  ctx.translate(-sprite.width / 2, -sprite.height / 2);
  sprite.children.forEach(child => {
    displaySprite(child);
  });
}
```

If the parent contains children, the context is repositioned to the parent's top-left corner. This lets us draw the child sprites at x and y coordinates that are local to the parent's coordinate space. The code then loops through each child sprite and calls displaySprite for each of them, which runs this very same code. If any of those child sprites have children of their own, displaySprite will be called on them as well. This hierarchy can be as deep as you need it to be, although it's rare for sprites to have nested children deeper than three or four levels at most.

Now that we have all our new components in place, let's find out how to use them.

Nesting Sprites

Figure 4-3 illustrates four rectangle sprites nested four levels deep. The dashed line shows the top and left boundaries of the canvas.

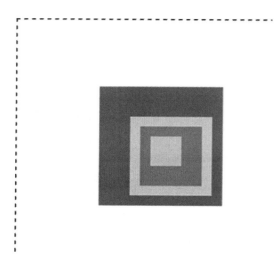

Figure 4-3. *A Nested parent-child sprite hierarchy*

The following code shows how these rectangles were created and displayed using the new functions you've just learned:

```
//Make the canvas
let canvas = makeCanvas(312, 312);
```

```
//Make the first parent sprite: the blueBox
let blueBox = rectangle(96, 96, "blue", "none", 0, 64, 54);
```

```
//Make the goldBox and add it as a child of the blueBox
let goldBox = rectangle(64, 64, "gold");
blueBox.addChild(goldBox);
```

```
//Assign the goldBox's local coordinates (relative to the blueBox)
goldBox.x = 24;
goldBox.y = 24;
```

```
//Add a grayBox to the goldBox
let grayBox = rectangle(48, 48, "gray");
goldBox.addChild(grayBox);
grayBox.x = 8;
grayBox.y = 8;
```

//Add a pinkBox to the grayBox
```
let pinkBox = rectangle(24, 24, "pink");
grayBox.addChild(pinkBox);
pinkBox.x = 8;
pinkBox.y = 8;
```

//Render the canvas
```
render(canvas);
```

Local and Global Coordinates

The main parent, the blueBox, is a child of the stage object. The stage has the same size and position as the canvas, with its 0,0 x/y registration point at the top-left corner. The means when the blueBox is created, its x and y position refers to its distance from the canvas's top-left corner. Its x position is 64, and its y position is 54, as highlighted here:

```
let blueBox = rectangle(96, 96, "blue", "none", 0, 64, 54);
```

64 and 54 are its **local coordinates**, relative to its parent, the stage. But because the blueBox is at the top of the sprite hierarchy, those local coordinates are also the same as its global coordinates.

What happens if you add a sprite as a child to the blueBox? The child's x and y position is *relative to its parent*.

```
let goldBox = rectangle(64, 64, "gold");
blueBox.addChild(goldBox);
goldBox.x = 24;
goldBox.y = 24;
```

The goldBox is offset 24 pixels from the blueBox's top-left corner; those are its local coordinates. You can use the goldBox's gx and gy properties to find out what its global coordinates are:

```
goldBox.gx;
goldBox.gy;
```

In this example goldBox.gx is 88 and goldBox.gy is 78.

In most game scenarios you'll only need to use a sprite's local coordinates, but if you ever need the global coordinates, you now know how to access them.

Rotation

If you rotate a parent sprite, all the children rotate along with it.

```
blueBox.rotation = 0.8;
```

Figure 4-4 shows the effect of this code. The actual rotation values of the child sprites don't change: they still all have rotation values of zero. But because they're bonded to the parent's coordinate system, they stay aligned with its axis of rotation.

Figure 4-4. *If you rotate a parent, its children match its axis of rotation*

You can test this by rotating the inner grayBox:

```
grayBox.rotation = 0.3;
```

Figure 4-5 shows the effect: the grayBox and its child the pinkBox rotate by 0.3 radians, in addition to the blueBox's rotation.

Figure 4-5. *Rotation values of the children are relative to the parent*

The same way that you and I stay fixed to the Earth's rotation, without being aware that it's spinning at about 1600km/hour, child sprites aren't aware of their parents' rotation values.

Scale

Scale works in the same way. Change a parent's scale, and all the children will match the scale effect.

```
blueBox.scaleX = 1.5;
```

Figure 4-6 shows the effect of this code on the children. They all stretch to match the parent.

Figure 4-6. *If you scale a parent, its children are also scaled*

Alpha Transparency

Transparency works in a similar way. What happens if you set a parent's alpha to 0.5, and the child's alpha to the same value, 0.5?

```
blueBox.alpha = 0.5
grayBox.alpha = 0.5;
```

Although it's difficult to see in print, Figure 4-7 shows that the effect is compounded. When it's rendered, the grayBox and its child the pinkBox appear to have an alpha of 0.25. It's a natural looking effect, and is how you would expect the transparency of nested objects to behave in the real world.

Figure 4-7. *A child's alpha transparency is relative to its parent*

Depth Layering

Sprites appear stacked on top of each other, from bottom to top, in the order in which they occur in their parent's children array. For example, if you create three overlapping rectangles, the last ones created will appear to be stacked above the earlier ones.

```
let redBox = rectangle(64, 64, "red", "black", 4, 220, 180);
let greenBox = rectangle(64, 64, "yellowGreen", "black", 4, 200, 200);
let violetBox = rectangle(64, 64, "violet", "black", 4, 180, 220);
```

Figure 4-8 shows what this code produces.

Figure 4-8. *The depth stacking order of sprites is determined by the order in which they're rendered*

The render method loops though the children array in sequence, and so sprites at the end of the array are the last ones to be rendered. What this means is that you can change the depth layer of a sprite by changing its position in the children array it belongs to.

Our new rectangle sprites have a layer setter property that does just that. If you change the value of layer, the code sorts the sprite's parent's children array based on that value. Sprites with a higher layer value are sorted to the end of the children array, so that they'll display last.

```
layer: {
  get() {
    return o._layer;
  },
  set(value) {
    o._layer = value;
    if (o.parent) {
      o.parent.children.sort((a, b) => a.layer - b.layer);
    }
  },
  enumerable: true, configurable: true
}
```

How does the array's sort method work? It takes a custom function with two arguments, a and b, where a is the current element being sorted and b is its neighbor to the right. The sort method loops through all the elements and compares their layer values. If a.layer minus b.layer is less than 0, then b is sorted to a higher position in the array. If the result is greater than zero, then a is sorted to a higher position. If the result is exactly 0, then there's no change in the position of either element.

All the rectangle sprites have a default layer value of 0. That means you can make a sprite display above another sprite by giving it any number higher than 0. In this example you can make the redBox appear above the other sprites by setting its layer property to 1.

```
redBox.layer = 1;
```

Figure 4-9 shows the effect.

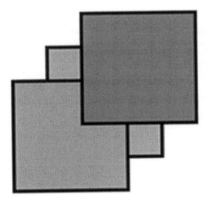

Figure 4-9. *Change a sprite's depth layer*

Now if you wanted the greenBox to appear above the redBox, you could set the greenBox's layer property to 2.

■ **Note**   Be careful! Sorting arrays is very computationally **expensive**. In a game you should avoid doing it unless absolutely necessary, and never sort arrays inside a continuous loop.

And that's it for our scene graph! Those are all the basics you need to know to make a nested sprite hierarchy for games.

Sprites for Games

You now know how to make rectangles, but you need a few more sprite types if you want to start making games. The following are the most important core sprite types that you need in order to make almost any kind of 2D action game:

- Circle
- Line
- Text
- Image
- Group (a special kind of sprite that, as you'll learn later in the chapter, is used just to group other sprites together)
- Rectangle

In the second half of this chapter, we're going to take all the concepts we learned about making rectangle sprites and use them to create these new sprite types. And we're going to do that by leveraging the strengths of ES6's class inheritance system.

The DisplayObject Class

In the previous examples we used *functional composition* to create rectangle sprites. In this technique the sprite is created by a function that composes an object and then returns that object to the main program. This is a really neat way to make sprites or any kinds of reusable objects. If you like that style of coding, keep doing it!

But in the interest of teaching you something new, I'm going to show you how to implement a game sprite system using a shallow inheritance pattern. This is exactly the kind of programming task that ES6's class system was designed for.

First, create a base class called DisplayObject that contains properties and methods shared by all the different sprite types.

```
class DisplayObject {
  constructor(properties) {
    //Initialize the sprite
  }
  commonMethod() {
  }
}
```

Next, create a specific sprite type that extends `DisplayObject` and implements its own unique methods and properties:

```
class SpriteType extends DisplayObject {
  constructor() {
    //Call DisplayObject's constructor to initialize
    //all the default properties
    super();
    //Initialize the sprite's specific properties
  }
  specificMethod() {
  }
}
```

We're going to create seven sprite types that extend `DisplayObject`: Circle, Rectangle, Line, Text, Sprite (for images), Group (to group sprites together), and Stage (the root parent container for all the sprites). This pattern will keep our code compact and give us a well-defined structure.

If `DisplayObject` is going to be the base class for all our sprites, which properties and methods does it need to contain? At a minimum, it needs to have all the properties and methods we gave the latest version of our rectangle sprite. Those include the basics like a `children` array, a `layer` property, `addChild`/`removeChild` methods, and all the rest. But because we're going to use our sprites to make a wide variety of games, we're also going to add some new features to help make the game development process as smooth and fun as possible.

First let's add some properties that will help us position sprites and calculate their size:

- `pivotX`, `pivotY`: Define the sprite's axis point, around which it should rotate.

- `halfWidth`, `halfHeight`: Properties that return half the width and height values.

- `centerX`, `centerY`: Define the sprite's center position.

- `localBounds`, `globalBounds`: Each of these properties returns a single object that tells you the *x*, *y*, width and height of the sprite (using either local or global coordinates). You can use them as a quick shortcut to get the position and size of the sprite in boundary-checking calculations.

- `circular`: If you set the `circular` property to `true`, diameter and radius properties will be created on the sprite. Setting it to `false` deletes the `diameter` and `radius` properties. You'll see how this feature will become useful for collision detection in the chapters to come.

A few enhanced visual effects will be nice to have:

- `blendMode`: Sets the sprite's blend mode.

- `shadow`, `shadowColor`, `shadowOffsetX`, `shadowOffsetY`, `shadowBlur`: Properties that let you add a drop shadow to the sprite.

We're also going to implement some convenient "luxury" properties and methods. They're not essential, but nice to have:

- `position`: A getter that returns the sprite's position as an object with *x* and *y* properties.

- `setPosition`. A method that lets you set a sprite's *x* and *y* values in one line of code, like this: `sprite.setPosition(120, 45);`

- **empty**: A Boolean property that returns `false` if the sprite's `children` array is empty.

- **putCenter, putTop, putRight, putBottom, and putLeft**: Methods that let you position any sprites relative to this sprite.

- **swapChildren**: A method that swaps the positions of two sprites in the `children` array. Use it to swap the depth layers of two child sprites.

- **add and remove**: Shortcuts for `addChild` and `removeChild` that let you add or remove many child sprites with one line of code, like this: `sprite.remove (firstChild, secondChild, thirdChild)`.

We're also going to add some advanced features. We won't use them in this chapter, but you'll learn all about how they work and how we'll use them in the chapters that follow:

- **draggable**: Defines whether the sprite can be dragged with the pointer (mouse or touch).

- **interactive**: Lets you make the sprite interactive, so that it become sensitive to pointer events.

- **frame, currentFrame, loop, and playing**: Properties we'll need to change a sprite's image states or animate it.

All these methods and properties will be inherited by all the sprite types, including the root `stage` object.

Coding the `DisplayObject` Class

Here's the complete `DisplayObject` class that implements all these features. (You'll find the working code in `library/display` in the chapter's source files.)

```
class DisplayObject {
  constructor() {

    //The sprite's position and size
    this.x = 0;
    this.y = 0;
    this.width = 0;
    this.height = 0;

    //Rotation, alpha, visible, and scale properties
    this.rotation = 0;
    this.alpha = 1;
    this.visible = true;
    this.scaleX = 1;
    this.scaleY = 1;

    //`pivotX` and `pivotY` let you set the sprite's axis of rotation
    //(0.5 represents the sprite's center point)
    this.pivotX = 0.5;
    this.pivotY = 0.5;
```

```
//Add `vx` and `vy` (velocity) variables that will help you move the sprite
this.vx = 0;
this.vy = 0;

//A "private" `_layer` property
this._layer = 0;

//A `children` array on the sprite that will contain all the
//child sprites in this container
this.children = [];

//The sprite's `parent` property
this.parent = undefined;

//The sprite's `children` array
this.children = [];

//Optional drop shadow properties.
//Set `shadow` to `true` if you want the sprite to display a shadow
this.shadow = false;
this.shadowColor = "rgba(100, 100, 100, 0.5)";
this.shadowOffsetX = 3;
this.shadowOffsetY = 3;
this.shadowBlur = 3;

//Optional blend mode property
this.blendMode = undefined;

//Properties for advanced features:

//Image states and animation
this.frames = [];
this.loop = true;
this._currentFrame = 0;
this.playing = false;

//Can the sprite be dragged?
this._draggable = undefined;

//Is the sprite circular? If it is, it will be given a `radius`
//and `diameter`
this._circular = false;

//Is the sprite `interactive`? If it is, it can become clickable
//or touchable
this._interactive = false;
}
```

```
/* Essentials */

//Global position
get gx() {
  if (this.parent) {

    //The sprite's global x position is a combination of
    //its local x value and its parent's global x value
    return this.x + this.parent.gx;
  } else {
    return this.x;
  }
}
get gy() {
  if (this.parent) {
    return this.y + this.parent.gy;
  } else {
    return this.y;
  }
}

//Depth layer
get layer() {
  return this._layer;
}
set layer(value) {
  this._layer = value;
  if (this.parent) {
    this.parent.children.sort((a, b) => a.layer - b.layer);
  }
}

//The `addChild` method lets you add sprites to this container
addChild(sprite) {
  if (sprite.parent) {
    sprite.parent.removeChild(sprite);
  }
  sprite.parent = this;
  this.children.push(sprite);
}

removeChild(sprite) {
  if(sprite.parent === this) {
    this.children.splice(this.children.indexOf(sprite), 1);
  } else {
    throw new Error(sprite + "is not a child of " + this);
  }
}
```

```
//Getters that return useful points on the sprite
get halfWidth() {
  return this.width / 2;
}
get halfHeight() {
  return this.height / 2;
}
get centerX() {
  return this.x + this.halfWidth;
}
get centerY() {
  return this.y + this.halfHeight;
}

/* Conveniences */

//A `position` getter. It returns an object with x and y properties
get position() {
  return {x: this.x, y: this.y};
}

//A `setPosition` method to quickly set the sprite's x and y values
setPosition(x, y) {
  this.x = x;
  this.y = y;
}

//The `localBounds` and `globalBounds` methods return an object
//with `x`, `y`, `width`, and `height` properties that define
//the dimensions and position of the sprite. This is a convenience
//to help you set or test boundaries without having to know
//these numbers or request them specifically in your code.
get localBounds() {
  return {
    x: 0,
    y: 0,
    width: this.width,
    height: this.height
  };
}
get globalBounds() {
  return {
    x: this.gx,
    y: this.gy,
    width: this.gx + this.width,
    height: this.gy + this.height
  };
}
```

```
//`empty` is a convenience property that will return `true` or
//`false` depending on whether this sprite's `children`
//array is empty
get empty() {
  if (this.children.length === 0) {
    return true;
  } else {
    return false;
  }
}


//The following "put" methods help you position
//another sprite in and around this sprite. You can position
//sprites relative to this sprite's center, top, right, bottom or
//left sides. The `xOffset` and `yOffset`
//arguments determine by how much the other sprite's position
//should be offset from this position.
//In all these methods, `b` is the second sprite that is being
//positioned relative to the first sprite (this one), `a`

//Center `b` inside `a`
putCenter(b, xOffset = 0, yOffset = 0) {
  let a = this;
  b.x = (a.x + a.halfWidth - b.halfWidth) + xOffset;
  b.y = (a.y + a.halfHeight - b.halfHeight) + yOffset;
}

//Position `b` above `a`
putTop(b, xOffset = 0, yOffset = 0) {
  let a = this;
  b.x = (a.x + a.halfWidth - b.halfWidth) + xOffset;
  b.y = (a.y - b.height) + yOffset;
}

//Position `b` to the right of `a`
putRight(b, xOffset = 0, yOffset = 0) {
  let a = this;
  b.x = (a.x + a.width) + xOffset;
  b.y = (a.y + a.halfHeight - b.halfHeight) + yOffset;
}

//Position `b` below `a`
putBottom(b, xOffset = 0, yOffset = 0) {
  let a = this;
  b.x = (a.x + a.halfWidth - b.halfWidth) + xOffset;
  b.y = (a.y + a.height) + yOffset;
}
```

```
//Position `b` to the left of `a`
putLeft(b, xOffset = 0, yOffset = 0) {
  let a = this;
  b.x = (a.x - b.width) + xOffset;
  b.y = (a.y + a.halfHeight - b.halfHeight) + yOffset;
}

//Some extra conveniences for working with child sprites

//Swap the depth layer positions of two child sprites
swapChildren(child1, child2) {
  let index1 = this.children.indexOf(child1),
      index2 = this.children.indexOf(child2);
  if (index1 !== -1 && index2 !== -1) {

    //Swap the indexes
    child1.childIndex = index2;
    child2.childIndex = index1;

    //Swap the array positions
    this.children[index1] = child2;
    this.children[index2] = child1;
  } else {
    throw new Error(`Both objects must be a child of the caller ${this}`);
  }
}

//`add` and `remove` let you add and remove many sprites at the same time
add(...spritesToAdd) {
  spritesToAdd.forEach(sprite => this.addChild(sprite));
}
remove(...spritesToRemove) {
  spritesToRemove.forEach(sprite => this.removeChild(sprite));
}

/* Advanced features */

//If the sprite has more than one frame, return the
//value of `_currentFrame`
get currentFrame() {
  return this._currentFrame;
}

//The `circular` property lets you define whether a sprite
//should be interpreted as a circular object. If you set
//`circular` to `true`, the sprite is given `radius` and `diameter`
//properties. If you set `circular` to `false`, the `radius`
//and `diameter` properties are deleted from the sprite
```

```
  get circular() {
    return this._circular;
  }
  set circular (value) {

    //Give the sprite `diameter` and `radius` properties
    //if `circular` is `true`
    if (value === true && this._circular === false) {
      Object.defineProperties(this, {
        diameter: {
          get () {
            return this.width;
          },
          set (value) {
            this.width = value;
            this.height = value;
          },
          enumerable: true, configurable: true
        },
        radius: {
          get() {
            return this.halfWidth;
          },
          set(value) {
            this.width = value * 2;
            this.height = value * 2;
          },
          enumerable: true, configurable: true
        }
      });

      //Set this sprite's `_circular` property to `true`
      this._circular = true;
    }

    //Remove the sprite's `diameter` and `radius` properties
    //if `circular` is `false`
    if (value === false && this._circular === true) {
      delete this.diameter;
      delete this.radius;
      this._circular = false;
    }
  }
}

//Is the sprite draggable by the pointer? If `draggable` is set
//to `true`, the sprite is added to a `draggableSprites`
//array. All the sprites in `draggableSprites` are updated each
//frame to check whether they're being dragged.
//(You'll learn how to implement this in Chapter 6.)
```

```
  get draggable() {
    return this._draggable;
  }
  set draggable(value) {
    if (value === true) {
      draggableSprites.push(this);
      this._draggable = true;
    }

    //If it's `false`, remove it from the `draggableSprites` array
    if (value === false) {
      draggableSprites.splice(draggableSprites.indexOf(this), 1);
    }
  }

  //Is the sprite interactive? If `interactive` is set to `true`,
  //the sprite is run through the `makeInteractive` function.
  //`makeInteractive` makes the sprite sensitive to pointer
  //actions. It also adds the sprite to the `buttons` array,
  //which is updated each frame.
  //(You'll learn how to implement this in Chapter 6.)
  get interactive() {
    return this._interactive;
  }
  set interactive(value) {
    if (value === true) {

      //Add interactive properties to the sprite
      //so that it can act like a button
      makeInteractive(this);

      //Add the sprite to the global `buttons` array so
      //it can be updated each frame
      buttons.push(this);

      //Set this sprite's private `_interactive` property to `true`
      this._interactive = true;
    }
    if (value === false) {

      //Remove the sprite's reference from the
      //`buttons` array so that it's no longer affected
      //by mouse and touch interactivity
      buttons.splice(buttons.indexOf(this), 1);
      this._interactive = false;
    }
  }
}
```

As a bonus, let's also create a universal remove function that will remove any sprite, or list of sprites, from any parent:

```
function remove(...spritesToRemove) {
  spritesToRemove.forEach(sprite => {
    sprite.parent.removeChild(sprite);
  });
}
```

If you need to remove a sprite from a game and don't know or care what its parent is, use this universal remove function.

A Full-featured Render Function

We've added some new features to our sprites—shadows, blend modes, and rotation pivot points. Let's update our render function to allow us to use all these features. We're also going to add a further optimization: sprites will only be drawn on the canvas if they're within the canvas's visible area.

```
function render(canvas) {

  //Get a reference to the context
  let ctx = canvas.ctx;

  //Clear the canvas
  ctx.clearRect(0, 0, canvas.width, canvas.height);

  //Loop through each sprite object in the stage's `children` array
  stage.children.forEach(sprite => {

    //Display a sprite
    displaySprite(sprite);
  });

  function displaySprite(sprite) {

    //Only display the sprite if it's visible
    //and within the area of the canvas
    if (
      sprite.visible
      && sprite.gx < canvas.width + sprite.width
      && sprite.gx + sprite.width >= -sprite.width
      && sprite.gy < canvas.height + sprite.height
      && sprite.gy + sprite.height >= -sprite.height
    ) {

      //Save the canvas's present state
      ctx.save();
```

```
//Shift the canvas to the center of the sprite's position
ctx.translate(
  sprite.x + (sprite.width * sprite.pivotX),
  sprite.y + (sprite.height * sprite.pivotY)
);

//Set the sprite's `rotation`, `alpha` and `scale`
ctx.rotate(sprite.rotation);
ctx.globalAlpha = sprite.alpha * sprite.parent.alpha;
ctx.scale(sprite.scaleX, sprite.scaleY);

//Display the sprite's optional drop shadow
if(sprite.shadow) {
  ctx.shadowColor = sprite.shadowColor;
  ctx.shadowOffsetX = sprite.shadowOffsetX;
  ctx.shadowOffsetY = sprite.shadowOffsetY;
  ctx.shadowBlur = sprite.shadowBlur;
}

//Display the optional blend mode
if (sprite.blendMode) ctx.globalCompositeOperation = sprite.blendMode;

//Use the sprite's own `render` method to draw the sprite
if (sprite.render) sprite.render(ctx);

if (sprite.children && sprite.children.length > 0) {

  //Reset the context back to the parent sprite's top-left corner,
  //relative to the pivot point
  ctx.translate(-sprite.width * sprite.pivotX , -sprite.height * sprite.pivotY);

  //Loop through the parent sprite's children
  sprite.children.forEach(child => {

    //display the child
    displaySprite(child);
  });
}

//Restore the canvas to its previous state
ctx.restore();
  }
 }
}
```

Now that we have a base `DisplayObject` class and a renderer, let's start building our game sprites.

The Stage

The stage is the root parent container for all the sprites, so that's the first new thing we should make. The stage is just a sprite that doesn't display any of its own graphics. That means you can create the stage directly from the DisplayObject, with this syntax:

```
let stage = new DisplayObject();
```

Then just give it width and height values that match the canvas, and you're all set:

```
stage.width = canvas.width;
stage.height = canvas.height;
```

The Rectangle Class

The code for the Rectangle sprite will be very familiar, but it implements a few neat tricks that I'll explain after the code listing.

```
class Rectangle extends DisplayObject {
  constructor(
    width = 32,
    height = 32,
    fillStyle = "gray",
    strokeStyle = "none",
    lineWidth = 0,
    x = 0,
    y = 0
  ){

    //Call the DisplayObject's constructor
    super();

    //Assign the argument values to this sprite
    Object.assign(
      this, {width, height, fillStyle, strokeStyle, lineWidth, x, y}
    );

    //Add a `mask` property to enable optional masking
    this.mask = false;
  }

  //The `render` method explains how to draw the sprite
  render(ctx) {
    ctx.strokeStyle = this.strokeStyle;
    ctx.lineWidth = this.lineWidth;
    ctx.fillStyle = this.fillStyle;
    ctx.beginPath();
    ctx.rect(
      //Draw the sprite around its `pivotX` and `pivotY` point
      -this.width * this.pivotX,
      -this.height * this.pivotY,
```

```
      this.width,
      this.height
    );
    if (this.strokeStyle !== "none") ctx.stroke();
    if (this.fillStyle !== "none") ctx.fill();
    if (this.mask && this.mask === true) ctx.clip();
  }
}

//A higher-level wrapper for the rectangle sprite
function rectangle(width, height, fillStyle, strokeStyle, lineWidth, x, y) {

  //Create the sprite
  let sprite = new Rectangle(width, height, fillStyle, strokeStyle, lineWidth, x, y);

  //Add the sprite to the stage
  stage.addChild(sprite);

  //Return the sprite to the main program
  return sprite;
}
```

That's the code for the Rectangle class; now let's look at three new tricks it implements: masking, API Insurance, and rotating around the sprite's pivot point.

Masking

You learned in Chapter 2 how to use shapes to mask areas of the canvas. The Rectangle class introduces a useful new mask property that lets you optionally use any rectangle sprite as a mask.

```
this.mask = false;
```

It's initialized to false. If you set the mask property to true anywhere in your game code, the rectangle will mask any sprites that are children of this rectangle sprite. This bit of code from the rectangle's render function is what makes masking work:

```
if (this.mask && this.mask === true) ctx.clip();
```

As you'll see ahead, circle sprites also have this mask property.

API Insurance

Take a look at the last part of the Rectangle class code. You can see that a function called rectangle is used to create and return a sprite made using the Rectangle class. Why did I add what appears to be an extra unnecessary step? Why not just create the sprite directly using new Rectangle() without wrapping it in another function?

This is what I call **API Insurance**. It works like this: the rectangle function is a higher-level wrapper for the Rectangle class constructor. This extra wrapper means that you can use a consistent API for creating the sprite, even if at some future point your underlying code changes radically. For example, if you suddenly decide you want to use a completely different class to make rectangles, you can just swap out the old Rectangle constructor with the new one, like this:

```
function rectangle(width, height, fillStyle, strokeStyle, lineWidth, x, y) {
  let sprite = new BetterRectangle(width, height, fillStyle, strokeStyle, lineWidth, x, y);
  stage.addChild(sprite);
  return sprite;
}
```

The code you use to create rectangle sprites in your games won't change; the rectangle function just redirects the arguments to a different class constructor.

Using a wrapper function also means that you can run useful secondary tasks when you create the sprite, like adding the sprite to the stage. That's important, and something you need to do for every sprite you create. But to keep everything modular, it's a task that probably shouldn't be baked into the main sprite class. (API Insurance is a term I made up—don't look for it in any computer science textbook!)

Pivoting Around the Rotation Axis

Use a pivot point if you want to rotate your sprites off-center. You can think of the pivot point as a pin that you can stick into the sprite. When you rotate the sprite, it rotates around that pin. The pivotX and pivotY properties take values between 0.1 and 0.99, which represent a percentage of the sprite's width or height. (Percentage values between 0 and 1 like this are often called **normalized** values.) pivotX and pivotY are initialized with a value of 0.5, which means the sprite will rotate around its center. Let's test this by using our new code to create a rectangle, set its pivot values to 0.25, and rotate it.

```
let box = rectangle(96, 96, "blue", "none", 0, 54, 64);
box.pivotX = 0.25;
box.pivotY = 0.25;
box.rotation = 0.8;
```

The third image in Figure 4-10 shows the result.

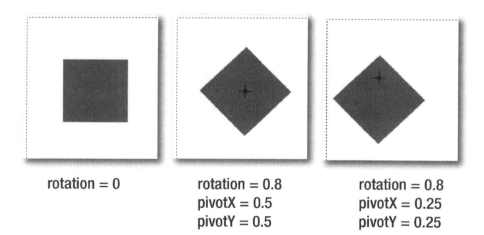

Figure 4-10. Set the pivot point

The pivot point doesn't change the sprite's *x* and *y* positions; those remain fixed to the sprite's unrotated top-left corner.

How do pivotX and pivotY work to create this effect? The rectangle's render function draws the shape *around the pivot point.*

```
ctx.rect(
  -this.width * this.pivotX,
  -this.width * this.pivotY,
  this.width,
  this.height
);
```

You can use pivotX and pivotY with all the new sprite types in this chapter.

The Circle Class

The Circle class follows the same format as the Rectangle class, but it draws a circle instead. Like rectangles, circles also have a mask property, so that you can use them to optionally mask any other sprites.

```
class Circle extends DisplayObject {
  constructor(
    diameter = 32,
    fillStyle = "gray",
    strokeStyle = "none",
    lineWidth = 0,
    x = 0,
    y = 0
  ){

    //Call the DisplayObject's constructor
    super();

    //Enable `radius` and `diameter` properties
    this.circular = true;

    //Assign the argument values to this sprite
    Object.assign(
      this, {diameter, fillStyle, strokeStyle, lineWidth, x, y}
    );

    //Add a `mask` property to enable optional masking
    this.mask = false;

  }
  //The `render` method
  render(ctx) {
    ctx.strokeStyle = this.strokeStyle;
    ctx.lineWidth = this.lineWidth;
    ctx.fillStyle = this.fillStyle;
    ctx.beginPath();
```

```
    ctx.arc(
      this.radius + (-this.diameter * this.pivotX),
      this.radius + (-this.diameter * this.pivotY),
      this.radius,
      0, 2*Math.PI,
      false
    );
    if (this.strokeStyle !== "none") ctx.stroke();
    if (this.fillStyle !== "none") ctx.fill();
    if (this.mask && this.mask === true) ctx.clip();
  }
}
```

```
//A higher level wrapper for the circle sprite
export function circle(diameter, fillStyle, strokeStyle, lineWidth, x, y) {
  let sprite = new Circle(diameter, fillStyle, strokeStyle, lineWidth, x, y);
  stage.addChild(sprite);
  return sprite;
}
```

Here's how to use this code to draw a circle with a cyan (light blue) fill and red outline, shown in Figure 4-11.

```
let cyanCircle = circle(64, "cyan", "red", 4, 64, 280);
```

Figure 4-11. *Use the* Circle *class to draw a circle*

The circle's *x* and *y* values refer to the top-left corner of an imaginary box that bounds the circle.

Circles have diameter and radius properties, which were created by this line of code in the Circle class constructor:

```
this.circular = true;
```

The DisplayObject base class has a setter called circular that creates diameter and radius properties on any sprite when it's set to true. You might also find this feature useful if you have sprites that display circular images that you want to use with collision detection functions for circles, which you'll learn all about in Chapter 7.

The Line Class

The Line class creates a sprite that helps you draw lines:

```
class Line extends DisplayObject {
  constructor(
    strokeStyle = "none",
    lineWidth = 0,
    ax = 0,
    ay = 0,
    bx = 32,
    by = 32
  ){

    //Call the DisplayObject's constructor
    super();

    //Assign the argument values to this sprite
    Object.assign(
      this, {strokeStyle, lineWidth, ax, ay, bx, by}
    );

    //The `lineJoin` style.
    //Options are "round", "mitre" and "bevel".
    this.lineJoin = "round";
  }

  //The `render` method
  render(ctx) {
    ctx.strokeStyle = this.strokeStyle;
    ctx.lineWidth = this.lineWidth;
    ctx.lineJoin = this.lineJoin;
    ctx.beginPath();
    ctx.moveTo(this.ax, this.ay);
    ctx.lineTo(this.bx, this.by);
    if (this.strokeStyle !== "none") ctx.stroke();
  }
}

//A higher-level wrapper for the line sprite
function line(strokeStyle, lineWidth, ax, ay, bx, by) {
  let sprite = new Line(strokeStyle, lineWidth, ax, ay, bx, by);
  stage.addChild(sprite);
  return sprite;
}
```

To create a line sprite, set its color and width, and then define its start and end points. The values ax and ay define the start point of the line, and bx and by define its end point:

```
let blackLine = line(fillStyle, lineWidth, ax, ay, bx, by);
```

You can change the values of ax, ay, bx, and by at any time to change the line's position. The following code produces the image of crisscrossing lines in Figure 4-12.

```
let blackLine = line("black", 4, 200, 64, 264, 128);
let redLine = line("red", 4, 200, 128, 264, 64);
let greenLine = line("green", 4, 264, 96, 200, 96);
let blueLine = line("blue", 4, 232, 128, 232, 64);
```

Figure 4-12. *Draw some lines with the Line class*

The Text Class

The Text class gives you a quick way to add some dynamic text to a game:

```
class Text extends DisplayObject {
  constructor(
    content = "Hello!",
    font = "12px sans-serif",
    fillStyle = "red",
    x = 0,
    y = 0
  ){
    //Call the DisplayObject's constructor
    super();

    //Assign the argument values to this sprite
    Object.assign(
      this, {content, font, fillStyle, x, y}
    );

    //Set the default text baseline to "top"
    this.textBaseline = "top";

    //Set `strokeText` to "none"
    this.strokeText = "none";
  }
```

```
//The `render` method describes how to draw the sprite
render(ctx) {
  ctx.font = this.font;
  ctx.strokeStyle = this.strokeStyle;
  ctx.lineWidth = this.lineWidth;
  ctx.fillStyle = this.fillStyle;

  //Measure the width and height of the text
  if (this.width === 0) this.width = ctx.measureText(this.content).width;
  if (this.height === 0) this.height = ctx.measureText("M").width;

  ctx.translate(
    -this.width * this.pivotX,
    -this.height * this.pivotY
  );
  ctx.textBaseline = this.textBaseline;
  ctx.fillText(
    this.content,
    0,
    0
  );
  if (this.strokeText !== "none") ctx.strokeText();
  }
}

//A higher level wrapper
function text(content, font, fillStyle, x, y) {
  let sprite = new Text(content, font, fillStyle, x, y);
  stage.addChild(sprite);
  return sprite;
}
```

Here's how to make a text sprite that displays the words "Hello World!":

```
let message = text("Hello World!", "24px Futura", "black", 330, 230);
```

The second argument defines the font that the text should use. You can use any standard font built into the browser, or any font file loaded with the @font-face CSS rule or the assets object we built in Chapter 3.

Text sprites have a property called content that you can use to change the words the text displays:

```
message.content = "Anything you like";
```

You can change the content at any time during a game, which is useful for updating dynamic text, like the player's score.

The Group Class

Group is a special kind of sprite that doesn't display any of its own graphics. Instead, it's used to group other sprites together. You can think of it as a big container for sprites. But because a group has all the same DisplayObject properties as the other sprites, you can use it as the root parent for complex game characters, game scenes, or levels.

A group's height and width is calculated dynamically based on the content that it contains. The Group class implements custom addChild and removeChild methods that recalculate the size of the group each time a sprite is added to or removed from it. The Group class's calculateSize method loops through each of the group's children and sets the group's width and height to the maximum width and height that any of its children occupy.

```
class Group extends DisplayObject {
  constructor(...spritesToGroup){

    //Call the DisplayObject's constructor
    super();

    //Group all the sprites listed in the constructor arguments
    spritesToGroup.forEach(sprite => this.addChild(sprite));
  }

  //Groups have custom `addChild` and `removeChild` methods that call
  //a `calculateSize` method when any sprites are added or removed
  //from the group

  addChild(sprite) {
    if (sprite.parent) {
      sprite.parent.removeChild(sprite);
    }
    sprite.parent = this;
    this.children.push(sprite);

    //Figure out the new size of the group
    this.calculateSize();
  }

  removeChild(sprite) {
    if(sprite.parent === this) {
      this.children.splice(this.children.indexOf(sprite), 1);

      //Figure out the new size of the group
      this.calculateSize();
    } else {
      throw new Error(`${sprite} is not a child of ${this}`);
    }
  }

  calculateSize() {

    //Calculate the width based on the size of the largest child
    //that this sprite contains
    if (this.children.length > 0) {

      //Some temporary private variables to help track the new
      //calculated width and height
      this._newWidth = 0;
      this._newHeight = 0;
```

```
    //Find the width and height of the child sprites furthest
    //from the top left corner of the group
    this.children.forEach(child => {

      //Find child sprites that combined x value and width
      //that's greater than the current value of `_newWidth`
      if (child.x + child.width > this._newWidth) {

        //The new width is a combination of the child's
        //x position and its width
        this._newWidth = child.x + child.width;
      }
      if (child.y + child.height > this._newHeight) {
        this._newHeight = child.y + child.height;
      }
    });

    //Apply the `_newWidth` and `_newHeight` to this sprite's width
    //and height
    this.width = this._newWidth;
    this.height = this._newHeight;
  }
 }
}


//A higher level wrapper for the group sprite
function group(...spritesToGroup) {
  let sprite = new Group(...spritesToGroup);
  stage.addChild(sprite);
  return sprite;
}
```

To create a group, list the sprites you want to group in the group's constructor:

```
let squares = group(squareOne, squareTwo, squareThree);
```

As an alternative, you could create an empty group and use addChild or add to group sprites together:

```
let squares = group();
squares.addChild(squareOne);
squares.add(squareTwo, squareThree);
```

Groups have many versatile uses in games, as you'll see in the chapters to come.

The Sprite Class

Sprite is a powerful class that displays images. It lets you display images from single image files, texture atlas frames, or subimages from a tileset. It also lets you store multiple image states and initialize the sprite with an array of images. To help display different image states, the Sprite class also implements a new method called gotoAndStop. (We're going to use these features as the basis for making interactive buttons in Chapter 7 and for doing keyframe animation in Chapter 8.)

This is a lot of work for one sprite type to handle, and so the Sprite class is pretty big. But the biggest part of this code is just figuring out what kind of image information is being supplied to it. Let's take a look at the entire code listing for the Sprite class, and I'll then walk you through how each feature works.

```
class Sprite extends DisplayObject {
  constructor(
    source,
    x = 0,
    y = 0
  ){

    //Call the DisplayObject's constructor
    super();

    //Assign the argument values to this sprite
    Object.assign(this, {x, y});

    //We need to figure out what the source is, and then use
    //that source data to display the sprite image correctly

    //Is the source a JavaScript Image object?
    if(source instanceof Image) {
      this.createFromImage(source);
    }

    //Is the source a tileset from a texture atlas?
    //(It is if it has a `frame` property)
    else if (source.frame) {
      this.createFromAtlas(source);
    }

    //If the source contains an `image` subproperty, this must
    //be a `frame` object that's defining the rectangular area of an inner subimage.
    //Use that subimage to make the sprite. If it doesn't contain a
    //`data` property, then it must be a single frame
    else if (source.image && !source.data) {
      this.createFromTileset(source);
    }

    //If the source contains an `image` subproperty
    //and a `data` property, then it contains multiple frames
    else if (source.image && source.data) {
      this.createFromTilesetFrames(source);
    }
```

```
//Is the source an array? If so, what kind of array?
else if (source instanceof Array) {
  if (source[0] && source[0].source) {

    //The source is an array of frames on a texture atlas tileset
    this.createFromAtlasFrames(source);
  }

  //It must be an array of image objects
  else if (source[0] instanceof Image){
    this.createFromImages(source);
  }

  //throw an error if the sources in the array aren't recognized
  else {
    throw new Error(`The image sources in ${source} are not recognized`);
  }
}
//Throw an error if the source is something we can't interpret
else {
  throw new Error(`The image source ${source} is not recognized`);
}
}

createFromImage(source) {

  //Throw an error if the source is not an Image object
  if (!(source instanceof Image)) {
    throw new Error(`${source} is not an image object`);
  }

  //Otherwise, create the sprite using an Image
  else {
    this.source = source;
    this.sourceX =  0;
    this.sourceY =  0;
    this.width = source.width;
    this.height = source.height;
    this.sourceWidth = source.width;
    this.sourceHeight = source.height;
  }
}

createFromAtlas(source) {
  this.tilesetFrame = source;
  this.source = this.tilesetFrame.source;
  this.sourceX = this.tilesetFrame.frame.x;
  this.sourceY = this.tilesetFrame.frame.y;
  this.width = this.tilesetFrame.frame.w;
```

```
    this.height = this.tilesetFrame.frame.h;
    this.sourceWidth = this.tilesetFrame.frame.w;
    this.sourceHeight = this.tilesetFrame.frame.h;
  }

  createFromTileset(source) {
    if (!(source.image instanceof Image)) {
      throw new Error(`${source.image} is not an image object`);
    } else {
      this.source = source.image;
      this.sourceX = source.x;
      this.sourceY = source.y;
      this.width = source.width;
      this.height = source.height;
      this.sourceWidth = source.width;
      this.sourceHeight = source.height;
    }
  }

  createFromTilesetFrames(source) {
    if (!(source.image instanceof Image)) {
      throw new Error(`${source.image} is not an image object`);
    } else {
      this.source = source.image;
      this.frames = source.data;

      //Set the sprite to the first frame
      this.sourceX = this.frames[0][0];
      this.sourceY = this.frames[0][1];
      this.width = source.width;
      this.height = source.height;
      this.sourceWidth = source.width;
      this.sourceHeight = source.height;
    }
  }

  createFromAtlasFrames(source) {
    this.frames = source;
    this.source = source[0].source;
    this.sourceX = source[0].frame.x;
    this.sourceY = source[0].frame.y;
    this.width = source[0].frame.w;
    this.height = source[0].frame.h;
    this.sourceWidth = source[0].frame.w;
    this.sourceHeight = source[0].frame.h;
  }

  createFromImages(source) {
    this.frames = source;
    this.source = source[0];
    this.sourceX = 0;
```

```
    this.sourceY = 0;
    this.width = source[0].width;
    this.height = source[0].width;
    this.sourceWidth = source[0].width;
    this.sourceHeight = source[0].height;
}

//Add a `gotoAndStop` method to go to a specific frame
gotoAndStop(frameNumber) {
  if (this.frames.length > 0 && frameNumber < this.frames.length) {

    //a. Frames made from tileset subimages.
    //If each frame is an array, then the frames were made from an
    //ordinary Image object using the `frames` method
    if (this.frames[0] instanceof Array) {
      this.sourceX = this.frames[frameNumber][0];
      this.sourceY = this.frames[frameNumber][1];
    }

    //b. Frames made from texture atlas frames.
    //If each frame isn't an array, and it has a subobject called `frame`,
    //then the frame must be a texture atlas ID name.
    //In that case, get the source position from the atlas's `frame` object
    else if (this.frames[frameNumber].frame) {
      this.sourceX = this.frames[frameNumber].frame.x;
      this.sourceY = this.frames[frameNumber].frame.y;
      this.sourceWidth = this.frames[frameNumber].frame.w;
      this.sourceHeight = this.frames[frameNumber].frame.h;
      this.width = this.frames[frameNumber].frame.w;
      this.height = this.frames[frameNumber].frame.h;
    }

    //c. Frames made from individual Image objects.
    //If neither of the above is true, then each frame must be
    //an individual Image object
    else {
      this.source = this.frames[frameNumber];
      this.sourceX = 0;
      this.sourceY = 0;
      this.width = this.source.width;
      this.height = this.source.height;
      this.sourceWidth = this.source.width;
      this.sourceHeight = this.source.height;
    }

    //Set the `_currentFrame` value to the chosen frame
    this._currentFrame = frameNumber;
  }
```

```
      //Throw an error if this sprite doesn't contain any frames
      else {
        throw new Error(`Frame number ${frameNumber} does not exist`);
      }
    }

    //The `render` method
    render(ctx) {
      ctx.drawImage(
        this.source,
        this.sourceX, this.sourceY,
        this.sourceWidth, this.sourceHeight,
        -this.width * this.pivotX,
        -this.height * this.pivotY,
        this.width, this.height
      );
    }
  }

//A higher-level wrapper
function sprite(source, x, y) {
  let sprite = new Sprite(source, x, y);
  stage.addChild(sprite);
  return sprite;
}
```

The Sprite class is designed for maximum flexibility so that you can display images from a wide variety of sources. Let's find out what image sources you can use and how.

Making Sprites from Single Images

To make a sprite using a single image file, first load the image using assets.load, which you learned how to use in Chapter 3.

```
assets.load(["images/cat.png"]).then(() => setup());
```

Then supply a reference to the image object as the sprite function's first argument. The second and third arguments are the sprite's *x* and *y* position:

```
function setup() {
  let cat = sprite(assets["images/cat.png"], 64, 410);
}
```

That's the most basic way to make a sprite from an image, but you have many more options.

Making Sprites from Texture Atlas Frames

Using a texture atlas frame is just as easy as using a single image file. First load the texture atlas:

```
assets.load(["images/animals.json"]).then(() => setup());
```

Then supply the atlas frame as the sprite's source:

```
let tiger = sprite(assets["tiger.png"], 192, 410);
```

(Remember, "tiger.png" is the texture atlas frame ID, *not an image file*.) The Sprite class knows that this is a texture atlas frame because when it examines the source argument, it finds a property called frame. That's the fingerprint of a texture atlas.

This is convenient, but what if you want to blit a subimage from a single tileset image directly without using a texture atlas?

Blitting a Subimage from a Tileset

Imagine that you've got a single tileset image that contains a game character's four animation frames. Figure 4-13 shows an example.

Figure 4-13. *A tileset with four character animation frames*

You don't have an accompanying JSON file that tells you anything about the position or size of these frames; you just want to blit one of the subimages directly from the image. How can you do that?

We're going to use a new function called frame that helps you capture individual tileset frames.

```
function frame(source, x, y, width, height) {
  var o = {};
  o.image = source;
  o.x = x;
  o.y = y;
  o.width = width;
  o.height = height;
  return o;
};
```

To use it, supply the name of the tileset image you want to blit from. Then supply the *x*, *y*, width, and height of the subimage that you want to use. The frame function returns an object that you'll be able to use to create the sprite using that subimage. Here's how to blit the first frame from the example fairy character tileset using this new frame function (each frame in the example tileset is 48 pixels wide and 32 pixels high):

```
let fairyFrame = frame(
  assets["images/fairy.png"],   //the tileset source image
  0, 0, 48, 32                  //The subimage's x, y, width and height
);
```

Next, initialize the sprite using the returned fairyFrame object.

```
let fairy = sprite(fairyFrame, 164, 326);
```

This creates a sprite that displays the first frame of the tileset, shown in Figure 4-14.

Figure 4-14. *Blit a subimage from a tileset*

fairyFrame is the sprite's source argument. The Sprite class detects that you're blitting a single subimage because the source contains an image property that was created by the frame function. Here's the snippet of code from the Sprite class that checks for this:

```
else if (source.image && !source.data) {

  //The source is a single subimage from a tileset
  this.createFromTileset(source);
}
```

(You'll find out what source.data is in the next section.)

The Sprite class calls its createFromTileset method to blit the subimage onto the canvas, using the same technique you learned in Chapter 2.

Blitting Multiple Tileset Frames

An important feature of the Sprite class is that it can load up a sprite with multiple images. You can then use sprite.gotoAndStop(frameNumber) to change the image that the sprite displays. This feature will form the basis for keyframe animation and button interactivity, which you'll learn about in the chapters ahead.

But how can you load multiple images into a sprite? There are a few different ways, but let's first find out how to do it with tileset images. We're going to use a new function called frames (with an "s") that lets you specify an array of *x* and *y* positions for the subimages you want to use.

```
function frames(source, arrayOfPositions, width, height) {
  var o = {};
  o.image = source;
  o.data = arrayOfPositions;
  o.width = width;
  o.height = height;
  return o;
};
```

The second argument lets you supply a 2D array of the subimage *x* and *y* positions on the tileset. That 2D array is copied into a property called data on the object returned by the function. Here's how you can use it with our example fairy tileset to specify that you want to use the first three frames:

```
let fairyFrames = frames(
  assets["images/fairy.png"],    //The tileset image
  [[0,0],[48,0],[96,0]],         //The 2D array of x/y frame positions
  48, 32                         //The width and height of each frame
);
```

Now create the sprite by supplying fairyFrames as the source:

```
let fairy = sprite(fairyFrames, 224, 326);
```

The fairy sprite now has three image frames stored in an internal array property called frames. The first frame is displayed by default, but you can use gotoAndStop to make the sprite display another frame. Here's how to make the fairy display the third frame, shown in Figure 4-15.

```
fairy.gotoAndStop(2);
```

Figure 4-15. *Use gotoAndStop to change the frame that a sprite displays*

The gotoAndStop method does this by setting the sprite's sourceX and sourceY values to the *x/y* position 2D array specified by the frame number. Here's the code from the Sprite class that does this:

```
if (this.frames[0] instanceof Array) {
  this.sourceX = this.frames[frameNumber][0];
  this.sourceY = this.frames[frameNumber][1];
}
```

You can apply a similar technique to loading multiple texture atlas frames as well, as you'll see next.

Using Multiple Texture Atlas Frames

Imagine that you want to make a clickable button for a game with three image states: up, over, and down. You create each state in an image editor and use those images to make a texture atlas, as shown in Figure 4-16. The button frame ID names are up.png, over.png, and down.png.

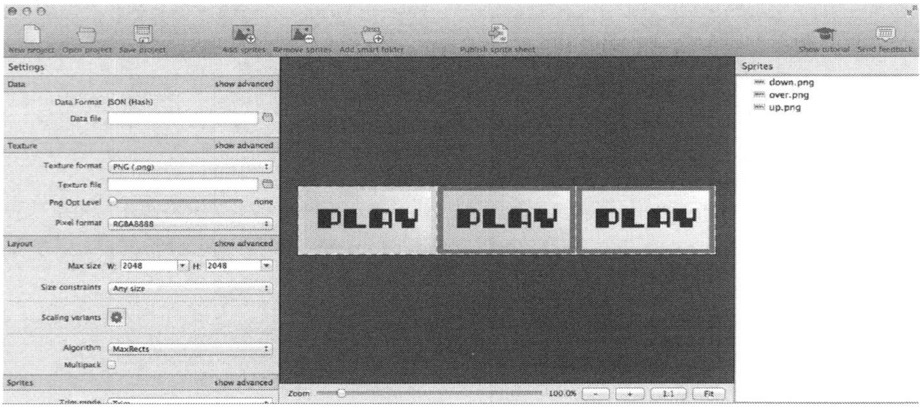

Figure 4-16. *Use a texture atlas to create sprite image states*

Next, you load the texture atlas into your game:

```
assets.load([
  "images/button.json"
]).then(() => setup());
```

You want to create a sprite that can use all three button image states. First, create an array that references the three frame ID names:

```
let buttonFrames = [
  assets["up.png"],
  assets["over.png"],
  assets["down.png"]
];
```

Then create a sprite and supply the `buttonFrames` array as the source:

```
let button = sprite(buttonFrames, 300, 280);
```

The `Sprite` class loads these up into the sprite's `frames` array, and sets up the sprite to display the first frame. You can now use `gotoAndStop` to display any of these frames selectively. Here's how you would display the `"over.png"` frame (the second element in the frames array):

```
button.gotoAndStop(1);
```

The `gotoAndStop` method does this by switching the sprite's `sourceX` and `sourceY` to the correct *x* and *y* frame values in the texture atlas. Here's the snippet of code from the `gotoAndStop` method that does this:

```
else if (this.frames[frameNumber].frame) {
  this.sourceX = this.frames[frameNumber].frame.x;
  this.sourceY = this.frames[frameNumber].frame.y;
}
```

You can load a sprite with as many frames as you like, and you'll learn in Chapter 8 how to use `gotoAndStop` as the essential building block for building a keyframe animation player.

Using Multiple Image Files

For maximum flexibility, the Sprite class also lets you load individual image files into sprites. Imagine you want to make a sprite that contains images of three animals, each as individual frames. First, load your image files into the assets object:

```
assets.load([
  "images/cat.png",
  "images/tiger.png",
  "images/hedgehog.png"
]).then(() => setup());
```

Next, create an array that references each of those image files:

```
let animalImages = [
  assets["images/hedgehog.png"],
  assets["images/tiger.png"],
  assets["images/cat.png"]
];
```

Then use that array of images to initialize the sprite:

```
let animals = sprite(animalImages, 320, 410);
```

The first image in the array, the hedgehog, will be displayed on the sprite by default. If you want the sprite to display the cat image, use gotoAndStop to display the third array element, like this:

```
animals.gotoAndStop(2);
```

Take a look at the gotoAndStop method in the source code and you'll see that this works just by switching the sprite's source to the correct image.

Making Your Own Sprites

You've now got a flexible and useful system for making sprites, and you'll see in the chapters to come how all this new code will help us make games in a fun and productive way. These sprite types are all you need to make almost any 2D action game you can think of. You'll find all this new code in the library/display folder in the chapter's source files. If you want to use these new classes and functions to start making your own sprites, import them as follows:

```
import {
  makeCanvas, rectangle, circle, sprite,
  line, group, text, stage, render, remove,
  frame, frames
} from "../library/display";
```

And, don't forget to import the assets object from library/utilities if you need to preload any image, font, or JSON files:

```
import {assets} from "../library/utilities";
```

Then use `assets.load` to load any files you might need, and call the `setup` function:

```
assets.load([
  "fonts/puzzler.otf",
  "images/cat.png",
  "images/animals.json",
  "images/fairy.png",
  "images/tiger.png",
  "images/hedgehog.png",
  "images/button.json"
]).then(() => setup());
```

Next, use the `setup` function to create the canvas, set up the stage, and create your sprites. Call the render function to display them.

```
function setup() {

  //Create the canvas and stage
  let canvas = makeCanvas(512, 512);
  stage.width = canvas.width;
  stage.height = canvas.height;

  //..Use the code from this chapter to make sprites here...

  //Then render them on the canvas:
  render(canvas);
}
```

In the chapter's source files you'll find a file called `allTheSprites.html`, shown in Figure 4-17, which demonstrates the new code in this chapter. Take a close look at how the code produces the images you see on the canvas, and try making your own changes and additions.

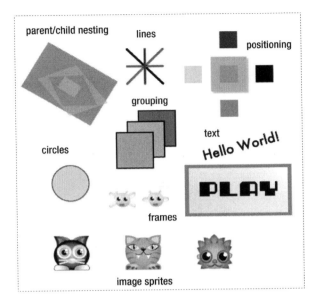

Figure 4-17. *All the new techniques you learned in this chapter*

Summary

In this chapter you've learned how useful sprites can be for quickly displaying images on the screen. You've created a hierarchical scene graph using parent/child nesting, created sprites that display rectangles, circles, lines, text, and images, and even made sprites with multiple frames. You've also had an in-depth look at how to render sprites, how to make sprites using a texture atlas, and how to use ES6 classes to build a useful class inheritance system, and you've learned the principles of code abstraction.

Now that we know how to create sprites, how can we make them move? In the next chapter you'll learn all about scripted animation, the essential techniques every game designer needs to know to move sprites around the screen.

CHAPTER 5

■ ■ ■

Making Things Move

It's almost curtain time! Your sprites are all dressed up, they've memorized their lines, arrived punctually at the rehearsal hall, and are standing patiently on the stage waiting for you to direct them. Now what? You need to animate them!

There are two main ways of animating sprites in games:

- **Scripted animation**: Make the sprite move around the screen.

- **Keyframe animation**: Change the appearance of a sprite. Display a series of slightly different prerendered images, in the same way that you would do hand-drawn cartoon or flipbook animation.

Keyframe animation is about animating a sprite's appearance, while scripted animation is about animating its *x, y* position on the screen. In this chapter you're going to learn how to make sprites move using scripted animation. In Chapter 8 you'll learn how to do keyframe animation to create effects like walking game characters.

In this chapter we're also going to take a detailed look at the game loop: the looping function that makes your sprites move. You'll learn some strategies for separating your game's update logic from its rendering logic to achieve the smoothest possible sprite animation.

Basic Movement

To animate a sprite using scripted animation, you need to change its *x, y* position inside a **game loop**. A game loop is a function that's updated 60 times per second so that you can incrementally change a sprite's position to create the illusion of motion. All your sprite animation, and most of your game logic, happens inside the game loop. The best way to make a game loop with JavaScript and HTML5 is to use a method called window.requestAnimationFrame. Here's some code to illustrate how you can use this method to make a ball bounce off the edges of the canvas. (Figure 5-1 illustrates what this code does.)

```
//Import code from the library
import {makeCanvas, circle, stage, render} from "../library/display";

//Create the canvas and stage
let canvas = makeCanvas(256, 256);
stage.width = canvas.width;
stage.height = canvas.height;
```

```
//Create a ball sprite
//`circle` arguments: diameter, fillStyle, strokeStyle, lineWidth, x, y
let ball = circle(32, "gray", "black", 2, 96, 128);

//Set the ball's velocity
ball.vx = 3;
ball.vy = 2;

//Start the game loop
gameLoop();

function gameLoop() {
  requestAnimationFrame(gameLoop);

  //Move the ball
  ball.x += ball.vx;
  ball.y += ball.vy;

  //Bounce the ball off the canvas edges.
  //Left and right
  if(ball.x < 0
  || ball.x + ball.diameter > canvas.width) {
    ball.vx = -ball.vx;
  }

  //Top and bottom
  if(ball.y < 0
  || ball.y + ball.diameter > canvas.height) {
    ball.vy = -ball.vy;
  }

  //Render the animation
  render(canvas);
}
```

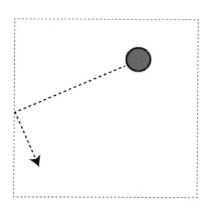

Figure 5-1. *Bounce a ball around the canvas at 60 frames per second*

■ **Note** This code uses methods and objects imported from the `display` module in the `library` folder. Chapter 4 shows how to import and use these tools. You'll find the `library` folder in the chapter's source files.

Velocity is the speed and direction that the ball is travelling. It's represented by two sprite properties: vx and vy.

```
ball.vx = 3;
ball.vy = 2;
```

vx represents the ball's horizontal velocity: how fast it moves right or left. vy represents its vertical velocity: how fast it moves up and down.

■ **Note** The two properties vx and vy actually represent a vector. See the Appendix for everything you need to know about what vectors are and how to leverage their power in your games.

The ball moves because its velocity is added to its current position inside the `requestAnimationFrame` loop:

```
gameLoop();

function gameLoop() {
  requestAnimationFrame(gameLoop);

  ball.x += ball.vx;
  ball.y += ball.vy;

  //...
}
```

With each new frame, the ball's *x* position will change by 3 pixels, and its *y* position will change by 2 pixels. Because the change in motion is small, and the code is being updated 60 times per second, it creates the illusion of motion. This is the basis of scripted animation.

The `requestAnimationFrame` method is the engine that drives the continuously looping code. Its argument is the function that should be called in a loop:

```
requestAnimationFrame(functionToLoop);
```

`requestAnimationFrame` tells the browser that it should call the loop function at intervals of—usually—16 milliseconds (60 times per second). Each loop update is called an **animation frame**, because the effect simulates a running video or filmstrip. (Videos and films are made up of a series of still images, called **frames**, which play in sequence to create the illusion of motion.) The actual rate at which these frames are displayed is synchronized to your monitor's screen refresh rate, which is usually 60Hz (but not always; you'll learn some strategies near the end of this chapter for dealing with these variances). This synchronization makes the loop highly optimized, because the browser will only call the looping code when it's most optimal to do so, and it's not busy performing other tasks.

───

■ **Note** It doesn't matter whether you call `requestAnimationFrame` at the beginning of the loop function or the end. That's because `requestAnimationFrame` doesn't call the loop function at the point where it appears in the code; it just gives the browser permission to call the loop function at any time it's ready to do so.

───

`requestAnimationFrame` can pass an optional **timestamp** argument to the loop function. The timestamp tells you how many milliseconds have passed since `requestAnimationFrame` first started the loop. Here's how to access the timestamp:

```
function gameLoop(timestamp) {
  requestAnimationFrame(gameLoop);
  console.log(`elapsed time: ${timestamp}`);
}
```

At the end of this chapter you'll learn how to use this timestamp to fine-tune the game loop.

───

■ **Note** You can also use `Date.now()` to capture the current UTC time in milliseconds. UTC (Coordinated Universal Time), also known as Unix Time, is a standard measure of time that tells you how many milliseconds have elapsed since January 1, 1970. You can use it as a general timestamp by capturing the current UTC time, comparing it with an earlier or later time, and using the difference to work out the elapsed time. For even greater precision, use `Performance.now()`, which gives you a time accurate to one thousandth millisecond.

───

In this first example, the ball bounces off the edges of the canvas. How does it do this? Two `if` statements check to see if the edges of the ball hit the edges of the canvas. If this is true, the ball's velocity is reversed.

```
//Left and right
if(ball.x < 0
|| ball.x + ball.diameter > canvas.width) {
  ball.vx = -ball.vx;
}
```

```
//Top and bottom
if(ball.y < 0
|| ball.y + ball.diameter > canvas.height) {
  ball.vy = -ball.vy;
}
```

Prefixing the velocities (`ball.vx` and `ball.vy`) with a minus sign causes the ball to reverse its direction when it hits the edge of the canvas.

Adding Acceleration and Friction

You can make an object move in a more natural way by adding physics properties, like acceleration and friction. Acceleration makes an object gradually speed up, and friction slows it down. Figure 5-2 shows an example of a ball that gradually speeds up. When it hits the edges of the canvas, it bounces back and slows to a stop.

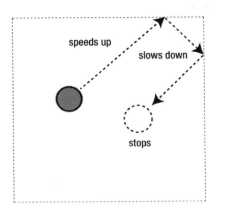

Figure 5-2. *Speed up with acceleration and slow down with friction*

To make this work, add some new acceleration and friction properties to the sprite, and initialize its velocity to zero:

```
let ball = circle(32, "gray", "black", 2, 64, 96);
```

//Set the ball's velocity to 0
```
ball.vx = 0;
ball.vy = 0;
```

//Acceleration and friction properties
```
ball.accelerationX = 0.2;
ball.accelerationY = -0.2;
ball.frictionX = 1;
ball.frictionY = 1;
```

The acceleration *x* and *y* values, 0.2 and –0.2, are the amount by which you want the ball's velocity to increase with each frame. The friction *x* and *y* value, 1, is the amount by which the velocity should be multiplied to slow it down. You don't want to apply any friction to the ball initially, so assigning a value of 1 essentially means "no friction." (That's because the velocity multiplied by 1 just results in the same velocity value without any change. 1 times 1 equals 1, right?) Any friction value less than 1, such as 0.98, will make the object gradually slow down. Acceleration and friction can affect the *x* and *y* axes differently, so that's why there are friction and acceleration properties for each axis.

Here's the game loop that uses these properties to make the ball speed up. As soon as the ball hits the edge of the canvas, the acceleration is set to zero and friction is set to 0.98 to make the ball gradually slow down and stop.

//Start the game loop
```
gameLoop();

function gameLoop() {
  requestAnimationFrame(gameLoop);

  //Apply acceleration to the velocity
  ball.vx += ball.accelerationX;
  ball.vy += ball.accelerationY;
```

169

```
//Apply friction to the velocity
ball.vx *= ball.frictionX;
ball.vy *= ball.frictionY;

//Move the ball by applying the new calculated velocity
//to the ball's x and y position
ball.x += ball.vx;
ball.y += ball.vy;

//Bounce the ball off the canvas edges and slow it to a stop

//Left and right
if(ball.x < 0
|| ball.x + ball.diameter > canvas.width) {

  //Turn on friction
  ball.frictionX = 0.98;
  ball.frictionY = 0.98;

  //Turn off acceleration
  ball.accelerationX = 0;
  ball.accelerationY = 0;

  //Bounce the ball on the x axis
  ball.vx = -ball.vx;
}

//Top and bottom
if(ball.y < 0
|| ball.y + ball.diameter > canvas.height) {

  //Turn on friction
  ball.frictionX = 0.98;
  ball.frictionY = 0.98;

  //Turn off acceleration
  ball.accelerationX = 0;
  ball.accelerationY = 0;

  //Bounce the ball on the y axis
  ball.vy = -ball.vy;
}

//Render the animation
render(canvas);
}
```

You can see in the preceding code that acceleration is *added to* the ball's velocity:

```
ball.vx += ball.accelerationX;
ball.vy += ball.accelerationY;
```

Friction is *multiplied by* the ball's velocity:

```
ball.vx *= ball.frictionX;
ball.vy *= ball.frictionY;
```

To make the ball move, add its new velocity to its current position:

```
ball.x += ball.vx;
ball.y += ball.vy;
```

By changing the ball's friction and acceleration values somewhere in the game, such as when it hits the edge of the canvas, this code will recalculate the ball's velocity correctly. In the next chapter you'll learn how you can change a sprite's acceleration and friction using the mouse, keyboard, and touch.

Gravity

Gravity is a constant downward force on an object. You can add it to a sprite by applying a constant positive value to the sprite's vertical velocity (vy), like this:

```
ball.vy += 0.3;
```

■ **Note**　Remember, canvas *y* positions increase as you move from the top to the bottom of the canvas. That means if you want to pull an object down, you have to add a value to its *y* position, not subtract from it.

If you mix gravity with a bounce effect, you can create a very realistic simulation of a bouncing ball. Run the gravity.html file from the chapter's source code for a working example. The ball starts off with a random velocity, bounces around the canvas, and gradually rolls to a stop at the bottom. Figure 5-3 illustrates what you'll see.

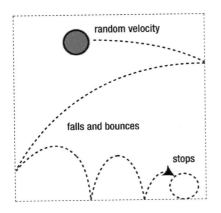

Figure 5-3. *Add some gravity to make a realistic bouncing ball*

It's not just gravity that helps create this effect. To add a bit more realism, the ball also has mass and friction. When the ball hits one of the canvas edges, its mass is deducted from its velocity to simulate the surface absorbing some of the impact force. When the ball is on the ground, some friction is applied to its velocity on the x axis. Both forces slow the ball down in a very realistic way. Without them, the ball would continue to bounce endlessly around the canvas, without losing any momentum. Let's look at the code that does all this.

The ball sprite adds four new properties: gravity, mass, frictionX, and frictionY. It's also initialized with random vx and vy velocities so that the ball moves with different force and direction values each time the program is run:

```
let ball = circle(32, "gray", "black", 2, 96, 128);
```

```
//Random velocity
ball.vx = randomInt(5, 15);
ball.vy = randomInt(5, 15);
```

```
//Physics properties
ball.gravity = 0.3;
ball.frictionX = 1;
ball.frictionY = 0;
ball.mass = 1.3;
```

The mass should be any number greater than 1.

You can see that the random vx and vy properties are initialized to random numbers between 5 and 15. Our code does this with the help of the custom randomInt function you learned in Chapter 1:

```
function randomInt(min, max) {
  return Math.floor(Math.random() * (max - min + 1)) + min;
}
```

If you ever need random floating-point (decimal) numbers in a game, you can use the related function randomFloat:

```
function randomFloat(min, max) {
  return min + Math.random() * (max - min);
}
```

Here's the game loop that uses these properties to make the ball fall downward and bounce off the canvas edges:

```
//Start the game loop
gameLoop();
```

```
function gameLoop() {
  requestAnimationFrame(gameLoop);

  //Apply gravity to the vertical velocity
  ball.vy += ball.gravity;

  //Apply friction. `ball.frictionX` will be 0.96 if the ball is
  //on the ground, and 1 if it's in the air
  ball.vx *= ball.frictionX;
```

```
//Move the ball by applying the new calculated velocity
//to the ball's x and y position
ball.x += ball.vx;
ball.y += ball.vy;
```

```
//Bounce the ball off the canvas edges and slow it to a stop
```

```
//Left
if (ball.x < 0) {
  ball.x = 0;
  ball.vx = -ball.vx / ball.mass;
}
```

```
//Right
if (ball.x + ball.diameter > canvas.width) {
  ball.x = canvas.width - ball.diameter;
  ball.vx = -ball.vx / ball.mass;
}
```

```
//Top
if (ball.y < 0) {
  ball.y = 0;
  ball.vy = -ball.vy / ball.mass;
}
```

```
//Bottom
if(ball.y + ball.diameter > canvas.height) {

  //Position the ball inside the canvas
  ball.y = canvas.height - ball.diameter;

  //Reverse its velocity to make it bounce, and dampen the effect with mass
  ball.vy = -ball.vy / ball.mass;

  //Add some friction if it's on the ground
  ball.frictionX = 0.96;
} else {

  //Remove friction if it's not on the ground
  ball.frictionX = 1;
}
```

```
//Render the animation
  render(canvas);
}
```

You can see that gravity is *added to* the ball's vy property:

```
ball.vy += ball.gravity;
```

Over time, this gradually pulls the ball toward the bottom of the canvas.

■ **Note** In this example gravity is a property of the ball, but in a game you might want to create it as a global value that affects all sprites equally.

Four `if` statements check for collisions between the ball and the canvas edges. If the ball crosses the canvas boundary, it is moved back so that it's just inside the boundary. For example, if the ball crosses the right side of the canvas, its *x* position is set to be equal to the width of the canvas, minus half the ball's diameter.

```
ball.x = canvas.width - ball.diameter;
```

These checks ensure that the ball is completely free of the canvas boundaries and won't get stuck to them when its velocity changes.

Next, the ball's velocity is reversed to make it bounce. The code also divides the ball's velocity by its `mass` (1.3) so that a bit of force is lost in the impact. This is what happens when the ball hits the right side of the canvas:

```
ball.vx = -ball.vx / ball.mass;
```

This will make the ball gradually slow down each time it hits a surface.

The `if` statement that checks whether the ball is hitting the bottom of the canvas does one more thing. It sets the ball's friction to 0.96, so that the ball slows down even more if it's on the ground.

```
if(ball.y + ball.diameter > canvas.height) {
  ball.y = canvas.height - ball.radius;
  ball.vy = -ball.vy / ball.mass;
  ball.frictionX = 0.96;
} else {
  ball.frictionX = 1;
}
```

If the ball isn't on the ground, the `else` block sets the ball's friction back to 1 so that it moves freely through the air.

You can see from these examples that it's very easy to make sprites behave in complex and interesting ways with just a few simple physics properties and a bit of logic. I hope this quick introduction to physics will inspire you start to start playing around with it in your own games. It's really not more complex than this.

Containing Sprites Inside an Area

Containing a sprite inside an area, like the edges of the canvas, is a very common game design requirement. So let's create a function called `contain` that you can use with any of your game projects, like this:

```
let collision = contain(sprite, bounds, bounce, callbackFunction)
```

The first argument is the sprite you want to contain, and the second argument, `bounds`, is an object with *x*, *y*, width, and height properties that define the containment area. Set `bounce` (the third argument) to `true` if the sprite should bounce off the boundary edges. You can also supply an optional extra callback function (the fourth argument) that should run if the sprite hits any of boundary edges. The contain function returns a variable called collision that tells you if the sprite has hit the "top", "left", "bottom" or "right" edges of the boundary. Here's the complete contain function:

```
export function contain (sprite, bounds, bounce = false, extra = undefined){

  let x = bounds.x,
      y = bounds.y,
      width = bounds.width,
      height = bounds.height;

  //The `collision` object is used to store which
  //side of the containing rectangle the sprite hits
  let collision;

  //Left
  if (sprite.x < x) {

    //Bounce the sprite if `bounce` is true
    if (bounce) sprite.vx *= -1;

    //If the sprite has `mass`, let the mass
    //affect the sprite's velocity
    if(sprite.mass) sprite.vx /= sprite.mass;
    sprite.x = x;
    collision = "left";
  }

  //Top
  if (sprite.y < y) {
    if (bounce) sprite.vy *= -1;
    if(sprite.mass) sprite.vy /= sprite.mass;
    sprite.y = y;
    collision = "top";
  }

  //Right
  if (sprite.x + sprite.width > width) {
    if (bounce) sprite.vx *= -1;
    if(sprite.mass) sprite.vx /= sprite.mass;
    sprite.x = width - sprite.width;
    collision = "right";
  }

  //Bottom
  if (sprite.y + sprite.height > height) {
    if (bounce) sprite.vy *= -1;
    if(sprite.mass) sprite.vy /= sprite.mass;
    sprite.y = height - sprite.height;
    collision = "bottom";
  }
```

```
    //The `extra` function runs if there was a collision
    //and `extra` has been defined
    if (collision && extra) extra(collision);

    //Return the `collision` object
    return collision;
};
```

Here's how you can use this contain function to replace the four if statements in the original version of the gravity code from the previous example:

```
let collision = contain(ball, stage.localBounds, true);
```

If the ball hits any of the stage's boundaries, the collision variable will have the value "top", "right", "bottom", or "left". The second argument shows how you can use a sprite's localBounds property, which you learned about in Chapter 4. localBounds is an object with *x*, *y*, width, and height properties that define a rectangular area. You could alternatively achieve the same effect by providing a custom bounds object as the second argument, like this:

```
let collision = contain(
  ball,
  {x: 0, y: 0, width: canvas.width, height: canvas.height},
  true
);
```

Using the stage's localBounds property is a convenient shortcut.

If the ball has hit the stage's boundaries, the collision variable will tell you on what side of the stage the collision occurred. In this gravity example, you want to make the ball slow down if it hits the bottom of the canvas. That means you can check whether collision has the value of "bottom" and, if it does, apply some friction to the ball:

```
if (collision === "bottom") {
  ball.frictionX = 0.96;
} else {
  ball.frictionX = 1;
}
```

Another feature of the contain function is that you can add an extra optional callback function as the fourth argument. Here's how:

```
let collision = contain(
  ball, stage.localBounds, true,
  () => {
    console.log("Hello from the extra function!");
  }
);
```

Each time the ball hits the stage boundaries, the code in that extra callback function will run. This is a convenient way to inject some custom code into the contain function, without modifying the function itself. The contain function checks for the existence of this extra callback and runs it just before it returns the collision value. Here's the code from the contain function that does this:

```
if (collision && extra) extra(collision);
```

You can see that the extra callback also has access to the `collision` value, so it can use that information if it needs it. This is a really useful trick that you'll see many more example of in this book.

Just for your reference, here's the entire `gameLoop` for the gravity example, with the four `if` statements replaced by the `contain` function:

```
function gameLoop() {
  requestAnimationFrame(gameLoop);

  //Move the ball
  ball.vy += ball.gravity;
  ball.vx *= ball.frictionX;
  ball.x += ball.vx;
  ball.y += ball.vy;

  //Check for a collision between the ball and the stage boundaries
  let collision = contain(ball, stage.localBounds, true);
  if (collision === "bottom") {
    //Slow the ball down if it hits the bottom
    ball.frictionX = 0.96;
  } else {
    ball.frictionX = 1;
  }

  //Render the animation
  render(canvas);
}
```

This is a lot less code than the original, and you can reuse the `contain` function in any other project.

Fine-Tuning the Game Loop

Now you know all the basics to making sprites move with code. Pretty easy, isn't it? But there's a little more you'll need to know about the game loop to give you maximum control over how your sprites move around the screen. In this second half of the chapter you're going to learn how to set a game's frame rate, and how to fine-tune the game loop for the smoothest possible sprite animations.

The first, most essential step, is to separate your game logic from your render logic. You're halfway there already: all the sprite rendering happens in the `render` function that you learned to write in the previous chapter. The only new thing you need to do is keep the game logic in its own function called `update`. When the game loop runs, it will first update the game logic and then render the sprites:

```
gameLoop();

function gameLoop() {
  requestAnimationFrame(gameLoop);

  //update the game logic
  update();

  //Render the sprites
  render(canvas);
}
```

177

```
function update() {
  //All your game logic goes here
}

function render(canvas) {
  //The same rendering code from Chapter 4
}
```

You'll see how important this extra bit of modularization will become in the examples ahead.

Setting the Frame Rate

The speed at which you display a sequence of animation frames is called the **frame rate**, which is measured in frames per second, or **fps**. It's the number of times that an animation is updated or changed each second. Higher frame rates give you smoother animation, and lower frame rates make the animation appear choppier. The frame rate for any animation is often determined by the value of a variable called fps. If you wanted your animation to play at 12 frames per second, you could set the fps like this:

```
fps = 12
```

Fps is an easily understandable measurement for us humans, but JavaScript counts milliseconds, not frames. So if we want to use the fps value to the play the frames at regular intervals, we need to use a frame rate based on milliseconds. Divide the fps by 1000 to figure out how many milliseconds should elapse between each frame, like this:

```
frameRate = 1000 / fps
```

If the fps is 12, the frameRate will be 83 milliseconds. This is the general idea, but how can we use it to control the frame rate of our games?

requestAnimationFrame updates the canvas at 60Hz on most systems, and that means that your game loop will run at about 60 frames per second. That's fast and smooth. requestAnimationFrame gives you the smoothest possible animation because the browser draws all the screen graphics at fixed frame intervals in a single screen refresh. It makes the most optimal use of precious CPU time.

A frame rate of 60 frames per second means you've got about 16 milliseconds free between frames to run your game code. Actually, you only have about 13 milliseconds between frames, because browser processes can eat up a few extra milliseconds here and there. To play it safe, add a few more milliseconds and pretend that you really only have 10. So that's a budget of 10 milliseconds of free CPU time to do all your game logic, physics, UI handling, and graphics rendering. That's not much, and it's why game developers tend to obsess about performance and optimization. If you can save only one millisecond of processing somewhere, that's about 10 percent of your performance budget. If your game code needs more than about 10 milliseconds to run, the frame rate will drop, and animations will become **janky**. We all know what jankiness is: jittery, jumpy, and stuttering animations that break a game world's illusion of immersion.

Jank Busting

Jankiness is often caused by JavaScript's **garbage collector** doing automated memory management tasks. Unfortunately you have no control over when the garbage collector runs or how efficiently it's doing its work. Garbage collection is managed by the JavaScript runtime environment (usually the web browser), and you just have to hope that it's doing its job well.

Most web browser developer tools have a frame rate graph that tells you how fast your game is running. If you watch the graph while your game is running you might notice that everything seems fine, and then, out of nowhere, there will be a momentary drop in the frame rate. This is called a **spike**, shown in Figure 5-4. Spikes are a common cause of jankiness.

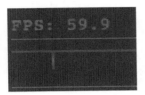

Figure 5-4. *The game designer's nemesis: a frame rate spike!*

A spike happens when there is any sudden increase in the amount of processing that your game or the browser has to do. You can see what causes it by opening the browser's frame Timeline viewer in the developer tools and viewing the Frames graph. The Frames graph tells you how many milliseconds each frame of your game has taken to process. It also shows exactly how much time each piece of code in your game took to run during each frame. If you notice any unusual spikes, check to see what's causing them. Typically, the biggest spikes are caused by the browser doing automated garbage collection, as shown in Figure 5-5.

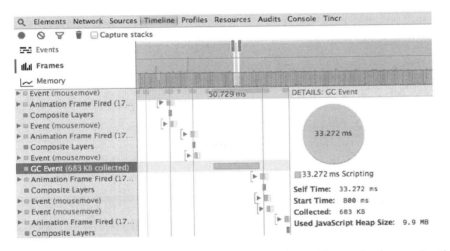

Figure 5-5. *A garbage collection event that consumed 33 milliseconds of processing time*

The garbage collection event in Figure 5-5 took 33 milliseconds. So even if your game were running along at a smooth 60 fps, the garbage collection event would suddenly make it drop to 20 fps, causing a brief stutter of jankiness. So what's the garbage collector actually doing that's taking it 33 milliseconds to run?

It's sometimes hard to tell. But often the biggest garbage collection spikes are caused by the browser clearing out temporary data that it needs for graphics rendering. The best solution for that is to use Canvas or WebGL to render your sprites whenever you can, because they are so much more resource-efficient that DOM rendering. If you don't think you have a rendering bottleneck, do you have any loops, recursive functions, or sorting algorithms that could be causing it? Are you using a physics library that's doing lots of intensive calculations? If you've done all the optimization that you think you can, and your game is still janky, consider lowering your game's frame rate.

■ **Note**   Modern garbage collectors learn how to manage your game's memory while the game is running. So you may see a lot of memory spikes in the first few seconds, and then fewer and fewer as the game continues to run.

Setting the Game's Frame Rate

If you set the game's frame rate to between 30 and 50 fps, you'll win a nice bit of overhead, and your game will still appear to run smoothly. 30 fps is about the lowest you should consider going.

Here's how to set the frame rate:

1. Decide on your rate: 12 fps, 30 fps, 40 fps, or any other rate you want to use.

2. Figure out the frame duration. How many milliseconds should elapse between each frame? This will be 1000 milliseconds divided by the frame rate. For example, if your frame rate is 30 fps, the duration for each frame should be 33 milliseconds.

3. Update the frame only if the elapsed time since the last frame matches the frame duration.

4. Set the update time for the next frame to be the current time plus the frame duration.

Here's an example of some code that does all this to make a game run at 30 frames per second:

```
//Set the frame rate and find the frame duration in milliseconds
let fps = 30,
    start = 0,
    frameDuration = 1000 / fps;

//Start the game loop
gameLoop();

function gameLoop(timestamp) {
  requestAnimationFrame(gameLoop);
  if (timestamp >= start) {

    //update the game logic
    update();

    //Render the sprites
    render(canvas);

    //Reset the frame start time
    start = timestamp + frameDuration;
  }
}
```

This code doesn't guarantee that your game won't run slower than 30 fps, just that it won't run faster than 30fps. The code **clamps** the frame rate at an upper limit of 30 fps. If it's running slower, you probably have bigger problems in your game code somewhere that no amount of tweaking of the frame rate is likely to solve. That's when it's time to dig into your code to search for memory leaks or to do some really aggressive optimization.

Clamping the frame rate like this has another advantage: it makes your game run at a consistent speed across all devices. The `requestAnimationFrame` method is synchronized with your monitor's refresh rate, which is usually 60Hz—but not always. Many newer monitors and device screens have a 120Hz refresh rate, and this makes `requestAnimationFrame` run at double speed: 120 frames per second. By setting the frame rate, you can ensure that your game won't run too fast on any platform.

Fixed Update Time, Variable Rendering Time

There's a further way to optimize the game loop. Instead of running the `update` and `render` functions at the same frame rate, you can run them at different rates. For example, you could run the `update` game logic at a fixed 30 frames per second, and let the `render` function run at the maximum speed that each user's system is capable of running—60 fps, 120 fps, or higher. To do this, your sprites need two positions: one set by the game logic, and another position on the screen that's set by the renderer. But you also want to smooth out fluctuations in the frame rate caused by system processing overhead, so that the animation isn't janky. With the help of some simple math you can make the positions of the rendered sprites stay closely synchronized to the game logic, even though they're being called at different times, and even though there might be small hiccups in the frame rate. This is a technique called **fixed timestep, variable rendering**. In a perfect world, it will give you the most room for game logic calculations. And as long as your game logic frame rate is less than your rendering frame rate, your sprite animation will look smooth and jank-free.

How does it work? Imagine that you decide to update your game logic at 15 fps, and your render logic at 60 fps. You run an ordinary `requestAnimationFrame` loop, which runs at around 60 fps. You call the `render` function each frame, but you don't update the game logic until the time passed since the last frame equals 15 fps. Ideally, you'll end up with calls to `update` and `render` that look like this:

```
update
render
render
render
render
update
render
render
render
render
update
```

But because of unavoidable real-world jankiness, some of the rendering calls might intermittently dip down to 30 fps or less. That means the calls to `update` and `render` might actually look something like this:

```
update
render
render
update
render
```

```
update
render
render
render
update
```

You can see that update is still being called at a fixed rate, but render fluctuates. What happens if you get a lagging render call stuck between two update calls?

```
update
render
update
```

The animation will still look janky unless we employ a technique called **interpolation**, which averages out a sprite's rendered position between update calls. Interpolation irons out inconsistencies in the frame rate so that you can have very smooth sprite animation even at low frame rates. Let's find out how it works.

Writing the Code

Here's the new game loop that implements all these concepts. Notice that the code calls a new function called renderWithInterpolation to render the sprites. I'll explain how that works ahead.

```
let fps = 30,
    previous = 0,
    frameDuration = 1000 / fps,
    lag = 0;

function gameLoop(timestamp) {
  requestAnimationFrame(gameLoop);

  //Calculate the time that has elapsed since the last frame
  if (!timestamp) timestamp = 0;
  let elapsed = timestamp - previous;

  //Optionally correct any unexpected huge gaps in the elapsed time
  if (elapsed > 1000) elapsed = frameDuration;

  //Add the elapsed time to the lag counter
  lag += elapsed;

  //Update the frame if the lag counter is greater than or
  //equal to the frame duration
  while (lag >= frameDuration) {

    //Update the game logic
    update();

    //Reduce the lag counter by the frame duration
    lag -= frameDuration;
  }
```

```
//Calculate the lag offset. This tells us how far
//we are into the next frame
let lagOffset = lag / frameDuration;

//Render the sprites using the `lagOffset` to
//interpolate the sprites' positions
renderWithInterpolation(canvas, lagOffset);

//Capture the current time to be used as the previous
//time in the next frame
previous = timestamp;
}
```

The gameLoop first figures out how much time has elapsed since the previous frame:

```
let elapsed = timestamp - previous;
```

Take a look at the final line in the gameLoop and you'll see that previous is a reference to the current value of timestamp:

```
previous = timestamp;
```

So when the next frame swings around, previous will still contain that old value. That's why we can use it at the beginning of the loop to help calculate the elapsed time since the previous frame.

As an extra precaution, the code first checks whether the elapsed time isn't greater than some extremely large amount, like 1 second. If thats the case, the game code might have crashed or the user may have switched browser tabs:

```
if (elapsed > 1000) elapsed = frameDuration;
```

This is just a safety net to set the elapsed time back to a sensible amount.

A variable called lag is used to count the amount of elapsed time between frames:

```
lag += elapsed;
```

When lag accumulates an amount that's greater than or equal to the frame rate, it resets and calls the update function:

```
while (lag >= frameDuration) {
  update();
  lag -= frameDuration;
}
```

It's this while loop that acts as a kind of shock absorber for frame rate inconsistencies. It will call the update function as many times as needed until lag has caught up with the current frame rate.

Next, the code uses the lag amount to figure out the difference between the update frame rate and the render frame rate. That value is saved in a variable called lagOffset:

```
let lagOffset = lag / frameDuration;
```

The `lagOffset` value gives you the proportional difference between the update frame rate and the rendered frame rate. It will be a normalized number between 0 and 1. (This value is often called the delta time, or dt.) This is the value we need to help figure out the precise position at which the sprites should be rendered, using the new `renderWithInterpolation` function.

```
renderWithInterpolation(canvas, lagOffset);
```

How does `renderWithInterpolation` work to find the compromise sprite positions between the update frame rate and the render frame rate?

Interpolation

Let's imagine that the game logic is being updated at 15 frames per second, and the sprites are being rendered at 60 frames per second. That means there will be four render calls for each update call. To keep the animation smooth, the renderer needs to guess at which positions the sprites should be displayed between each update, and draw the sprites at those positions. This is called interpolation. Here's the basic formula for figuring it out:

```
renderedPosition = (currentPosition - previousPosition) * lagOffset + previousPosition;
```

The key part of the formula is that the sprite's velocity is worked out dynamically by subtracting its position in the previous frame from its position in the current frame. How do you know what the sprite's previous position is? You capture the sprite's current position each frame as your very first step, before you make any changes to it. You can then use that captured position as the sprite's previous position in the following frame. Here's how to implement this strategy:

```
function update() {

  sprite.previousX = sprite.x;
  sprite.previousY = sprite.y;

  //Next, change the sprite's velocity and position
  //as you normally would for the current frame
}
```

Here's how to implement this in our bouncing ball example:

```
function update() {

  //Capture the ball's previous positions
  ball.previousX = ball.x;
  ball.previousY = ball.y;

  //Move the ball and bounce it off the stage's edges
  ball.vy += ball.gravity;
  ball.vx *= ball.frictionX;
  ball.x += ball.vx;
  ball.y += ball.vy;
```

```
  let collision = contain(ball, stage.localBounds, true);
  if (collision === "bottom") {
    ball.frictionX = 0.96;
  } else {
    ball.frictionX = 1;
  }
}
```

ball.previousX and ball.previousY will still contain the sprite's position values from the previous frame when this current frame has finished updating.

Now you can use the renderWithInterpolation function to take all this new data and use it to interpolate the sprite's position. The renderWithInterpolation function is the same as the old render function you learned to use in the previous chapter, with the exception of this new bit of code that calculates the sprites' rendered positions.

```
function renderWithInterpolation(canvas, lagOffset) {

  //...

  //Interpolate the position
  if (sprite.previousX) {
    sprite.renderX = (sprite.x - sprite.previousX) * lagOffset + sprite.previousX;
  } else {
    sprite.renderX = sprite.x;
  }

  if (sprite.previousY) {
    sprite.renderY = (sprite.y - sprite.previousY) * lagOffset + sprite.previousY;
  } else {
    sprite.renderY = sprite.y;
  }

  //Draw the sprite at its interpolated position
  ctx.translate(
    sprite.renderX + (sprite.width * sprite.pivotX),
    sprite.renderY + (sprite.height * sprite.pivotY)
  );

  //...
}
```

(You'll find the complete renderWithInterpolation function in the library/display folder in the book's source code.)

Now if you set the game's fps to 15, the sprites will still render at 60 fps, giving you smooth, jank-free animation and minimal overhead.

▧ **Note**   You can interpolate other sprite properties like rotation and alpha using these same techniques.

Interpolating Multiple Sprites

If you have lots of sprites in your game, you need to capture all of their previous positions before you change their current positions. A simple way to do that is to run a `capturePreviousPositions` function before you call `update` in the game loop, like this:

```
while (lag >= frameDuration) {
  capturePreviousPositions(stage);
  update();
  lag -= frameDuration;
}
```

The `capturePreviousPositions` function just loops through all the sprites and their children and sets their previous position values to their current positions.

```
function capturePreviousPositions(stage) {

  //Loop through all the children of the stage
  stage.children.forEach(sprite => {
    setPreviousPosition(sprite);
  });

  function setPreviousPosition(sprite) {

    //Set the sprite's `previousX` and `previousY`
    sprite.previousX = sprite.x;
    sprite.previousY = sprite.y;

    //Loop through all the sprite's children
    if (sprite.children && sprite.children.length > 0) {
      sprite.children.forEach(child => {

        //Recursively call `setPosition` on each sprite
        setPreviousPosition(child);
      });
    }
  }
}
```

The rest of the code will be the same. Figure 5-6 shows an example of 500 balls animated smoothly with the game logic running at 15 fps and the renderer running at 60 fps. You'll find the full source code in the chapter's source files.

Figure 5-6. *Interpolation allows for smooth animation at low frame rates*

Should You Do It?

What's the trade-off with interpolation? There are a few.

Because the interpolated positions are based on the sprite's previous positions, the rendered view into the game world will always be just slightly behind the game logic. If the logic is being run at 30 fps and the renderer is running at 60 fps, the time difference will be about 33 milliseconds. This isn't significant—players won't ever notice it—but you should be aware that it's happening.

The other trade-off is that your code becomes much more complex. If you have a physics-heavy game that requires a lot of processing overhead, it might be worth it. But the biggest bottleneck for most games is usually the rendering, not the game logic calculations.

There's another side-effect to be aware of. If there's an unusually big system spike and it takes longer to update the game logic than it does to render the sprites, you'll see a jump in the animation. The animation will appear to stop, and then a moment later you'll see the sprite appear in the position it would have been if the animation had continued without interruption. In the less sophisticated game loops we looked at earlier, a big spike would just cause the animation to slow down. Neither of these effects is necessarily better or worse; you just have to decide which you prefer.

Finally, I should offer a general warning about premature optimization. There's simplicity to the first, most basic game loop we looked at. This is where the update and render functions are both called in the same loop and at the maximum frame rate:

```
gameLoop();
function gameLoop() {
  requestAnimationFrame(gameLoop);
  update();
  render(canvas);
}
```

That might be all you need. Browser vendors are continuously tweaking, changing, improving, and experimenting with how they render graphics, sometimes in inscrutable ways. You need to be careful that you don't accidentally write some code that fights against the browser's own rendering engine and end up with poorer performance than before you started. Fine-tuning the game loop and sprite rendering is an art much more than it is a science, so keep an open mind, try everything, and remember this: if your game looks good and it runs good, then it is good.

Summary

In the previous chapter you learned how to create sprites, and in this one you learned how to make them move. You learned how to update a sprite's position by modifying its velocity inside a game loop using `requestAnimationFrame`. You saw how easy it was to add physics properties to sprites by applying acceleration, friction, and gravity, and also how to bounce a sprite off boundary walls. We took a closer look at modularizing your code with a reusable `contain` function, and you learned some detailed strategies for optimizing game logic and rendering performance.

Now that we can make sprites and move them, how can we interact with them? HTML5 and JavaScript have built-in capabilities for controlling games using the mouse, keyboard, and touch, and you'll find out all about how those work in the next chapter.

CHAPTER 6

■ ■ ■

Interactivity

Welcome to the greatest-hits countdown of the most important pieces of game code you need to know to add interactivity to your sprites. Now that you know how to make sprites move, you're going to learn all about how to make them interact with the game world they live in.

You're also going to learn how to create two of the most useful interactive objects for games: clickable buttons and draggable sprites. Everything you need to know about adding rich interactivity to your game world is right here in this chapter.

Keyboard, Mouse, and Touch

The first step to adding keyboard, mouse, or touch interactivity is to set up an **event listener**. The event listener is a bit of code that's built into the browser and "listens" for whether the player is pressing a key on the keyboard, touching the screen or moving or clicking the mouse. If the listener detects an event, it calls an **event handler**, which is just a function that does some kind of action that's important in your game. The event handler might make a player's character move, calculate the speed of the mouse, or accept some input. The event listeners and handlers are like the bridge between our human world and the game world. In this first section of the chapter you're going to learn how to add event listeners and handlers for keyboard, touch, and mouse events, and how to use them to make something interesting happen in the game world. Let's start with keyboard interactivity.

■ **Note** The HTML5 specification also includes a Gamepad API that lets you capture input from game controller buttons. Check out the specification at `dvcs.w3.org`. It's as easy to use as keyboard, mouse, and touch events.

Capturing Keyboard Events

If you want to find out whether a player has pressed a key on the keyboard, add an event listener with a keydown event. Then write a keyDownHandler that uses an ASCII keyCode number to find out which key was pressed. Here's how you can find out if a player pressed the space key. (The keycode for the space key is 32, and a quick web search for "ASCII keycodes" will bring up a complete list.)

```
window.addEventListener("keydown", keydownHandler, false)
function keydownHandler(event) {
  if(event.keyCode === 32) {
    console.log("Space key pressed");
  }
}
```

This code works fine, but for most games you'll also need to use a keyup event to tell you if the key has been released. A good way to check for this is to create a key object with properties called isDown and isUp. Set these properties to true or false, depending on the key's state. This will let you check for keystrokes with if statements, like this:

```
if (space.isDown) {
  //do this!
}
if (space.isUp) {
  //do this!
}
```

Here's the space key object that will let you write the if statements just shown:

```
let space = {
  code: 32,
  isDown: false,
  isUp: true,
  downHandler(event) {
    if(event.keyCode === this.code) {
      this.isDown = true;
      this.isUp = false;
    }
  },
  upHandler(event) {
    if(event.keyCode === this.code) {
      this.isUp = true;
      this.isDown = false;
    }
  }
};
```

```
//Add the event listeners and bind them to the space object
window.addEventListener(
  "keydown", space.downHandler.bind(space), false
);
window.addEventListener(
  "keyup", space.upHandler.bind(space), false
);
```

■ **Note**   Notice how the `bind` method is used to connect the listener to the `space.downHandler` and `space.upHandler` methods. It makes sure that references to "this" in the space object refer to the space object itself, and not the window object.

This works well, but what if we also wanted to also add listeners for the four keyboard arrow keys (up, right, down, and left)? We don't want to have to write these 20 lines of repetitive code five times over. We can do better!

Let's make a keyboard function that creates key objects that listen for specific keyboard events. We'll be able to create a new key object like this:

```
let keyObject = keyboard(asciiKeyCodeNumber);
```

We'll then be able to assign `press` and `release` methods to the key object as follows:

```
keyObject.press = function() {
  //key object pressed
};
keyObject.release = function() {
  //key object released
};
```

Our key objects will also have `isDown` and `isUp` Boolean properties that you can check if you need to. Here's the keyboard function that lets us implement this:

```
export function keyboard(keyCode) {
  let key = {};
  key.code = keyCode;
  key.isDown = false;
  key.isUp = true;
  key.press = undefined;
  key.release = undefined;

  //The `downHandler`
  key.downHandler = function(event) {
    if (event.keyCode === key.code) {
      if (key.isUp && key.press) key.press();
      key.isDown = true;
      key.isUp = false;
    }

    //Prevent the event's default behavior
    //(such as browser window scrolling)
    event.preventDefault();
  };
```

```
//The `upHandler`
key.upHandler = function(event) {
  if (event.keyCode === key.code) {
    if (key.isDown && key.release) key.release();
    key.isDown = false;
    key.isUp = true;
  }
  event.preventDefault();
};

//Attach event listeners
window.addEventListener(
  "keydown", key.downHandler.bind(key), false
);
window.addEventListener(
  "keyup", key.upHandler.bind(key), false
);

//Return the `key` object
return key;
}
```

You'll find this complete keyboard function in the library/interactive.js file in the chapter's source code.

Open keyObject.html in this chapter's source files for a working example of this code in action. Press and release the space key, and you'll see "pressed" and "released" displayed on the canvas (Figure 6-1).

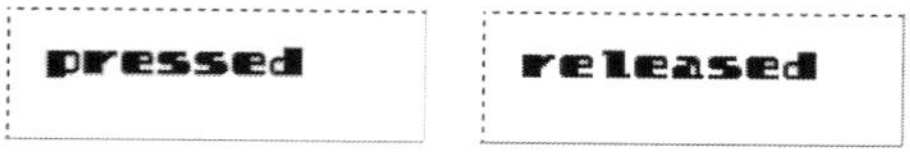

Figure 6-1. *Use a text sprite to tell you whether a key is pressed or released*

This works by using a game loop to display the string contents of a text sprite. This sprite's content is set by the press and release methods of a space key object. The code also uses the assets object to load a custom font and call the setup function when it's ready. Here's the complete code that accomplishes all this:

```
//Import code from the library
import {makeCanvas, text, stage, render} from "../library/display";
import {assets} from "../library/utilities";
import {keyboard} from "../library/interactive";

//Load a custom font
assets.load(["fonts/puzzler.otf"]).then(() => setup());

//Declare any variables shared between functions
let canvas;
```

```
function setup() {

  //Make the canvas and initialize the stage
  canvas = makeCanvas(256, 256);
  stage.width = canvas.width;
  stage.height = canvas.height;

  //Make a text sprite
  let message = text("Press space", "16px puzzler", "black", 16, 16);

  //Make a space key object
  let space = keyboard(32);

  //Assign `press` and `release` methods
  space.press = () => message.content = "pressed";
  space.release = () => message.content = "released";

  //Use a loop to display any changes to the text sprite's
  //`content` property
  gameLoop();
}

function gameLoop() {
  requestAnimationFrame(gameLoop);
  render(canvas);
}
```

You've now got a general-purpose system for quickly creating and listening for keyboard input. Further into this chapter you'll find an example of how to use key objects to control an interactive game character.

Capturing Pointer Events

Now that you know how to add keyboard interactivity, let's find out how to create interactive mouse and touch events. Mouse and touch both behave in a similar way, so it's useful to think of them as a single thing called a "pointer." In this section you're going to learn how to create a universal pointer object that unifies both mouse and touch events. You're then going to learn how to use the new pointer object to add interactivity to games.

▦ **Note** At the time of writing, an HTML5 specification called Pointer Events was in the works. If it's widely implemented when you read this, it means you no longer need to fork your code to accommodate both mouse and touch; Pointer Events work for both. And, as a great convenience, the Pointer Events API is almost identical to the Mouse Event API, so there's nothing really new for you to learn. Just swap "mouse" for "pointer" in any mouse event code and you're good to go. Then set the CSS touch-action property on the pointer-sensitive element to "none" to disable the browser's default pan and zoom actions. Keep your eye on this specification and use it if you can (http://www.w3.org/TR/pointerevents/).

To create mouse or touch events, attach an event listener to the HTML element that you want to make sensitive to the pointer, such as the canvas. Then make the listener call an event handler when the event happens:

```
canvas.addEventListener("mousedown", downHandler, false);

function downHandler(event) {
  console.log("Pointer pressed down");
}
```

There's one small problem for us game developers, however. How do you detect whether a player has tapped or clicked something? A tap or click is just a very rapid down-up action of the pointer. Anything faster than about 200 milliseconds could be defined as a tap or click. You can figure out if this has happened by comparing the time between a down and an up event. If it's less than 200 milliseconds, you can assume the player has tapped or clicked. Here's the general way to figure this out.

First, when the pointer is down, capture the current time with Date.now():

```
function downHandler(event) {
  downTime = Date.now();
}
```

The downTime value now contains the exact time in milliseconds that the pointer was pressed down. When the pointer is up, capture the new time, and figure out how much time has elapsed since the downTime. If it's less than 200 milliseconds, then you know there was a tap or click.

```
function upHandler(event) {
  elapsedTime = Math.abs(downTime - Date.now());
  if (elapsedTime <= 200) {
    console.log("Tap or click!");
  }
}
```

To help us manage all this, let's create a pointer object. In addition to tapping or clicking, the pointer should also be able to tell us its *x* and *y* positions, and also whether it's currently up or down. For maximum flexibility, we're also going to let the user define optional press, tap, and release methods that can run some custom code if either of those events happen. In addition, we're going to give the pointer centerX, centerY, and position properties so its API closely mirrors the API of our sprites from the previous chapter. As you'll see later in this book, this is a convenience that will make it easier for us to use the pointer with the collision detection functions you're going to learn to use in Chapter 7.

The pointer will also have a forward-looking property called scale. The scale property will help us adjust the pointer's coordinates if the canvas is scaled up or down inside the browser window. For most games, the default scale value of 1 is all you need. But if you change the game's display size, you'll need to proportionately modify the pointer's *x* and *y* coordinates by the scale value. (You'll see how helpful this will be in Chapter 11.)

Here's a makePointer function that creates and returns a pointer object that does all this for us. The nitty-gritty details of how it works are in the comments, and I'll show you how to use it after the code listing.

```
export function makePointer(element, scale = 1) {

  let pointer = {
    element: element,
    scale: scale,

    //Private x and y properties
    _x: 0,
    _y: 0,

    //The public x and y properties are divided by the scale. If the
    //HTML element that the pointer is sensitive to (like the canvas)
    //is scaled up or down, you can change the `scale` value to
    //correct the pointer's position values
    get x() {
      return this._x / this.scale;
    },
    get y() {
      return this._y / this.scale;
    },

    //Add `centerX` and `centerY` getters so that we
    //can use the pointer's coordinates with easing
    //and collision functions
    get centerX() {
      return this.x;
    },
    get centerY() {
      return this.y;
    },

    //`position` returns an object with x and y properties that
    //contain the pointer's position
    get position() {
      return {x: this.x, y: this.y};
    },

    //Booleans to track the pointer state
    isDown: false,
    isUp: true,
    tapped: false,

    //Properties to help measure the time between up and down states
    downTime: 0,
    elapsedTime: 0,

    //Optional, user-definable `press`, `release`, and `tap` methods
    press: undefined,
    release: undefined,
    tap: undefined,
```

```
//The pointer's mouse `moveHandler`
moveHandler(event) {

  //Get the element that's firing the event
  let element = event.target;

  //Find the pointer's x,y position (for mouse).
  //Subtract the element's top and left offset from the browser window
  this._x = (event.pageX - element.offsetLeft);
  this._y = (event.pageY - element.offsetTop);

  //Prevent the event's default behavior
  event.preventDefault();
},

//The pointer's `touchmoveHandler`
touchmoveHandler(event) {
  let element = event.target;

  //Find the touch point's x,y position
  this._x = (event.targetTouches[0].pageX - element.offsetLeft);
  this._y = (event.targetTouches[0].pageY - element.offsetTop);
  event.preventDefault();
},

//The pointer's `downHandler`
downHandler(event) {

  //Set the down states
  this.isDown = true;
  this.isUp = false;
  this.tapped = false;

  //Capture the current time
  this.downTime = Date.now();

  //Call the `press` method if it's been assigned by the user
  if (this.press) this.press();
  event.preventDefault();
},

//The pointer's `touchstartHandler`
touchstartHandler(event) {
  let element = event.target;

  //Find the touch point's x,y position
  this._x = event.targetTouches[0].pageX - element.offsetLeft;
  this._y = event.targetTouches[0].pageY - element.offsetTop;
```

```
//Set the down states
this.isDown = true;
this.isUp = false;
this.tapped = false;

//Capture the current time
this.downTime = Date.now();

//Call the `press` method if it's been assigned by the user
if (this.press) this.press();
event.preventDefault();
},

//The pointer's `upHandler`
upHandler(event) {

  //Figure out how much time the pointer has been down
  this.elapsedTime = Math.abs(this.downTime - Date.now());

  //If it's less than 200 milliseconds, it must be a tap or click
  if (this.elapsedTime <= 200 && this.tapped === false) {
    this.tapped = true;

    //Call the `tap` method if it's been assigned
    if (this.tap) this.tap();
  }
  this.isUp = true;
  this.isDown = false;

  //Call the `release` method if it's been assigned by the user
  if (this.release) this.release();
  event.preventDefault();
},

//The pointer's `touchendHandler`
touchendHandler(event) {

  //Figure out how much time the pointer has been down
  this.elapsedTime = Math.abs(this.downTime - Date.now());

  //If it's less than 200 milliseconds, it must be a tap or click
  if (this.elapsedTime <= 200 && this.tapped === false) {
    this.tapped = true;

    //Call the `tap` method if it's been assigned by the user
    if (this.tap) this.tap();
  }
  this.isUp = true;
  this.isDown = false;
```

```
      //Call the `release` method if it's been assigned by the user
      if (this.release) this.release();
      event.preventDefault();
    },

  //Bind the events to the handlers'
  //Mouse events
  element.addEventListener(
    "mousemove", pointer.moveHandler.bind(pointer), false
  );
  element.addEventListener(
    "mousedown", pointer.downHandler.bind(pointer), false
  );

  //Add the `mouseup` event to the `window` to
  //catch a mouse button release outside of the canvas area
  window.addEventListener(
    "mouseup", pointer.upHandler.bind(pointer), false
  );

  //Touch events

  element.addEventListener(
    "touchmove", pointer.touchmoveHandler.bind(pointer), false
  );
  element.addEventListener(
    "touchstart", pointer.touchstartHandler.bind(pointer), false
  );

  //Add the `touchend` event to the `window` object to
  //catch a mouse button release outside the canvas area
  window.addEventListener(
    "touchend", pointer.touchendHandler.bind(pointer), false
  );

  //Disable the default pan and zoom actions on the `canvas`
  element.style.touchAction = "none";

  //Return the pointer
  return pointer;
}
```

You'll find the complete makePointer function in the source code's library/display folder. Here's how you can use this function to create and initialize a pointer object:

```
pointer = makePointer(canvas);
```

Open and run the pointer.html program for a working example of how to use it; a sample run is shown in Figure 6-2. When you move, tap, click, press, or release the pointer over the canvas, the HTML text displays the pointer's status. Here's the complete program, including the HTML code, so that you can see how all the pieces fit together.

Pointer properties:
pointer.x: 123
pointer.y: 115
pointer.isDown: false
pointer.isUp: true
pointer.tapped: true

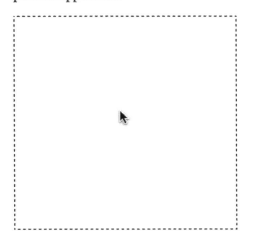

Figure 6-2. *A universal pointer object for mouse and touch*

```
<!doctype html>
<meta charset="utf-8">
<title>Pointer</title>
<p id="output"></p>
<script type="module">
```

//Import code from the library
```
import {makeCanvas, stage, render} from "../library/display";
import {assets} from "../library/utilities";
import {makePointer} from "../library/interactive";
```

//Make the canvas and initialize the stage
```
let canvas = makeCanvas(256, 256);
stage.width = canvas.width;
stage.height = canvas.height;
```

//Get a reference to the output <p> tag
```
let output = document.querySelector("p");
```

//Make the pointer
```
let pointer = makePointer(canvas);
```

//Add a custom `press` method
```
pointer.press = () => console.log("The pointer was pressed");
```

```
//Add a custom `release` method
pointer.release = () => console.log("The pointer was released");

//Add a custom `tap` method
pointer.tap = () => console.log("The pointer was tapped");

//Use a loop to display changes to the output text
gameLoop();

function gameLoop() {
  requestAnimationFrame(gameLoop);

  //Display the pointer properties in the
  //HTML <p> tag called `output`
  output.innerHTML
    = `Pointer properties: <br>
  pointer.x: ${pointer.x} <br>
  pointer.y: ${pointer.y} <br>
  pointer.isDown: ${pointer.isDown} <br>
  pointer.isUp: ${pointer.isUp} <br>
  pointer.tapped: ${pointer.tapped}`;

}
</script>
```

■ **Note** This example also demonstrates the minimum HTML5 code you need to write and still have a valid HTML document. Short and simple! The `<html>` and `<body>` tags are optional. You might still need a `<body>` tag as a hook for adding and removing HTML elements, but if you leave it out, the HTML5 specification assumes that it's implied.

Notice how the optional press, release, and tap functions have been defined:

```
pointer.press = () => console.log("The pointer was pressed");
pointer.release = () => console.log("The pointer was released");
pointer.tap = () => console.log("The pointer was tapped");
```

These are convenient methods that let you inject some custom code whenever any of these actions happen. You'll see how to use them in the chapters ahead.

We've now got keyboard, mouse, and touch interactivity—cool! Now that we know how to interact with the game world, let's start doing it!

Interactive Movement

Let's take what you learned in the previous chapter about how to move sprites and combine it with what you've learned about interactivity so far in this chapter. In this next section you're going to learn some of the most useful snippets of code to make sprites move. These are the classic techniques that the history of video games was built on, and you'll find countless uses for them in your games. You'll find all the custom functions we're using in this section in the source code's library/utilities folder.

Finding the Distance between Sprites

Your games will often need to calculate the number of pixels between sprites. This is useful for finding out whether sprites are colliding, or close to colliding. If your sprites have centerX and centerY properties, you can figure out the distance between them using the following function (s1 stands for "sprite 1" and s2 stands for "sprite 2"):

```
function distance(s1, s2) {
  let vx = s2.centerX - s1.centerX,
      vy = s2.centerY - s1.centerY;
  return Math.sqrt(vx * vx + vy * vy);
}
```

The vx and vy values describe a line from the center of the first sprite to the center of the second sprite. (The "v" stands for "vector." You can think of a vector as just a line between any two *x,y* positions. See the Appendix for everything you need to know about vectors). Math.sqrt is then used to apply the Pythagorean Theorem, which tells you how long this line is, in pixels.

In the chapter's source files you'll find an example program called distance.html that shows this function in action. There are two circle sprites with a line connecting them. When you move the pointer, a text sprite tells you the distance in pixels between the two circles. Figure 6-3 illustrates this.

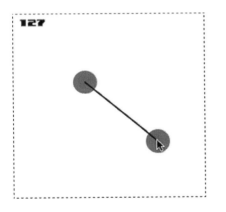

Figure 6-3. *Find the distance between sprites*

Let's look at how the program uses this distance function, and also take this opportunity to learn more about how to work with sprites. Here's the complete JavaScript code for the distance.html program:

```
import {makeCanvas, text, circle, line, stage, render} from "../library/display";
import {assets, distance} from "../library/utilities";
import {makePointer} from "../library/interactive";

//Load a custom font
assets.load(["fonts/puzzler.otf"]).then(() => setup());
```

```
//Declare any variables shared between functions
let canvas, c1, c2, message, connection, pointer;

function setup() {

  //Make the canvas and initialize the stage
  canvas = makeCanvas(256, 256);
  stage.width = canvas.width;
  stage.height = canvas.height;

  //Make a text sprite
  message = text("", "12px puzzler", "black", 8, 8);

  //Create a circle sprite offset by 32 pixels to the
  //left and top of the stage
  c1 = circle(32, "gray");
  stage.putCenter(c1, -32, -32);

  //Create a circle sprite offset by 32 pixels to the
  //right and bottom of the stage
  c2 = circle(32, "gray");
  stage.putCenter(c2, 32, 32);

  //Create a line between the centers of the circles
  connection = line(
    "black", 2, c1.centerX, c1.centerY, c2.centerX, c2.centerY
  );

  //Make the pointer
  pointer = makePointer(canvas);

  //Use a loop to update the sprites' positions
  gameLoop();
}

function gameLoop() {
  requestAnimationFrame(gameLoop);

  //Keep the center of c2 aligned with the
  //pointer's position
  c2.x = pointer.x - c2.halfWidth;
  c2.y = pointer.y - c2.halfHeight;

  //Draw the connecting line between the circles
  connection.ax = c1.centerX;
  connection.ay = c1.centerY;
  connection.bx = c2.centerX;
  connection.by = c2.centerY;
```

```
//Use the imported `distance` function to figure
//out the distance between the circles
let distanceBetweenCircles = distance(c1, c2);

//Use the message text sprite to display the distance.
//Use `Math.floor` to truncate the decimal values
message.content = Math.floor(distanceBetweenCircles);

//Render the canvas
render(canvas);
}
```

There are quite a few display elements working together in this program: circle, line, and text sprites, as well as the stage. The game loop is also dynamically calculating the distance between the circles and continuously redrawing the connecting line each frame.

Positioning Sprites with the put Methods

This is also the first time you've seen one of the mysterious "put" sprite methods in action (we added the "put" methods to sprites in Chapter 4). All Display objects (sprites and the stage) have methods called putCenter, putTop, putRight, putBottom, and putLeft that you can use to conveniently align and position sprites. In this example program the stage object is using putCenter to position the circles inside the stage:

```
c1 = circle(32, "gray");
stage.putCenter(c1, -32, -32);

c2 = circle(32, "gray");
stage.putCenter(c2, 32, 32);
```

The first argument is the sprite that should be centered: c1 or c2. The second and third arguments define by how much the sprite should be offset from the center on the *x*- and *y*-axes. This code places c1 in the top-left portion of the stage and c2 in the bottom-right portion. You'll find that you're often going to need to do this kind of positioning in games, and the "put" methods save you from having to write a lot of tedious positioning code.

Easing

In the previous example, the circle followed the pointer's position exactly. You can make the circle move with a little more grace by using a standard formula called **easing**. Easing makes the sprite gently settle into position over its destination point. Here's a followEase function that you can use to make a sprite follow another sprite with easing.

```
function followEase(follower, leader, speed) {

  //Figure out the distance between the sprites
  let vx = leader.centerX - follower.centerX,
      vy = leader.centerY - follower.centerY,
      distance = Math.sqrt(vx * vx + vy * vy);
```

```
  //Move the follower if it's more than 1 pixel
  //away from the leader
  if (distance >= 1) {
    follower.x += vx * speed;
    follower.y += vy * speed;
  }
}
```

The function calculates the distance between the sprites. If they're more than 1 pixel apart, the code moves the follower at a speed which decreases proportionally as it approaches the leader. Speed values between 0.1 and 0.3 are a good place to start (higher numbers make the sprites move faster). The follower will gradually slow to a stop over the leader's position. Open the easing.html file in the chapter's source files to see how to can use this function to make a sprite follow the mouse with easing. Figure 6-4 illustrates what you'll see.

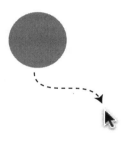

Figure 6-4. *Move a sprite with easing*

The program code is very similar to the previous example. The followEase function is used in the game loop like this:

```
function gameLoop() {
  requestAnimationFrame(gameLoop);
  followEase(c1, pointer, 0.1);
  render(canvas);
}
```

Making a sprite follow another sprite is a common requirement for games, so let's look at another way you can do it.

Following at a Constant Speed

The easing formula from the previous sections makes a sprite move at a variable speed that is proportional to the distance from its destination. With a small change to the formula you can make it move at a fixed, constant speed. Here's a `follow` function that implements this:

```
function followConstant(follower, leader, speed) {

  //Figure out the distance between the sprites
  let vx = leader.centerX - follower.centerX,
      vy = leader.centerY - follower.centerY,
      distance = Math.sqrt(vx * vx + vy * vy);

  //Move the follower if it's more than 1 move
  //away from the leader
  if (distance >= speed) {
    follower.x += (vx / distance) * speed;
    follower.y += (vy / distance) * speed;
  }
}
```

The speed value should be the number of pixels per frame that you want the follower to move; in the following example code it is 3 pixels per frame:

```
function gameLoop() {
  requestAnimationFrame(gameLoop);
  followConstant(c1, pointer, 3);
  render(canvas);
}
```

This is a really useful function for creating an enemy AI sprite that chases the player.

Rotating toward Something

You can find the angle of rotation between two sprites using the following function:

```
function angle(s1, s2) {
  return Math.atan2(
    s2.centerY - s1.centerY,
    s2.centerX - s1.centerX
  );
}
```

It returns the angle of rotation in radians. You can apply it to a sprite's `rotation` property to make the sprite rotate toward another sprite, or the pointer, with this statement:

```
box.rotation = angle(box, pointer);
```

You can see a working example of this in the `rotateTowards.html` file in the chapter's source files; the output is shown in Figure 6-5. The box rotates toward the pointer, and a red line 32 pixels long extends from the center of the box in the direction of rotation.

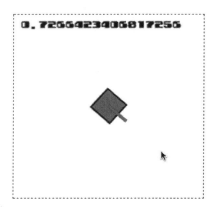

Figure 6-5. *Rotate a sprite toward the pointer*

With a bit of imagination, you might realize that the box with red line is actually a staple video game component: a rotating gun turret. How was it made? It's a good example of how to build a simple compound sprite using a parent/child hierarchy. The `turret` (the red line) is the child of the box. Here's the code:

```
//Make a square and center it in the stage
box = rectangle(32, 32, "gray", "black", 2);
stage.putCenter(box);

//Make a turret by drawing a red, 4 pixel wide
//line that's 32 pixels long
turret = line("red", 4, 0, 0, 32, 0);

//Add the line as a child of the box and place its
//start point at the box's center
box.addChild(turret);
turret.x = 16;
turret.y = 16;
```

Now when the game loop uses the `angle` function to make the box rotate toward the `pointer`, the `turret` automatically follows the box's rotation.

```
function gameLoop() {
  requestAnimationFrame(gameLoop);
  box.rotation = angle(box, pointer);
  render(canvas);
}
```

This is where all the extra work we did in Chapter 4 to create our hierarchical scene graph pays off. It has saved us from having to write some complex math to manually keep the turret's rotation aligned to the box.

Rotate around a Sprite

Use the following rotateSprite function to make a sprite rotate around another sprite:

```
function rotateSprite(rotatingSprite, centerSprite, distance, angle) {
  rotatingSprite.x
    = centerSprite.centerX - rotatingSprite.parent.x
    + (distance * Math.cos(angle))
    - rotatingSprite.halfWidth;

  rotatingSprite.y
    = centerSprite.centerY - rotatingSprite.parent.y
    + (distance * Math.sin(angle))
    - rotatingSprite.halfWidth;
}
```

Here's how to use it to make a ball rotate around a box, as shown in Figure 6-6.

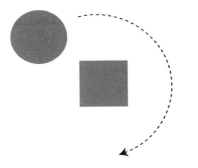

Figure 6-6. *Rotate a sprite around another sprite*

```
//Create a box and position it
box = rectangle(32, 32, "gray");
stage.putCenter(box, 32, -48);

//Create a circle sprite offset by 32 pixels to the
//left of the box
ball = circle(32, "gray");
box.putLeft(ball, -32);

//Add an `angle` property to the ball that we'll use to
//help make the ball rotate around the box
ball.angle = 0;

//Start the game loop
gameLoop();
```

```
function gameLoop() {
  requestAnimationFrame(gameLoop);

  //Update the ball's rotation angle
  ball.angle += 0.05;

  //Use the ball's `angle` value to make it rotate around the
  //box at a distance of 48 pixels from the box's center
  rotateSprite(ball, box, 48, ball.angle);
}
```

Rotate around a Point

Sometimes it's useful just to be able to rotate a single point in space around another point. For example, you could create a "wobbly line" effect by making the two ends of a line rotate around invisible points in space, as illustrated in Figure 6-7. By joining wobbly lines together like this, you could create wobbly shapes.

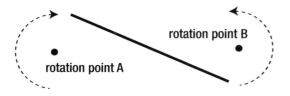

Figure 6-7. *Make points rotate around other points. You can use a function called* rotatePoint *to help create this effect*

```
export function rotatePoint(pointX, pointY, distanceX, distanceY angle) {
  let point = {};
  point.x = pointX + Math.cos(angle) * distanceX;
  point.y = pointY + Math.sin(angle) * distanceY;
  return point;
}
```

The rotatePoint function returns a point object with *x* and *y* values that represent the axis of rotation. The distanceX and distanceY arguments define the radius from the center of rotation to the edge of the imaginary circle that's being traced in space. If distanceX and distanceY have the same values, the function will trace a circle. If you give them different values, the function will trace an ellipse. You can use the point object that rotatePoint returns to make any other *x/y* point rotate around that axis. Here's some code that uses rotatePoint to create the wobbly line effect shown in Figure 6-7.

```
movingLine = line("black", 4, 64, 160, 192, 208);

//We're going to make the line's start and end points
//rotate in space. The line will need two new angle properties
//to help us do this. Both are initialized to 0
movingLine.angleA = 0;
movingLine.angleB = 0;
```

```
//Start the game loop
gameLoop();

function gameLoop() {
  requestAnimationFrame(gameLoop);

  //Make the line's `ax` and `ay` points rotate clockwise around
  //point 64, 160. `rotatePoint` returns an
  //object with `x` and `y` properties
  //containing the point's new rotated position
  movingLine.angleA += 0.02;
  let rotatingA = rotatePoint(64, 160, 20, 20, movingLine.angleA);
  movingLine.ax = rotatingA.x;
  movingLine.ay = rotatingA.y;

  //Make the line's `bx` and `by` point rotate counter-
  //clockwise around point 192, 208
  movingLine.angleB -= 0.03;
  let rotatingB = rotatePoint(192, 208, 20, 20, movingLine.angleB);
  movingLine.bx = rotatingB.x;
  movingLine.by = rotatingB.y;

  //Render the canvas
  render(canvas);
}
```

The effect is like a crankshaft turning an invisible wheel. It's fun to watch and even slightly spooky, so make sure you check out the working example of this code in the rotateAround.html file in the chapter's source code.

Move in the Direction of Rotation

If you know a sprite's angle, you can make it move in the direction that it's pointing. Run the moveTowards.html file and you'll find an example of a sprite that you can move using the arrow keys. Left and right rotate the sprite, and up makes it move in the direction that it's pointing. Release the up-arrow key and it will slow to a stop. Figure 6-8 shows what you'll see.

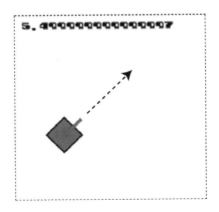

Figure 6-8. *Use the arrow keys to rotate a sprite and move it in the direction that it's pointing*

209

Let's exercise our imaginative powers again and pretend that the move box with the red line is a "tank." Now let's rethink the way we built this object from the earlier example. It might make sense to enclose the box and turret together in a single group called tank. We can use the group function we created in Chapter 4 to do this; here's how:

```
//Make the box and turret
let box = rectangle(32, 32, "gray");
let turret = line("red", 4, 0, 0, 32, 0);
turret.x = 16;
turret.y = 16;
```

```
//Group them together as a compound sprite called `tank`
tank = group(box, turret);
stage.putCenter(tank);
```

The tank group is now the parent container for the box and turret sprites. This is just another approach you can take to making compound sprites. The tank group is now the main sprite that you control. Add some properties to it to help make it move:

```
//Add some physics properties
tank.vx = 0;
tank.vy = 0;
tank.accelerationX = 0.2;
tank.accelerationY = 0.2;
tank.frictionX = 0.96;
tank.frictionY = 0.96;
```

```
//The speed at which the tank should rotate,
//initialized to 0
tank.rotationSpeed = 0;
```

```
//Whether or not the tank should move forward
tank.moveForward = false;
```

The rotationSpeed determines how fast the tank will rotate, either to the left or the right, and moveForward is just a Boolean that tells us whether the code in the game loop should make the tank move. Both of these properties are set by the arrow keys: the right and left keys make the tank rotate, and the up key makes it move forward. Here's the code that uses the keyboard function we wrote earlier in this chapter to program the arrow keys:

```
//Make key objects
let leftArrow = keyboard(37),
    rightArrow = keyboard(39),
    upArrow = keyboard(38);
```

```
//Set the tank's `rotationSpeed` to -0.1 (to rotate left) if the
//left arrow key is being pressed
leftArrow.press = () => tank.rotationSpeed = -0.1;
```

```
//If the left arrow key is released and the right arrow
//key isn't being pressed down, set the `rotationSpeed` to 0
leftArrow.release = () => {
  if (!rightArrow.isDown) tank.rotationSpeed = 0;
}

//Do the same for the right arrow key, but set
//the `rotationSpeed` to 0.1 (to rotate right)
rightArrow.press = () => tank.rotationSpeed = 0.1;
rightArrow.release = () => {
  if (!leftArrow.isDown) tank.rotationSpeed = 0;
}

//Set `tank.moveForward` to `true` if the up arrow key is
//pressed, and set it to `false` if it's released
upArrow.press = () => tank.moveForward = true;
upArrow.release = () => tank.moveForward = false;
```

We can now use these properties, along with what we learned about acceleration and friction from the previous chapter, to make the tank move in the direction of its rotation. Here's the code in the game loop that does that:

```
function gameLoop() {
  requestAnimationFrame(gameLoop);

  //Use the `rotationSpeed` to set the tank's rotation
  tank.rotation += tank.rotationSpeed;

  //If `tank.moveForward` is `true`, use acceleration with a
  //bit of basic trigonometry to make the tank move in the
  //direction of its rotation
  if (tank.moveForward) {
    tank.vx += tank.accelerationX * Math.cos(tank.rotation);
    tank.vy += tank.accelerationY * Math.sin(tank.rotation);
  }

  //If `tank.moveForward` is `false`, use
  //friction to slow the tank down
  else {
    tank.vx *= tank.frictionX;
    tank.vy *= tank.frictionY;
  }

  //Apply the tank's velocity to its position to make the tank move
  tank.x += tank.vx;
  tank.y += tank.vy;

  //Display the tank's angle of rotation
  message.content = tank.rotation;

  //Render the canvas
  render(canvas);
}
```

211

The secret to making the tank move in the direction of its rotation is these two lines of code:

```
tank.vx += tank.accelerationX * Math.cos(tank.rotation);
tank.vy += tank.accelerationY * Math.sin(tank.rotation);
```

It's just a bit of basic trigonometry which combines the tank's acceleration with its rotation. The resulting vx and vy values will make the tank move in the correct direction when they're applied to the tank's *x,y* position.

```
tank.x += tank.vx;
tank.y += tank.vy;
```

You can use this basic system as the starting point for many kinds of rotating video game objects, like spaceships or cars. In this example our tank actually behaves more like a spaceship than a real tank. That's because when it rotates left or right, it continues to drift forward, rather than changing direction with the rotation, the way a vehicle with wheels would. We'll fix this in a short while. First, let's give the tank the ability to fire bullets.

Firing Bullets

With only a little more code, you can make your sprites fire bullets. Run bullets.html and press the space bar to fire bullets in the direction that the tank is pointing, as shown in Figure 6-9.

Figure 6-9. *Fire bullets in all directions*

A feature of this code is that the bullets are removed when they hit the edges of the canvas, and a text sprite tells you which edge the bullet hit.

The first step to making bullets is to create an array to store the new bullet sprites that you're going to make:

```
let bullets = [];
```

Next, you need a shoot function that lets you create bullets using some parameters:

```
shoot(
  tank,              //The shooter
  tank.rotation,     //The angle at which to shoot
  32,                //The bullet's offset from the center
  7,                 //The bullet's speed (pixels per frame)
  bullets,           //The array used to store the bullets

  //A function that returns the sprite that should
  //be used to make each bullet
  () => circle(8, "red")
);
```

The shoot function assigns all the parameters you need to shoot a bullet. The most important is the last one:

```
() => circle(8, "red")
```

That's a function that creates and returns the kind of sprite you want to use as a bullet. In this case, it's a red circle 8 pixels in diameter. You can use any of the sprite-creation functions you've learned in the book so far, or create your own custom function.

Here's the shoot function definition that uses these parameters to create a new bullet sprite and add it to the bullets array.

```
function shoot(
  shooter, angle, offsetFromCenter,
  bulletSpeed, bulletArray, bulletSprite
) {

  //Make a new sprite using the user-supplied `bulletSprite` function
  let bullet = bulletSprite();

  //Set the bullet's start point
  bullet.x
    = shooter.centerX - bullet.halfWidth
    + (offsetFromCenter * Math.cos(angle));
  bullet.y
    = shooter.centerY - bullet.halfHeight
    + (offsetFromCenter * Math.sin(angle));

  //Set the bullet's velocity
  bullet.vx = Math.cos(angle) * bulletSpeed;
  bullet.vy = Math.sin(angle) * bulletSpeed;

  //Push the bullet into the `bulletArray`
  bulletArray.push(bullet);
}
```

You can see that the shoot function is using the shooter sprite's rotation angle to figure out the bullet's start point and velocity. The shoot function is designed to be flexible and generic, so you can use it in a wide variety of different game projects.

How is your game going to let the player fire a bullet? In this example a bullet is fired once, and only once, each time the space key is pressed. Releasing the space key resets the bullet firing mechanism so that you can fire again the next time it's pressed. This is an easy mechanism to set up using the keyboard function we created earlier in the chapter. First, create a space key object:

```
let space = keyboard(32);
```

Then assign the space key's press method so that it calls the shoot function to fire a bullet:

```
space.press = () => {
  shoot(
    tank, tank.rotation, 32, 7, bullets,
    () => circle(8, "red")
  );
};
```

Now that we're able to shoot bullets, we need to move them across the canvas. We also need to check their screen boundaries so that we can remove the bullets if they hit the edges of the canvas (actually the root parent stage object). This has to happen inside the game loop:

```
function gameLoop() {
  requestAnimationFrame(gameLoop);
  //Move the bullets here...
}
```

The code that moves the bullets and checks for a collision with the stage boundaries also happens inside a loop. We're going to use a filter loop so that if a bullet hits the edges of the stage, it will be removed from the bullets array. We're also going to use a custom function called outsideBounds that will tell us if the bullet has crossed the stage's boundary, and also which side of the boundary the bullet hit. Here's the filter loop that does all this:

```
bullets = bullets.filter(bullet => {

  //Move the bullet
  bullet.x += bullet.vx;
  bullet.y += bullet.vy;

  //Check for a collision with the stage boundary
  let collision = outsideBounds(bullet, stage.localBounds);

  //If there's a collision, display the side that the collision
  //happened on, remove the bullet sprite, and filter it out of
  //the `bullets` array
  if(collision) {

    //Display the boundary side that the bullet crossed
    message.content = "The bullet hit the " + collision;
```

```
//The `remove` function will remove a sprite from its parent
//to make it disappear
remove(bullet);

//Remove the bullet from the `bullets` array
return false;
}

//If the bullet hasn't hit the edge of the stage,
//keep it in the `bullets` array
return true;
});
```

The outsideBounds function returns a collision variable that will have the value "top", "right", "bottom" or "left", depending on which side of the boundary the bullet crossed. It will return undefined if there's no collision. outsideBounds is very similar to the contain function you learned in the previous chapter—it's just much simpler. It checks whether the entire shape of the sprite has crossed the containment boundary, and leaves it up to you to decide what to do with that information.

```
function outsideBounds(sprite, bounds, extra = undefined){

  let x = bounds.x,
      y = bounds.y,
      width = bounds.width,
      height = bounds.height;

  //The `collision` object is used to store which
  //side of the containing rectangle the sprite hits
  let collision;

  //Left
  if (sprite.x < x - sprite.width) {
    collision = "left";
  }
  //Top
  if (sprite.y < y - sprite.height) {
    collision = "top";
  }
  //Right
  if (sprite.x > width) {
    collision = "right";
  }
  //Bottom
  if (sprite.y > height) {
    collision = "bottom";
  }
```

```
//The `extra` function runs if there was a collision
//and `extra` has been defined
if (collision && extra) extra(collision);

//Return the `collision` object
return collision;
};
```

You'll find both the shoot and outsideBounds functions in the library/display folder in the book's source files.

Moving the Tank

In this new example the tank behaves like a real wheeled vehicle. Changing its rotation also changes the direction of its forward movement, as illustrated in Figure 6-10. This is not a difficult effect to achieve; we just have to rethink slightly how to calculate and apply the tank's physics properties.

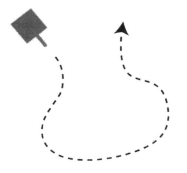

Figure 6-10. *The tank moves in the direction of its rotation*

First, give the tank new speed and friction values. We'll use speed to help decide how fast the tank should go, and friction to help us slow it down. (This new friction value replaces frictionX and frictionY from the previous example.)

```
tank.friction = 0.96;
tank.speed = 0;
```

Here are all the initial values of the tank's new physics properties:

```
tank.vx = 0;
tank.vy = 0;
tank.accelerationX = 0.1;
tank.accelerationY = 0.1;
tank.rotationSpeed = 0;
tank.moveForward = false;
tank.friction = 0.96;
tank.speed = 0;
```

The game loop makes the tank move using speed and friction to figure out how fast the tank should go. The tank's acceleration is calculated by applying its speed to its rotation:

```
//Use the `rotationSpeed` to set the tank's rotation
tank.rotation += tank.rotationSpeed;
```

```
//If `tank.moveForward` is `true`, increase the speed
if (tank.moveForward) {
  tank.speed += 0.1;
}
```

```
//If `tank.moveForward` is `false`, use
//friction to slow the tank down
else {
  tank.speed *= tank.friction;
}
```

```
//Use the `speed` value to figure out the acceleration in the
//direction of the tank's rotation
tank.accelerationX = tank.speed * Math.cos(tank.rotation);
tank.accelerationY = tank.speed * Math.sin(tank.rotation);
```

```
//Apply the acceleration to the tank's velocity
tank.vx = tank.accelerationX;
tank.vy = tank.accelerationY;
```

```
//Apply the tank's velocity to its position to make the tank move
tank.x += tank.vx;
tank.y += tank.vy;
```

This tweak to the code eliminates the spaceship-style drift effect from the first example. You can use it as the basis for moving any kind of wheeled vehicle.

Interactive Mouse and Touch Events

So far in this chapter you've learned how to make sprites move by assigning press and release methods to keyboard keys, and also how to make sprites follow the pointer's position. But what if you want to interact with sprites in a more sophisticated way? Your game sprites might need to respond to being clicked, touched, or dragged, and you might want to make buttons to build a UI for your game.

In this second half of this chapter you will learn how to do exactly that. We're going to build a general framework for making interactive sprites of all kinds, and then customize it to make buttons and drag-and-drop sprites. Let's find out how!

Find Out If the Pointer Is Touching a Sprite

The most important first step is that we need some way to figure out whether the pointer is touching a sprite. We can do that by adding a method to the pointer object called hitTestSprite. Its job is to check whether the pointer's *x/y* position is inside the area of the sprite. We're going to add hitTestSprite to the same pointer object that we created using the makePointer function at the beginning of the chapter:

```
function makePointer(element, scale = 1) {
  let pointer = {

    //... the pointer's previous properties and methods...

    hitTestSprite(sprite) {
      //The new code goes here
    }
  };

  //... the rest of the makePointer function...

  return pointer;
}
```

What does hitTestSprite do? It compares the pointer's position against the area defined by the sprite. If the pointer is inside that area, the method returns true; if not, it returns false. As a bonus feature, hitTestSprite works with circular sprites as well as rectangular ones. (You'll remember from Chapter 4 that all our sprites have a Boolean property called circular that you can use to find the sprite's general shape.)

```
hitTestSprite(sprite) {

  //The `hit` variable will become `true` if the pointer is
  //touching the sprite and remain `false` if it isn't
  let hit = false;

  //Is the sprite rectangular?
  if (!sprite.circular) {

    //Yes, it is.
    //Get the position of the sprite's edges using global
    //coordinates
    let left = sprite.gx,
        right = sprite.gx + sprite.width,
        top = sprite.gy,
        bottom = sprite.gy + sprite.height;

    //Find out if the pointer is intersecting the rectangle.
    //`hit` will become `true` if the pointer is inside the
    //sprite's area
    hit
      = this.x > left && this.x < right
      && this.y > top && this.y < bottom;
  }
```

```
//Is the sprite circular?
else {

  //Yes, it is.
  //Find the distance between the pointer and the
  //center of the circle
  let vx = this.x - (sprite.gx + sprite.radius),
      vy = this.y - (sprite.gy + sprite.radius),
      distance = Math.sqrt(vx * vx + vy * vy);

  //The pointer is intersecting the circle if the
  //distance is less than the circle's radius
  hit = distance < sprite.radius;
}

  return hit;
}
```

In the case of rectangular sprites, the code checks whether the pointer's *x,y* position is inside the sprite's area. In the case of circular sprites, it checks whether the distance between the center of the pointer and the center of the sprite is less than the circle's radius. In both cases, the code will set hit to true if the pointer is touching the sprite. The pointer's *x,y* coordinates will always be relative to the canvas, which is why the code uses the sprite's global gx and gy coordinates.

Use hitTestSprite in your game code as shown here:

```
pointer.hitTestSprite(anySprite);
```

Run the pointerCollision.html file for an interactive demonstration of how hitTestSprite works, as shown in Figure 6-11. A text sprite will tell you whether or not the pointer is touching the box or ball sprites.

Figure 6-11. *Find out if the pointer is touching a sprite*

Here's the code from the game loop that makes this work:

```
if(pointer.hitTestSprite(ball)) {
  message.content = "Ball!"
} else if(pointer.hitTestSprite(box)) {
  message.content = "Box!"
} else {
  message.content = "No collision..."
}
```

This example has actually been a sneaky introduction to a game design topic called **collision detection**, which you'll learn about in the next chapter. But, for now, how can we use hitTestPoint to make interactive sprites? Let's find out by learning how to make the most useful interactive sprites of all: buttons.

Buttons

Buttons are an important UI component that you'll definitely want to use in your games. You can easily make them using HTML and CSS, but there's a lot to be said for creating your own custom buttons for a canvas-based sprite rendering system such as the one we've developed in this book. You'll be able to integrate the buttons into your existing scene graph and renderer, manipulate them just like you would any other game sprite, and keep your code base unified in JavaScript without having to jump the fence to HTML and CSS. Using what we learned about pointer interactivity in the last section, and by making a small addition to our sprite system, we can create a versatile new button sprite object. You can think of the buttons we're going to make as "clickable/touchable sprites" that you'll be able to use for a wide variety of games.

The most important thing you need to know about buttons is that they have **states** and **actions**. States define what the button looks like, and actions define what it does.

Most buttons have three states:

- **Up**: When the pointer is not touching the button

- **Over**: When the pointer is over the button

- **Down**: When the pointer is pressing down on the button

Figure 6-12 shows an example of these three button states.

Figure 6-12. *Up, Over, and Down button states*

Touch-based games need only two states: up and down.

With the button sprite that we're going to create, you'll be able to access these states as a string property, like this:

```
playButton.state
```

The state property could have the value "up", "over", or "down", which you could use in your game logic. Buttons also have **actions**:

- Press: When the pointer presses the button

- Release: When the pointer is released from the button

- Over: When the pointer moves into the button's area

- Out: When the pointer moves out of the button's area

- Tap: When the button has been tapped (or clicked)

You can define these actions as user-definable methods, like this:

```
playButton.press = () => console.log("pressed");
playButton.release = () => console.log("released");
playButton.over = () => console.log("over");
playButton.out = () => console.log("out");
playButton.tap = () => console.log("tapped");
```

You should also be able to access the button's "pressed" and "released" actions in a string property, like this:

```
playButton.action
```

Got it? Good! So how do we actually make buttons?

Creating Buttons

First, start with three images that define the three button states. You might call them "up.png", "over.png", and "down.png". Then add those three images to a tileset, or as frames in a texture atlas. Figure 6-13 shows a simple texture atlas that contains these three states.

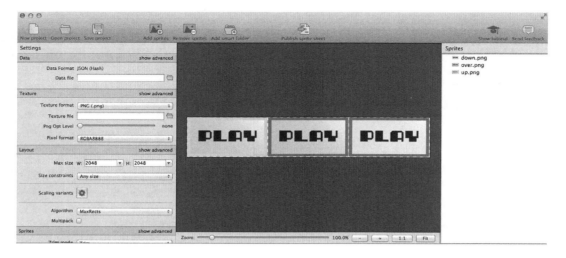

Figure 6-13. *Add the button image states to a texture atlas*

■ **Note** Although having three image states is standard, sometimes buttons have only two image states. This is particularly true of touch-only buttons, which don't have an "over" state. The Button sprite that we're going to create ahead will use three images if they're available, but if it only has two, the code will assume they refer to the "up" and "down" states.

Next, load the texture atlas into your game program:

```
assets.load(["images/button.json"]).then(() => setup());
```

Also initialize a new button sprite by using the three frames as the button's source argument:

```
let buttonFrames = [
  assets["up.png"],
  assets["over.png"],
  assets["down.png"]
];

playButton = button(buttonFrames, 32, 96);
```

To see this button in action, run the button.html file, whose output is shown in Figure 6-14. When you move the pointer over the button, the cursor changes to a hand icon. The game loop updates some text that displays the button's state and action.

```
stateMessage.content = `State: ${playButton.state}`;
actionMessage.content = `Action: ${playButton.action}`;
```

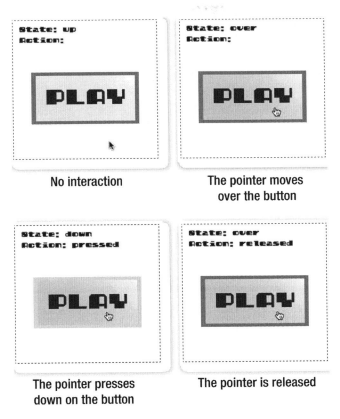

No interaction

The pointer moves over the button

The pointer presses down on the button

The pointer is released

Figure 6-14. *An interactive button sprite*

This is ultimately what we want to achieve, but we need to write a bit more code to make all these details work. Let's find out exactly what we need to do to create these fully interactive buttons.

The New Button Class

You might have many buttons in a game, and, as you'll soon see, you'll need to update them each frame. So the first thing you need is a `buttons` array to store all the buttons in your game:

```
export let buttons = [];
```

Keep this `buttons` array in your `display` module along with the `stage` object and the sprite classes. Make sure to export it, because you'll need to import it into your application code for any game that requires buttons.

Next, make a Button class. All it does is extend the Sprite class and set the sprite's `interactive` property to `true`. Making a whole new class for buttons isn't really essential, but as you'll soon see, doing so will help us automatically display image states based on pointer interactivity.

```
class Button extends Sprite {
  constructor(source, x = 0, y = 0) {
    super(source, x, y);
    this.interactive = true;
  }
}

export function button(source, x, y) {
  let sprite = new Button(source, x, y);
  stage.addChild(sprite);
  return sprite;
}
```

What does setting `interactive` to `true` actually do?

```
this.interactive = true;
```

You'll recall that when we made our sprite system in Chapter 4, we gave all our sprites a property called `interactive` that you could set to `true`. Here's the excerpted code from the `DisplayObject` class that does this (check back to Chapter 4 to see this code in its full context if you need to).

```
get interactive() {
  return this._interactive;
}

set interactive(value) {

  if (value === true) {

    //Add interactive properties to the sprite
    //so that it can act like a button
    makeInteractive(this);

    //Add the sprite to the global `buttons` array so
    //it can be updated each frame
    buttons.push(this);

    this._interactive = true;
  }

  if (value === false) {

    //Remove the sprite's reference from the
    //`buttons` array so that it's no longer affected
    //by mouse and touch interactivity
    buttons.splice(buttons.indexOf(this), 1);
    this._interactive = false;
  }
}
```

Setting interactive to true sends the sprite to a function called makeInteractive and adds it to the buttons array. Setting it to false splices it out of the buttons array. Let's find out what that makeInteractive function does, and how it can transform any sprite into a clickable, touchable button. You'll remember that I told you in Chapter 4, "don't worry about all this stuff now—I'll explain it later!" Well, now's the time!

Adding Interactivity

The makeInteractive function assigns a handful of new methods to the sprite: press, release, over, tap, and out. It also adds some properties to the sprite so that we can monitor its interactive state. These methods will make *any* sprite behave like a button. But if the sprite is actually an instance of the Button class, makeInteractive adds a bonus feature: it sets the sprite's image state to "up", "over", or "down" depending on what the pointer is doing.

makeInteractive is a reasonably complex bit of code, even for me. That's because it has to work out what the button's current state is based on what its previous state was and what the pointer is doing. This happens to be an unavoidably delicate enterprise—a bit like juggling daggers. The comments explain how it works, but the best way to really understand its subtleties is to read the code while observing the effect in the button.html example file. Writing this code was just a gradual process of trial and error, and lots and lots of testing. And I didn't fully understand the problem I was trying to solve until I was done. That kind of exploration and discovery is one of the reasons programming is so much fun! Here's the complete makeInteractive function from the library/display file.

```
function makeInteractive(o) {

  //The `press`, `release`, `over`, `out`, and `tap` methods. They're `undefined`
  //for now, but they can be defined in the game program
  o.press = o.press || undefined;
  o.release = o.release || undefined;
  o.over = o.over || undefined;
  o.out = o.out || undefined;
  o.tap = o.tap || undefined;

  //The `state` property tells you the button's
  //current state. Set its initial state to "up"
  o.state = "up";

  //The `action` property tells you whether it's being pressed or
  //released
  o.action = "";

  //The `pressed` and `hoverOver` Booleans are mainly for internal
  //use in this code to help figure out the correct state.
  //`pressed` is a Boolean that helps track whether
  //the sprite has been pressed down
  o.pressed = false;

  //`hoverOver` is a Boolean that checks whether the pointer
  //has hovered over the sprite
  o.hoverOver = false;
```

```
//The `update` method will be called each frame
//inside the game loop
o.update = (pointer, canvas) => {

  //Figure out if the pointer is touching the sprite
  let hit = pointer.hitTestSprite(o);

  //1. Figure out the current state
  if (pointer.isUp) {

    //Up state
    o.state = "up";

    //Show the first image state frame, if this is a `Button` sprite
    if (o instanceof Button) o.gotoAndStop(0);
  }

  //If the pointer is touching the sprite, figure out
  //if the over or down state should be displayed
  if (hit) {

    //Over state
    o.state = "over";

    //Show the second image state frame if this sprite has
    //3 frames and it's a `Button` sprite
    if (o.frames && o.frames.length === 3 && o instanceof Button) {
      o.gotoAndStop(1);
    }

    //Down state
    if (pointer.isDown) {
      o.state = "down";

      //Show the third frame if this sprite is a `Button` sprite and it
      //has only three frames, or show the second frame if it
      //has only two frames
      if(o instanceof Button) {
        if (o.frames.length === 3) {
          o.gotoAndStop(2);
        } else {
          o.gotoAndStop(1);
        }
      }
    }
  }
}
```

```
//Perform the correct interactive action

//a. Run the `press` method if the sprite state is "down" and
//the sprite hasn't already been pressed
if (o.state === "down") {
  if (!o.pressed) {
    if (o.press) o.press();
    o.pressed = true;
    o.action = "pressed";
  }
}

//b. Run the `release` method if the sprite state is "over" and
//the sprite has been pressed
if (o.state === "over") {
  if (o.pressed) {
    if (o.release) o.release();
    o.pressed = false;
    o.action = "released";

    //If the pointer was tapped and the user assigned a `tap`
    //method, call the `tap` method
    if (pointer.tapped && o.tap) o.tap();
  }

  //Run the `over` method if it has been assigned
  if (!o.hoverOver) {
    if (o.over) o.over();
    o.hoverOver = true;
  }
}

//c. Check whether the pointer has been released outside
//the sprite's area. If the button state is "up" and it has
//already been pressed, then run the `release` method
if (o.state === "up") {
  if (o.pressed) {
    if (o.release) o.release();
    o.pressed = false;
    o.action = "released";
  }

  //Run the `out` method if it has been assigned
  if (o.hoverOver) {
    if (o.out) o.out();
    o.hoverOver = false;
  }
}
};
}
```

An important feature in the preceding code is that makeInteractive adds to the sprite a method called update:

```
o.update = (pointer, canvas) => { /*...*/ }
```

This update method is what actually figures out what the button's state should be. The only way it can work is if it's called on *every animation frame*. That means every button in the game needs to have its update method called inside the game loop. Luckily, every sprite that has had interactive set to true is pushed into the buttons array. That means you can update all the buttons in the game with a function like this:

```
function gameLoop() {
  requestAnimationFrame(gameLoop);

  //Only run the code if there are buttons in the array
  if (buttons.length > 0) {

    //Set the mouse pointer to the default arrow icon
    canvas.style.cursor = "auto";

    //Loop through all the buttons
    buttons.forEach(button => {

      //Update the buttons
      button.update(pointer, canvas);

      //Figure out if the mouse arrow should be a hand icon
      if (button.state === "over" || button.state === "down") {

        //If the button (or interactive sprite) isn't the
        //stage, change the cursor to a pointer.
        //(This works because the `stage` object has a
        //`parent` value of `undefined`)
        if(button.parent !== undefined) {

          //Display the mouse arrow as a hand
          canvas.style.cursor = "pointer";
        }
      }
    });
  }

  //Render the canvas
  render(canvas);
}
```

The code loops through all the buttons and calls the update method on all of them. As a bonus, this code also figures out whether the mouse arrow should display a hand icon. If the button state is "over" or "down", and the interactive sprite isn't the stage object, then the hand icon is displayed.

Putting It All Together

Now that you know how all these component pieces work, let's take a look at the complete JavaScript code for the button.html file. You can use this as the starting point for using buttons in your own projects.

```javascript
//Import code from the library
import {
  makeCanvas, button, buttons, frames,
  text, stage, render
} from "../library/display";
import {assets} from "../library/utilities";
import {makePointer} from "../library/interactive";

//Load the button's texture atlas and the custom font
assets.load([
  "fonts/puzzler.otf",
  "images/button.json"
]).then(() => setup());

//Declare any variables shared between functions
let canvas, playButton, stateMessage, actionMessage, pointer;

function setup() {

  //Make the canvas and initialize the stage
  canvas = makeCanvas(256, 256);
  stage.width = canvas.width;
  stage.height = canvas.height;

  //Define the button's frames
  let buttonFrames = [
    assets["up.png"],
    assets["over.png"],
    assets["down.png"]
  ];

  //Make the button sprite
  playButton = button(buttonFrames, 32, 96);

  //Define the button's actions
  playButton.over = () => console.log("over");
  playButton.out = () => console.log("out");
  playButton.press = () => console.log("pressed");
  playButton.release = () => console.log("released");
  playButton.tap = () => console.log("tapped");

  //Add some message text
  stateMessage = text("State:", "12px puzzler", "black", 12, 12);
  actionMessage = text("Action:", "12px puzzler", "black", 12, 32);
```

```
  //Make the pointer
  pointer = makePointer(canvas);

  //Start the game loop
  gameLoop();
}

function gameLoop() {
  requestAnimationFrame(gameLoop);

  //Update the buttons
  if (buttons.length > 0) {
    canvas.style.cursor = "auto";
    buttons.forEach(button => {
      button.update(pointer, canvas);
      if (button.state === "over" || button.state === "down") {
        if(button.parent !== undefined) {
          canvas.style.cursor = "pointer";
        }
      }
    });
  }

  //Display the button's state and action
  stateMessage.content = `State: ${playButton.state}`;
  actionMessage.content = `Action: ${playButton.action}`;

  //Render the canvas
  render(canvas);
}
```

I mentioned earlier that buttons are just a kind of interactive sprite, one that happen to have three defined image states. What this means is that you can add button-like interactivity to any sprite. Let's find out how.

Making an Interactive Sprite

You can make any sprite behave like a button by setting its interactive property to true:

```
anySprite.interactive = true;
```

This adds the sprite to the buttons array and gives it the same method properties as any other button. That means you can assign press or release methods to the sprite, and access its state and action properties.

■ **Note** You can also make the stage object interactive. This can be useful if you want to find out whether a player has tapped or pressed the canvas.

Run interacteractiveSprites.html for a demonstration of this feature, shown in Figure 6-15. If you click on the circle, its fill and stroke colors will change at random.

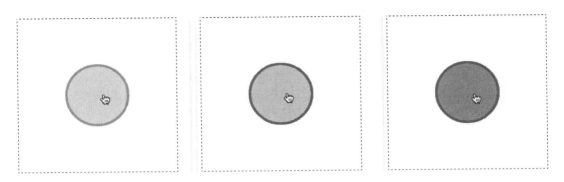

Figure 6-15. *Click to make the circle display random colors*

Here's the code that achieves this effect:

```
//Make the pointer
pointer = makePointer(canvas);

//Create the sprite and put it in the center of the stage
ball = circle(96, "red", "blue", 8);
stage.putCenter(ball);

//Make the ball interactive
ball.interactive = true;

//Assign the ball's `press` method
ball.press = () => {

  //An array of color names
  var colors = ["Gold", "Lavender", "Crimson", "DarkSeaGreen"];

  //Set the ball's `fillStyle` and `strokeStyle` to a random color
  ball.fillStyle = colors[randomInt(0, 3)];
  ball.strokeStyle = colors[randomInt(0, 3)];
};
```

If you want to make a clickable/tappable sprite that interacts with the pointer, you now have a way to do that.

■ **Note** Remember that if you set a sprite's interactive property to `true`, you also need to import the `buttons` array and update all the buttons in the game loop.

Drag and Drop

The last thing we need to make our sprites fully interactive is to give them drag-and-drop capabilities.
In Chapter 4 we added a `draggable` property to sprites that you could set to `true` or `false`:

```
anySprite.draggable = true;
```

This was another of my "I'll tell you about it later!" moments. What setting `draggable` to `true`
does is let you use the pointer to drag the sprite around the canvas. Figure 6-16 shows the output of the
`draggableSprites.html` example file that lets you do this. You can drag sprites around the canvas and stack
them on top of each other. Selected sprites are displayed at the top of the stack, and the mouse arrow cursor
changes to a hand when it's over a draggable sprite.

Figure 6-16. *Dragging and dropping sprites*

What actually happens when you set `draggable` to `true`, and how does this work?
First, you need an array called `draggableSprites`. You'll find it in the `library/display` module.

```
export let draggableSprites = [];
```

The draggable property on the DisplayObject class pushes the sprite into draggableSprites when it's set to true, and splices it out if it's set to false. Here's the code from the DisplayObject class that does this:

```
get draggable() {
  return this._draggable;
}

set draggable(value) {

  if (value === true) {

    //Push the sprite into the `draggableSprites` array
    draggableSprites.push(this);
    this._draggable = true;
  }

  if (value === false) {

    //Splice the sprite from the `draggableSprites` array
    draggableSprites.splice(draggableSprites.indexOf(this), 1);
  }
}
```

Next, you need some new properties and a new method on the pointer object to help you control the drag-and-drop behavior. They're added to the pointer in the makePointer function we created earlier in the chapter:

```
function makePointer(element, scale = 1) {

  let pointer = {

    //... the pointer's existing properties and methods...

    //New drag and drop properties:

    dragSprite: null,
    dragOffsetX: 0,
    dragOffsetY: 0,

    //New `updateDragAndDrop` method:

    updateDragAndDrop(sprite) {
      //The new code goes here
    }

  };

  //... the rest of the `makePointer` function...

  return pointer;
}
```

The dragSprite object is the sprite that the pointer is currently dragging, and dragOffsetX and dragOffsetY are used to help move the dragSprite. The updateDragAndDrop method does all the work of selecting draggable sprites, dragging them around the canvas, and making selected sprites appear stacked above the unselected ones.

```
updateDragAndDrop(draggableSprites) {

  //Check whether the pointer is pressed down
  if (this.isDown) {

    //You need to capture the coordinates at which the pointer was
    //pressed down and find out if it's touching a sprite

    //Only run this code if the pointer isn't already dragging a sprite
    if (this.dragSprite === null) {

      //Loop through the `draggableSprites` in reverse so that
      //you start searching at the top of the stack.
      //This means the last array element
      //will be the first one checked.
      //(Sprites at the end of the array are displayed
      //above sprites at the beginning of the array)
      for (let i = draggableSprites.length - 1; i > -1; i--) {
        let sprite = draggableSprites[i];

        //Check for a collision with the pointer using `hitTestSprite`
        if (this.hitTestSprite(sprite) && sprite.draggable) {

          //Calculate the difference between the pointer's
          //position and the sprite's position
          this.dragOffsetX = this.x - sprite.gx;
          this.dragOffsetY = this.y - sprite.gy;

          //Set the sprite as the pointer's `dragSprite` property
          this.dragSprite = sprite;

          //The next two lines reorder the `sprites` array so that the
          //selected sprite is displayed above all the others.
          //First, splice the sprite out of its current position in
          //its parent's `children` array
          let children = sprite.parent.children;
          children.splice(children.indexOf(sprite), 1);

          //Next, push the `dragSprite` to the end
          //of its `children` array so that it's
          //displayed last, above all the other sprites
          children.push(sprite);
```

```
    //Reorganize the `draggableSprites` array in the same way
    draggableSprites.splice(draggableSprites.indexOf(sprite), 1);
    draggableSprites.push(sprite);

    //Break the loop, because we only need to drag the topmost sprite
    break;
    }
  }
}

//If the pointer is down and it has a `dragSprite`, make the
//sprite follow the pointer's position, with the calculated offset
else {
  this.dragSprite.x = this.x - this.dragOffsetX;
  this.dragSprite.y = this.y - this.dragOffsetY;
}
}

//If the pointer is up, drop the `dragSprite` by setting it to `null`
if (this.isUp) {
  this.dragSprite = null;
}

//Change the mouse arrow pointer to a hand if it's over a
//draggable sprite
draggableSprites.some(sprite => {
  if (this.hitTestSprite(sprite) && sprite.draggable) {
    this.element.style.cursor = "pointer";
    return true;
  } else {
    this.element.style.cursor = "auto";
    return false;
  }
});
}
```

To make this work, you need to call the pointer's updateDragAndDrop method inside the game loop. That keeps the sprite and pointer positions synchronized with the frame rate.

```
function gameLoop() {
  requestAnimationFrame(gameLoop);
  pointer.updateDragAndDrop(draggableSprites);
  render(canvas);
}
```

So that you can see how all this works in its proper context, here's all the JavaScript code from the draggableSprites.html file, which creates the three draggable animal sprites shown in Figure 6-16.

```
//Import code from the library, including the `draggableSprites` array
import {makeCanvas, stage, draggableSprites, sprite, render} from "../library/display";
import {assets} from "../library/utilities";
import {makePointer} from "../library/interactive";

//Load the texture atlas containing the animal sprite images
assets.load(["images/animals.json"]).then(() => setup());

//Declare any variables shared between functions
let canvas, cat, tiger, hedgehog, pointer;

function setup() {

  //Make the canvas and initialize the stage
  canvas = makeCanvas(256, 256);
  stage.width = canvas.width;
  stage.height = canvas.height;

  //Make three sprites and set their `draggable` properties to `true`
  cat = sprite(assets["cat.png"]);
  stage.putCenter(cat, -32, -32);
  cat.draggable = true;

  tiger = sprite(assets["tiger.png"]);
  stage.putCenter(tiger);
  tiger.draggable = true;

  hedgehog = sprite(assets["hedgehog.png"]);
  stage.putCenter(hedgehog, 32, 32);
  hedgehog.draggable = true;

  //Make the pointer
  pointer = makePointer(canvas);

  //Start the game loop
  gameLoop();
}

function gameLoop() {
  requestAnimationFrame(gameLoop);

  //Update the pointer's drag and drop system
  pointer.updateDragAndDrop(draggableSprites);

  //Render the canvas
  render(canvas);
}
```

You can use this code as a basic model for adding drag-and-drop capabilities to any sprite.

Summary

Games are all about interactivity, and in this chapter you've learned the most important techniques you need to know to add interactivity to any game. You've learned the classic functions for calculating distance, making sprites rotate toward other sprites, making sprites follow other sprites or the pointer, and making sprites move in the direction of their rotation. You also learned how to write and implement a useful keyboard function to quickly add keyboard interactivity to games, and how to create a universal `pointer` object that works both for the mouse and touch. And if that weren't enough, you found out how to make clickable and touchable buttons, and how to drag and drop sprites around the canvas.

But we need to fill in one more important piece of the puzzle before we can really start making games. We have to learn what to do when sprites bump into one another. That's what the next chapter is all about: collision.

CHAPTER 7

■ ■ ■

Collision Detection

What happens when two sprites collide? That's what this chapter is all about: **collision detection**. You're going to learn how to determine if two sprites are touching, and make them react in interesting ways when they do. For 2D games, there are four essential collision detection techniques you need to know, and we're going to cover all of them in this chapter:

- **Point vs. Shape**: When a point intersects a shape
- **Circle vs. Circle**: When two circles intersect
- **Rectangle vs. Rectangle**: When two rectangles intersect
- **Circle vs. Rectangle**: When a rectangle and a circle intersect

With these four techniques in your back pocket, a whole universe of game design possibilities opens up to you. You're going to learn some useful, reusable functions that will help you do collision detection with the sprite system we've developed in this book, and how to apply those functions to a variety of practical game prototypes.

You'll find all the collision functions that we're going to use in this chapter in the `library/collision.js` file in the chapter's source files. We're going to use the following collision functions in this chapter:

```
hitTestPoint
hitTestCircle
hitTestRectangle
rectangleCollision
circleCollision
movingCircleCollision
hitTestCirclePoint
circlePointCollsion
hitTestCircleRectangle
circleRectangleCollision
hit
```

Make sure to import these functions into your application code before you use them. They'll work with any sprites that have the following properties:

```
x, y, centerX, centerY, vx, vy, width, height,
halfWidth, halfHeight, radius, diameter
```

As long as your sprites have these properties, the collision functions will work—even if you're using some other display system or game engine than the one we've built in this book. Let's find out how you can use these collision functions to start making some compelling games.

■ **Note**   In this chapter I'm not going to delve into all the messy details of how the collision functions in this chapter work under the hood. They've been designed so that you can drop them into any game project—just let them do their magic and enjoy it. You're a game designer, not a mathematician, so relax! This chapter is all about how to use these collision functions in fun and interesting ways. You'll find all the collision functions meticulously commented in the source code, so if you're really curious, take a look. And if you want to get deep into the math behind how these collision functions work, you'll learn everything you need to know as we examine vectors in the Appendix.

Point vs. Shape

The most basic collision test is to check whether a point is intersecting a shape. You can use a function called `hitTestPoint` to figure this out. `hitTestPoint` takes two arguments: a point object with *x* and *y* properties, and a sprite.

```
hitTestPoint(
  {x: 128, y: 128}, //An object with `x` and `y` properties
  sprite            //A sprite
)
```

`hitTestPoint` will return `true` if the point intersects the sprite, and `false` if it doesn't. Here's how you can use it to check for a collision between the pointer and a rectangular sprite called box:

```
if (hitTestPoint(pointer.position, box) {
  //The point is touching the box
}
```

(You'll remember from the previous chapter that the pointer's `position` property is an object that contains an *x, y* value.)

The `hitTestPoint` function works equally well with rectangular and circular sprites. If the sprite has a `radius` property, `hitTestPoint` assumes that the sprite is circular and applies a point collision detection algorithm for circles. If the sprite doesn't have a `radius` property, the function assumes it is a square. You'll find a working example of `hitTestPoint` in the `pointVsShape.html` file, shown in Figure 7-1.

Figure 7-1. *Check whether a single point, like the pointer, is touching a sprite*

Surprise! `hitTestPoint` is almost identical to the pointer's `hitTestSprite` method you learned in the previous chapter. The only difference is that you can use `hitTestPoint` with any point you define, not just the pointer. Here's the code from the game loop in the example `pointVsShape.html` file that achieves the effect shown in Figure 7-1:

```
if(hitTestPoint(pointer.position, ball)) {
  message.content = "Ball!"
} else if(hitTestPoint(pointer.position, box)) {
  message.content = "Box!"
} else {
  message.content = "No collision..."
}
```

Circle vs. Circle

If you want to check for a collision between two circular sprites, use the `hitTestCircle` function:

```
hitTestCircle(sprite1, sprite2)
```

Use it with any sprite that has a `radius` property. It returns `true` if the circles are touching, so you can use an `if` statement to check for a collision, with syntax like this:

```
if (hitTestCircle(sprite1, sprite2)) {
  //The circles are touching
}
```

■ **Note**   All the collision functions in the chapter use the sprites' local coordinates by default. If you want to force the function to use global coordinates, set the final optional argument, `global`, to `true`. Here's how:

```
hitTestCircle(sprite1, sprite2, true)
```

All the collision functions in this chapter have this optional final `global` argument.

Run the `circleCollision.html` file to see how you can use this function along with the drag-and-drop pointer system we created in the previous chapter, as shown in Figure 7-2.

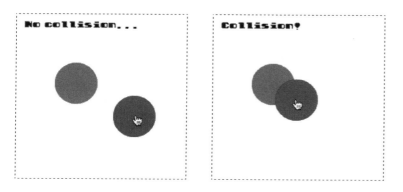

Figure 7-2. *Check whether two circles are touching*

Here's the code from the game loop that uses `hitTestCircle` to achieve this effect. The red circle is called `c1` (for "circle 1"), and the blue circle is called `c2` (for "circle 2").

```
if(hitTestCircle(c1, c2)) {
  message.content = "Collision!"
} else {
  message.content = "No collision..."
}
```

This is the basic system you need in place to create a puzzle or drag-and-drop shape-matching game.

Reactive Circle Collisions

In the previous example you could detect that a collision occurred, but the circles didn't react to the collisions in any way. In most action games you'll want your sprites to block the movements of other sprites or bounce off each other when they collide. There are two functions you can use to make sprites with this kind of realistic collision reaction: `circleCollision` and `movingCircleCollision`. Why are there two? Because moving circles react slightly differently depending on whether they hit a stationary circle or another moving circle. In the next two sections you'll learn how to use both functions with some very practical game prototypes.

Collisions Between a Moving Circle and a Stationary Circle

If a moving circle hits a nonmoving circle, you can create a collision reaction using the `circleCollision` function:

```
circleCollision(circle1, circle2, true);
```

The first argument is the moving ball, and the second is the nonmoving ball. The third argument is an optional Boolean that determines whether the first circle should bounce off the second. (The Boolean will default to `false` if you leave it out, so if you want the circles to bounce, set it to `true`.)

■ **Note** Setting an optional fourth argument to `true` makes the function use the sprites' global coordinates. This is important if you want to check for collisions between sprites that have different parent containers. You'll see how this will be helpful in the example ahead.

Any sprite with a `radius` property can be used in this function. If the sprite also has a `mass` property, the `circleCollision` function will use its value to dampen the bounce effect proportionately.

Run `pegs.html` to see how you can use this function to make a ball that bounces through a grid of circular pegs. The ball bounces off each peg and settles to a stop at the bottom of the canvas. The size and color of each peg in the grid are random, as are the ball's size, mass, and start velocity, so the effect is different each time it runs. Figure 7-3 shows what you'll see.

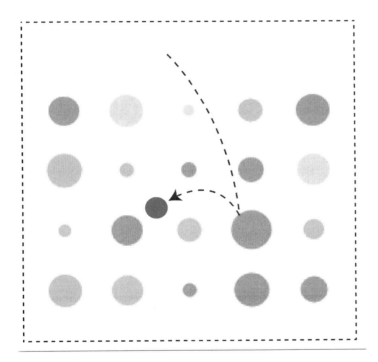

Figure 7-3. *A ball falls and bounces through a grid of pegs*

The pegs are in an array called pegs, and the ball's collision reaction is created in the game loop using this bit of code:

```
pegs.children.forEach(peg => {
  circleCollision(ball, peg, true, true);
});
```

That's all that's needed to create the bounce effect. But there are a few more interesting things going on in this program that you might find a use for in your own games. Let's see how the grid of pegs was made.

Plotting the Grid

Take a close look and you'll notice that each peg is laid out inside an invisible grid of five columns by five rows, as illustrated in Figure 7-4.

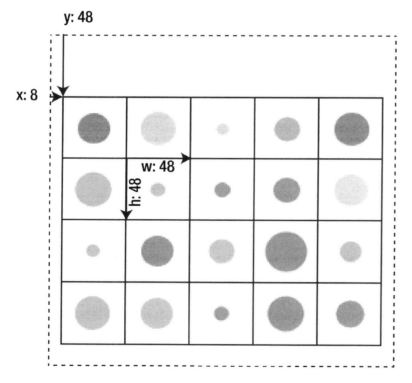

Figure 7-4. *Each peg is centered inside a cell in an invisible grid*

You can see that each peg is centered inside a grid cell with a width and height of 48 pixels. Each peg has a random diameter between 8 and 32 pixels, and a random color chosen from an array of color values. The grid is offset from the left of the canvas by 8 pixels and from the top by 48 pixels. The grid is a parent group container, and each circular peg is a child of that group. How was this grid made?

Plotting sprites in a grid shape like this is an extremely common video game design task—so common, in fact, that it's helpful to assign the work to a reusable function that will do it for you automatically. In the library/display folder you'll find a function called grid that does exactly this. Here's how the grid function is used in the example file to make the pegs grid:

```
pegs = grid(
    5,            //The number of columns
    4,            //The number of rows
    48,           //The width of each cell
    48,           //The height of each cell
    true,         //Should the sprite be centered in the cell?
    0,            //The sprite's xOffset from the left of the cell
    0,            //The sprite's yOffset from the top of the cell

    //A function that describes how to make each peg in the grid.
    //A random diameter and color are selected for each one
    () => {
      let peg = circle(randomInt(8, 32));
      let colors = [
        "#FFABAB", "#FFDAAB", "#DDFFAB", "#ABE4FF", "#D9ABFF"
      ];
      peg.fillStyle = colors[randomInt(0, 4)];
      return peg;
    },

    //Run any optional extra code after each
    //peg is made
    () => console.log("extra!")
);
```

The function returns a group called pegs. All the sprites inside each cell of the grid are children of that pegs group. Because it's a group, you can manipulate the entire grid just like any other sprite. That means you can use the setPosition method we created in Chapter 4 to position the group inside the canvas, like this:

```
pegs.setPosition(8, 48);
```

Testing for collisions between the ball and the pegs is just a matter of looping through pegs.children and calling the circleCollision function for each one. Because the positions of the sprites inside the group are relative to the group's local coordinates, you need to set circleCollision's global flag to true.

```
pegs.children.forEach(peg => {
  circleCollision(ball, peg, true, true);
});
```

If you don't use the global coordinates, all the collisions will appear to be off by the same amount that the grid is offset from the left and top of the canvas (8 pixels on the *x* axis, and 48 pixels on the *y* axis).

245

Here's the complete grid function that creates all the pegs, plots them on the grid, and adds them to the group:

```
export function grid(
    columns = 0, rows = 0, cellWidth = 32, cellHeight = 32,
    centerCell = false, xOffset = 0, yOffset = 0,
    makeSprite = undefined,
    extra = undefined
  ){

  //Create an empty group called `container`. This `container`
  //group is what the function returns to the main program.
  //All the sprites in the grid cells will be added
  //as children to this container
  let container = group();

  //The `create` method plots the grid
  let createGrid = () => {
    //Figure out the number of cells in the grid
    let length = columns * rows;

    //Create a sprite for each cell
    for(let i = 0; i < length; i++) {

      //Figure out the sprite's x/y placement in the grid
      let x = (i % columns) * cellWidth,
          y = Math.floor(i / columns) * cellHeight;

      //Use the `makeSprite` function supplied in the constructor
      //to make a sprite for the grid cell
      let sprite = makeSprite();

      //Add the sprite to the `container`
      container.addChild(sprite);

      //Should the sprite be centered in the cell?

      //No, it shouldn't be centered
      if (!centerCell) {
        sprite.x = x + xOffset;
        sprite.y = y + yOffset;
      }

      //Yes, it should be centered
      else {
        sprite.x
          = x + (cellWidth / 2)
          - sprite.halfWidth + xOffset;
        sprite.y
          = y + (cellHeight / 2)
          - sprite.halfHeight + yOffset;
      }
```

```
    //Run any optional extra code. This calls the
    //`extra` function supplied by the constructor
    if (extra) extra(sprite);
  }
};

//Run the `createGrid` method
createGrid();

//Return the `container` group back to the main program
return container;
}
```

There's a little bit of magic in this code. It's the calculation that finds the correct *x, y* position for each cell in the grid:

```
let x = (i % columns) * cellWidth,
    y = Math.floor(i / columns) * cellHeight;
```

This lets you plot the grid using a single for loop, instead of having to use two nested loops. It's a handy shortcut. (If you want to know exactly why this works, it's explained in detail in the platform game example later in this chapter.)

▦ **Tip** Here's a fun extension to this example. If you ever need to make a ball appear to roll, you can do so by dividing the ball's vx by its radius, and adding the result to its rotation, as shown here:
`ball.rotation += ball.vx / ball.radius;`

In this example you saw how to make a moving ball interact with stationary balls, but what if all the balls are moving, as in a game of billiards or marbles?

Collisions Between Moving Circles

You can create a collision reaction between two moving circles using the movingCircleCollision function. Supply two circle sprites as arguments:

```
movingCircleCollision(circle1, circle2)
```

If the circles have a mass property, it will be used to help figure out the force with which the circles should bounce off each other. The movingCircleCollision makes the sprites bounce apart by default.

An important feature of this function is that when two moving circles collide, they transfer their velocities to each other in a way that makes them bounce apart very realistically. This opens up a whole new world of game possibilities. You're now very close to being able to make a game of billiards or marbles. Run marbles.html for a working prototype of just such a game, shown in Figure 7-5. Hold the pointer down over any marble, and pull and release it to flick the marble away. A yellow line appears between the marble and the pointer when you start dragging. This line represents a kind of elastic band or sling that snaps the marble in the opposite direction that you pull. The length of the line determines the force at which the marble will move. When you release the sling, the marble will bounce off the edges of the canvas and off all the other marbles, causing them to bounce around and against each other as well.

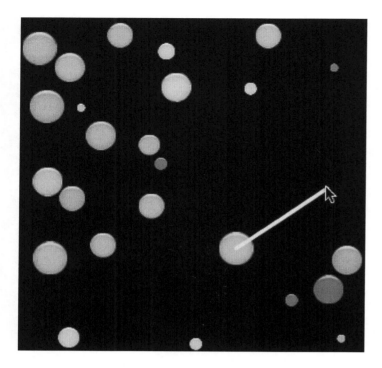

Figure 7-5. *Pull and release to make multiple circles bounce off each other and around the canvas*

There's some really interesting stuff going on here that brings together many techniques that you've learned in the book so far. Let's go on a step-by-step tour of how this game prototype was made.

Making the Marbles

How is each marble made? The marbles are actually images from a single tileset image called `marbles.png`, shown in Figure 7-6. Each tile is 32 by 32 pixels.

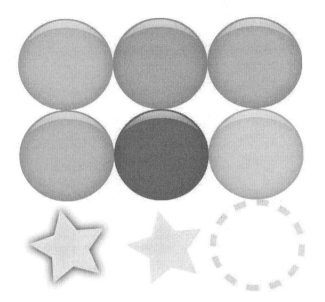

Figure 7-6. *The marbles tileset*

The game uses only the first two rows of images: the six colored circles. In Chapter 4 you learned how to use the frames function to capture multiple images on a tileset. Here's how to use it to capture references to all six colored circles:

```
let marbleFrames = frames(
  assets["images/marbles.png"],   //The tileset image
  [
    [0,0],[32,0],[64,0],          //A 2D array that defines the
    [0,32],[32,32],[64,32]        //x and y image positions
  ],
  32, 32                          //The width and height of each image
);
```

You can now initialize a sprite using these frames:

```
let marble = sprite(marbleFrames);
```

The marble sprite now has references to all six image frames, and you can display any of them by using gotoAndStop. Here's how to use randomInt to make the marble display a random frame:

```
marble.gotoAndStop(randomInt(0, 5));
```

Set the marble's `circular` property to `true` so that it will have the `diameter` and `radius` properties that the collision function needs:

```
marble.circular = true;
```

What if you want to give the marble a random diameter? Create an array of sizes and randomly assign one to the marble's `diameter` property:

```
let sizes = [8, 12, 16, 20, 24, 28, 32];
marble.diameter = sizes[randomInt(0, 6)];
```

Of course, you're not just making one marble—the game prototype has 25 of them. So it makes sense to initialize them in a grid. Here's all the code from the game's `setup` function that uses the `grid` function to create all 25 marble sprites.

```
marbles = grid(

  //Set the grid's properties
  5, 5, 64, 64,
  true, 0, 0,

  //A function that describes how to make each marble
  () => {
    let marbleFrames = frames(
      assets["images/marbles.png"],
      [
        [0,0],[32,0],[64,0],
        [0,32],[32,32],[64,32]
      ],
      32, 32
    );

    //Initialize a marble with the frames
    let marble = sprite(marbleFrames);

    //Set the marble to a random frame
    marble.gotoAndStop(randomInt(0, 5));

    //Give it circular properties (`diameter` and `radius`)
    marble.circular = true

    //Give the marble a random diameter
    let sizes = [8, 12, 16, 20, 24, 28, 32];
    marble.diameter = sizes[randomInt(0, 6)];

    //Give it a random initial velocity
    marble.vx = randomInt(-10, 10);
    marble.vy = randomInt(-10, 10);
```

```
//Assign the rest of the marble's physics properties
marble.frictionX = 0.99;
marble.frictionY = 0.99;
marble.mass = 0.75 + (marble.diameter / 32);

//Return the marble sprite so that it can
//be added to the grid cell
return marble;
  }
);
```

You can see in this code that the marbles are also assigned random initial velocities, from –10 to 10:

```
marble.vx = randomInt(-10, 10);
marble.vy = randomInt(-10, 10);
```

That means they'll fly away in different directions as soon as their positions are updated in the game loop. The code also works out each marble's mass:

```
marble.mass = 0.75 + (marble.diameter / 32);
```

Lighter marbles with less mass will bounce apart with greater speed than heavier marbles with more mass.

Making the Slingshot

A key feature of this example is the slingshot effect that you get when you hold the pointer down over a marble, drag, and then release it. The marble snaps away against the direction you pulled and bounces against any other marbles it hits, creating a complex chain of collisions, as illustrated in Figure 7-7.

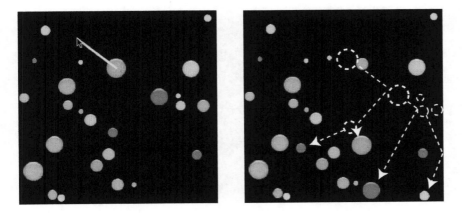

Figure 7-7. *Press, drag, and release the pointer over a marble for a slingshot effect*

This slingshot device is an important feature for many games, like Angry Birds, so let's take a quick look at how it's done.

The black line, known as the **sling**, that you see when you press down and drag over a marble is just a `line` sprite. Its `visible` property is set to `false` in the `setup` function when the game first starts so that you can't see it:

```
sling = line("Yellow", 4);
sling.visible = false;
```

The game uses a variable called `capturedMarble` that keeps track of which marble has been selected by the pointer. It's initialized to `null` when the game first starts:

```
capturedMarble = null;
```

On each frame the game loops through all the marbles and checks for a collision with the `pointer`. If the `pointer` is down, and a marble hasn't already been captured, the code uses `hitTestPoint` to find out if there's a marble under the `pointer`. If there is, the code sets the marble as the `capturedMarble`, and sets the marble's velocity to zero to stop it from moving:

```
marbles.children.forEach(marble => {

  //Check for a collision with the pointer and marble
  if (pointer.isDown && capturedMarble === null) {
    if (hitTestPoint(pointer, marble)) {

      //If there's a collision, capture the marble
      capturedMarble = marble;
      capturedMarble.vx = 0;
      capturedMarble.vy = 0;
    }
  }
  //... make the marbles move and set screen boundaries...
});
```

If a marble has been captured, the sling becomes visible and is drawn from the `pointer` to the center of the marble:

```
if (capturedMarble !== null) {
  sling.visible = true;
  sling.ax = capturedMarble.centerX;
  sling.ay = capturedMarble.centerY;
  sling.bx = pointer.x;
  sling.by = pointer.y;
}
```

When the `pointer` is released, the length of the sling is converted into a velocity that makes the marble shoot away in the opposite direction with proportional speed. The further you drag the sling, the greater the marble's velocity will be. It's just like an elastic band. This is really a just a slight variation on the code that we used to fire bullets in the previous chapter.

```
if (pointer.isUp) {

  //Make the sling invisible when it is released
  sling.visible = false;

  if (capturedMarble !== null) {

    //Find out how long the sling is
    sling.length = distance(capturedMarble, pointer);

    //Get the angle between the center of the marble and the pointer
    sling.angle = angle(pointer, capturedMarble);

    //Shoot the marble away from the pointer with a velocity
    //proportional to the sling's length
    let speed = 5;
    capturedMarble.vx = Math.cos(sling.angle) * sling.length / speed;
    capturedMarble.vy = Math.sin(sling.angle) * sling.length / speed;

    //Release the captured marble
    capturedMarble = null;
  }
}
```

Checking for Multiple Collisions

On every frame you need to check for a collision between each marble and every other marble. You need to make sure that no pair of marbles is checked for collisions with each other more than once. The key to making this work is to use a **nested for loop** and to start the counter of the inner loop by one greater than the outer loop. Here's the nested for loop that does this using the movingCircleCollision function to make the marbles bounce off each other:

```
for (let i = 0; i < marbles.children.length; i++) {

  //The first marble to use in the collision check
  var c1 = marbles.children[i];

  for (let j = i + 1; j < marbles.children.length; j++) {

    //The second marble to use in the collision check
    let c2 = marbles.children[j];

    //Check for a collision and bounce the marbles apart if they collide
    movingCircleCollision(c1, c2);
  }
}
```

You can see that the inner loops starts a number that's one greater than the outer loop:

```
let j = i + 1
```

This prevents any pair of objects from being checked for collisions more than once.

■ **Note**   The `library/collision` file contains a convenience method called `multipleCircleCollision` that automates this entire nested `for` loop for you. You can use it in a game loop to check all the sprites in an array with all the other sprites in the same array, without duplication. Use it like this:

```
multipleCircleCollision(marbles.children)
```

It will automatically call `movingCircleCollision` on each pair of sprites to make them bounce off one another.

You now know most of the important techniques you need to make a wide range of games using circular sprites. Next, we'll look at how you can handle collisions between rectangular sprites.

■ **Note**   Do you need to do a collision check between a circle and a single point? Just think of a point as a very small circle with a diameter of 1 pixel and a radius of 0.5 pixels. Then use that very small circle with any collision function that works with ordinary circles. To make this easier for you, the `library/collision` module contains two "circle vs. point" functions: `hitTestCirclePoint` tests for a collision, and `circlePointCollision` bounces the circle off the point. The first argument should be a circle sprite, and the second should be a point object with x and y properties.

Rectangle vs. Rectangle

To find out whether two rectangular sprites are overlapping, use a function called `hitTestRectangle`:

```
hitTestRectangle(rectangle1, rectangle2)
```

Run the file `rectangleCollision.html` for a simple example. Drag the squares with the pointer and watch the output text display "Hit!" when they collide, as shown in Figure 7-8.

Figure 7-8. *Check for collisions between rectangles*

Using `hitTestRectangle` inside a simple `if` statement is what changes the output text:

```
if (hitTestRectangle(rectangle1, rectangle2)) {
  output.text = "Hit!";
} else {
  output.text = "No collision...";
}
```

Checking for collisions between rectangular shapes like this is by far the most common kind of collision detection you're likely to do in your games. In fact, there are countless games you could make using nothing more sophisticated than `hitTestRectangle`. Let's take a close at how to use it to make a simple object collection and enemy avoidance game called Treasure Hunter.

Treasure Hunter

Treasure Hunter (Figure 7-9) is a good example of one of the simplest complete games you can make using the tools we've built in this book so far. (Play through `treasureHunter.html` in the chapter's source files to get a feel for it.) Use the arrow keys to help the explorer find the treasure and carry it to the exit. Six blob monsters move up and down between the dungeon walls, and if they hit the explorer he becomes semi-transparent, and the health meter at the top-right corner shrinks. If all the health is used up, "You lost" is displayed in the canvas; if the player character reaches the exit with the treasure, "You won!" is displayed. Although it's a basic prototype, Treasure Hunter contains most of the elements you'll find in much bigger games: texture atlas graphics, interactivity, collision, and multiple game scenes. Let's take a quick look at how it was put together so that you can use it as a starting point for one of your own games.

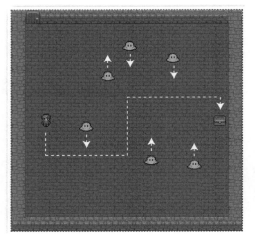

Don't get caught by a blob.

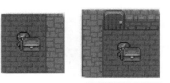

Carry the treasure to the exit.

Figure 7-9. *Find the treasure, avoid the enemies, and reach the exit*

Making the Game Sprites

Each of the sprites started out as an individual image file. I used Texture Packer to turn them into a texture atlas (shown in Figure 7-10), and imported the texture atlas with `assets.load`.

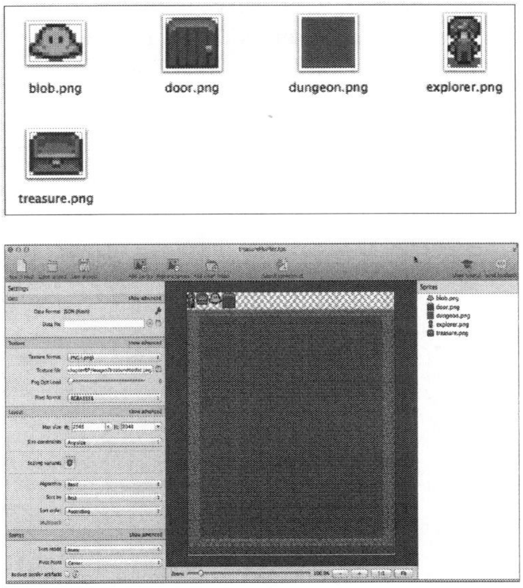

Figure 7-10. Make the texture atlas out of individual image files

```
assets.load(["images/treasureHunter.json"]).then(() => setup());
```

The player character, exit door, treasure chest and the dungeon background image are all sprites from texture atlas frames.

```
//The dungeon background image
dungeon = sprite(assets["dungeon.png"]);
```

```
//The exit door
exit = sprite(assets["door.png"]);
exit.x = 32;
```

```
//The player character sprite
player = sprite(assets["explorer.png"]);
stage.putCenter(player, -128);
```

```
//Create the treasure
treasure = sprite(assets["treasure.png"]);
```

```
//Position the treasure next to the right edge of the canvas
stage.putRight(treasure, -64);
```

All the sprites are grouped together in a single gameScene:

```
gameScene = group(dungeon, exit, player, treasure);
```

Keeping them together in a group will make it easy for us to hide the gameScene and display the gameOverScene when the game is finished.

The six blob monsters are created in a loop. Each blob is given a random initial position and velocity. The vertical velocity is alternately multiplied by 1 or –1 for each blob, and that's what causes each blob to move in the opposite direction to the one next to it:

```
let numberOfEnemies = 6,
    spacing = 48,
    xOffset = 150,
    speed = 2,
    direction = 1;

//An array to store all the enemies
enemies = [];

//Make as many enemies as there are `numberOfEnemies`
for (let i = 0; i < numberOfEnemies; i++) {

  //Each enemy is made from a blob texture atlas frame
  let enemy = sprite(assets["blob.png"]);

  //Space each enemy horizontally according to the `spacing` value.
  //`xOffset` determines the point from the left of the screen
  //at which the first enemy should be added
  let x = spacing * i + xOffset;

  //Give the enemy a random y position
  let y = randomInt(0, canvas.height - enemy.height);

  //Set the enemy's direction
  enemy.x = x;
  enemy.y = y;

  //Set the enemy's vertical velocity. `direction` will be either `1` or
  //`-1`. `1` means the enemy will move down and `-1` means the enemy will
  //move up. Multiplying `direction` by `speed` determines the enemy's
  //vertical direction
  enemy.vy = speed * direction;

  //Reverse the direction for the next enemy
  direction *= -1;

  //Push the enemy into the `enemies` array
  enemies.push(enemy);

  //Add the enemy to the `gameScene`
  gameScene.addChild(enemy);
}
```

You'll notice that when the player touches one of the enemies, the width of the health bar at the top-right corner of the screen decreases. How was this health bar made? It's just two rectangle sprites at the same position: a black rectangle behind, and a red rectangle in front. They're grouped together to make a single compound sprite called healthBar. The healthBar is then added to the gameScene.

```
//Make the inner and outer bars
let outerBar = rectangle(128, 8, "black"),
    innerBar = rectangle(128, 8, "red");
```

```
//Group the inner and outer bars
healthBar = group(outerBar, innerBar);
```

```
//Set the `innerBar` as a property of the `healthBar`
healthBar.inner = innerBar;
```

```
//Position the health bar
healthBar.x = canvas.width - 164;
healthBar.y = 4;
```

```
//Add the health bar to the `gameScene`
gameScene.addChild(healthBar);
```

You can see that a property called inner has been added to the healthBar. It just references the innerBar (the red rectangle) so that it will be convenient to access later:

```
healthBar.inner = innerBar;
```

You don't have to include this property; but why not! It means that if you want to control the width of the innerBar, you can write some smooth code that looks like this:

```
healthBar.inner.width = 30;
```

That's pretty neat and readable, so we'll keep it!

When the game is finished, some text displays "You won!" or "You lost!", depending on the outcome. We create this text by using a text sprite and adding it to a group called gameOverScene. The gameOverScene's visible property is set to false when the game starts so that you can't see this text. Here's the code from the setup function that creates the gameOverScene and the message text:

```
//Add some text for the game over message
message = text("Game Over!", "64px Futura", "black", 20, 20);
message.x = 120;
message.y = canvas.height / 2 - 64;
```

```
//Create a `gameOverScene` group and add the message sprite to it
gameOverScene = group(message);
```

```
//Make the `gameOverScene` invisible for now
gameOverScene.visible = false;
```

When the game is over, gameOverScene.visible will be set to true to reveal the outcome.

Moving and Containing the Sprites

The player is controlled using the keyboard, and the code that does that is very similar to the keyboard control code you learned in the previous chapter. The keyboard objects modify the player's velocity, and that velocity is added to the player's position in the game loop. An important detail of Treasure Hunter is that all the player and enemy sprites are contained inside the dungeon's wall, in a way that matches the 2.5D perspective of the artwork. This area is just slightly smaller than the total canvas area, and is shown by the green rectangle in Figure 7-11.

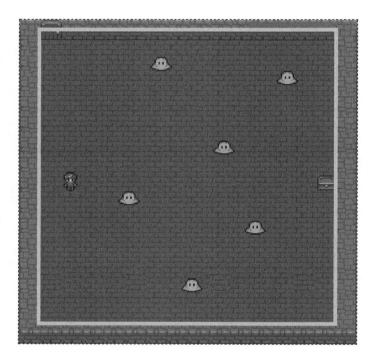

Figure 7-11. *The sprites are contained inside the dungeon walls*

This was easy to do with the help of the custom `contain` function we wrote in the previous chapter. The `contain` function's second argument is an object that defines the rectangular area to which the sprite should be contained. In Treasure Hunter this is an area that's offset from and slightly smaller than the canvas's area.

```
contain(
  player,
  {
    x: 32, y: 16,
    width: canvas.width - 32,
    height: canvas.height - 32
  }
);
```

The game loop also moves the enemies, keeps them contained inside the dungeon, and checks each one for a collision with the player. If an enemy bumps into the dungeon's top or bottom walls, its direction is reversed. A forEach loop does all this work on every frame:

```
//Loop through all the enemies
enemies.forEach(enemy => {

  //Move the enemy
  enemy.x += enemy.vx;
  enemy.y += enemy.vy;

  //Check the enemy's screen boundaries
  let enemyHitsEdges = contain(
    enemy,
    {
      x: 32, y: 16,
      width: canvas.width - 32,
      height: canvas.height - 32
    }
  );

  //If the enemy hits the top or bottom of the stage, it reverses
  //its direction
  if (enemyHitsEdges === "top" || enemyHitsEdges === "bottom") {
    enemy.vy *= -1;
  }

  //Test for a collision. If any of the enemies are touching
  //the player, set `playerHit` to `true`
  if(hitTestRectangle(player, enemy)) {
    playerHit = true;
  }
});
```

The last if statement checks for a collision between the enemy and the player—let's take a closer look at how it works.

Checking for Collisions

hitTestRectangle is used to figure out if any of the enemies have touched the player. If hitTestRectangle returns true, it means there's been a collision. The code then sets a variable called playerHit to true.

```
if(hitTestRectangle(player, enemy)) {
  playerHit = true;
}
```

If playerHit is true, the game loop makes the player semitransparent and reduces the width of the health bar by 1 pixel:

```
if(playerHit) {

  //Make the player semitransparent
  player.alpha = 0.5;
```

```
//Reduce the width of the health bar's inner rectangle by 1 pixel
healthBar.inner.width -= 1;
} else {

  //Make the player fully opaque (nontransparent) if it hasn't been hit
  player.alpha = 1;
}
```

The game loop also checks for a collision between the treasure chest and the player. If there's a hit, the treasure is set to the player's position, with a slight offset, to make it look like the player is carrying it (Figure 7-12).

```
if (hitTestRectangle(player, treasure)) {
  treasure.x = player.x + 8;
  treasure.y = player.y + 8;
}
```

Figure 7-12. *The player character can pick up and carry the treasure chest*

Reaching the Exit Door and Ending the Game

There are two ways the game can end: You can win if you carry the treasure to the exit, or you can lose if you run out of health. To win the game, the treasure chest just needs to touch the exit door. If that happens, the gameScene that contains all the sprites is made invisible, and the gameOverScene, which displays the message text, is displayed. Here's the if statement in the game loop that does this:

```
if (hitTestRectangle(treasure, exit)) {
  gameScene.visible = false;
  gameOverScene.visible = true;
  message.content = "You won!";
}
```

To lose the game, the health bar's width has to be less than 0. If it is, then the gameOverScene is revealed in the same way. The game loop uses this if statement to check:

```
if (healthBar.inner.width < 0) {
  gameScene.visible = false;
  gameOverScene.visible = true;
  message.content = "You lost!";
}
```

And that's really all there is to it! With a little more work you could turn this simple prototype into a full game—try it!

Reactive Rectangle Collisions

In the previous examples you could check whether two rectangles were colliding, but there was nothing to prevent them from overlapping. With a new function called `rectangleCollision` we can go one step further and make the rectangles behave as though they have solid mass; `rectangleCollision` will prevent any of the rectangle sprites in its first two arguments from overlapping:

```
rectangleCollision(rectangle1, rectangle2)
```

`rectangleCollision` also returns a string, whose value may be `"left"`, `"right"`, `"top"`, or `"bottom"`, that tells you which side of the first rectangle touched the second rectangle. You can assign the return value to a variable and use the information in your game. Here's how:

```
let collision = rectangleCollision(rectangle1, rectangle2);

//On which side of the red square is the collision occurring?
switch (collision) {
  case "left":
    message.content = "Collision on left";
    break;
  case "right":
    message.content = "Collision on right";
    break;
  case "top":
    message.content = "Collision on top";
    break;
  case "bottom":
    message.content = "Collision on bottom";
    break;
  default:
    message.content = "No collision...";
}
```

`collision` has a default value of `undefined`.

This code prevents the rectangles from overlapping and displays the collision side in the `message` text sprite. Run `reactiveRectangles.html` for a working example, as shown in Figure 7-13. Use the pointer to drag the red square into the blue square. No matter how hard you try, the squares will stay cleanly separated and never overlap. The output text displays on which side of the red square the collision is occurring.

Figure 7-13. *The squares don't overlap, and the output text tells you the collision side*

The rectangleCollision function has a very useful side effect. The second sprite in the argument has the ability to push the first sprite out of the way. You can see this effect in the example by using the blue square to push the red square around the canvas, as illustrated in Figure 7-14.

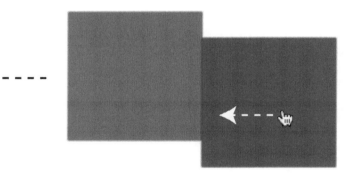

Figure 7-14. *The second sprite in the argument can push the first sprite*

If you need to add a block-pushing or tile-sliding feature to a game, this is how you can do it.

The rectangleCollision function has a third, optional Boolean argument, bounce:

```
rectangleCollision(rectangle1, rectangle2, true)
```

If bounce is true, it makes the first sprite bounce off the second sprite when they collide. Its default value is false. (As with the all the other collision functions in this chapter, you should set the final optional argument, global, to true if you want to use the sprites' global coordinates.)

Accurate rectangle collision reactions like this are among the most useful game design tools in your arsenal. To show you just how useful, we're going to take a detailed look at a practical example that should give you lots of inspiration for a multitude of game projects you can start working on right away.

Making a Platform Game

Platform games are a great technical and creative benchmark for game designers because they give you a chance to use all of the game-design toys in your toy box. If you can solve all the challenges you need to overcome to make a platform game, you'll find it easy to scale back and use those same techniques to make many other kinds of 2D action games.

Let's take all the tools we've created in this book so far to build a minimalist platform game prototype. Run the platforms.html file, shown in Figure 7-15, to try the working example. Move the red square left and right with the arrow keys, and use the space bar to jump. You can jump on either rock platforms (black squares) or grass platforms (green squares). The grass platforms are always above the rock platforms. Collect the treasure (the yellow squares) to increase your score. The game level map is generated procedurally, so it's different each time you play.

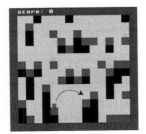

Figure 7-15. *Run and jump around a procedurally generated platform game*

There are two main parts to this game program. The first controls the mechanics of platform jumping and the way collision detection is used. The second part is the way the game level is created randomly using some simple rules. We'll look at the game mechanics first and then how the level is created. At the end of this section you'll learn how to swap these simple shape sprites for image sprites, so that you can easily customize the look of the game.

Platform Collisions

The game uses the rectangleCollision function to prevent the player character (the red square) from falling through the platforms (the black and green squares). When the player lands on a platform, the code needs to stop the player by setting its velocity to zero. The game also needs to know when the player is standing "on the ground." The "ground" in this game is any platform's top side. When the player is standing on top of a platform, we need to set a variable called isOnGround to false, and also neutralize the effect of gravity by subtracting it from the player's velocity.

Here's the code inside the game loop that does all this. It loops through all the platforms and uses the rectangleCollision function to find out if the player is touching any platforms. If it is, the code prevents the player from falling through. The code also uses the rectangleCollision's return value ("left", "right", "top", or "bottom") to find out on which side the player is touching the platform.

```
world.platforms.forEach(platform => {

  //Use `rectangleCollision` to prevent the player and platforms
  //from overlapping
  let collision = rectangleCollision(player, platform);

  //Use the `collision` variable to figure out what side of the player
  //is hitting the platform
  if (collision) {
    if(collision === "bottom" && player.vy >= 0) {

      //Tell the game that the player is on the ground if
      //it's standing on top of a platform
      player.isOnGround = true;

      //Neutralize gravity by applying its
      //exact opposite force to the character's vy
      player.vy = -player.gravity;
    }
    else if(collision === "top" && player.vy <= 0) {
      player.vy = 0;
    }
    else if(collision === "right" && player.vx >= 0) {
      player.vx = 0;
    }
    else if(collision === "left" && player.vx <= 0) {
      player.vx = 0;
    }

    //Set `isOnGround` to `false` if the bottom of the player
    //isn't touching the platform
    if(collision !== "bottom" && player.vy > 0) {
      player.isOnGround = false;
    }
  }
});
```

Each time the player picks up some treasure (a yellow square), the treasure disappears from the game and the score increases by one, as illustrated in Figure 7-16. The code does this by looping through each of the platform sprites and using `hitTestRectangle` to check for a collision.

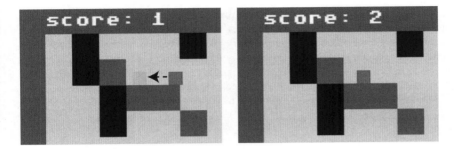

Figure 7-16. *Collect treasure to increase the score*

```
world.treasure = world.treasure.filter(box => {

  //Check for a collision between the player and the treasure
  if (hitTestRectangle(player, box)){

    //Increase the score by 1
    score += 1;

    //Remove the treasure sprite
    remove(box);

    //Remove the treasure from the array
    return false;
  } else {

    //Keep the treasure in the array
    return true;
  }
});


//Display the score
message.content = `score: ${score}`;
```

Now that you know how the collision detection in the game works, how does the player move around?

Making the Player Move and Jump

This platform game prototype uses all the physics forces that you learned in the previous chapters. It also adds a new one: a `jumpForce` that's applied when you press the space bar. `jumpForce` is a property of the player sprite:

```
player.jumpForce = -6.8;
```

It's set to a negative number to make the player jump up toward the top of the canvas. (Remember, negative *y* forces make things go up.) When the player presses the space bar, this jumpForce is added to the player's vertical velocity (vy). It's really just a matter of trial and error to find the right number that makes the player's jumping look natural.

The player should only be allowed to jump when it's standing on a platform. Luckily, the isOnGround variable that we set with the platform collisions can tell us that. Also, if the left and right arrow keys are being pressed, the player's movement shouldn't be affected by friction so that it can move smoothly across the platform surfaces. But what if the player is moving through the air? Some wind resistance should slow it down a bit so that the jump is more controlled. These are delicate details to get just right, but the final code is not too complex. Here's the code from the setup function that creates the player's keyboard controls.

```
leftArrow = keyboard(37);
rightArrow = keyboard(39);
space = keyboard(32);

//Left arrow key
leftArrow.press = () => {
  if(rightArrow.isUp) {
    player.accelerationX = -0.2;
  }
};
leftArrow.release = () => {
  if(rightArrow.isUp) {
    player.accelerationX = 0;
  }
};

//Right arrow key
rightArrow.press = () => {
  if(leftArrow.isUp) {
    player.accelerationX = 0.2;
  }
};
rightArrow.release = () => {
  if(leftArrow.isUp) {
    player.accelerationX = 0;
  }
};

//Space key (jump)
space.press = () => {
  if(player.isOnGround) {
    player.vy += player.jumpForce;
    player.isOnGround = false;
    player.frictionX = 1;
  }
};
```

The game loop then makes the player move by updating these physics properties and applying them to the player's position:

```
//Regulate the amount of friction acting on the player
if (player.isOnGround) {

  //Add some friction if the player is on the ground
  player.frictionX = 0.92;
} else {

  //Add less friction if it's in the air
  player.frictionX = 0.97;
}

//Apply the acceleration
player.vx += player.accelerationX;
player.vy += player.accelerationY;

//Apply friction
player.vx *= player.frictionX;

//Apply gravity
player.vy += player.gravity;

//Move the player
player.x += player.vx;
player.y += player.vy;
```

These are all the basic mechanics that you need to know to create most kinds of platform games. But how was the actual game world created?

Creating the Game World

The program's setup function creates the game world. All the level data is stored in an object called level, which describes how big the game world is. The world is made up of a grid of **tiles**: 16 tiles across and 16 tiles down. Each tile is 32 pixels wide and 32 pixels high, which means the size of the world in pixels is 512 by 512. The size of each tile matches the maximum size of the sprites we're gong to use to make the world.

```
level = {

  //The height and width of the level, in tiles
  widthInTiles: 16,
  heightInTiles: 16,

  //The width and height of each tile, in pixels
  tilewidth: 32,
  tileheight: 32
};
```

In a more complex game, you could add other kinds of data in the level object that is specific to the game level. These could be properties that store the locations of specific items, values that make the level easier or harder, or the size and type of the level that should be created. If you're creating a multilevel game, you could use different level objects like this for each level in your game. You could then store and access them all in a big array of game levels that you could load and create dynamically as your game progresses.

This level data is then used to make the game world:

```
world = makeWorld(level);
```

What is world and how does makeWorld work? world is a group, returned by makeWorld, that contains all the sprites in the game. The makeWorld function basically just creates the group, adds the game sprites to it, and then returns the group back to the game program. All of this happens in the setup function before the game loop starts running.

The makeWorld function has a lot of work to do, so before we look at the details, let's take a birds-eye view of what it does.

```
function makeWorld(level) {

  //create the `world` object
  let world = group();

  //Add some arrays to the world that will store the objects that we're
  //going to create
  world.map = [];
  world.itemLocations = [];
  world.platforms = [];
  world.treasure = [];

  //Initialize a reference to the player sprite
  world.player = null;

  //1. Make the map
  makeMap();

  //2. Terraform the map
  terraformMap();

  //3. Add the items
  addItems();

  //4. Make the sprites
  makeSprites();

  //The four functions that do all the work:

  function makeMap() {/* Make the map */}
  function terraformMap() {/* Add grass, rock, sky and clouds */}
  function addItems() {/* Add the player and treasure to the map */}
  function makeSprites() {/* Use the map data to make the actual game sprites */}
```

```
//Return the `world` group back to the main program
return world;
}
```

You can see that makeWorld methodically calls four functions in order: makeMap, terraformMap, addItems, and makeSprites. It's like a little assembly line. Each of those functions does a little bit of work, and then hands the job over to the next function to continue. When the last one, makeSprites, is finished, all the sprites have been made and the world group is returned back to the main game program. This all happens in sequence, so let's find out how each function works.

Making the Map

The first function, makeMap, fills the map array with random cells. The cells are just plain old familiar JavaScript objects:

```
cell = {};
```

Each cell has *x* and *y* properties that represent its position on a grid, based on the level's width and height. In this example they represent a 16 by 16 grid of cells. The cells have a terrain property, which can either be "rock" or "sky". Each cell has a 25% chance of being rock and a 75% chance of being sky, which is determined by a helper function called cellIsAlive. The cells also have a property called item, which we'll use in later steps to place game items: the player and the treasure boxes.

```
function makeMap() {

  //The `cellIsAlive` helper function.
  //Give each cell a 1 in 4 chance to live. If it's "alive", it will
  //be rock, if it's "dead" it will be sky.
  //`cellIsAlive` will be `undefined` unless the random number is 0
  let cellIsAlive = () => randomInt(0, 3) === 0;


  //First, figure out the number of cells in the grid
  let numberOfCells = level.heightInTiles * level.widthInTiles;

  //Next, create the cells in a loop
  for (let i = 0; i < numberOfCells; i++) {

    //Figure out the x and y position
    let x = i % level.widthInTiles,
        y = Math.floor(i / level.widthInTiles);

    //Create the `cell` object
    let cell = {
      x: x,
      y: y,
      item: ""
    };
```

```
  //Decide whether the cell should be "rock" or "sky"
  if (cellIsAlive()) {
    cell.terrain = "rock";
  } else {
    cell.terrain = "sky";
  }

  //Push the cell into the world's `map` array
  world.map.push(cell);
 }
}
```

After this function runs, the map array will contain 256 cell objects, 25% of which will randomly have their terrain set to "rock", and the rest set to "sky". Their x and y properties will also tell you where on the 16 by 16 grid they're positioned. Figure 7-17 shows an example of what one of these random maps could look like. (We haven't created the sprites for these cells yet, so Figure 7-17 just illustrates the array data we've created.)

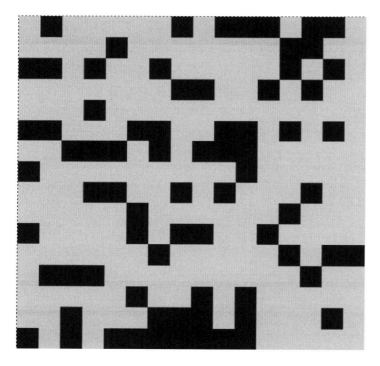

Figure 7-17. *Create a random map of rock (black squares) and sky (blue squares)*

It's a good start, but you'll see how we can improve this map in the steps ahead.

Using a 1D Array for a 2D Map

You'll notice that although we're creating a 2D grid of cells, we're only using a flat, 1D array. This is the same technique we used in the grid function that we wrote at the beginning of the chapter, so let's take a closer look at how it works.

You can figure out how long the 1D array should be by multiplying the grid's width (16) by its height (16):

```
let numberOfCells = this.height * this.width;
```

This will give you 256 array elements: 16 rows and 16 columns.

The reason we don't need to use a 2D array is that each cell object has x and y properties that store its position on the grid, but we don't need the row and column information that you can derive from a 2D array. Instead, the code uses this formula to convert the array's index counter, i, to x (column) and y (row) coordinates:

```
x = i % this.width;
y = Math.floor(i / this.width);
```

The x position will always be the remainder of the index counter divided by the grid's width: i % this.width. The y position will always be the value of the index counter divided by the grid's width, with the remainder truncated: Math.floor(i / this.width). This is a handy magic formula to keep in your back pocket!

Why not just use a 2D array? It's mostly a matter of style. By using a 1D array we can eliminate an inner nested for loop. And because each array element contains an object, we can store the grid position directly on that object, rather than having to use the loop index counters to calculate it. Also, we can pack the cell object with as many extra properties as we need to describe that cell of the map. This makes it an efficient storage container for map information. You'll see how this will prove helpful ahead as we continue to build the game level.

Terraforming the Map

Now that we've got a grid of random squares, we can improve it to make it better suited for a platform game environment. To **terraform** means to modify an existing environment – so that's what we're going to do next. There are four things that I've decided I want to do to improve this map:

- I want to add a border around the playing area.

- I want to find each rock that has a sky cell above it. These rocks should become "grass" cells. (You can see these as green squares in the finished prototype.) Grass cells are all the platforms that the player will be able to jump on.

- I've decided that there should be at least two cells of sky above each grass cell. This will make it easy for the game character to jump freely without bumping its head.

- It turns out that the cells *directly above* the grass cells are ideal places to use as starting positions for the player and treasure boxes. I want to find all these cells, push them into an array called itemLocations, and use them to randomly position the player and treasure boxes when the game first starts.

(You can see all these improvements illustrated in Figure 7-18, along with the code that finds these cells.)

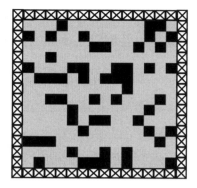

Find the map border cells

```
if (cell.x === 0 || cell.y === 0
|| cell.x === level.widthInTiles - 1
|| cell.y === level.heightInTiles - 1) {
  cell.terrain = "border";
}
```

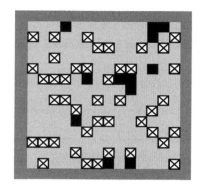

Find the "grass" cells

```
if (cell.terrain === "rock") {
  if (cellAbove && cellAbove.terrain === "sky") {
    cell.terrain = "grass";
  //...}
  //...}
```

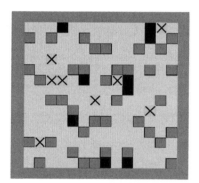

Make sure there are 2 sky cells
above each grass cell

```
if (cell.terrain === "rock") {
  if (cellAbove && cellAbove.terrain === "sky") {
    cell.terrain = "grass";
    if (cellTwoAbove.terrain === "rock"
    || cellTwoAbove.terrain === "grass") {
      cellTwoAbove.terrain = "sky";
    }
  }
}
```

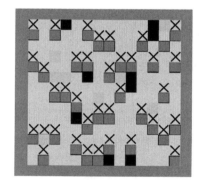

Find good spots to place
game items

```
world.map.forEach((cell, index, map) => {
  if (cell.terrain === "grass") {
    let cellAbove = world.map[getIndex(cell.x, cell.y - 1)];
    world.itemLocations.push(cellAbove);
  }
});
```

Figure 7-18. *Add features to improve the map*

To do all this, we'll need to loop through the map array and analyze each cell. We'll need to know what type of cell it is ("rock" or "grass"), its x/y position on the grid, and also what type of cells are surrounding it. The map is a 1D array, but the cells represent a 2D grid. How can we convert the cells' x and y positions to the correct array index number? We can use this simple helper function called getIndex:

```
let getIndex = (x, y) => x + (y * level.widthInTiles);
```

To use it, call getIndex inside the map array's square brackets. Use the current cell's x and y values to target the cell you want to find. Here's how you can use it to find the array index of the cell that's directly to the left of the current cell:

```
cellTotheLeft = map[getIndex(cell.x - 1, cell.y)]
```

And here's how to find the index number of the cell that's two grid cells above the current cell:

```
cellTwoAbove = map[getIndex(cell.x, cell.y - 2)]
```

We now have an easy way to navigate a 2D grid inside a 1D array.

■ **Note** If getIndex tries to reference an element in the array that's less than 0 or greater than the array's length, it will return undefined. If there's any chance your code might produce undefined values, such as if you reference cells that are outside the map boundaries, make sure you add an extra conditional check for this.

With this trick up our sleeve, we can loop through all the cells in the map array, analyze them and their neighboring cells, and use that information to improve the map. Here's the terraformMap function that does all this. Read the comments to see how the code works, and compare the code to Figure 7-18 to see how it changes the map.

```
function terraformMap() {

  //A `getIndex` helper function to convert the cell x and y position to an
  //array index number
  let getIndex = (x, y) => x + (y * level.widthInTiles);

  world.map.forEach((cell, index, map) => {

    //Some variables to help find the cells to the left, right, below
    //and above the current cell
    let cellToTheLeft = world.map[getIndex(cell.x - 1, cell.y)],
        cellToTheRight = world.map[getIndex(cell.x + 1, cell.y)],
        cellBelow = world.map[getIndex(cell.x, cell.y + 1)],
        cellAbove = world.map[getIndex(cell.x, cell.y - 1)],
        cellTwoAbove = world.map[getIndex(cell.x, cell.y - 2)];

    //If the cell is on the border of the map, change its terrain to "border"
    if (cell.x === 0 || cell.y === 0
    || cell.x === level.widthInTiles - 1
    || cell.y === level.heightInTiles - 1) {
      cell.terrain = "border";
    }

    //If the cell isn't on the border, find out if we can
    //grow some grass on it. Any rock with a sky cell above
    //it should be made into grass. Here's how to figure this out:
    else {
```

```
        //1. Is the cell a rock?
        if (cell.terrain === "rock") {

            //2. Is there sky directly above it?
            if (cellAbove && cellAbove.terrain === "sky") {

                //3. Yes there is, so change its name to "grass"
                cell.terrain = "grass";

                //4. Make sure there are 2 sky cells above grass cells
                //so that it's easy to jump to higher platforms
                //without bumping your head. Change any rock cells that are
                //2 above the current grass cell to "sky"
                if (cellTwoAbove) {
                    if (cellTwoAbove.terrain === "rock"
                    || cellTwoAbove.terrain === "grass") {
                        cellTwoAbove.terrain = "sky";
                    }
                }
            }
        }
    });

    //We now have the finished map.
    //Next, we're going to loop through the map one more time
    //to find all the item location cells and push them into the
    //`itemLocations` array. `itemLocations` is a list of cells that
    //we'll use later to place the player and treasure on the map

    world.map.forEach((cell, index, map) => {
        //Is the cell a grass cell?
        if (cell.terrain === "grass") {

            //Yes, so find the cell directly above it and push it
            //into the `itemLocations` array
            let cellAbove = world.map[getIndex(cell.x, cell.y - 1)];
            world.itemLocations.push(cellAbove);
        }
    });
}
```

Our platform game environment is now finished, and we have an array called itemLocations that we can use to place the player and the treasure.

> ■ **Note** There's obviously a lot more fine-tuning you could do to this map, such as making sure there are no enclosed spaces, making sure all platforms can be reached, and finding good places for traps and enemies. Just continue to apply these same principles to customize the map for you own games. It's just as easy to do as you think it might be. To learn more about procedurally generated game maps, do some research into game level design using **cellular automata**.

Adding Game Items

Adding the player and treasure boxes to the game is simply a matter of randomly choosing cells from the itemLocations array that we populated in the previous step. The cell's item property is then set to whatever item we want it to contain. The level object's addItems method does this for us.

```
function addItems() {

  //The `findStartLocation` helper function returns a random cell
  let findStartLocation = () => {

    //Randomly choose a start location from the `itemLocations` array
    let randomIndex = randomInt(0, world.itemLocations.length - 1);
    let location = world.itemLocations[randomIndex];

    //Splice the cell from the array so we don't choose the
    //same cell for another item
    world.itemLocations.splice(randomIndex, 1);
    return location;
  };

  //1. Add the player
  //Find a random cell from the `itemLocations` array
  let cell = findStartLocation();
  cell.item = "player";

  //2. Add 3 treasure boxes
  for (let i = 0; i < 3; i++) {
    cell = findStartLocation();
    cell.item = "treasure";
  }
}
```

The map is now complete. The last step is to use the cell information to create the sprites we can display on the canvas.

Making the Sprites

A function called makeSprites uses the map data to create the actual sprites you see on the canvas. The makeSprites function first loops through the map array and uses the cell's properties to create the border, rock, sky, and grass cells. The cell's *x* and *y* properties are just multiplied by the level's cellWidth and cellHeight to plot the sprite at the correct position on the canvas. The border, rock, and grass cells are also pushed into the platforms array so that they can be used in the platform collision code we looked at earlier.

After these terrain cells are made, the code loops through the map array a second time to add the player and treasure items. The game item sprites are created at half the size of the terrain sprites, and centered and positioned directly above them.

The item sprites will be added to the end of the sprites array, which means that when the render function displays them, they'll be the last sprites to render. That will make them overlap in front of the terrain sprites.

Here's the complete makeSprites function that does all this:

```
function makeSprites() {

  //Make the terrain
  world.map.forEach(cell => {
    let mapSprite = rectangle();
    mapSprite.x = cell.x * level.tilewidth;
    mapSprite.y = cell.y * level.tileheight;
    mapSprite.width = level.tilewidth;
    mapSprite.height = level.tileheight;

    switch (cell.terrain) {
      case "rock":
        mapSprite.fillStyle = "black";
        world.platforms.push(mapSprite);
        break;

      case "grass":
        mapSprite.fillStyle = "green";
        world.platforms.push(mapSprite);
        break;

      case "sky":
        mapSprite.fillStyle = "cyan";
        break;

      case "border":
        mapSprite.fillStyle = "blue";
        world.platforms.push(mapSprite);
        break;
    }
  });

  //Make the game items. (Do this after the terrain so
  //that the item sprites display above the terrain sprites)
  world.map.forEach(cell => {
```

```
//Each game object will be half the size of the cell.
//They should be centered and positioned so that they align
//with the bottom of the cell
if(cell.item !== "") {
  let mapSprite = rectangle();
  mapSprite.x = cell.x * level.tilewidth + level.tilewidth / 4;
  mapSprite.y = cell.y * level.tileheight + level.tilewidth / 2;
  mapSprite.width = level.tilewidth / 2;
  mapSprite.height = level.tileheight / 2;

  switch (cell.item) {
    case "player":
      mapSprite.fillStyle = "red";
      mapSprite.accelerationX = 0;
      mapSprite.accelerationY = 0;
      mapSprite.frictionX = 1;
      mapSprite.frictionY = 1;
      mapSprite.gravity = 0.3;
      mapSprite.jumpForce = -6.8;
      mapSprite.vx = 0;
      mapSprite.vy = 0;
      mapSprite.isOnGround = true;
      world.player = mapSprite;
      break;

    case "treasure":
      mapSprite.fillStyle = "gold";

      //Push the treasure into the treasures array
      world.treasure.push(mapSprite);
      break;
    }
  }
});
}
```

After this method runs, the world object is returned back to the main program and the game starts.

Using Image Sprites

Our platform game is nothing more than a lot of data. The code is completely agnostic about what the sprites actually look like. That means you can use exactly the same data from the map array and, instead of making simple shapes, create image sprites from a tileset. You can see an example of this by enabling the makeImageSprites method in the platforms.html example file. The game runs and plays in exactly the same way, but instead of colored blocks, the sprites are now real illustrations, as shown in Figure 7-19.

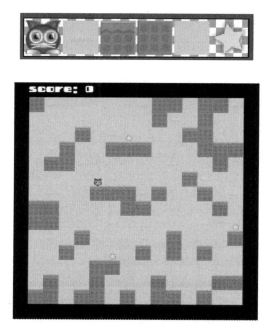

Figure 7-19. Use a tileset to completely customize the look of the game

Without changing the underlying code at all, you can completely change the look of the game just by using a different tileset. Take a look at the following makeImageSprites function for details, and you'll see that it's based on all the same techniques we've used for creating image sprites with a texture atlas that you've seen many examples of in this chapter.

```
function makeImageSprites() {

  //Make the terrain
  world.map.forEach((cell, index, map) => {
    let mapSprite,
        x = cell.x * level.tilewidth,
        y = cell.y * level.tileheight;

    switch (cell.terrain) {
      case "rock":
        mapSprite = sprite(assets["rock.png"]);
        mapSprite.setPosition(x, y);
        world.platforms.push(mapSprite);
        break;

      case "grass":
        mapSprite = sprite(assets["grass.png"]);
        mapSprite.setPosition(x, y);
        world.platforms.push(mapSprite);
        break;

      case "sky":
```

```
      //Add clouds every 6 cells and only on the top
      //80% of the level
      let sourceY = 0;
      if (index % 6 === 0 && index < map.length * 0.8) {
        mapSprite = sprite(assets["cloud.png"]);
      } else {
        mapSprite = sprite(assets["sky.png"]);
      }
      mapSprite.setPosition(x, y);
      break;

    case "border":
      mapSprite = rectangle(level.tilewidth, level.tileheight, "black");
      mapSprite.setPosition(x, y);
      world.platforms.push(mapSprite);
      break;
  }
});

//Make the game items

world.map.forEach(cell => {
  if (cell.item !== "") {
    let mapSprite,
        x = cell.x * level.tilewidth + level.tilewidth / 4,
        y = cell.y * level.tileheight + level.tilewidth / 2,
        width = level.tilewidth / 2,
        height = level.tileheight / 2;

    switch (cell.item) {
      case "player":
        mapSprite = sprite(assets["cat.png"]);
        mapSprite.width = width;
        mapSprite.height = height;
        mapSprite.setPosition(x, y);
        mapSprite.accelerationX = 0;
        mapSprite.accelerationY = 0;
        mapSprite.frictionX = 1;
        mapSprite.frictionY = 1;
        mapSprite.gravity = 0.3;
        mapSprite.jumpForce = -6.8;
        mapSprite.vx = 0;
        mapSprite.vy = 0;
        mapSprite.isOnGround = true;
        world.player = mapSprite;
        break;
```

```
        case "treasure":
          mapSprite = sprite(assets["star.png"]);
          mapSprite.width = width;
          mapSprite.height = height;
          mapSprite.setPosition(x, y);

          //Push the treasure into the `treasures` array
          world.treasure.push(mapSprite);
          break;
      }
    }
  });
}
```

Notice how this code places an image of a cloud for every sixth sky tile, and also how it limits placing the clouds to the top 80% of the map:

```
if (index % 6 === 0 && index < map.length * 0.8) { //...
```

Use this technique as a starting point to adding some variety to your own game environments.

■ **Tip**   Is your game fun to play? The sure-fire way to tell is to build your game prototype using simple elemental shapes and colors. In fact, in this platform game example I used the same font and color palette as a 1982-era Commodore 64, which is one of the first computers I learned to make games with. If your game isn't fun to play as a bunch of blocks and circles, the best graphics in the world won't be able to save it.

Circle vs. Rectangle

That last important collision check you need for games is to find out if a circular shape is hitting a rectangular shape. You can use a function called hitTestCircleRectangle to help you do this. The first argument is the circular sprite, and the second is the rectangular sprite:

```
let collision = hitTestCircleRectangle(ball, box);
```

If they're touching, the return value (collision) will tell you where the circle is hitting the rectangle. It can have the value "topLeft", "topMiddle", "topRight", "leftMiddle", "rightMiddle", "bottomLeft", "bottomMiddle", or "bottomRight". If there's no collision it will be undefined. Run the circleVsRectangle.html file for an interactive example. Drag the shapes to make them touch, and the text will tell you where the collision is happening. Figure 7-20 illustrates what you'll see.

Figure 7-20. *Check for a collision between a circle and a rectangle*

Here's the code from the example file's game loop that checks for a collision and displays the result:

```
let collision = hitTestCircleRectangle(ball, box);
if (collision) {
  message.content = collision;
} else {
  message.content = "No collision..."
}
```

You can use a companion function called `circleRectangleCollision` to make a circle bounce off a square's sides or corners:

```
circleRectangleCollision(ball, box, true);
```

(Setting the optional third argument to `true` makes the sprites bounce apart, and setting the fourth argument to `true` tells the function to use the sprites' global coordinates.)

Run the `bricks.html` file in the chapter's source code to see a working example. It's the same as the "pegs" example from earlier in the chapter, except that the round pegs have been exchanged for rectangular bricks. (Figure 7-21). The ball falls from the top of the canvas and bounces around the grid of bricks before settling on the ground.

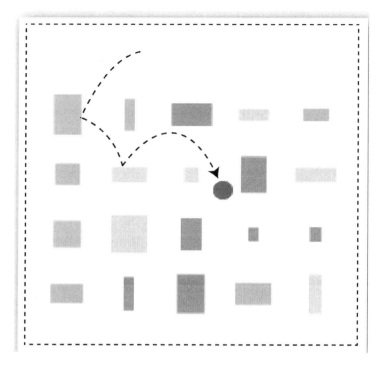

Figure 7-21. *A ball bounces through a grid of bricks*

Here's the code from the game loop that makes this work:

```
bricks.children.forEach(brick => {
  circleRectangleCollision(ball, brick, true, true);
});
```

And that's all you need to know to start making some truly captivating games!

A Universal Hit Function

To make your life a little easier, the `library/collision` file includes a universal collision function called `hit`. It automatically detects the kinds of sprites that are being used in the collision and chooses the appropriate collision function for you. This means that instead of having to remember which of the many collision functions from this chapter to use, you only need remember one: `hit`.

In its simplest form, you can use `hit` like this:

```
hit(spriteOne, spriteTwo)
```

The sprites can be circles or rectangles. If you want them to react to the collision, so that they don't intersect, set the third argument to true. If you want them to bounce apart, set the fourth argument to true. Setting the fifth argument to true makes the function use the sprites' global coordinates.

```
hit(spriteOne, spriteTwo, react, bounce, global)
```

If you want to check a point object for a collision against a sprite, use the point as the first argument, like this:

```
hit({x: 145, y:65}, sprite)
```

The hit function also lets you check for a collision between a sprite and an array of sprites. Just include the array as the second argument:

```
hit(ball, bricks.children, true, true, true);
```

You'll see that hit automatically loops through all the sprites in the array for you and checks them against the first sprite. This means you don't have to write your own for or forEach loop.

The hit function also returns a collision object, with a return value that matches the kinds of sprites you're checking. For example, if both sprites are rectangles, you could find the side on which the collision occurred like this:

```
let collision = hit(rectangleOne, rectangleTwo, true);
message.text = `collision side: ${collision}`;
```

collision will always be undefined if there's no collision.

A final feature is that you can use an optional callback function as the fifth argument. This lets you inject some extra code that should run when the collision occurs. This is especially useful for checking a collision between a single sprite and an array of sprites. If there's a collision, the callback will run, and you can access both the collision return value and the sprite involved in the collision. Here's how you could use this feature in the platform game example we looked at earlier in this chapter, to do the collision check between the player and the platforms:

```
let playerVsPlatforms = hit(
  player, world.platforms, true, false, false,
  (collision, platform) => {
    //`collision` tells you the side on player that the collision occurred on.
    //`platform` is the sprite from the `world.platforms` array
    //that the player is colliding with
  }
);
```

This is a compact way of doing complex collision checks that gives you a lot of information and low-level control but saves you from having to manually loop through all the sprites in the array.

If you're curious about how the hit function works, flip ahead to the Appendix where it's explained in detail. Essentially, it just analyzes the kinds of sprites provided in the arguments and sends them to the correct collision function.

Summary

Congratulations, you've just graduated from collision detection boot camp! This chapter covered all the most important collision functions you need to know for 2D action games: rectangle collisions, circle collisions, and point collisions. In fact, you now have all the skills you need to use HTML5 and JavaScript to re-create most of the classics of video game history, and there are very few 2D games that aren't now within your reach. Use the working prototypes from this chapter as the starting points for you own games, and, with a bit of imagination, you'll be amazed at what you can do.

But there's an important tool missing from your toolkit: keyframe animation. In the next chapter you're going to learn some advanced animation techniques to help you make expressive animated game characters and special effects. But before you turn the page, why not go ahead and make a game with all the new skills you've learned in this chapter? I'll meet you at Chapter 8 when you're done!

CHAPTER 8

■ ■ ■

Juice It Up

With all the tools we've built in the book so far, you can actually start making real games. But what's missing so far is what game developers call **juice**: flashy effects and animation that make the game world feel alive. This chapter is all about three important ways to add juice to your games:

- **Keyframe animation**: Make your game characters play a sequence of prerendered animation frames, like a film strip.

- **Particle effects**: Create explosion or stream effects using lots of tiny particles.

- **Tiling sprites**: These are a quick and easy way to add an infinite scrolling background, especially for creating a parallax depth effect.

By carefully using these effects together, you can transform even a very simple game into a compelling and immersive alternate universe that your players will find irresistible.

Keyframe Animation

In Chapter 2 you learned how to move sprites around the screen by interactively changing their x and y positions. That's an animation technique called **scripted animation**: using mathematical formulas to make things move. In this chapter you're going to learn another animation technique, called **keyframe animation**. Keyframe animation displays a sequence of prerendered images that make sprites appear to perform an action. These could be any actions that change the way the sprite looks, like changing its color, breaking it into pieces, or moving its feet to make it walk. Keyframe animation is about changing what the sprite looks like when its state changes. If you combine scripted animation (changing a sprite's position) with keyframe animation (changing a sprite's appearance) you can start to develop rich and complex sprite interactivity.

In this first section of the chapter we're going to take a detailed look at how to play and control a set of animation sequences on a sprite. But before we do, let's look at the first step in the process: how to change a sprite's state.

Changing States

Figure 8-1 shows a tileset called `states.png`. It contains an elf character shown in four states: up, left, down, and right. Each state is represented by one image frame.

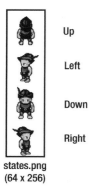

states.png
(64 x 256)

Figure 8-1. *A tileset with four character states*

Imagine that you're creating a game where this elf character should change the direction it's facing depending on which arrow key you're pressing. How can you do that?

The first step is to create an array of frames: one for each of the four frames in the image. You can do this using the `frames` method you learned to use in Chapter 4.

```
let elfFrames = frames(
  assets["images/states.png"],          //The tileset image to use
  [[0,0], [0,64], [0,128], [0, 192]],   //Array of x/y positions of each frame
  64, 64                                //The width and height of each frame
);
```

`elfFrames` is now an array that contains four frames that match each of the elf's image states. (You'll find the `frames` method in `library/display` in the book's source files.)

Now use the `elfFrames` array to make a sprite:

```
elf = sprite(elfFrames);
```

Next, define four state properties: `up`, `left`, `down`, and `right`. They're wrapped in an object called `states`. Give each one a value that corresponds to the index number of its frame in the array.

```
elf.states = {
  up: 0,
  left: 1,
  down: 2,
  right: 3
};
```

Then just use `gotoAndStop` to display the state you want to show:

```
elf.gotoAndStop(elf.states.right);
```

Was that too easy? Hey, enjoy the simplicity!

These are just static image states, but in most games you will want to do something more complex than this. Wouldn't it be nice to load the sprite up with a series of animation sequences, and then play those sequences selectively depending on what the sprite is doing in the game? If the sprite is walking, play its walking animation; if it's jumping, play its jumping animation. This is a basic feature that you'll want most of your game sprites to have. Let's build our own animation state player that does this.

Creating a State Player

We're going to build our state player in two phases. In this first phase, we'll use it only to display a single static image state, as we did in the previous section. This is just to give you a bare-bones idea of how it works. In the next section we'll adapt it so that our sprites can play a continuous sequence of frames.

Before we create the state player, let's first see how you'll be able to use it when we're done. If you want to display the elf's left state, you'll be able to do so using a new method called show:

```
elf.show(elf.states.left);
```

The show method just calls gotoAndStop on the sprite based on the values we defined in the state. How can we set this up?

We're going to add the show method to the sprite with the help of a function called addStatePlayer. Its job is to create the show method and add it to the sprite. Here's how it does that:

```
function addStatePlayer(sprite) {

  //The `show` function (to display static states)
  function show(frameNumber) {

    //Find the new state on the sprite
    sprite.gotoAndStop(frameNumber);
  }

  //Add the `show` method to the sprite
  sprite.show = show;
}
```

You can see that the function takes the sprite as an argument, creates the show method, and then, in the last line, adds the show method to the sprite.

You can now apply the state player to the sprite with this statement:

```
addStatePlayer(elf);
```

The elf object now has its own new method, called show:

```
elf.show(anyFrameNumber)
```

The show method is just a wrapper for gotoAndStop. That in itself is not very useful, but later in the chapter we're going to use this basic addStatePlayer function as a stepping stone to build something more complex. Before we do that, let's find out how we can change a sprite's static image state in a game.

Run the statePlayer.html file in the chapter's source files for a working example. Use the arrow keys to move the elf around the canvas as shown in Figure 8-2.

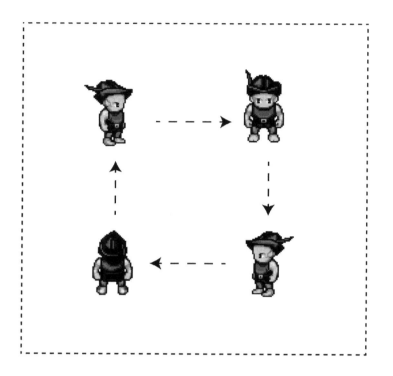

Figure 8-2. *Use the arrow keys to make the elf move and change direction*

Here's the code that makes this state-changing strategy work:

```
function setup() {

  //...Create the sprite...

  //Create the keyboard objects
  let leftArrow = keyboard(37),
      upArrow = keyboard(38),
      rightArrow = keyboard(39),
      downArrow = keyboard(40);

  //Assign key `press` methods
  leftArrow.press = () => {

    //Display the elf's new state and set its velocity
    elf.show(elf.states.left);
    elf.vx = -1;
    elf.vy = 0;
  };
```

```
  upArrow.press = () => {
    elf.show(elf.states.up);
    elf.vy = -1;
    elf.vx = 0;
  };

  rightArrow.press = () => {
    elf.show(elf.states.right);
    elf.vx = 1;
    elf.vy = 0;
  };

  downArrow.press = () => {
    elf.show(elf.states.down);
    elf.vy = 1;
    elf.vx = 0;
  };

  //Start the game loop
  gameLoop();
}

function gameLoop() {
  requestAnimationFrame(gameLoop);

  //Move the elf
  elf.x += elf.vx;
  elf.y += elf.vy;

  //Render the canvas
  render(canvas);
}
```

Being able to set sprite states this way is really easy to do and has wide application for games. For many games that don't require complex animation, a simple state machine like this might be all you need. It's just gotoAndStop!

But what if you want to make the elf character actually appear to walk, by moving its arms and legs?

Playing Frames

Instead of displaying just one image for a given state, you can play a series of image frames in sequence to create an animated action. Figure 8-3 shows a tileset with a nine-frame sequence of our elf character walking.

Figure 8-3. An animation sequence

Wouldn't it be nice to have methods called play and stop that you could use to control the animation? Let's see how to build such a character animation player for games.

In Chapter 6 you learned how to set the frames-per-second and calculate the frame rate, like this:

```
fps = 12
frameRate = 1000 / this.fps
```

If the fps is 12, the frameRate will be approximately 83 milliseconds.

For our character animation player we're going to use JavaScript's setInterval timer to control how quickly successive frames are displayed. Using setInterval has the advantage of letting you use a frame rate for character animation that is independent of your game's frame rate. It also means you can use different frame rates for different kinds of animations in the same game. You can use setInterval to advance an animation frame at set intervals. In this example we're going to use setInterval to run a function called advanceFrame every 83 milliseconds. Here's how:

```
let timerInterval = setInterval(advanceFrame, frameRate);
```

The job of advanceFrame is to display the next frame in the animation sequence:

```
function advanceFrame() {
  sprite.gotoAndStop(sprite.currentFrame + 1);
}
```

This displays the next image in the sprite's frames array every 83 milliseconds. That's really all there is to it.

These are the absolute basics of keyframe animation. But in practice you'll need to add a few more features to make a completely robust and flexible system for games.

Adding Features

To build a fully featured animation frame player, you'll need to address these issues:

- How can you make the animation stop when it reaches the last frame? Or, how can you make it loop back to the beginning?

- How can you play and loop a specific range of frames? For example, if your character's complete animation is 36 frames, but you just want to loop the frames between 10 and 17, how can you do that?

- If you want to stop and restart an animation, you have to clear the current timer interval, and reset the animation to the beginning again. How?

Your sprites will also need properties that help you control their animations. In Chapter 4 we added some properties to each sprite's DisplayObject parent class to help us with these tasks:

```
this.frames = [];
this.loop = true;
this._currentFrame = 0;
get currentFrame() {
  return this._currentFrame;
}
```

At the time I told you, "don't worry about these properties now; you'll find out how to use them later." You've been very patient for waiting, but "later" has become "now"! So let's find out how to make all this work.

Looping the Animation

To make an animation loop, you first need to know how many frames it has, and which frame is currently playing. Use some variables to help you track this. These new variables will get you started:

```
startFrame, endFrame, numberOfFrames, frameCounter
```

If you're going to loop within a range of frames, you need to know what those frame numbers are. For example, if you want to loop through all the frames between 1 and 8, you could use these `startFrame` and `endFrame` values:

```
startFrame = 1;
endFrame = 8;
```

Then use those values to calculate the total number of frames:

```
numberOfFrames = endFrame - startFrame;
```

The value of `numberOfFrames` will be 7. Because we start number frames at 0, frame number 7 will actually be the eighth frame in the sequence.

Figure 8-4 shows an example of how the frame sequence works. The nine frames of our elf animation are numbered from 0 to 8. The first frame, 0, just shows what the elf looks like when he's standing still. Frames 1 to 8 show what the elf looks like when he's walking. If we want to make the elf appear to walk, we have to exclude frame 0, and play only frames 1 to 8 in a continuous loop.

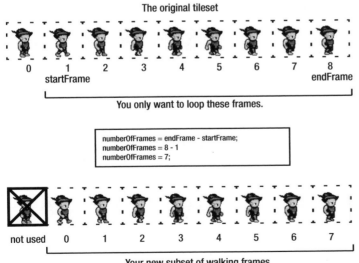

Figure 8-4. A sub-sequence of frames

As you'll see shortly, we're going to use these startFrame and endFrame values to play this looping sub-sequence of frames.

We also need to count the number of frames that have elapsed while the animation is playing; so a frameCounter variable can help track this:

```
frameCounter = 0;
```

Do we want the animation to loop or not? We can use the Boolean loop property that's already built into our sprites to determine this (its default value is true).

Here's our new advanceFrame function that implements the loop feature. If loop is true, it will restart the animation from the startFrame. If loop is false, it will stop at the last frame.

```
function advanceFrame() {

  //Advance the frame if `frameCounter` is less than the total frames
  if (frameCounter < numberOfFrames) {

    //Advance the frame
    sprite.gotoAndStop(sprite.currentFrame + 1);

    //Update the frame counter
    frameCounter += 1;

  //If we've reached the last frame and `loop`
  //is `true`, then start from the first frame again
  } else {
    if (sprite.loop) {
      sprite.gotoAndStop(startFrame);
      frameCounter = 1;
    }
  }
}
```

Now we've got a simple animation loop system.

Resetting the Animation

In a real game development project you won't just be running an animation once and then forgetting about it; more likely, you'll need to start, stop, and restart it multiple times. You'll probably also have many other animations that could be playing at the same time. So it's a good idea to be able to track whether an animation is currently playing so that you can fine-tune its start and stop conditions. In Chapter 4 we created a property called playing on the DisplayObject class to help manage this.

```
this.playing = false;
```

Now, before you start a new animation, you can check this variable to make sure the animation isn't already playing. If it isn't, start it, and then set `playing` to `true`:

```
if(!sprite.playing) {
  timerInterval = setInterval(advanceFrame, frameRate);
  sprite.playing = true;
}
```

If you've already played the animation once, and then need to restart it, you'll have to reset it back to its initial conditions. You'll also need to clear the `timerInterval` so that you can create a new timer. Here's a reset function that does all these things.

```
function reset() {
  if (timerInterval !== undefined && sprite.playing === true) {
    sprite.playing = false;
    frameCounter = 0;
    startFrame = 0;
    endFrame = 0;
    numberOfFrames = 0;
    clearInterval(timerInterval);
  }
}
```

You're now all set to play the animation from the beginning again.

These are all the important concepts you need to know to build a robust sprite animator for games. But how can we put all this into practice?

Improving the `addStatePlayer` Function

Earlier in this chapter we built a fun little function called `addStatePlayer` that let us change a sprite's image state when we pressed the arrow keys. We're going to improve it by giving it a few new methods.

If you want to play the all the frames in the sprite's frames array, use the `play` method.

```
elf.play();
```

The frames will play from beginning to end and will loop if the sprite's `loop` property is `true`. If you want the animation to stop, use the `stop` method:

```
elf.stop();
```

If you just want to play a specific range of frames, use a method called `playSequence`. For example, if you want to play all the frames between 10 and 17, you can do that with this statement:

```
elf.playSequence([10, 17]);
```

The sequence will loop if the sprite's `loop` property is `true`.

You can set the animation's frames-per-second this way:

```
elf.fps = 12;
```

Here's the complete, new, addStatePlayer function with comments explaining how each section works. (You'll find the working code in the library/display folder.) At its heart, all this new code is the same as the basic animation code we just looked at.

```
function addStatePlayer(sprite) {
  let frameCounter = 0,
      numberOfFrames = 0,
      startFrame = 0,
      endFrame = 0,
      timerInterval = undefined;

  //The `show` function (to display static states)
  function show(frameNumber) {

    //Reset any possible previous animations
    reset();

    //Find the new state on the sprite
    sprite.gotoAndStop(frameNumber);
  }

  //The `play` function plays all the sprite's frames
  function play() {
    playSequence([0, sprite.frames.length - 1]);
  }

  //The `stop` function stops the animation at the current frame
  function stop() {
    reset();
    sprite.gotoAndStop(sprite.currentFrame);
  }

  //The `playSequence` function, to play a sequence of frames
  function playSequence(sequenceArray) {

    //Reset any possible previous animations
    reset();

    //Figure out how many frames there are in the range
    startFrame = sequenceArray[0];
    endFrame = sequenceArray[1];
    numberOfFrames = endFrame - startFrame;

    //Compensate for two edge cases:

    //1. If the `startFrame` happens to be `0`
    if (startFrame === 0) {
      numberOfFrames += 1;
      frameCounter += 1;
    }
```

```
//2. If only a two-frame sequence was provided
if(numberOfFrames === 1){
  numberOfFrames = 2;
  frameCounter += 1;
};

//Calculate the frame rate. Set the default fps to 12
if (!sprite.fps) sprite.fps = 12;
let frameRate = 1000 / sprite.fps;

//Set the sprite to the starting frame
sprite.gotoAndStop(startFrame);

//If the state isn't already `playing`, start it
if(!sprite.playing) {
  timerInterval = setInterval(advanceFrame.bind(this), frameRate);
  sprite.playing = true;
}
}

//`advanceFrame` is called by `setInterval` to display the next frame
//in the sequence based on the `frameRate`. When the frame sequence
//reaches the end, it will either stop or loop
function advanceFrame() {

  //Advance the frame if `frameCounter` is less than
  //the state's total frames
  if (frameCounter < numberOfFrames) {

    //Advance the frame
    sprite.gotoAndStop(sprite.currentFrame + 1);

    //Update the frame counter
    frameCounter += 1;

  //If we've reached the last frame and `loop`
  //is `true`, then start from the first frame again
  } else {
    if (sprite.loop) {
      sprite.gotoAndStop(startFrame);
      frameCounter = 1;
    }
  }
}

function reset() {
```

```
    //Reset `sprite.playing` to `false`, set the `frameCounter` to 0,
    //and clear the `timerInterval`
    if (timerInterval !== undefined && sprite.playing === true) {
      sprite.playing = false;
      frameCounter = 0;
      startFrame = 0;
      endFrame = 0;
      numberOfFrames = 0;
      clearInterval(timerInterval);
    }
  }

  //Add the `show`, `play`, `stop`, and `playSequence` methods to the sprite
  sprite.show = show;
  sprite.play = play;
  sprite.stop = stop;
  sprite.playSequence = playSequence;
}
```

There's one more thing we should do. These animation methods are so useful that it would help if they were automatically added to any sprite that has multiple image frames. To do that, we need to modify the **sprite** function in the library/display module that creates and returns each sprite. Make it call this new addStatePlayer function for any sprite that has more than one element in its frames array:

```
export function sprite(source, x, y) {
  let sprite = new Sprite(source, x, y);
  if (sprite.frames.length > 0) addStatePlayer(sprite);
  stage.addChild(sprite);
  return sprite;
}
```

Great—we're all ready to roll! How can we use all the techniques we've just explored in a practical game project?

Building a Walking Sprite

Run the animation.html file for an interactive example that uses these new techniques to make a walking sprite. Use the arrow keys to make the elf walk all around the forest landscape. Four different walk cycle animations match the four directions that the elf can walk in. When the keys are released, the elf stops and faces the direction it was moving. Figure 8-5 illustrates what you'll see.

Figure 8-5. *An animated walking sprite*

Capturing the Frames

The elf's animation is based on a single tileset image that contains all the frames, shown in Figure 8-6.

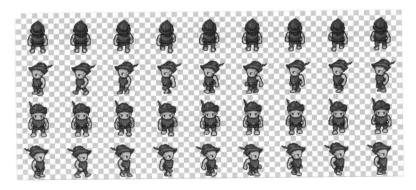

Figure 8-6. *A tileset image contains all the animation frames*

Before you can animate the sprite, you need an array containing all these frames as separate images. You know that you can use the frames function to turn an array of frame position values into an array of images. But there are 36 frames in this tileset, spanning four rows, so you definitely don't want to enter these position values by hand. Let's use a new custom function called filmstrip that figures out the x/y position of each frame for us and returns all the animation frames:

```
export function filmstrip(image, frameWidth, frameHeight, spacing = 0){

  //An array to store the x and y positions of each frame
  let positions = [];

  //Find out how many columns and rows there are in the image
  let columns = image.width / frameWidth,
      rows = image.height / frameHeight;

  //Find the total number of frames
  let numberOfFrames = columns * rows;

  for(let i = 0; i < numberOfFrames; i++) {

    //Find the correct row and column for each frame
    //and figure out its x and y position
    let x = (i % columns) * frameWidth,
        y = Math.floor(i / columns) * frameHeight;

    //Compensate for any optional spacing (padding) around the frames if
    //there is any. This bit of code accumulates the spacing offsets from the
    //left side of the tileset and adds them to the current tile's position
    if (spacing && spacing > 0) {
      x += spacing + (spacing * i % columns);
      y += spacing + (spacing * Math.floor(i / columns));
    }

    //Add the x and y value of each frame to the `positions` array
    positions.push([x, y]);
  }

  //Create and return the animation frames using the `frames` method
  return frames(image, positions, frameWidth, frameHeight);
};
```

(You'll find the filmstrip function in the library/display file.)

You can now use this filmstrip function to create a sprite's frames array. Supply as arguments the image you want to use, the width and height of each frame, and any optional spacing between frames:

```
let elfFrames = filmstrip(assets["images/walkcycle.png"], 64, 64);
```

Then use elfFrames to initialize the sprite:

```
elf = sprite(elfFrames);
```

The elf is now loaded up with 36 frames, and it's ready to start being animated.

300

Defining the Elf's States

The elf has eight states in total: four standing states and four walking states. Figure 8-7 shows the tileset with these eight states. The black lines in the illustration define the states' boundaries.

Static   **Animated**

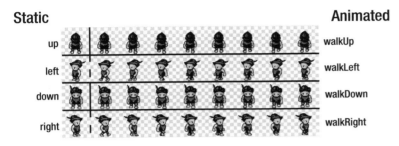

Figure 8-7. *The tileset contains the sprite's eight states*

The up, left, down, and right states are static, which means they don't contain any animation frames. We'll display them using the show method, just as we did at the beginning of the chapter. The walkUp, walkLeft, walkDown, and walkRight states are animated, and we'll display them using playSequence. The first frame of the walkLeft and walkRight animations also happen to be the left and right static states, which is why there's dashed line separating them in Figure 8-7.

Here are the elf's states that set this all up:

```
elf.states = {
  up: 0,
  left: 9,
  down: 18,
  right: 27,
  walkUp: [1, 8],
  walkLeft: [10, 17],
  walkDown: [19, 26],
  walkRight: [28, 35]
};
```

Next, set the elf's frame rate:

```
elf.fps = 12;
```

Now you just need to figure out which state to display depending on which keys are up or down. With a bit of experimentation, you might come up with some code that looks like this:

```
leftArrow.press = function() {

  //Play the elf's `walkLeft` animation sequence
  elf.playSequence(elf.states.walkLeft);
  elf.vx = -1;
  elf.vy = 0;
};
```

301

```
leftArrow.release = function() {
  if (!rightArrow.isDown && elf.vy === 0) {

    //Show the elf's `left` state
    elf.show(elf.states.left);
    elf.vx = 0;
  }
};
```

The three other keys, `rightArrow`, `upArrow`, and `downArrow`, all follow the same format.

Is that all there is to know about keyframe animation? Pretty much, yes! The state player that we've created can be used in a wide variety of different games, and you can customize it as much as you need to. Combine these techniques with the scripted animation you learned to do in Chapter 6, and there'll be no end to the rich and complex sprites you'll be able to fill your games with.

■ **Tip** How can you design complex character animations like our walking elf? You'll obviously need some artistic ability and graphic design skills, but there are many tools available to help you out. Here's some software you can try: ShoeBox, Spine, Spriter, DragonBones, Animo Sprites, Piskel, and Flash Professional (if you're using Flash Professional, export an animation as a sprite sheet).

Next let's find out how to add a dash of magic to your games.

Particle Effects

How do you create effects like fire, smoke, magic, and explosions? You make lots of tiny sprites; dozens, hundreds or thousands of them. Then apply some physical or gravitational constraints to those sprites so that they behave like the element you're trying to simulate. You also need to give them some rules about how they should appear and disappear, and what kinds of patterns they should form. These tiny sprites are called **particles**. You can use them to make a wide range of special effects for games.

With only a few dozen lines of code you can write a general-purpose particle effects engine that will be all you'll ever need for most 2D action games. To see the particle engine in action, run the `particleEffect.html` file, shown in Figure 8-8. Click the pointer, and a little explosion of stars bursts over the canvas, radiating from the pointer's position. The stars are pulled down by gravity, and each one has a different speed, rotation, fade, and scale rate.

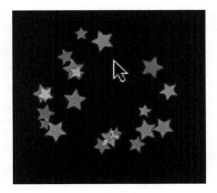

Figure 8-8. *Particle effects*

This was created by a custom function called `particleEffect`, which you'll find in the `library/display` folder. Here's how to use it, including all the arguments used to produce the explosion in the example.

```
particleEffect(
  pointer.x,                              //The particle's starting x position
  pointer.y,                              //The particle's starting y position
  () => sprite(assets["images/star.png"]), //Particle function
  20,                                     //Number of particles
  0.1,                                    //Gravity
  true,                                   //Random spacing
  0, 6.28,                                //Min/max angle
  12, 24,                                 //Min/max size
  1, 2,                                   //Min/max speed
  0.005, 0.01,                            //Min/max scale speed
  0.005, 0.01,                            //Min/max alpha speed
  0.05, 0.1                               //Min/max rotation speed
);
```

You can see that most of the arguments describe a range between the minimum and maximum values that should be used to change the sprites' speed, rotation, scale, or alpha. You can also assign the number of particles that should be created, and add optional gravity.

You can make particles using any sprites by customizing the third argument. Just supply a function that returns the kind of sprite you want to use for each particle:

```
() => sprite(assets["images/star.png"]),
```

If you supply a sprite that has multiple frames, the `particleEffect` function will automatically choose a random frame for each particle.

The minimum and maximum angle values are important for defining the circular spread of particles as they radiate out from the origin point. For a completely circular explosion effect, use a minimum angle of 0 and a maximum angle of 6.28.

```
0, 6.28
```

(These values are radians; the equivalent in degrees is 0 and 360.) 0 starts at the 3 o'clock position, pointing directly to the right. 3.14 is the 9 o'clock position, and 6.28 takes you around back to 0 again.

If you want to constrain the particle range to a narrower angle, just supply the minimum and maximum values that describe that range. Here are values you could use to constrain the angle to a pizza-slice with the crust pointing left.

```
2.4, 3.6
```

You could use a constrained angle range like this to create a particle stream, like those used to create a fountain or rocket engine flames. (You'll see exactly how to do this in the example game at the end of this chapter.) The random spacing value (the sixth argument) determines whether the particles should be spaced evenly (`false`) or randomly (`true`) within this range.

By carefully choosing the sprite for the particle and finely adjusting each parameter, you can use this all-purpose `particleEffect` function to simulate everything from liquid to fire. Let's find out exactly how the `particleEffect` function works under the hood and how you can use it in your games.

Building the `particleEffect` Function

All the particles in the game need to have their properties updated on every frame. Before you can start making particles, you need to create a single `particles` array to store them.

```
export let particles = [];
```

As you'll see, we're going to update all the particles by looping through this array on each frame, which is the same strategy we used for updating buttons in Chapter 6.

The `particleEffect` function takes all the arguments you've assigned and uses them to create each particle. It works out a unique angle for each particle, and uses that angle value to assign the particle's velocity, along with all the other properties. If the sprite function you've supplied returns a sprite with multiple image frames, a new random frame is chosen for every particle. Each particle is also created with an `update` method that describes how the particle's properties should change. This `update` method has to be called on each particle by the game loop to make the particles move, fade, rotate, and scale. When the function has finished creating each particle, it pushes that particle into the `particles` array.

```
export function particleEffect(
  x = 0,
  y = 0,
  spriteFunction = () => circle(10, "red"),
  numberOfParticles = 10,
  gravity = 0,
  randomSpacing = true,
  minAngle = 0, maxAngle = 6.28,
  minSize = 4, maxSize = 16,
  minSpeed = 0.1, maxSpeed = 1,
  minScaleSpeed = 0.01, maxScaleSpeed = 0.05,
  minAlphaSpeed = 0.02, maxAlphaSpeed = 0.02,
  minRotationSpeed = 0.01, maxRotationSpeed = 0.03
) {
```

```
//`randomFloat` and `randomInt` helper functions
let randomFloat = (min, max) => min + Math.random() * (max - min),
    randomInt = (min, max) => Math.floor(Math.random() * (max - min + 1)) + min;

//An array to store the angles
let angles = [];

//A variable to store the current particle's angle
let angle;

//Figure out by how many radians each particle should be separated
let spacing = (maxAngle - minAngle) / (numberOfParticles - 1);

//Create an angle value for each particle and push that
//value into the `angles` array
for(let i = 0; i < numberOfParticles; i++) {

  //If `randomSpacing` is `true`, give the particle any angle
  //value between `minAngle` and `maxAngle`
  if (randomSpacing) {
    angle = randomFloat(minAngle, maxAngle);
    angles.push(angle);
  }

  //If `randomSpacing` is `false`, space each particle evenly,
  //starting with the `minAngle` and ending with the `maxAngle`
  else {
    if (angle === undefined) angle = minAngle;
    angles.push(angle);
    angle += spacing;
  }
}

//Make a particle for each angle
angles.forEach(angle => makeParticle(angle));

//Make the particle
function makeParticle(angle) {

  //Create the particle using the supplied sprite function
  let particle = spriteFunction();

  //Display a random frame if the particle has more than 1 frame
  if (particle.frames.length > 0) {
    particle.gotoAndStop(randomInt(0, particle.frames.length - 1));
  }

  //Set the x and y position
  particle.x = x - particle.halfWidth;
  particle.y = y - particle.halfHeight;
```

```
//Set a random width and height
let size = randomInt(minSize, maxSize);
particle.width = size;
particle.height = size;

//Set a random speed to change the scale, alpha and rotation
particle.scaleSpeed = randomFloat(minScaleSpeed, maxScaleSpeed);
particle.alphaSpeed = randomFloat(minAlphaSpeed, maxAlphaSpeed);
particle.rotationSpeed = randomFloat(minRotationSpeed, maxRotationSpeed);

//Set a random velocity at which the particle should move
let speed = randomFloat(minSpeed, maxSpeed);
particle.vx = speed * Math.cos(angle);
particle.vy = speed * Math.sin(angle);

//The particle's `update` method is called on each frame of the
//game loop
particle.update = () => {

  //Add gravity
  particle.vy += gravity;

  //Move the particle
  particle.x += particle.vx;
  particle.y += particle.vy;

  //Change the particle's `scale`
  if (particle.scaleX - particle.scaleSpeed > 0) {
    particle.scaleX -= particle.scaleSpeed;
  }
  if (particle.scaleY - particle.scaleSpeed > 0) {
    particle.scaleY -= particle.scaleSpeed;
  }

  //Change the particle's rotation
  particle.rotation += particle.rotationSpeed;

  //Change the particle's `alpha`
  particle.alpha -= particle.alphaSpeed;

  //Remove the particle if its `alpha` reaches zero
  if (particle.alpha <= 0) {
    remove(particle);
    particles.splice(particles.indexOf(particle), 1);
  }
};

//Push the particle into the `particles` array.
//The `particles` array needs to be updated by the game loop each frame
particles.push(particle);
  }
}
```

An important detail to notice in `particleEffect` is that if the particle's `alpha` value reaches zero, the update method splices the particle out of the `particles` array. It does so using the following code:

```
if (particle.alpha <= 0) {
  remove(particle);
  particles.splice(particles.indexOf(particle), 1);
}
```

(You learned how to use the `remove` function in Chapter 4 to remove any sprite from its parent.) Any time you write code like this, in which an object is responsible for its own removal, you have to be really careful! It's undoubtedly convenient, but always stop and ask: are there any other dependencies that need to be notified that this object has been removed? If there are, and you forget about them, you could be setting yourself up for some nail-biting debugging sessions.

This is especially true if the object is splicing itself out of an array, in the context of a loop, which is what our particles are going to do. To do this safely, without throwing the loop index counter off by one, you need to loop through all the elements in the array **in reverse**. You'll learn how to do that next.

Using the `particleEffect` Function in a Game

To use this `particleEffect` function, first import it and the `particles` array into your game program:

```
import {particles, particleEffect} from "../library/display";
```

Then loop through all the particles on every frame and call the `update` method for each one. You need to loop through particles in reverse (starting with the last element in the array), so that if one of them is spliced out it won't affect the loop index counter. You can make a `for` loop run in reverse by initializing the counter variable (`i`) to the `length` of the array, and then decrementing it on each iteration. Here's the code:

```
function gameLoop() {
  requestAnimationFrame(gameLoop);

  if (particles.length > 0) {

    //Loop through the particles in reverse
    for(let i = particles.length - 1; i >= 0; i--) {
      let particle = particles[i];
      particle.update();
    }
  }
  render(canvas);
}
```

The particle's `update` method can now safely remove the particle when the particle's `alpha` reaches zero.

To start the `particleEffect`, just call it with any custom arguments whenever you want the effect to happen. In the example, this happens when the pointer's `press` method is called:

```
pointer.press = () => {
  particleEffect(
    //Assign the particle's arguments...
  );
};
```

307

But of course you can call `particleEffect` whenever you want at any point in your game. You'll see a few more examples at the end of this chapter.

The `particleEffect` function is great for creating a single burst of particles. But what if you want to produce particles in a continuous stream, as you would to simulate water drops flowing from a tap or flames from a rocket's engine? For that, you need the help of a **particle emitter**.

Adding a Particle Emitter

A particle emitter is just a simple timer that creates particles at fixed intervals. That means instead of just calling the `particleEffect` function once, the emitter calls it periodically. In this next section we're going to build an `emitter` function that you'll be able to use to create a constant stream of particles, at any time interval you need. Here's how you'll be able to use it:

```
let particleStream = emitter(
  100,                          //The interval
  () => particleEffect(         //The `particleEffect` function
    //Assign particle parameters...
  )
);
```

The `emitter` function just wraps around the `particleEffect` function we created in the previous section. Its first argument is a number, in milliseconds, that determines how frequently the particles should be created. The second argument is the `particleEffect` function, which you can customize however you like.

The `emitter` function returns an object with `play` and `stop` methods that you can use to control the particle stream. You can use them just like the `play` and `stop` methods we created at the beginning of the chapter to control a sprite's animation.

```
particleStream.play();
particleStream.stop();
```

The emitter object also has a `playing` property that will be either `true` or `false` depending on the emitter's current state. Here's the complete function that creates the emitter object and adds the methods and properties to it. (You'll find this working code in the `library/display` folder.)

```
export function emitter(interval, particleFunction) {
  let emitter = {},
      timerInterval = undefined;

  emitter.playing = false;

  function play() {
    if (!emitter.playing) {
      particleFunction();
      timerInterval = setInterval(emitParticle.bind(this), interval);
      emitter.playing = true;
    }
  }
```

```
function stop() {
  if (emitter.playing) {
    clearInterval(timerInterval);
    emitter.playing = false;
  }
}

function emitParticle() {
  particleFunction();
}

emitter.play = play;
emitter.stop = stop;
return emitter;
}
```

Run the `particleEmitter.html` file to see this code in action, as shown in Figure 8-9. Press and hold the left mouse button to produce a continuous stream of particles. When you release the button, the stream will stop.

Figure 8-9. *A particle emitter produces a continuous stream of particles*

Here's the code from the setup function that creates the pointer and the particle emitter. The emitter's play method is called when the pointer is pressed, and its stop method is called when the pointer is released.

```
pointer = makePointer(canvas);

let particleStream = emitter(
  100,                                        //The timer interval
  () => particleEffect(                       //The function
    pointer.x, pointer.y,                     //x and y position
    () => sprite(assets["images/star.png"]),  //Particle sprite
    10,                                       //Number of particles
    0.1,                                      //Gravity
    false,                                    //Random spacing
    3.14, 6.28,                               //Min/max angle
    16, 32,                                   //Min/max size
    2, 5                                      //Min/max speed
  )
);

pointer.press = () => {
  particleStream.play();
};

pointer.release = () => {
  particleStream.stop();
};
```

By using the particleEffect and emitter functions together this way, you'll be able to create most of the particle explosion and stream effects you'll need for your games.

Tiling Sprites

The last special effect that you'll learn how to create in this chapter is actually a new type of sprite: a **tiling sprite**. It's special kind of rectangle that has a repeating, tiled background image pattern. The tiling sprite has two new properties, tileX and tileY, that let you control the position of the tiled background. The tiled background wraps seamlessly, so that if you change the values of tileX and tileY in the game loop, you can create an infinitely scrolling background effect.

Run the tilingSprite.html file to see an example of a tiling sprite in action, as shown in Figure 8-10. It's a simple rectangle with a tile.png image set as its repeating background. The background pattern scrolls from the top left to the bottom right in an unbroken loop.

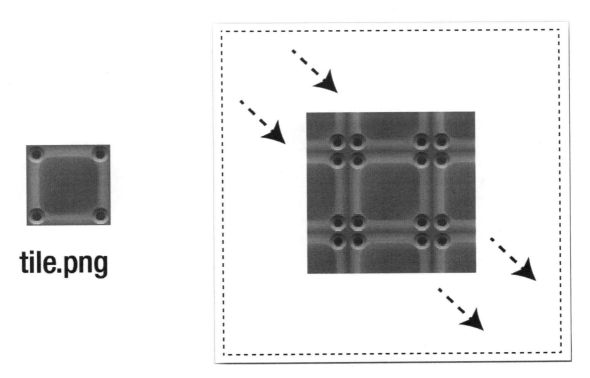

Figure 8-10. *A tiling sprite has a continuously repeating background pattern made from a single tile*

The tiling sprite was made using a new function called `tilingSprite`. You can think of it as a rectangle sprite with an image assigned as its fill:

```
box = tilingSprite(128, 128, assets["images/tile.png"]);
```

The tile image can either be an image file or a texture atlas frame. Because the tiling sprite is at heart just an ordinary rectangle sprite, you use it like any other rectangle sprite in your games. The one important difference is that it has `tileX` and `tileY` properties that let you reposition the origin point of the repeating background pattern. By changing the values of `tileX` and `tileY` in the game loop, you can create an infinite scroll effect:

```
box.tileY += 1;
box.tileX += 1;
```

The tiling sprite is a great example of how you can use many different tricks in your toy box to create a complex compound sprite. So how does it work?

Building the Tiling Sprite

The tiling sprite is essentially a single rectangle that masks a grid of sprites made from the tile image. The grid is one row and one column larger than the maximum number of tiles needed to fill the rectangle. This means that there's always a row and column just outside the visible area of the rectangle. If the background pattern is shifted up, down, left or right, the sprites from the hidden row or column are moved to the

311

opposite side of the grid to compensate. This creates the illusion of a seamless scrolling pattern. But all you're really doing is shifting the inner tile sprites around. Figure 8-11 illustrates how the hidden row and column is masked and repositioned to match the shifted pattern.

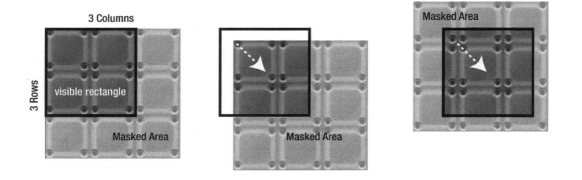

Figure 8-11. *When the pattern is shifted, sprites from the extra hidden row and column are repositioned to create the illusion of a seamless, infinitely scrolling background*

The most important thing to realize about the tiling sprite is that it's just a rectangle that masks a grid of child sprites. You might remember in Chapter 4 that rectangle sprites have an optional mask property that defaults to false. If you set mask to true, this following line is enabled in the rectangle's render method:

```
if (this.mask && this.mask === true) ctx.clip();
```

This will cause any of the rectangle's child sprites to be masked by the rectangle. (You can enable masking in circle sprites in the same way.)

In the library/display folder you'll find the tilingSprite function, which sets all this up and returns the masked grid. It's not really complicated, but it does have a lot of work to do. To help make sense of what it's doing, you can break down all its jobs down into these major steps:

1. Figure out whether the supplied tile image is from an image file or a texture atlas frame, and then capture the image's width and height values.

2. Figure out how many tiles can fit inside the dimensions of the rectangle.

3. Make a grid object that's larger than the dimensions of the sprite by one row and one column.

4. Create a rectangle sprite and add the grid as its child.

5. Set the rectangle's mask property to true.

6. Add tileX and tileY properties to the rectangle. The setters for these properties that shift the positions of the grid tiles proportionally based on the supplied offset values.

7. Return the rectangle sprite back to the main program.

Here's the `tilingSprite` function that does all of this. The comments explain in detail how each bit of code works.

```
export function tilingSprite(width, height, source, x = 0, y = 0) {

  //Figure out the tile's width and height
  let tileWidth, tileHeight;

  //If the source is a texture atlas frame, use its
  //`frame.w` and `frame.h` properties
  if(source.frame) {
    tileWidth = source.frame.w;
    tileHeight = source.frame.h;
  }

  //If it's an image, use the image's
  //`width` and `height` properties
  else {
    tileWidth = source.width;
    tileHeight = source.height;
  }

  //Figure out the rows and columns.
  //The number of rows and columns should always be
  //one greater than the total number of tiles
  //that can fit into the rectangle. This give us one
  //additional row and column that we can reposition
  //to create the infinite scroll effect

  let columns, rows;

  //1. Columns
  //If the width of the rectangle is greater than the width of the tile,
  //calculate the number of tile columns
  if (width >= tileWidth) {
    columns = Math.round(width / tileWidth) + 1;
  }

  //If the rectangle's width is less than the width of the
  //tile, set the columns to 2, which is the minimum
  else {
    columns = 2;
  }

  //2. Rows
  //Calculate the tile rows in the same way
  if (height >= tileHeight) {
    rows = Math.round(height / tileHeight) + 1;
  } else {
    rows = 2;
  }
```

```
//Create a grid of sprites that's just one sprite larger
//than the `totalWidth` and `totalHeight`
let tileGrid = grid(
 columns, rows, tileWidth, tileHeight, false, 0, 0,
 () => {

   //Make a sprite from the supplied `source`
   let tile = sprite(source);
   return tile;
 }
);

//Declare the grid's private properties that we'll use to
//help scroll the tiling background
tileGrid._tileX = 0;
tileGrid._tileY = 0;

//Create an empty rectangle sprite without a fill or stroke color.
//Set it to the supplied `width` and `height`
let container = rectangle(width, height, "none", "none");
container.x = x;
container.y = y;

//Set the rectangle's `mask` property to `true`. This switches on `ctx.clip()`
//In the rectangle sprite's `render` method
container.mask = true;

//Add the tile grid to the rectangle container
container.addChild(tileGrid);

//Define the `tileX` and `tileY` properties on the parent container
//so that you can scroll the tiling background
Object.defineProperties(container, {
  tileX: {
    get() {
      return tileGrid._tileX;
    },

    set(value) {

      //Loop through all of the grid's child sprites
      tileGrid.children.forEach(child => {

        //Figure out the difference between the new position
        //and the previous position
        let difference = value - tileGrid._tileX;

        //Offset the child sprite by the difference
        child.x += difference;
```

```
        //If the x position of the sprite exceeds the total width
        //of the visible columns, reposition it to just in front of the
        //left edge of the container. This creates the wrapping
        //effect
        if (child.x > (columns - 1) * tileWidth) {
          child.x = 0 - tileWidth + difference;
        }

        //Use the same procedure to wrap sprites that
        //exceed the left boundary
        if (child.x < 0 - tileWidth - difference) {
          child.x = (columns - 1) * tileWidth;
        }
      });

      //Set the private `_tileX` property to the new value
      tileGrid._tileX = value;
    },
    enumerable: true, configurable: true
  },
  tileY: {
    get() {
      return tileGrid._tileY;
    },

    //Follow the same format to wrap sprites on the y axis
    set(value) {
      tileGrid.children.forEach(child => {
        let difference = value - tileGrid._tileY;
        child.y += difference;
        if (child.y > (rows - 1) * tileHeight) child.y = 0 - tileHeight + difference;
        if (child.y < 0 - tileHeight - difference) child.y = (rows - 1) * tileHeight;
      });
      tileGrid._tileY = value;
    },
    enumerable: true, configurable: true
  }
});

//Return the rectangle container
return container;
}
```

One of the most common video game requirements is an infinitely scrolling background, and the tiling sprite was designed to make it easy for you to implement this. Let's find out how to use it in a game next.

Case Study: Flappy Fairy

Keyframe animation, particle effects, and tiling sprites help add a whole new dimension of interest and immersion to a game. As your game design skills and confidence grow, you'll probably find that most games you make will use at least one or probably all of these effects. In the last section of this chapter we're going to take a detailed look at a game prototype called Flappy Fairy—an homage to one of the most infamous games in video game history. It uses all three effects, and will give you a good starting point for integrating them into your own games.

Run the `flappyFairy.html` file to play the game. Tap the screen to make the fairy fly, and help her navigate through the gaps in 15 pillars to reach finish, as shown in Figure 8-12. A trail of multicolored fairy dust follows her as she flies through the maze. If she hits one of the green blocks she explodes in a shower of dust. But if she manages to navigate through the increasingly narrowing gaps between all 15 pillars, she reaches a big floating "Finish" sign.

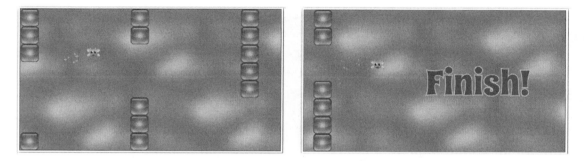

Figure 8-12. *Help Flappy Fairy fly through the maze of pillars to reach the finish*

Creating the Scrolling Background

Flappy Fairy is a side-scrolling game using a **parallax** effect. Parallax is a shallow 3D effect that creates the illusion of depth by making the background scroll at a slower rate than the foreground. This makes the background look as if it's further away.

To make sky background I started with a seamless 512 × 512 image of some clouds. It's a frame in the game's texture atlas, shown in Figure 8-13.

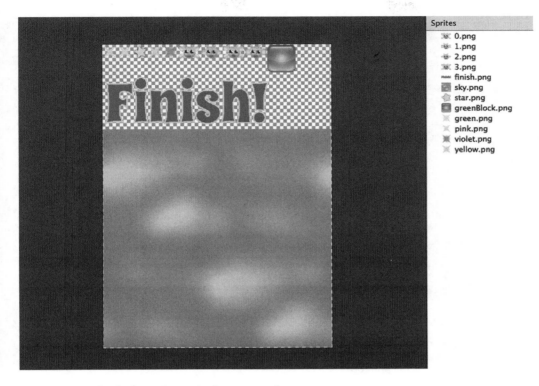

Figure 8-13. *The sky frame image in the texture atlas*

In the setup function I used the "sky.png" frame to create a tiling sprite called sky.

```
sky = tilingSprite(canvas.width, canvas.height, assets["sky.png"]);
```

The game loop then moves the tileX position by a small amount to the left each frame.

```
sky.tileX -= 1;
```

And that's all there is to it—infinite scrolling!

Creating the Pillars

There are fifteen pillars in the game. Every five pillars, the gap between the top and bottom sections become narrower. The first five pillars have a gap of four blocks, the next five have a gap of three blocks and the last five have a gap of two blocks. This makes the game increasingly difficult as Flappy Fairy flies further. The exact position of the gap is random for each pillar, and different every time game is played. Each pillar is spaced by 384 pixels, but Figure 8-14 shows what they would look like if they were right next to each other.

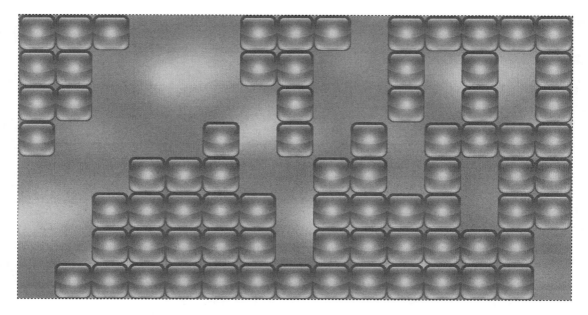

Figure 8-14. *The gap between the top and bottom of each pillar gradually narrows*

You can see how the gap gradually narrows from four spaces on the left down to two on the right. All the blocks that make up the pillars are in a group called `blocks`.

```
blocks = group();
```

A nested for loop creates each block and adds it to the `blocks` container. The outer loop runs 15 times; once to create each pillar. The inner loop runs eight times; once for each block in the pillar. The blocks are only added if they're not occupying the range that's been randomly chosen for the gap. Every fifth time the outer loop runs, the size of the gap narrows by one.

```
//What should the initial size of the gap be between the pillars?
let gapSize = 4;

//How many pillars?
let numberOfPillars = 15;

for (let i = 0; i < numberOfPillars; i++) {

  //Randomly place the gap somewhere inside the pillar
  let startGapNumber = randomInt(0, 8 - gapSize);

  //Reduce the `gapSize` by one after every fifth pillar. This is
  //what makes gaps gradually become narrower
  if (i > 0 && i % 5 === 0) gapSize -= 1;

  //Create a block if it's not within the range of numbers
  //occupied by the gap
  for (let j = 0; j < 8; j++) {
```

```
    if (j < startGapNumber || j > startGapNumber + gapSize - 1) {
      let block = sprite(assets["greenBlock.png"]);
      blocks.addChild(block);

      //Space each pillar 384 pixels apart. The first pillar will be
      //placed at an x position of 512
      block.x = (i * 384) + 512;
      block.y = j * 64;
    }
  }

  //After the pillars have been created, add the finish image
  //right at the end
  if (i === numberOfPillars - 1) {
    finish = sprite(assets["finish.png"]);
    blocks.addChild(finish);
    finish.x = (i * 384) + 896;
    finish.y = 192;
  }
}
```

The last part of the code adds the big finish sprite to the world, which Flappy Fairy will see if she manages to make it through to the end.

The game loop moves the group of blocks by 2 pixels to the right each frame, but only while the finish sprite is off-screen:

```
if (finish.gx > 256) {
  blocks.x -= 2;
}
```

When the finish sprite scrolls into the center of the canvas, the blocks container will stop moving. Notice that the code uses the finish sprite's global *x* position (gx) to test whether it's inside the area of the canvas. Because global coordinates are relative to the canvas, not the parent container, they're really useful for just these kinds of situations where you want to want to find a nested sprite's position on the canvas.

Making Flappy Fairy Fly

The fairy character is an animated sprite made using three texture atlas frames. Each frame is one image in the fairy's wing flapping animation. (Figure 8-15 illustrates these three texture atlas frames.)

```
let fairyFrames = [
  assets["0.png"],
  assets["1.png"],
  assets["2.png"]
];
fairy = sprite(fairyFrames);
fairy.fps = 24;
fairy.setPosition(232, 32);
fairy.vy = 0;
fairy.oldVy = 0;
```

The fairy sprite has a new property called oldVy which, as you'll see ahead, is going to help us calculate the fairy's vertical velocity.

To make the fairy move, the game loop applies –0.05 to her vertical velocity each frame to create gravity.

```
fairy.vy += -0.05;
fairy.y -= fairy.vy;
```

The player can make her fly by tapping or clicking anywhere on the canvas. Each tap adds 1.5 to the Flappy Fairy's vertical velocity, pushing her upward.

```
pointer = makePointer(canvas);
pointer.tap = () => {
  fairy.vy += 1.5;
};
```

Emitting Fairy Dust

The fairy emits a stream of multicolored particles while she's flapping her wings. The particles are constrained to an angle between 2.4 and 3.6 radians, so they're emitted in a cone-shaped wedge to the left of the fairy, as shown in Figure 8-15. The particle stream randomly emits pink, yellow, green, or violet particles, each of which is a separate frame on the texture atlas.

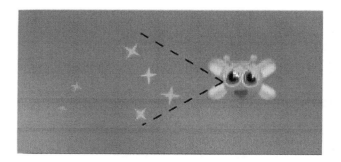

Figure 8-15. *A stream of multicolored particles is emitted when the fairy flaps her wings*

As you learned earlier in this chapter, the particleEffect function that we wrote will randomly display a frame on a sprite, if that sprite contains multiple frames. To make this work, first define an array of texture atlas frames that you want to use:

```
dustFrames = [
  assets["pink.png"],
  assets["yellow.png"],
  assets["green.png"],
  assets["violet.png"]
];
```

Next, use those frames to initialize the sprite function that's supplied to the emitter:

```
dust = emitter(
  300,                                     //The interval
  () => particleEffect(                    //The function
    fairy.x + 8,                           //x position
    fairy.y + fairy.halfHeight + 8,        //y position
    () => sprite(dustFrames),              //Particle sprite
    3,                                     //Number of particles
    0,                                     //Gravity
    true,                                  //Random spacing
    2.4, 3.6,                              //Min/max angle
    12, 18,                               //Min/max size
    1, 2,                                 //Min/max speed
    0.005, 0.01,                          //Min/max scale speed
    0.005, 0.01,                          //Min/max alpha speed
    0.05, 0.1                             //Min/max rotation speed
  )
);
```

You now have a particle emitter called dust. Just call its play function to make it start emitting particles:

```
dust.play();
```

Fine-Tuning the Fairy's Animation

When Flappy Fairy is going up, she flaps her wings and emits magical fairy dust. When she's going down, the dust stops and she stops flapping her wings. But how do we know whether she's flying upward or downward?

We have to find the difference in her velocity between the current frame and the previous frame. If her current velocity is greater than her previous velocity, she's going up. If it's less, and the previous velocity is greater than zero, she's doing down. The code stores the fairy's vy value from the current frame in a property called oldVy. When oldVy is accessed in the **next** frame, it tells you what the fairy's previous vy value was.

```
//If she's going up, make her flap her wings and emit fairy dust
if (fairy.vy > fairy.oldVy) {
  if(!fairy.playing) {
    fairy.play();
    if (fairy.visible && !dust.playing) dust.play();
  }
}
```

```
//If she's going down, stop flapping her wings, show the first frame
//and stop the fairy dust
if (fairy.vy < 0 && fairy.oldVy > 0) {
  if (fairy.playing) fairy.stop();
  fairy.show(0);
  if (dust.playing) dust.stop();
}

//Store the fairy's current vy so we can use it
//to find out if the fairy has changed direction
//in the next frame. (You have to do this as the last step)
fairy.oldVy = fairy.vy;
```

The oldVy property will be used to calculate the difference in velocity between frames when the next frame swings around. This is a very well-worn trick that you can use whenever you want to compare a sprite's difference in velocity between two frames.

Collisions with the Blocks

When Flappy Fairy hits a block, she disappears in a puff of dust, as shown in Figure 8-16. How does that behavior work?

Figure 8-16. *Poof! She's gone!*

The game loop does this with the help of the hitTestRectangle function, which you learned to use in the previous chapter. The code loops through the blocks.children array and tests for a collision between each block and the fairy. If hitTestRectangle returns true, the loop quits and a collision object called fairyVsBlock becomes true.

```
let fairyVsBlock = blocks.children.some(block => {
  return hitTestRectangle(fairy, block, true);
});
```

■ **Tip** You can see that code uses the some method to loop through all the blocks. The advantage to using some is that the loop will quit as soon it finds a value that equals true.

---

hitTestRectangle's third argument needs to be true so that the collision detection is done using the sprite's global coordinates (gx and gy). That's because the fairy is a child of the stage, but each block is a child of the blocks group. That means they don't share the same local coordinate space. Using their global coordinates forces the hitTestRectangle to use the sprites' positions relative to the canvas.

If fairyVsBlock is true, and the fairy is currently visible, the collision code runs. It makes the fairy invisible, creates the particle explosion, and calls the game's reset function after a delay of 3 seconds.

```
if (fairyVsBlock && fairy.visible) {

  //Make the fairy invisible
  fairy.visible = false;

  //Create a fairy dust explosion
  particleEffect(
    fairy.centerX, fairy.centerY, //x and y position
    () => sprite(dustFrames),     //Particle sprite
    20,                           //Number of particles
    0,                            //Gravity
    false,                        //Random spacing
    0, 6.28,                      //Min/max angle
    16, 32,                       //Min/max size
    1, 3                          //Min/max speed
  );

  //Stop the dust emitter that's trailing the fairy
  dust.stop();

  //Wait 3 seconds and then reset the game
  wait(3000).then(() => reset());
}
```

The reset function just repositions the fairy and the blocks to their initial positions and makes the fairy visible again.

```
function reset() {
  fairy.visible = true;
  fairy.y = 32;
  dust.play();
  blocks.x = 0;
}
```

As an alternative to looping through each block with some and testing for a collision with hitTestRectangle, you could use the universal hit function. As you learned at the end of the previous chapter, hit is a higher-level "luxury" function that does a lot of work for you automatically. If you supply it with an array of sprites as the second argument, hit will automatically loop through them for you and check them for a collision with the sprite in the first argument. Here's how you could use hit to perform the same collision test between the fairy and the blocks:

```
let fairyVsBlock = hit(
  fairy, blocks.children, false, false, true,
  () => {
    if (fairy.visible) {
      fairy.visible = false;
      particleEffect(/*...particle arguments...*/);
      dust.stop();
      wait(3000).then(() => reset());
    }
  }
);
```

Use whichever collision detection function you prefer.

Flappy Fairy: The Complete Code

Flappy Fairy uses all the techniques you've learned in this book so far, and it contains most of the elements that a complete game needs. How would you code a game like this from scratch? It's not always obvious how to begin or structure a complete, full-featured game, so here, for your reference, is the complete JavaScript code. Use it as a model for starting your own new games.

```
//Import code from the library
import {
  makeCanvas, sprite, group, particles, particleEffect,
  tilingSprite, emitter, stage, render
} from "../library/display";
import {assets, randomInt, contain, wait} from "../library/utilities";
import {makePointer} from "../library/interactive";
import {hit, hitTestRectangle} from "../library/collision";

//Load the assets
assets.load([
  "images/flappyFairy.json"
]).then(() => setup());

//Declare any variables shared between functions
let pointer, canvas, fairy, sky, blocks,
    finish, dust, dustFrames;

function setup() {

  //Make the canvas and initialize the stage
  canvas = makeCanvas(910, 512);
  canvas.style.backgroundColor = "black";
  stage.width = canvas.width;
  stage.height = canvas.height;
```

```
//Make the sky background
sky = tilingSprite(canvas.width, canvas.height, assets["sky.png"]);

//Create a `group` for all the blocks
blocks = group();

//What should the initial size of the gap be between the pillars?
let gapSize = 4;

//How many pillars?
let numberOfPillars = 15;

//Loop 15 times to make 15 pillars
for (let i = 0; i < numberOfPillars; i++) {

  //Randomly place the gap somewhere inside the pillar
  let startGapNumber = randomInt(0, 8 - gapSize);

  //Reduce the `gapSize` by one after every fifth pillar. This is
  //what makes gaps gradually become narrower
  if (i > 0 && i % 5 === 0) gapSize -= 1;

  //Create a block if it's not within the range of numbers
  //occupied by the gap
  for (let j = 0; j < 8; j++) {
    if (j < startGapNumber || j > startGapNumber + gapSize - 1) {
      let block = sprite(assets["greenBlock.png"]);
      blocks.addChild(block);

      //Space each pillar 384 pixels apart. The first pillar will be
      //placed at an x position of 512
      block.x = (i * 384) + 512;
      block.y = j * 64;
    }
  }

  //After the pillars have been created, add the finish image
  //right at the end
  if (i === numberOfPillars - 1) {
    finish = sprite(assets["finish.png"]);
    blocks.addChild(finish);
    finish.x = (i * 384) + 896;
    finish.y = 192;
  }
}
```

```
//Make the fairy
let fairyFrames = [
  assets["0.png"],
  assets["1.png"],
  assets["2.png"]
];
fairy = sprite(fairyFrames);
fairy.fps = 24;
fairy.setPosition(232, 32);
fairy.vy = 0;
fairy.oldVy = 0;

//Create the frames array for the fairy dust images
//that trail the fairy
dustFrames = [
  assets["pink.png"],
  assets["yellow.png"],
  assets["green.png"],
  assets["violet.png"]
];

//Create the particle emitter
dust = emitter(
  300,                              //The interval
  () => particleEffect(            //The function
    fairy.x + 8,                    //x position
    fairy.y + fairy.halfHeight + 8, //y position
    () => sprite(dustFrames),       //Particle sprite
    3,                              //Number of particles
    0,                              //Gravity
    true,                           //Random spacing
    2.4, 3.6,                       //Min/max angle
    12, 18,                         //Min/max size
    1, 2,                           //Min/max speed
    0.005, 0.01,                    //Min/max scale speed
    0.005, 0.01,                    //Min/max alpha speed
    0.05, 0.1                       //Min/max rotation speed
  )
);

//Make the particle stream start playing when the game starts
dust.play();

//Make the pointer and increase the fairy's
//vertical velocity when it's tapped
pointer = makePointer(canvas);
pointer.tap = () => {
  fairy.vy += 1.5;
};
```

```
  //Start the game loop
  gameLoop();
}

function gameLoop() {
  requestAnimationFrame(gameLoop);

  //Update all the particles in the game
  if (particles.length > 0) {
    for(let i = particles.length - 1; i >= 0; i--) {
      let particle = particles[i];
      particle.update();
    }
  }

  //The `play` function contains all the game logic
  play();
}

function play() {

  //Make the sky background scroll by shifting the `tileX`
  //of the `sky` tiling sprite
  sky.tileX -= 1;

  //Move the blocks 2 pixels to the left each frame.
  //This will just happen while the finish image is off-screen.
  //As soon as the finish image scrolls into view, the blocks
  //container will stop moving
  if (finish.gx > 256) {
    blocks.x -= 2;
  }

  //Add gravity to the fairy
  fairy.vy += -0.05;
  fairy.y -= fairy.vy;

  //Decide whether the fairy should flap her wings
  //If she's going up, make her flap her wings and emit fairy dust
  if (fairy.vy > fairy.oldVy) {
    if(!fairy.playing) {
      fairy.play();
      if (fairy.visible && !dust.playing) dust.play();
    }
  }
```

```
//If she's going down, stop flapping her wings, show the first frame
//and stop the fairy dust
if (fairy.vy < 0 && fairy.oldVy > 0) {
  if (fairy.playing) fairy.stop();
  fairy.show(0);
  if (dust.playing) dust.stop();
}

//Store the fairy's current vy so we can use it
//to find out if the fairy has changed direction
//in the next frame. (You have to do this as the last step)
fairy.oldVy = fairy.vy;

//Keep the fairy contained inside the stage and
//neutralize her velocity if she hits the top or bottom boundary
let fairyVsStage = contain(fairy, stage.localBounds);
if (fairyVsStage === "bottom" || fairyVsStage === "top") {
  fairy.vy = 0;
}

//Loop through all the blocks and check for a collision between
//each block and the fairy. (`some` will quit the loop as soon as
//`hitTestRectangle` returns `true`.) Set `hitTestRectangle`s third argument
//to `true` to use the sprites' global coordinates

let fairyVsBlock = blocks.children.some(block => {
  return hitTestRectangle(fairy, block, true);
});

//If there's a collision and the fairy is currently visible,
//create the explosion effect and reset the game after
//a three second delay

if (fairyVsBlock && fairy.visible) {

  //Make the fairy invisible
  fairy.visible = false;

  //Create a fairy dust explosion
  particleEffect(
    fairy.centerX, fairy.centerY, //x and y position
    () => sprite(dustFrames),     //Particle sprite
    20,                           //Number of particles
    0,                            //Gravity
    false,                        //Random spacing
    0, 6.28,                      //Min/max angle
    16, 32,                       //Min/max size
    1, 3                          //Min/max speed
  );
```

```
    //Stop the dust emitter that's trailing the fairy
    dust.stop();

    //Wait 3 seconds and then reset the game
    wait(3000).then(() => reset());
  }

  //Alternatively, you can achieve the same collision effect
  //using the higher-level universal `hit` function

  //Render the canvas
  render(canvas);
}

function reset() {

  //Reset the game if the fairy hits a block
  fairy.visible = true;
  fairy.y = 32;
  dust.play();
  blocks.x = 0;
}
```

If you're ever confused or uncertain where or how to apply a certain technique while building your own games, take a look back at this source code and use it as a framework and guide.

Summary

You've now got all the skills to start making some pretty sophisticated and compelling games. Far from being frivolous extras, techniques like keyframe animation, particle effects, and parallax scrolling add a whole new dimension of immersion to your games. They can transform a merely fun game into a living, breathing alternate universe.

You've also learned how leverage the power of code abstraction to make a fairy complex game prototype in less than 200 lines of code. By creating reusable objects and functions, and by burying all that code away in your code library, your final game code is lightweight and readable. You've now got a solid foundation for making a wide range of games, and you have an easy-to-understand structure to build on.

Before you turn the page, I want you to do one last thing. Play Flappy Fairy one more time and turn up the volume on your computer. What do you hear? That's right: nothing! We're going to fix that in the next chapter.

CHAPTER 9

■ ■ ■

Sound with the Web Audio API

HTML5 has two different systems for playing sounds: the older HTML5 Audio element and the newer Web Audio API. Which one should you use? For games, use the incredibly powerful Web Audio API. It loads sounds reliably, lets you play multiple sounds at the same time, and gives you precise playback control. In addition, it lets you apply effects, create your own synthesized sounds, and specify different kinds of input and output sources. Once you get over the small learning curve, you'll be able to use the Web Audio API to quickly create any kind of sound system you can imagine.

In this chapter you're going to learn everything you need to know about the Web Audio API to use and create all the music and sound effects you'll need for your games. You'll learn how to load sound files, access them, control how they play, and add special effects like echo and reverb. You'll also learn how to generate sounds from scratch with pure code, and how to build your own custom library of game sound effects.

Before we dive into the new Web Audio API, though, let's learn a bit more about the original HTML Audio element.

The HTML Audio Element

The HTML5 Audio element is specifically designed for playing audio files in websites and is generally too limited to be of good use for games. The JavaScript format for loading and playing sounds with the HTML5 Audio element is the same as the format for loading images. Create a new Audio object, listen for a canplaythrough event, and then call an event handler when the sound has finished loading. You can start the sound with a play method, and set other attributes like volume and loop. Here's a typical example:

```
let sound = new Audio();
sound.addEventListener("canplaythrough", playSoundHandler, false);
sound.src = "sounds/music.wav";

function playSoundHandler(event) {
  sound.play();
  sound.volume = 0.5;
  sound.loop = true;
}
```

It's sensible and familiar, but unfortunately, very limited. Playback control is imprecise, and simultaneous overlapping sounds either don't work or behave in quirky ways. And even though at the time of writing the HTML5 Audio element specification has been stable for years, none of the browser vendors have implemented it fully, or seem likely to do so soon. So if you run this example in a browser, first just hope that the loop property works. If it does, you might hear the music loop repeat, but you'll almost certainly hear a gap of a few milliseconds before it does. The HTML5 Audio element could be adequate for a game with undemanding sound design, but for anything else, you'll need much more control.

Enter, the Web Audio API!

Understanding the Web Audio API

No matter how hard you look through the Web Audio API specification, you won't find any method called play, or any properties called loop or volume. You have to build those yourself. What the Web Audio API gives you is a big toy box full of audio components that you can use to create any audio system you might need. Your job is to empty that box onto your kitchen table and spend a sunny afternoon connecting those components together into any combination that seems useful to you. The best thing about the Web Audio API is that it's completely modular, so you can connect different components in any way you like. You could build your own analog-style synthesizer or sampler, a 3D holographic music player, a music notation interpreter, a procedural music generator, or a sound visualizer. Or, you can do what we're going to do in this chapter: create reusable sound effect and music players and generators for games.

▤ **Note** The Web Audio API is complex and deep enough that it deserves a whole book on its own. In this chapter I'm not going to touch on each and every feature of the API, just those that you need to know to create a practical system for using sounds in games. You can think of this as a broad introduction to the Web Audio API, which will give you a strong foundation if you want to explore it further on your own.

Here's the basic procedure you need to follow to load and play a sound using the Web Audio API:

1.   Load the sound file with XHR and decode it. You end up with a raw audio file called a **buffer**.

2.   Connect the buffer to audio effects **nodes**. Think of each node as a little sound effects box with knobs you can tweak—that is, parameters and properties you can set with code. You might have a box that controls the volume, another box that controls left/right panning, and yet another box that controls reverb. Any electric guitar players out there can think of your guitar as the sound buffer and the nodes as effects pedals. You can connect as many nodes together as you like, in any order.

3.   To hear the sound, connect the last node in the effects chain to the **destination**. The destination is usually the default playback device on your system; it could be a speaker, headphones, 7.1 surround sound, or a TV. However, the destination could also be a new sound file.

4.   Start the sound.

Figure 9-1 shows what this process looks like.

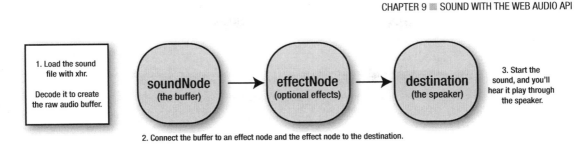

Figure 9-1. *How to play a sound with the Web Audio API*

This is a lot easier to understand in real code, so let's look at a practical example next.

Loading and Playing a Sound File

Let's start with the simplest example possible. We're going to load a sound file and play it by pressing the number 1 on the keyboard. The comments explain step-by-step how it all works.

```
//1. Create an audio context
    let actx = new AudioContext();

//2. Declare a variable to hold the sound we're going to load
    let soundBuffer;

//3. Load the sound.
//a. Use an XMLHttpRequest object to load the sound
    let xhr = new XMLHttpRequest();

//b. Set properties for the file we want to load.
//Use GET and set the path to the sound file.
//`true` means that the file will load asynchronously and will create
//an event when the file has finished loading
    xhr.open("GET", "sounds/test.wav", true);

//c. Set the `responseType`, which is the file format we're expecting to
//load. Sound files should be loaded as binary files, so the `responseType`
//needs to be `arraybuffer`
    xhr.responseType = "arraybuffer";

//d. Load the sound into the program
    xhr.send();

//e. Create a `loadHandler` that runs when the sound has been loaded
    xhr.addEventListener("load", loadHandler, false);

    function loadHandler(event) {

//f. Decode the audio file and store it in the `soundBuffer`
//variable. The `buffer` is the raw audio data
    actx.decodeAudioData(
      xhr.response,
      buffer => {
```

333

```
//g. Copy the audio file into the `soundBuffer` variable
soundBuffer = buffer;
},

//Optionally throw an error if the audio can't be decoded
error => {
  throw new Error("Audio could not be decoded: " + error);
  }
 );
}

//f. Play a sound when a key is pressed
window.addEventListener("keydown", keydownHandler, false);

function keydownHandler(event) {
  switch (event.keyCode) {
    case 49:
      if (soundBuffer) {

        //4. Play the sound
        //a. Create a new `soundNode` and tell it to use the
        //sound that we loaded as its audio source
        let soundNode = actx.createBufferSource();
        soundNode.buffer = soundBuffer;

        //b. Connect the sound to the destination.
        //(There are no effects in this example.)
        soundNode.connect(actx.destination);

        //c. Finally, play the sound. Use the `start` method to
        //play the sound "right now", which is the audio context's `currentTime`
        soundNode.start(actx.currentTime);
      }
      break;
  }
}
```

The first step is to create an AudioContext. This is the programming space where you'll create and control your sounds:

```
var actx = new AudioContext();
```

It is just like the canvas's context, except that it's for sounds instead of images.

Next, create a variable called soundBuffer that will be used to store the raw binary sound file.

```
let soundBuffer;
```

Load the sound using XHR. The responseType is "arrayBuffer", which just tells XHR that you're loading a binary file, not a text file.

```
let xhr = new XMLHttpRequest();
xhr.open("GET", "sounds/test.wav", true);
xhr.responseType = "arraybuffer";
xhr.send();
xhr.addEventListener("load", loadHandler, false);
```

The loadHandler uses the audio context's decodeAudioData method to convert the sound file into raw audio data. It saves this data in the soundBuffer:

```
function loadHandler(event) {
  actx.decodeAudioData(
    xhr.response,
    buffer => {
      soundBuffer = buffer;
    },
    error => {
      throw new Error("Audio could not be decoded: " + error);
    }
  );
}
```

The decodeAudioData method has an optional third argument, which is a function that runs if there was an error decoding the audio. You should always add this, because you definitely need to be informed if the audio didn't decode properly for some reason. You could get a decoding error if you're trying to load an incompatible audio format.

The last step is to actually play the sound, which in this example happens by pressing the number 1 on the keyboard. These are the minimum four lines of code you have to run to play a sound:

```
let soundNode = actx.createBufferSource();
soundNode.buffer = soundBuffer;
soundNode.connect(actx.destination);
soundNode.start(actx.currentTime);
```

Here's how these four lines work. First create a soundNode that will be used to play the sound. It holds references to the buffer that we loaded (the raw audio data). Then connect the soundNode to the audio context's destination, which, in this case is your computer's speaker. Finally, use the start method to play the sound. The argument actx.currentTime means "play the sound now."

```
soundNode.start(actx.currentTime);
```

The start method is used to schedule when the sound should be played, as offset from the current time. If you supply it with the audio context's currentTime value, it means "play the sound immediately, without any delay." If you want a 2 second delay before the sound starts, you could use this syntax:

```
start(actx.currentTime + 2)
```

Note that the Web Audio API works with units of time in seconds, not milliseconds.

■ **Tip** Alternatively, you can make a sound play immediately by supplying the **start** method with a value of 0, this way: **start(0)**. That's because any value that's less than the **currentTime** will cause the audio context to play the sound immediately. You can use whichever style you prefer.

Here's a very important thing you need to know: *you have to run these last four lines of code every time you want to play the sound.* That might seem like a lot of code to write for just one sound, but we're going to fix that soon.

You've seen how to load and play a basic sound, but what if you want to add a few more advanced features?

Volume, Pan, and Looping

To change the volume and panning, create a volumeNode and a panNode:

```
let volumeNode = actx.createGain();
let panNode = actx.createStereoPanner()
```

You can think of these as two audio effects boxes that you can connect between the sound and the speaker. Here's how to connect these nodes to the soundNode and the destination:

```
soundNode.connect(volumeNode);
volumneNode.connect(panNode);
panNode.connect(actx.destination);
```

You can see that you're creating a chain of connections: soundNode ➤ volumeNode ➤ panNode ➤ destination. The last effect node, which in this example is the panNode, should always be connected to the destination so that you can hear the sound.

■ **Note** Use the disconnect method if you need to disconnect a node. For example, you could disconnect the panNode with this syntax:

```
panNode.disconnect()
```

This disconnects the panNode from whatever it was connected to, which in this example is the volumeNode. But keep in mind that if you do this, you've broken the connection chain between the original sound and the destination. That means you won't hear anything when you start the sound unless you connect the volumeNode directly to the destination or to another connected node in the chain.

Now that they're connected, adjust the settings on these new nodes to achieve the effect you desire. Here's how to set the volume level to 50%:

```
volumeNode.gain.value = 0.5;
```

A gain.value of 0 is no sound, and a value of 1 is full volume. (Note that *gain* is the technical audio term for volume. More specifically, it refers to how much an audio signal is amplified.)

To set the left and right speaker panning, set the panNode.pan.value property to a number between –1 and 1. A value of –1 directs the sound to the left speaker, and a value of 1 directs it to the right speaker. A value of 0 makes the sound equal volume in both speakers. For example, here's how you could set the pan to be slightly more prominent in the left speaker:

```
panNode.pan.value = -0.2;
```

■ **Note**   You can also create a more advanced pan object using the createPanner method, which returns a pan node that lets you position sounds in 3D space, using x, y and z spatial coordinates. It's great for creating sophisticated sound environments for 3D games. For more information, see the Web Audio specification for the createPanner method at http://webaudio.github.io/web-audio-api/.

Do you want your sound to repeat when it finishes? Set the loop property of the soundNode to true:

```
soundNode.loop = true;
```

The sound will now repeat when it reaches the end.

■ **Tip**   Do you hear a short delay before the looping sound repeats? If so, open your sound file in any audio editing software. You'll probably find that the file contains a few extra milliseconds of silence before the sound starts. This is really common with MP3 files. Also consider removing MP3 header or metadata, which has been known to cause some audio rendering engines to hiccup for a millisecond or two before repeating the sound.

Now let's put all these new techniques together. Here's the complete code you'll need to run if you want to play a sound that loops with volume and pan control:

```
let soundNode = actx.createBufferSource();
soundNode.buffer = soundBuffer;

//Create volume and pan nodes
let volumeNode = actx.createGain();
let panNode = actx.createStereoPanner();

//Connect the sound source to the pan node, the pan node to
//volume node, and the volume node to the destination
soundNode.connect(panNode);
panNode.connect(volumeNode);
volumeNode.connect(actx.destination);

//Set the volume
volumeNode.gain.value = 0.5;

//Set the pan fully to the left
panNode.pan.value = -1;
```

```
//Optionally loop the sound
soundNode.loop = true;
```

```
//Finally, play the sound
soundNode.start(actx.currentTime);
```

And, just like our first example, you'll need to run all this code every time you want to play the sound.

This seems like a lot of work just to play one sound, doesn't it? But there's a reason for this: It's because the Web Audio API doesn't want you to write all this code each time you play a sound. Instead, it wants to give you powerful and flexible fine-grained tools so that you can build any kind of sound system you need from scratch. Instead of prescribing an API that you should use to play sounds, it gives you the building blocks you need to *make your own API*.

So that's exactly what we're going to do next: Build an easy-to-use and reusable sound object to play sound effects and music in games.

WEB AUDIO API NODES

We've only used four nodes in these examples so far: The audio source node (the loaded sound file) the gain node (for volume) the panner node and the destination node (the speaker.) But the Web Audio API has a rich collection of different nodes for you to play around with:

- DelayNode: Creates echo, phase, and flanger effects.

- ConvolverNode: Lets you simulate an acoustic environment like a cathedral, a speaker cabinet, or a telephone speaker.

- AnalyserNode: Gets data about your sound to help you make something like a music visualizer or graphic EQ.

- ChannelSplitterNode and ChannelMergerNode: Let you capture left and right stereo signal as mono outputs, and then, if you want to, remix them into a new stereo signal.

- DynamicsCompressorNode: Normalizes very quiet or very loud sounds to a mid-range volume level.

- BiquadFilterNode: Helps you build a bass, mid, and treble equalizer.

- WaveShaperNode: Distorts the sound.

- OscillatorNode: Generates synthesized sounds. Make your own Moog synthesizer!

- ScriptProcessorNode: If you need your sound to do something that isn't covered by the built-in nodes, create your own custom effect node using JavaScript.

In addition to these nodes, the Web Audio API lets you set up a moving AudioListener. Sound intensities and direction will change depending on where the listener is in 3D space. You can also capture sounds from a microphone or line-in source, as well as write sound files to disk. For details, check out the full, well-written and readable Web Audio API spec at http://webaudio.github.io/web-audio-api/.

A Web Audio Sound Object

How do you want to be able to control sound in your games? You should be able to load sounds and play them. It would be nice if you could pause them, restart them, and maybe play them from a specific position. You should also be able to control the volume and set the left and right speaker panning. In a perfect world, we'd be able to control our sound with simple properties and methods that might look something like this:

```
sound.load();
sound.play();
sound.pause();
sound.restart();
sound.volume = 0.8;
sound.pan = -0.5;
sound.playFrom(15);
```

Thanks to the Web Audio API, this perfect world exists. Well, almost... not yet. We have to build it first!

How do we build a sound object like this? Our dream API layout gives you some clues. The sound object needs methods called load, play, pause, restart, and playFrom. And it needs properties called volume and pan. We want to be able to make as many sound objects as we need for all the sounds in our game. That means we can think of each sound as a kind of *audio sprite*. But instead of displaying images, the audio sprites will play sounds. What that means is that we can use the same model we've used for visual sprites, and just adapt it so that it works for sounds.

In this next section we'll make a Sound class that does all this. As you'll see, it's just a combination of different patterns that you already know. It fuses what we've just learned about the Web Audio API and what we know about how to make objects using classes. The only really new thing is the system it uses to pause, restart, and play sounds. But we'll look at that in detail ahead, along with how to implement this class to make new sounds. Here's the complete Sound class. Read through it carefully, and I'll meet you on the other side when you're done!

```
//Create the audio context
let actx = new AudioContext();

//The sound class
class Sound {
  constructor(source, loadHandler) {

    //Assign the `source` and `loadHandler` values to this object
    this.source = source;
    this.loadHandler = loadHandler;

    //Set the default properties
    this.actx = actx;
    this.volumeNode = this.actx.createGain();
    this.panNode = this.actx.createStereoPanner();
    this.soundNode = null;
    this.buffer = null;
    this.loop = false;
    this.playing = false;

    //Values for the pan and volume getters/setters
    this.panValue = 0;
    this.volumeValue = 1;
```

```
    //Values to help track and set the start and pause times
    this.startTime = 0;
    this.startOffset = 0;

    //Load the sound
    this.load();
  }

  //The sound object's methods

  load() {

    //Use xhr to load the sound file
    let xhr = new XMLHttpRequest();
    xhr.open("GET", this.source, true);
    xhr.responseType = "arraybuffer";
    xhr.addEventListener("load", () => {

      //Decode the sound and store a reference to the buffer
      this.actx.decodeAudioData(
        xhr.response,
        buffer => {
          this.buffer = buffer;
          this.hasLoaded = true;

          //This next bit is optional, but important.
          //If you have a load manager in your game, call it here so that
          //the sound is registered as having loaded.
          if (this.loadHandler) {
            this.loadHandler();
          }
        },

        //Throw an error if the sound can't be decoded
        error => {
          throw new Error("Audio could not be decoded: " + error);
        }
      );
    });

    //Send the request to load the file
    xhr.send();
  }

  play() {

    //Set the start time (it will be `0` when the first sound starts)
    this.startTime = this.actx.currentTime;

    //Create a sound node
    this.soundNode = this.actx.createBufferSource();
```

```
  //Set the sound node's buffer property to the loaded sound
  this.soundNode.buffer = this.buffer;

  //Connect the sound to the volume, connect the volume to the
  //pan, and connect the pan to the destination
  this.soundNode.connect(this.volumeNode);
  this.volumeNode.connect(this.panNode);
  this.panNode.connect(this.actx.destination);

  //Will the sound loop? This can be `true` or `false`
  this.soundNode.loop = this.loop;

  //Finally, use the `start` method to play the sound.
  //The start time will be either `0`,
  //or a later time if the sound was paused
  this.soundNode.start(
    this.startTime,
    this.startOffset % this.buffer.duration
  );

  //Set `playing` to `true` to help control the
  //`pause` and `restart` methods
  this.playing = true;
}

pause() {

  //Pause the sound if it's playing, and calculate the
  //`startOffset` to save the current position
  if (this.playing) {
    this.soundNode.stop(this.actx.currentTime);
    this.startOffset += this.actx.currentTime - this.startTime;
    this.playing = false;
  }
}

restart() {

  //Stop the sound if it's playing, reset the start and offset times,
  //then call the `play` method again
  if (this.playing) {
    this.soundNode.stop(this.actx.currentTime);
  }
  this.startOffset = 0,
  this.play();
}

playFrom(value) {
  if (this.playing) {
    this.soundNode.stop(this.actx.currentTime);
  }
```

```
    this.startOffset = value;
    this.play();
  }

  //Volume and pan getters/setters

  get volume() {
    return this.volumeValue;
  }
  set volume(value) {
    this.volumeNode.gain.value = value;
    this.volumeValue = value;
  }

  get pan() {
    return this.panNode.pan.value;
  }
  set pan(value) {
    this.panNode.pan.value = value;
  }
}

//Create a high-level wrapper to keep our general API style consistent and flexible
function makeSound(source, loadHandler) {
  return new Sound(source, loadHandler);
}
```

To create a sound object using this class, initialize it with the sound's source path, and an optional load handler that should run when the sound has finished loading. Here's how you could create a new music sound:

```
let music = makeSound("sounds/music.wav", setupMusic);
```

The setup function will run as soon as the sound loads. Use it to set any of the sound's properties. Then decide how you want to control the sound. Here's some code that uses the keyboard function to listen for key presses. It lets you press the "a" key to play a sound, the "b" key to pause it, the "c" key to restart it and the "d" key to start playing it from the 10 second point.

```
function setupMusic() {

  //Make the music loop
  music.loop = true;

  //Set the pan
  music.pan = -0.8;

  //Set the volume
  music.volume = 0.3;

  //Capture keyboard key events
  let a = keyboard(65),
      b = keyboard(66),
      c = keyboard(67),
      d = keyboard(68);
```

```
//Use the key `press` methods to control the sound
//Play the music with the `a` key
a.press = () => {
  if (!music.playing) music.play();
  console.log("music playing");
};

//Pause the music with the `b` key
b.press = () => {
  music.pause();
  console.log("music paused");
};

//Restart the music with the `c` key
c.press = () => {
  music.restart();
  console.log("music restarted");
};

//Play the music from the 10 second mark
//with the `d` key
d.press = () => {
  music.playFrom(10);
  console.log("music start point changed");
};
}
```

To see (and hear!) this code in action, run the soundObject.html file in the chapter's source files, shown in Figure 9-2.

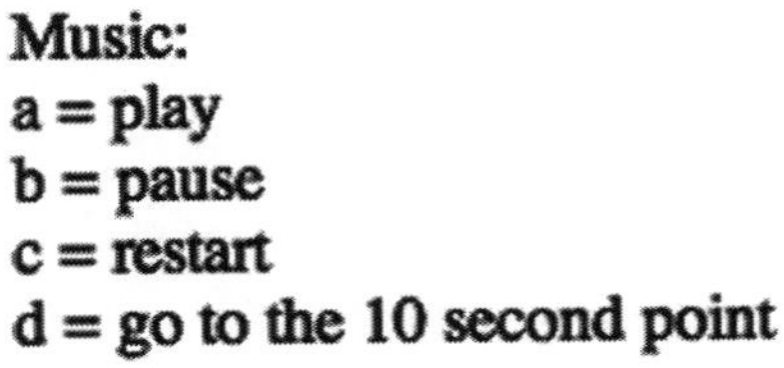

Music:
a = play
b = pause
c = restart
d = go to the 10 second point

Figure 9-2. Using a Sound class to load and control music

Pausing, Restarting and Playing from a Given Time

An important feature of the sound object is that the sounds can be paused, restarted, and played from any point. The AudioContext has a property called currentTime that tells you the time, in seconds, from the moment the context was created. It's like a clock's second hand, and is always moving forward. Counterintuitively, *it doesn't tell you the time at which the sound is playing*. That means if you pause a sound at the 10 second mark, wait 5 seconds, and then restart the sound from 0, the currentTime will be 15. The currentTime just keeps ticking forward, forever, until the sound object is destroyed.

Yes, it's weird. This is a totally different concept than timecode in video or audio. For example, in any audio application like Logic, Audacity, or Ableton Live, if you stop a sound, the timecode also stops. If you reverse the sound, the timecode moves backwards to match the section of time that you want to move to and if you advance the sound, the timecode also advances to that same position. That is not the case with time in the Web Audio API: it just keeps ticking forward and can't be paused, advanced, or reversed. But don't let this worry you: it's just a feature of the low-level nature of the Web Audio API and it gives you more flexibility in the long run. But it also means that you have to build your own system on top of this to start and play sounds at correct time points.

To help calculate the time start and stop points, use startTime and startOffset variables, which are initialized to zero:

```
this.startTime = 0;
this.startOffset = 0;
```

To pause a sound, first stop it using the stop method. Then calculate the startOffset time by adding whatever the currentTime is, minus the startTime.

```
pause() {
  if (this.playing) {
    this.soundNode.stop(this.actx.currentTime);
    this.startOffset += this.actx.currentTime - this.startTime;
    this.playing = false;
  }
},
```

When the sound is played again, capture the new startTime:

```
play() {
  this.startTime = this.actx.currentTime;
  //...
```

Play the sound by setting the start method's first parameter to currentTime. That means "play the sound now."

```
  //...
  this.soundNode.start(
    this.startTime,                        //1: "play right now"
    this.startOffset % this.buffer.duration //2: "Play the correct section of the sound"
  );
  this.playing = true;
},
```

The second parameter is the section of the sound file that you want to play. It's a simple calculation that specifies which part of the sound file to play. That point is calculated by finding the remainder of the startOffset divided by the buffer.duration. (The buffer.duration is the time, in seconds, of the loaded sound.) This makes the sound play from the point where it may have been paused.

Take a deep breath! This is probably the most complicated part of working with time in the Web Audio API, but we've now overcome it. Thanks to this little calculation we have a way of moving the audio back and forth in time, and resuming a sound from the point where it was paused.

■ **Note** The start method also has a third optional parameter, which is the duration, in seconds, that the sound should play for. If, for example, you have a sound that's 10 seconds long, but you only want to play the first 3 seconds of that sound, supply a duration of 3. If you want that portion of the sound to loop, you have to set the sounceNode's loopStart property to 0 (the start of the sound) and loopEnd property to 3 (the duration's end time.)

The restart method works in the same way. It sets the startOffset to currentTime, which causes the sound to play from the beginning again.

```
restart() {
  if (this.playing) {
    this.soundNode.stop(this.actx.currentTime);
  }
  this.startOffset = 0,
  this.play();
},
```

The third new feature is the playFrom method. This lets you play the sound from any time. Here's how to play the music from the 10 second mark:

```
music.playFrom(10);
```

It's almost the same as the restart method, but lets you specify the time, in seconds, from which to play.

```
playFrom(value) {
  if (this.playing) {
    this.soundNode.stop(this.actx.currentTime);
  }
  this.startOffset = value;
  this.play();
},
```

And now we have a neat, reusable sound object that we can add to any game.

■ **Note** You'll find the full Sound class and makeSound function in the library/sound.js file.

A Sound Asset Loader

Now that you know how to make sounds, you need some way to load sound files efficiently into your game program. Fortunately, we've already created a universal asset loader in Chapter 3. With just a few small modifications, we can extend it to help us load sound files just as easily as it loads fonts, images, and JSON data files. You'll find the assets object in the library/utilities.js file—flip back to Chapter 3 if you need a quick review on how it works.

The first step is to import the makeSound method from the library/sound module. Add this bit of code to the beginning of the utilities module:

```
import {makeSound} from "../library/sound";
```

Now find the assets object and add a property called audioExtensions, which is an array that lists all the file extensions for the kinds of audio files that you might need to load:

```
audioExtensions: ["mp3", "ogg", "wav", "webm"],
```

Then, in the loop that loads each source, check to see if any of the sources has one of those audio file extensions. If it does, the code should call a new method called loadSound:

```
sources.forEach(source => {
  //...

  else if (this.audioExtensions.indexOf(extension) !== -1) {
    this.loadSound(source, loadHandler);
  }

  //...
});
```

The loadSound method uses makeSound to create the sound object and load the sound file. It then assigns the sound object as a property of the assets object. It gives the sound object a name that matches the sound file's name.

```
loadSound(source, loadHandler) {

  //Create a sound object and alert the `loadHandler`
  //when the sound file has loaded
  let sound = makeSound(source, loadHandler);

  //Get the sound file name
  sound.name = source;

  //Assign the sound as a property of the assets object so
  //we can access it this way: `assets["sounds/sound.mp3"]`
  this[sound.name] = sound;
}
```

This means that after the sound is loaded, you'll be able to access the sound object in your game file with this syntax:

```
assets["sounds/soundFileName.mp3"];
```

How can you use this in a real game program? First, use the assets.load method to load the file, and call a setup function when it's finished. Here's how you could load two sound files into a game:

```
assets.load([
  "sounds/music.wav",
  "sounds/shoot.wav"
]).then(() => setup());
```

Of course, you can also list any other assets, like image or JSON files, that your game might need and load them at the same time.

Next, in the `setup` function, just use the `assets` object to get a reference to the loaded sounds you want to use. You can then use them just like any other sound objects from the earlier examples in this chapter.

```
function setup() {

  //Get references to the loaded sound objects
  let music = assets["sounds/music.wav"],
      shoot = assets["sounds/shoot.wav"];

  //Capture keyboard key events
  let a = keyboard(65),
      b = keyboard(66);

  //Play the music with the `a` key
  a.press = () => {
    if (!music.playing) music.play();
  };

  //Play the shoot sound with the `b` key
  b.press = () => {
    shoot.play();
  };
}
```

You've now got a unified and consistent interface for loading and using all the assets in your games.

Adding Effects

Loading and playing sound files for games is all well and good, but that only represents a tiny fraction of what the incredibly powerful Web Audio API is capable of. Now that you know the basics, let's explore a little further and see where our curiosity can take us. Maybe it would be nice to implement a few special effects to our sounds? With just a little more work, we can implement these three effects:

- Playback rate: Make the sound play back at a faster or slower speed.

- Echo: A decaying echo effect.

- Reverb: Simulate the sound of an acoustic space, like a large room or cave.

These effects are easy to implement on top of our current system, and will give you a good overview of some more advanced features of the Web Audio API. (Run the `specialEffects.html` file in the chapter's source code for working examples of this code in action.)

Changing the Playback Rate

Making sounds play back at faster or slower speeds is a fun and quick effect to start with. The sound buffer source (the `soundNode` object in our earlier examples) has a property called `playbackRate` that lets you change how quickly or slowly the sound plays. Its default value is 1, which is normal speed. You can make the sound play at half speed by setting `playbackRate` to 0.5, or make it play at double speed by setting it to 2. Changing the playbackRate doesn't affect the sound's pitch (pitch is the sound's note frequency, which is how high or low it sounds). Here's how to add a playback rate feature to the Sound class that lets you change the speed of any sound.

First, add a playBackrate property to the Sound class's constructor function:

```
this.playbackRate = 1;
```

Setting it to 1 means that the default playback rate will be normal speed.

Next, add the following line of code to the Sound class's play method, just before you call the start method. It sets the sound buffer source's playBackrate.value to the Sound class's own playBackrate value.

```
this.soundNode.playbackRate.value = this.playbackRate;
```

Finally, in your game program code, set the playbackRate property of any sound you make using the makeSound method. Here's how to make a sound called music play at half speed:

```
music.playbackRate = 0.5;
```

It you want it to play twice as fast, set it to 2. And now you've got an easy way to control any sound's playback speed!

Echo

Echo is an effect that you might want to use for some of your game sounds. The Web Audio API doesn't have a built-in way of automatically adding echo to sounds, but it's pretty easy to create your own echo system. To make it work, you need to use a **delay node**.

```
let delayNode = actx.createDelay();
```

The only thing the delay node does is delay a sound before playing it. If you wanted to set the delay for half a second, you could do it as follows:

```
delayNode.delayTime.value = 0.5;
```

But simply delaying a sound for half a second is not enough to create an echo effect. The sound needs to be delayed and then repeated, with each repetition become fainter. To make that work, you need another node, called **feedback,** that will make the sound get gradually quieter with each repetition. The feedbackNode is just a gain node, which is the same kind of node we used for setting the sound's volume.

```
let feedbackNode = actx.createGain();
```

If you want the echo to drop in volume by about 20 percent with each repetition, set the feedbackNode's value to 0.8.

```
feedbackNode.gain.value = 0.8;
```

(A value of 1 will mean there's no loss of volume, and the sound will repeat forever. Setting it to greater than 1 will gradually increase the volume of the echo.)

But we're not done yet! To make all this work you need to connect these nodes together. First, create a closed loop by sending the delay to the feedback, and then back into the delay. The connection path will look like this:

```
delay > feedback > delay
```

This loop is what creates the repeating echo effect. Each time the delayed sound is sent to the feedback, its volume is 20 percent less, so the sound gradually fades away with each repetition. Next, connect the delay node to your main sound chain. Insert it between the source and destination nodes:

```
source > delay > destination
```

The result is that the delay node gets the input from the source, sends it to the feedback loop, and then sends the resulting echo to the destination so that you can hear it.

What does this look like in real code? Let's simplify things a bit and ignore the volume and pan nodes for now. Here's the all the code you'd need to write to create a basic echo effect.

```
//Create the delay and feedback nodes
let delayNode = actx.createDelay(),
    feedbackNode = actx.createGain();

//Set their values
delayNode.delayTime.value = 0.2;
feedbackNode.gain.value = 0.8;

//Create the delay feedback loop
delayNode.connect(feedbackNode);
feedbackNode.connect(delayNode);

//Connect the source to the destination to play the first
//instance of the sound at full volume
source.connect(actx.destination);

//Capture the source and send it to the delay loop
//to create the echo effect. Then connect the delay to the
//destination so that you can hear the echo
source.connect(delayNode);
delayNode.connect(actx.destination);
```

The Web Audio API manages sound objects under the hood very efficiently, so there's no danger of memory leaks. The API runtime (the browser) will take care of destroying sounds that are no longer audible. That means you don't need to don't need to write your code to check for and remove sounds that have a volume level of zero.

This will get you started with a good, basic echo—but there's a little more we can do.

A More Organic Echo Effect

Our current echo repeats each sound as a perfect duplicate of the original sound, with just a drop in volume with each repetition. You can give the echo effect a much organic, fantasy quality by slightly changing the tone of each repeated sound. An easy way to do this is to add a **biquad filter** into the mix. A biquad filter just filters out any frequencies above a certain threshold. Here's how to create a biquad filter node, and set its frequency value.

```
let filterNode = actx.createBiquadFilter();
filterNode.frequency.value = 1000;
```

Giving the filter a frequency value of 1000 means that it will shear out any frequencies above 1000 Hz.

■ **Note**   The biquad filter is a low-pass filter, by default which means it lets through all frequencies that are under a given threshold. By setting the filter's type property, you can change its filtering behavior. The type property can be set to any of these string values: "lowpass", "highpass", "bandpass", "lowshelf", "highshelf", "peaking", "notch", and "allpass".

Add the filterNode to the delay loop, between the feedback and delay connection, like this:

delay > feedback > filter > delay

Here's the new delay loop code with the filter included:

```
delayNode.connect(feedbackNode);
feedbackNode.connect(filterNode);
filterNode.connect(delayNode);
```

You can achieve a wide variety of cool sci-fi effects by changing the filterNode's frequency value—it's perfect for fantasy or space games.

■ **Tip**   Biquad filters also have a fun property called detune, which lets you change the pitch of the source sound. Set it to a value in cents (percentage of a semitone) to change the pitch by that amount. An entire octave (12 semitones) is 1200 cents.

Adding an Echo Feature to the Sound Class

Now that we know how to create an echo effect, let's update our Sound class so that we can selectively apply an echo to any sound. First, create the new nodes we need in the constructor function:

```
this.delayNode = this.actx.createDelay();
this.feedbackNode = this.actx.createGain();
this.filterNode = this.actx.createBiquadFilter();
```

Then create some properties we can use to customize the effect on the sound object:

```
this.echo = false;
this.delayValue = 0.3;
this.feedbackValue = 0.3;
this.filterValue = 0;
```

Let's also create a method called setEcho that will let us set the delay time, feedback time, and optional filtering of the effect.

```
setEcho(delayValue = 0.3, feedbackValue = 0.3, filterValue = 0) {
  this.delayValue = delayValue;
  this.feedbackValue = feedbackValue;
  this.filterValue = filterValue;
  this.echo = true;
}
```

We can use the value of echo (true or false) to turn the echo effect on or off. To do that, let's add our echo code to the Sound class's play method. All the new code is highlighted.

```
play() {
  this.startTime = this.actx.currentTime;
  this.soundNode = this.actx.createBufferSource();
  this.soundNode.buffer = this.buffer;

  //Create the main node chain
  this.soundNode.connect(this.volumeNode);
  this.volumeNode.connect(this.panNode);
  this.panNode.connect(this.actx.destination);

  //Add optional echo
  if (this.echo) {

    //Set the values
    this.feedbackNode.gain.value = this.feedbackValue;
    this.delayNode.delayTime.value = this.delayValue;
    this.filterNode.frequency.value = this.filterValue;

    //Create the delay loop, with optional filtering
    this.delayNode.connect(this.feedbackNode);
    if (this.filterValue > 0) {
      this.feedbackNode.connect(this.filterNode);
      this.filterNode.connect(this.delayNode);
    } else {
      this.feedbackNode.connect(this.delayNode);
    }

    //Capture the sound from the main node chain, send it to the
    //delay loop, and send the final echo effect to the `panNode`, which
    //will then route it to the destination
    this.volumeNode.connect(this.delayNode);
    this.delayNode.connect(this.panNode);
  }
```

```
    this.soundNode.loop = this.loop;
    this.soundNode.playbackRate.value = this.playbackRate;
    this.soundNode.start(
      this.startTime,
      this.startOffset % this.buffer.duration
    );
    this.playing = true;
}
```

Now to create an echo effect with any sound, use the sound's setEcho method. Supply the values you need to set the delay time, feedback time, and, if you want to use the biquad filter, optionally supply the frequency ceiling you want to filter.

```
let bounce = assets["sounds/bounce.mp3"];
bounce.setEcho(0.2, 0.5, 1000);
```

If you need to turn the echo effect off at some point, just set the sound's echo property to false:

```
bounce.echo = false;
```

By varying these values you can create a huge range of echo effects for your games.

Reverb

Reverb is an effect that simulates an acoustic space, like a room, cathedral, or space cavern. It's the most complex effect we're going to create, and it will give you deeper insight into some of the more advanced workings of the Web Audio API. Before we get to the nuts and bolts, let's take a short break from coding and dip our toes into some theoretical waters so you're properly prepared for what's to come.

So What Is a Buffer, Really?

I've been throwing the word "buffer" around quite a bit in this chapter. I mentioned earlier that it was the "raw audio file," but it's actually a little more than that. You can think of the buffer as an array that stores binary data. The data are the ones and zeros that represent the sound. Each piece of that sound is called a **sample**. Samples are the equivalent of pixels in images, so I like to think of samples as "audio pixels." This means you can think of the buffer as an array in which each element represents the smallest unit that makes up each piece of the sound.

The buffer also contains **channels**. You can think of each channel as a separate array, containing its own sound samples. If you have a buffer with two channels, the first channel might contain the samples for the left speaker, and the second channel might contain the samples for the right speaker. You can visualize the buffer like this:

```
buffer = [
  [l0, l1, l2], //channel one sample data for the left speaker
  [r0, r1, r2]  //channel two sample data for the right speaker
];
```

So the buffer is a bit a like a multidimensional array, with each channel representing a subarray. Each index position in the array is called a **sample-frame**. This example buffer contains three sample-frames: l0 and r0 are both on sample-frame 0; l2 and r2 are both on sample-frame 2. Samples that occupy the same sample-frames will play at the same point in time. They're like separate tracks on a strip of audiotape. A single buffer can contain up to 32 channels of audio data.

■ **Note**   A monaural sound, which is the same in both speakers, uses only one channel. Dolby 5.1 surround sound uses 5 channels. Quad sound uses 4.

You can create an empty sound buffer at any time using the Web Audio API's createBuffer method. It takes three arguments: the number of channels, the length of the buffer in sample-frames, and the sample rate.

```
let emptyBuffer = actx.createBuffer(numberOfChannels, length, sampleRate);
```

Usually you'll only need two channels, one for the left speaker and one for the right speaker. The length defines how many sample-frames the buffer has. The sampleRate is the number of sample-frames that are played each second. The sample rate affects the resolution of the sound—the higher the sample rate, the higher the quality of the audio. The sample rate is measured in Hertz (Hz) and has to be in the range of 22050 to 96000. The Web Audio API's default sample rate is usually 44.1kHz, but it depends on the device that your code is running on. If you initialize an empty buffer as in the example just seen, the channel data will be filled with zeros, representing silence.

■ **Tip**   You can find out how long a sound buffer is, in seconds, by dividing the number of frames by the sample rate.

I've been talking about the buffer as an "array" to help you visualize it, but that's not precisely what it is. Yes, I lied again! It's actually an "array-like" data type called an ArrayBuffer. An ArrayBuffer is just a JavaScript storage container for binary data. However, you can convert an ArrayBuffer into a real, usable array with the help of the buffer's getChannelData method. Here's how to use it to convert the left and right speaker channel data into arrays:

```
let left = buffer.getChannelData(0),
    right = buffer.getChannelData(1);
```

left and right are now normal arrays packed with audio data. (0 represents the left channel, and 1 represents the right channel.) You can work with them just as you would work with any ordinary array. They're actually a special kind of high-resolution array called a Float32Array. But don't let that worry you—just think of them as normal arrays that are particularly efficient for storing and accessing binary data.

■ **Note**   Float32 arrays are also used in WebGL graphics rendering.

What's great about this is that you can change what the buffer sounds like by changing the channel data in the arrays. It also means that you can create sounds procedurally from pure code. Just use an algorithm that produces the kind of sound data you want, and push it into the channel data arrays. That's what we're going to do next.

Simulating Sound Reverberation

Now let's get back to reverb! The trick to creating believable reverb is that you combine two sounds together. The first sound is your original sound, without reverb. The second is a special recording of a neutral sound (white noise) in the kind of acoustic space that you want to simulate: for example, a room, cave, or theatre. These special recordings are called **impulse response** recordings. You then blend these two sounds together using an audio processor called a **convolver**. The convolver takes your original sound, compares it to the impulse response recording, and combines the two sounds together. The result is realistic reverb which sounds like the space that you're trying to simulate.

But where do you get the impulse response sound that models the reverb? There are thousands of professionally recorded impulse response recordings available, which model the acoustics of everything from guitar amplifier cabinets, to telephone speakers, to historic cathedrals. You can create your own too: just take an audio recorder to an abandoned power plant, factory, or insane asylum, and fire a few shots in the air with a pistol. Preferably, do this at 3 am. You'll get a great recording of the acoustic space that you can use with the convolver, and have a lot of fun in the process.

Or, if you have second thoughts about attracting the attention of the police, you can generate your configurable impulse response with just a few lines of code. The impulseResponse function listed next does just that. It creates an empty buffer with two channels, and fills each channel with random noise. A simple formula makes the noise decay exponentially, in the same way that sound does naturally when it bounces off the walls of a room. You can set the duration of the reverb, and the amount of decay, to simulate a wide variety of spaces. It's the exponential decay (not the white noise) that defines the impulse response, and hence the apparent size of your acoustic space. A short decay creates the illusion that the sound is happening in a small space, and a longer decay simulates a bigger space. The impulseResponse function also has a reverse parameter which, if true, creates a spooky reverse-reverb effect.

```
function impulseResponse(duration = 2, decay = 2, reverse = false) {

  //The length of the buffer
  //(The AudioContext's default sample rate is 44100)
  let length = actx.sampleRate * duration;

  //Create an audio buffer (an empty sound container) to store the reverb effect
  let impulse = actx.createBuffer(2, length, actx.sampleRate);

  //Use `getChannelData` to initialize empty arrays to store sound data for
  //the left and right channels
  let left = impulse.getChannelData(0),
      right = impulse.getChannelData(1);

  //Loop through each sample-frame and fill the channel
  //data with random noise
  for (let i = 0; i < length; i++){

    //Apply the reverse effect, if `reverse` is `true`
    let n;
    if (reverse) {
      n = length - i;
    } else {
      n = i;
    }
```

```
//Fill the left and right channels with random white noise that
//decays exponentially
left[i] = (Math.random() * 2 - 1) * Math.pow(1 - n / length, decay);
right[i] = (Math.random() * 2 - 1) * Math.pow(1 - n / length, decay);
}

//Return the `impulse`
return impulse;
}
```

The impulseResponse function returns a buffer, which is a model of the reverb effect that we want to apply to our sound. But how can we actually use it?

First, create a **convolver node**. This is the specialized audio processor that blends ordinary sounds with impulse responses to create the final reverb effect.

```
let convolverNode = actx.createConvolver();
```

Then set the impulse response to the convolver's own buffer.

```
convolverNode.buffer = impulseResponse(2, 2, false);
```

And finally, connect the convolver node to your sound chain.

```
soundNode.connect(convolverNode);
convolverNode.connect(destination);
```

When the sound is routed through the convolver, it blends the impulse response into it, and the result is a realistic reverb effect.

Adding a Reverb Feature to the Sound Class

Now let's update our Sound class to add a reusable reverb feature that we can enable on any sound. First, create the convolver node in the constructor function, as well as some properties that will help us control the effect.

```
this.convolverNode = this.actx.createConvolver();
this.reverb = false;
this.reverbImpulse = null;
```

Next, create a setReverb method that will allow us to apply reverb easily to any sound.

```
setReverb(duration = 2, decay = 2, reverse = false) {
  this.reverbImpulse = impulseResponse(duration, decay, reverse);
  this.reverb = true;
}
```

Then, in the play method, connect the convolver between the volume and pan nodes, and apply the impulse response to the convolver's buffer. If reverb is set to false, the effect will be bypassed. Here's the first part of the Sound class's play method, with all the new code highlighted.

```
play() {
  this.startTime = this.actx.currentTime;
  this.soundNode = this.actx.createBufferSource();
  this.soundNode.buffer = this.buffer;

  //Connect all the nodes
  this.soundNode.connect(this.volumeNode);

  //If there's no reverb, bypass the convolverNode
  if (this.reverb === false) {
    this.volumeNode.connect(this.panNode);
  }

  //If there is reverb, connect the `convolverNode` and apply
  //the impulse response
  else {
    this.volumeNode.connect(this.convolverNode);
    this.convolverNode.connect(this.panNode);
    this.convolverNode.buffer = this.reverbImpulse;
  }

  this.panNode.connect(this.actx.destination);


  //... the rest of the `play` method is the same
}
```

Now you can apply customized reverb to any sound using the setReverb method, with this syntax:

```
let music = assets["sounds/music.wav"];
music.setReverb(2, 5, false);
```

If you need to turn reverb off later, set the sound's reverb property to false:

```
music.reverb = false;
```

Play around with different duration and delay settings, and you'll be able to produce a huge variety of effects. If it's Halloween, set the reverse parameter to true!

■ **Tip**   Run the specialEffects.html file in the chapter's source files to play around with all these new features. And be sure to check out the complete Sound class in the library/Sound module to see all of this code in its full context.

Synthesizing Sounds

So far in this chapter, all the sounds we've loaded and controlled have been prerecorded audio files. But the Web Audio API also lets you create completely new sounds, with a versatile **oscillator node**. An oscillator generates a tone at any pitch you choose. It also has a bunch of useful properties you can set to shape that tone. You can connect the oscillator to any of the Web Audio API's other nodes, such as the delay node or convolver, to create an almost limitlessly rich spectrum of sounds for games. In this last section of the chapter I'll first introduce you to the basics of creating and working with oscillators, and we'll then build a simple SoundEffect class that you can use as the basis for building a wide variety of different game sounds.

It's extremely easy to create and play a sound with an oscillator. Here's the most basic code you need to do it:

```
//Create the audio context
let actx = new AudioContext();

//Create a new oscillator
let oscillator = actx.createOscillator();

//Connect it to the destination
oscillator.connect(actx.destination);

//Make it play
oscillator.start(actx.currentTime);
```

(Use the stop method to stop an oscillator.)

If you run this code it produces a tone at a default 200 Hz (which is a slightly sharp G.) You can change the note that the oscillator plays by setting its frequency.value property. Here's how to make it play middle-A (440 Hz):

```
oscillator.frequency.value = 440;
```

Oscillators also have a detune property, which is a value in cents that offsets the frequency.

You can change the basic waveform pattern that the oscillator's tone is based on by setting its type property, a string that can be set to "sine", "triangle", "square", or "sawtooth".

```
oscillator.type = "sawtooth";
```

Each of those waveform types produces a progressively harsher tone. If you want a really smooth, chime-like tone, use "sine". Try "triangle" if you still want a smooth tone, but with a touch of grittiness. "square" starts sounding a little harsh, with "sawtooth" the most jagged and harsh sounding of them all.

■ **Note** These four basic waveform types will probably be all you need to generate most sounds for games. But you can create your own custom waveforms with the help of the createPeriodicWave and setPeriodicWave methods. You can use them along with special data arrays called **Fourier transforms** to simulate a wide variety of tones, such as different musical instruments. See the Web Audio API specification for more details.

To show you just how ridiculously easy it is to make something really useful using oscillators, let's turn your computer into a musical instrument.

Making Music

We're going to create a mini-application that lets you play five notes using your keyboard's number keys. We'll start with a reusable function called playNote that lets you play any note value. It creates and plays a musical note that sounds just like what you'd expect if you pressed any key from any electronic keyboard you've played around with. You can set the note's value (frequency in Hertz), its waveform type, and its decay. The decay value determines for how long the note is audible while it fades from full volume to silence. The playNote function is basically just a reusable wrapper for the code we just looked at: it creates an oscillator and volume node, connects them together to the destination, and uses the oscillator's values to play the sound. (The only new thing in this code is the technique used to fade the note out—but I'll explain how that works ahead.)

```
function playNote(frequency, decay = 1, type = "sine") {

  //Create an oscillator and a gain node, and connect them
  //together to the destination
  let oscillator = actx.createOscillator(),
      volume = actx.createGain();

  oscillator.connect(volume);
  volume.connect(actx.destination);

  //Set the oscillator's wave form pattern
  oscillator.type = type;

  //Set the note value
  oscillator.frequency.value = frequency;

  //Fade the sound out
  volume.gain.linearRampToValueAtTime(1, actx.currentTime);
  volume.gain.linearRampToValueAtTime(0, actx.currentTime + decay);

  //Make it play
  oscillator.start(actx.currentTime)
}
```

You can use playNote to play a note at any frequency, like this:

```
playNote(440, 2, "square");
```

The Fade-Out Effect

The second parameter, decay, determines how long the note is audible while it fades out. The fade-out effect is created using these two lines of code:

```
volume.gain.linearRampToValueAtTime(1, actx.currentTime);
volume.gain.linearRampToValueAtTime(0, actx.currentTime + decay);
```

linearRampToValueAtTime is a really useful built-in function that lets you change any node value over time. In this example it's changing the value of the volume's gain from full volume (1) to silence (0) over a period that starts at the currentTime and finishes at whatever decay is set to. You can see that you need to use linearRampToValueAtTime twice to create the complete fade-out effect. The first use sets the start volume and start time. The second sets its end volume and end time. The Web Audio API's engine automatically interpolates all the in-between values for you, and gives you a completely smooth transition in volume.

Here's the basic format you can use to change any node value over time:

```
nodeProperty.linearRampToValueAtTime(startValue, startTime);
nodeProperty.linearRampToValueAtTime(endValue, endTime);
```

It works with any node values, including frequency, so you can use linearRampToValueAtTime to create a wide range of different effects for games.

■ **Note**   linearRampToValueAtTime changes a value linearly: in an even, gradual way. If you want the value to change exponentially, use exponentialRampToValueAtTime. An exponential change starts gradually and quickly falls off. Many sounds in nature have exponential changes in values.

Playing Notes

The only thing left to do is to hook the playNote function up with some kind of event. Here's the code that captures keyboard events for the 1 to 5 number keys. It then calls the playNote function at the correct note frequencies when they're pressed: D, E, G, A, or C. (In case you're curious, those five notes are all you need to play an ancient Indian classical raga called *megh*, which means *cloud*. They sound good together in any combination.)

```
//Capture keyboard events for the number keys 1 to 5
let one = keyboard(49),
    two = keyboard(50),
    three = keyboard(51),
    four = keyboard(52),
    five = keyboard(53);

//Define the note values
let D = 293.66,
    E = 329.63,
    G = 392.00,
    A = 440.00,
    C = 523.25;

//D
one.press = () => {
  playNote(D, 1);
};

//E
two.press = () => {
  playNote(E, 1);
}
```

```
//G
three.press = () => {
  playNote(G, 1);
}

//A
four.press = () => {
  playNote(A, 1)
}

//C
five.press = () => {
  playNote(C, 1);
}
```

■ **Tip**   A quick web search will bring up many charts that show you how to convert frequency values in Hertz to real note values.

With hardly any trouble at all, you've turned your computer keyboard into a musical instrument! You can just as easily add musical effects to your game. What about making blocks in a platform game play notes when a character jumps on them, or a simple random music generator? How about a game where the player composes a melody while exploring a game world? You're now just a few small steps away from entering a whole new dimension of music-based games, so go for it!

And that's just about it! There's really nothing complicated about oscillators—the real fun begins when you start hooking them up to some of the other nodes we've used in this chapter in imaginative ways. With a little bit of experimentation, you'll soon realize that you have a complete music and sound effect synthesizer sitting at your fingertips, with almost limitless potential to create any game sounds you might need.

Really? Yes, let's find out how!

Generating Sound Effects

Imagine this: a single, reusable function that, in less than 150 lines of code, can generate any sound effects or musical notes you might ever need for games, without having to download any sound files. Thanks to the Web Audio API, this promised land is possible, and it's exactly what we're going to build next: a universal sound effect generator that can produce almost any sound you might need for games.

The sound effect function we're going to build is called, sensibly, soundEffect. It has 13 low-level parameters that you can set to create a huge number of useful tones. Before we look at all the details of the how the function works its magic, let's take a close at how you can use it in a practical way. Here's a model for using it, including a description of what each parameter does.

```
soundEffect(
  frequencyValue,    //The sound's frequency pitch in Hertz
  attack,            //The time, in seconds, to fade the sound in
  decay,             //The time, in seconds, to fade the sound out
  type,              //waveform type: "sine", "triangle", "square", or "sawtooth"
  volumeValue,       //The sound's maximum volume
  panValue,          //The speaker pan. left: -1, middle: 0, right: 1
  wait,              //The time, in seconds, to wait before playing the sound
```

```
  pitchBendAmount,  //A frequency amount, in Hz, to bend the sound's pitch down
  reverse,          //If `reverse` is true the pitch will bend up
  randomValue,      //A range, in Hz., within which to randomize the pitch
  dissonance,       //A value in Hz. Creates 2 additional dissonant frequencies
  echo,             //An array: [delayTime, feedbackTime, filterValue]
  reverb            //An array: [duration, decayRate, reverse?]
);
```

The strategy for using this soundEffect function is to tinker with all these parameters and come up with your own custom library of sound effects for games. Think of it as a big soundboard with thirteen colorful flashing dials you can play with. And imagine that you're a mad scientist, and that thirteen is your lucky number!

To see how to set these parameters to create the kinds of sounds you want, let's try using soundEffect to produce four versatile game sounds: a laser shooting sound, a jumping sound, an explosion sound, and a musical motif. (Run the soundEffects.html file in the chapter's source files for working examples of this code, shown in Figure 9-3.)

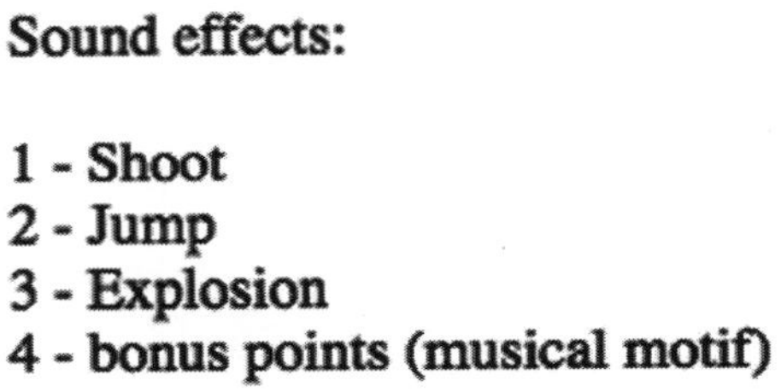

Sound effects:

1 - Shoot
2 - Jump
3 - Explosion
4 - bonus points (musical motif)

Figure 9-3. *Generate custom sound effects from pure code*

The Shooting Sound

Here's an example of how to use the soundEffect function to create a typical laser shooting sound:

```
function shootSound() {
  soundEffect(
    1046.5,            //frequency
    0,                 //attack
    0.3,               //decay
    "sawtooth",        //waveform
    1,                 //Volume
    -0.8,              //pan
    0,                 //wait before playing
    1200,              //pitch bend amount
    false,             //reverse bend
    0,                 //random frequency range
    25,                //dissonance
    [0.2, 0.2, 2000],  //echo array: [delay, feedback, filter]
    undefined          //reverb array: [duration, decay, reverse?]
  );
}
```

361

The "sawtooth" waveform setting gives the sound a biting harshness. The pitchBendAmount is 1200, which means the sound's frequency drops by 1200 Hz from start to finish. That makes it sound like every laser from every science fiction movie you've ever seen. The dissonance value of 25 means that two extra overtones are added to the sound at 25 Hz above and below the main frequency. Those extra overtones add an edgy complexity to the tone.

Because the soundEffect function is wrapped in a custom shootSound function, you can play the effect at any time in your application code, this way:

```
shootSound();
```

It will play immediately.

The Jumping Sound

Let's look at another example. Here's a jumpSound function that produces a typical platform game-character jumping sound.

```
function jumpSound() {
  soundEffect(
    523.25,        //frequency
    0.05,          //attack
    0.2,           //decay
    "sine",        //waveform
    3,             //volume
    0.8,           //pan
    0,             //wait before playing
    600,           //pitch bend amount
    true,          //reverse
    100,           //random pitch range
    0,             //dissonance
    undefined,     //echo array: [delay, feedback, filter]
    undefined      //reverb array: [duration, decay, reverse?]
  );
}
```

The jumpSound has an attack value of 0.05, which means there's a very quick fade-in to the sound. It's so quick that you can't really hear it, but it subtly softens the start of the sound. The reverse value is true, which means that the pitch bends up instead of down. (This makes sense because jumping characters jump upwards.) The randomValue is 100. That means the pitch will randomize within a range of 100 Hz around the target frequency, so that the sound's pitch will be slightly different every time. This adds organic interest to the sound and makes the game world feel alive.

The Explosion Sound

You can create a radically different explosionSound effect just by tweaking the same parameters:

```
function explosionSound() {
  soundEffect(
    16,            //frequency
    0,             //attack
    1,             //decay
```

```
  "sawtooth",    //waveform
  1,             //volume
  0,             //pan
  0,             //wait before playing
  0,             //pitch bend amount
  false,         //reverse
  0,             //random pitch range
  50,            //dissonance
  undefined,     //echo array: [delay, feedback, filter]
  undefined      //reverb array: [duration, decay, reverse?]
 );
}
```

This creates a low-frequency rumble. The starting point for the explosion sound is to set the frequency value extremely low: 16 Hz. It also has a harsh "sawtooth" waveform. But what makes it really work is the dissonance value of 50. This adds two overtones, 50 Hz above and below the target frequency, which interfere with each other and the main sound.

The Musical Motif

But it's not just for sound effects! You can use the soundEffect function to create musical notes, and play them at set intervals Here's a function called bonusSound which plays three notes (D, A and high D) in a rising pitch sequence. It's typical of the kind of musical motif you might hear when a game character scores some bonus points, like picking up stars or coins. (When you hear this sound, you might get a flashback to 1985!)

```
function bonusSound() {

  //D
  soundEffect(587.33, 0, 0.2, "square", 1, 0, 0);

  //A
  soundEffect(880, 0, 0.2, "square", 1, 0, 0.1);

  //High D
  soundEffect(1174.66, 0, 0.3, "square", 1, 0, 0.2);
}
```

The key to making it work is the last argument: the wait value (highlighted in the code just shown). The first sound's wait value is 0, which means the sound will play immediately. The second sound's wait value is 0.1, which means it will play after a delay of 100 milliseconds. The last sound's wait value is 0.2, which will make it play in 200 milliseconds. This means that all three notes play in sequence with a 100 millisecond gap between them.

With just a little more work you could use the wait parameter to build a simple music sequencer, and build your own mini-library of musical sound effects just for playing notes.

The Complete soundEffect Function

Here's the entire soundEffect function with comments that explain how it works. As you'll see, it's a bubbling witches' brew of all the techniques you've learned in this chapter. (You'll find this soundEffect function in the library/sound.js file.)

```
function soundEffect(
  frequencyValue,
  attack = 0,
  decay = 1,
  type = "sine",
  volumeValue = 1,
  panValue = 0,
  wait = 0,
  pitchBendAmount = 0,
  reverse = false,
  randomValue = 0,
  dissonance = 0,
  echo = undefined,
  reverb = undefined
) {

  //Create oscillator, gain and pan nodes, and connect them
  //together to the destination
  let oscillator = actx.createOscillator(),
      volume = actx.createGain(),
      pan = actx.createStereoPanner();

  oscillator.connect(volume);
  volume.connect(pan);
  pan.connect(actx.destination);

  //Set the supplied values
  volume.gain.value = volumeValue;
  pan.pan.value = panValue;
  oscillator.type = type;

  //Optionally randomize the pitch. If the `randomValue` is greater
  //than zero, a random pitch is selected that's within the range
  //specified by `frequencyValue`. The random pitch will be either
  //above or below the target frequency.
  let frequency;
  let randomInt = (min, max) => {
   return Math.floor(Math.random() * (max - min+ 1)) + min;
  }
  if (randomValue > 0) {
    frequency = randomInt(
      frequencyValue - randomValue / 2,
      frequencyValue + randomValue / 2
    );
  } else {
```

```
  frequency = frequencyValue;
}
oscillator.frequency.value = frequency;
```

//Apply effects
```
if (attack > 0) fadeIn(volume);
if (decay > 0) fadeOut(volume);
if (pitchBendAmount > 0) pitchBend(oscillator);
if (echo) addEcho(volume);
if (reverb) addReverb(volume);
if (dissonance > 0) addDissonance();
```

//Play the sound
```
play(oscillator);
```

//The helper functions:

//Reverb
```
function addReverb(volumeNode) {
  let convolver = actx.createConvolver();
  convolver.buffer = impulseResponse(reverb[0], reverb[1], reverb[2]);
  volumeNode.connect(convolver);
  convolver.connect(pan);
}
```

//Echo
```
function addEcho(volumeNode) {

  //Create the nodes
  let feedback = actx.createGain(),
      delay = actx.createDelay(),
      filter = actx.createBiquadFilter();

  //Set their values (delay time, feedback time, and filter frequency)
  delay.delayTime.value = echo[0];
  feedback.gain.value = echo[1];
  if (echo[2]) filter.frequency.value = echo[2];

  //Create the delay feedback loop, with
  //optional filtering
  delay.connect(feedback);
  if (echo[2]) {
    feedback.connect(filter);
    filter.connect(delay);
  } else {
    feedback.connect(delay);
  }

  //Connect the delay loop to the oscillator's volume
  //node, and then to the destination
  volumeNode.connect(delay);
```

```
    //Connect the delay loop to the main sound chain's
    //pan node, so that the echo effect is directed to
    //the correct speaker
    delay.connect(pan);
}

//Fade in (the sound's "attack")
function fadeIn(volumeNode) {

    //Set the volume to 0 so that you can fade in from silence
    volumeNode.gain.value = 0;

    volumeNode.gain.linearRampToValueAtTime(
      0, actx.currentTime + wait
    );
    volumeNode.gain.linearRampToValueAtTime(
      volumeValue, actx.currentTime + wait + attack
    );
}

//Fade out (the sound's "decay")
function fadeOut(volumeNode) {
    volumeNode.gain.linearRampToValueAtTime(
      volumeValue, actx.currentTime + attack + wait
    );
    volumeNode.gain.linearRampToValueAtTime(
      0, actx.currentTime + wait + attack + decay
    );
}

//Pitch bend.
//Uses `linearRampToValueAtTime` to bend the sound's frequency up or down
function pitchBend(oscillatorNode) {

    //Get the frequency of the current oscillator
    let frequency = oscillatorNode.frequency.value;

    //If `reverse` is true, make the sound drop in pitch.
    //(Useful for shooting sounds)
    if (!reverse) {
      oscillatorNode.frequency.linearRampToValueAtTime(
        frequency,
        actx.currentTime + wait
      );
      oscillatorNode.frequency.linearRampToValueAtTime(
        frequency - pitchBendAmount,
        actx.currentTime + wait + attack + decay
      );
    }
}
```

```
  //If `reverse` is false, make the note rise in pitch.
  //(Useful for jumping sounds)
  else {
    oscillatorNode.frequency.linearRampToValueAtTime(
      frequency,
      actx.currentTime + wait
    );
    oscillatorNode.frequency.linearRampToValueAtTime(
      frequency + pitchBendAmount,
      actx.currentTime + wait + attack + decay
    );
  }
}


//Dissonance
function addDissonance() {

  //Create two more oscillators and gain nodes
  let d1 = actx.createOscillator(),
      d2 = actx.createOscillator(),
      d1Volume = actx.createGain(),
      d2Volume = actx.createGain();

  //Set the volume to the `volumeValue`
  d1Volume.gain.value = volumeValue;
  d2Volume.gain.value = volumeValue;

  //Connect the oscillators to the gain and destination nodes
  d1.connect(d1Volume);
  d1Volume.connect(actx.destination);
  d2.connect(d2Volume);
  d2Volume.connect(actx.destination);

  //Set the waveform to "sawtooth" for a harsh effect
  d1.type = "sawtooth";
  d2.type = "sawtooth";

  //Make the two oscillators play at frequencies above and
  //below the main sound's frequency. Use whatever value was
  //supplied by the `dissonance` argument
  d1.frequency.value = frequency + dissonance;
  d2.frequency.value = frequency - dissonance;

  //Apply effects to the gain and oscillator
  //nodes to match the effects on the main sound
  if (attack > 0) {
    fadeIn(d1Volume);
    fadeIn(d2Volume);
  }
```

```
    if (decay > 0) {
      fadeOut(d1Volume);
      fadeOut(d2Volume);
    }
    if (pitchBendAmount > 0) {
      pitchBend(d1);
      pitchBend(d2);
    }
    if (echo) {
      addEcho(d1Volume);
      addEcho(d2Volume);
    }
    if (reverb) {
      addReverb(d1Volume);
      addReverb(d2Volume);
    }

    //Play the sounds
    play(d1);
    play(d2);
  }

  //The `play` function that starts the oscillators
  function play(oscillatorNode) {
    oscillatorNode.start(actx.currentTime + wait);
  }
}
```

Summary

You now have a powerful set of new tools to add sounds to games. You've learned all the basics of loading and playing sounds with the Web Audio API, and have a useful Sound class that you can use for all the music and sound effects in your games. You've also learned how to load and manage sounds with the assets object, and how to generate sounds from scratch with the universal soundEffect function.

But how do you actually use sounds in a game? You're going to learn how in Chapter 11. But before you do, let's look at one more essential tool you need to know to complete your game design toolkit: tweening.

CHAPTER 10

■ ■ ■

Tweening

Tweening is an animation technique that you can use to make a sprite change its appearance or position over time in very specific ways. You can use tweening to make a sprite move along a fixed path or curve, or make a sprite fade in, fade out, pulse, or wobble. Using tweening effects will add a whole new dimension of interactivity and engagement to your games that will make them come alive in new and exciting ways.

How is tweening different from the other ways you've learned to move sprites in this book? In Chapter 5 you learned how to make sprites move using velocity and physics properties. That's great for making things like bouncing balls that need to react on every frame to a constantly changing game environment. But sometimes you just want to tell your sprites something like "Go over there, then come back, and repeat that forever." Tweening is like giving your sprites a predictable fixed, unchanging script for movement, which isn't influenced by the physics of the game. It's like a train that runs on a track; it always follows the same route and stops at each station at the same time. Tweening is especially useful for handling some of the more tedious aspects of game animation, like animating the user interface. It's great for making titles and buttons slide or fade in and out, and also for creating transitions between game scenes. Generally you'll use physics-based movements for your main sprite animation, and tweening when you want to implement a quick motion special effect.

The word **tween** comes from "in between." It's a word used by animators to describe the positions of animated objects in between their start and finish points. If you know point A, and you know point B, and you know how long it should take an object to travel between those points, you can use tweening to calculate where all those in-between points are.

■ **Tip** Does that sound familiar? Yes, it does! In Chapter 5 you learned about the concept of interpolation—tweening and interpolation are the same thing. Use "interpolation" when you're chatting with your programming friends and "tweening" with your animator friends.

In this chapter you'll take a deep look at how to implement tweening techniques for games from the ground up, including:

- Low-level formulas and procedures to tween any sprite properties (or any other values).

- **Easing**: Gradually making a sprite speed up to or slow down to a specific destination over time.

- **Motion paths**: Making a sprite move along straight or curved paths.

You'll also learn how to build some useful reusable components that will let you easily apply easing effects to any sprites in your game.

Easing and Interpolation

Easing is a tween effect that creates a smooth transition from one state or position to another. Imagine that you have a sprite that you want to animate from the left side of the canvas to the right side, over a period of 60 frames (one second). It should start slowly, gradually speed up, and then slow down to a stop. Figure 10-1 illustrates the effect you want to achieve.

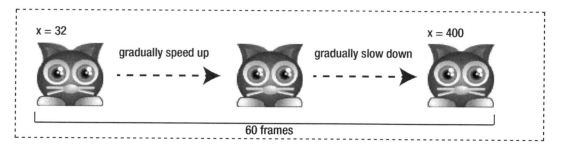

Figure 10-1. *Use easing to tween a sprite's position smoothly*

If you know only the sprite's startValue (32), its endValue (400), and the totalTime (60 frames) the animation should take, how can you work out the in-between positions?

The trick is to convert the time it takes for the sprite the move into a number between 0 and 1. This is called the **normalized time**. You can figure it out with this simple formula:

```
normalizedTime = currentTime / totalTime;
```

The normalizedTime is a magic number. You can use it to create a whole universe of easing functions to produce a huge range of different effects. All you need to do is take the normalizedTime value, drop it into a specialized easing function, and apply the result back to the sprite's position. You'll learn many of these easing functions in the pages ahead—but let's jump in quickly with a practical example.

Applying an Easing Function

The most useful easing function you need to know is called **smoothstep**. If you want a sprite to speed up and slow down in a natural-looking way, smoothstep is awaiting your command. This is it:

```
smoothstep = x => x * x * (3 - 2 * x);
```

Don't let it scare you! It's just an ordinary function that takes one argument, x, applies some math to it, and returns the result. All the easing functions you're going to learn will follow this same format.

What does the math in the smoothstep function do? It just describes a curve. Figure 10-2 shows what that curve looks like.

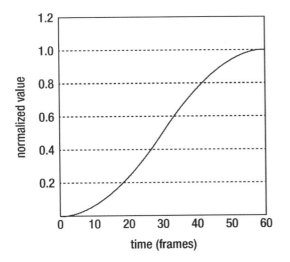

Figure 10-2. *The smoothstep function describes a pleasant curve*

If you apply that curve to the normalizedTime, you can control the flow of time to match the shape of the curve. Here's how to do that:

```
curvedTime = smoothstep(normalizedTime);
```

With this statement the time will start slow, speed up midway, and then slow down again near the end. The same way water takes on the shape of the container it's poured into, time takes on the shape of whatever easing function you use.

When you have that curved time value, you can use it to interpolate the sprite's *x* position with this calculation:

```
sprite.x = (endValue * curvedTime) + (startValue * (1 - curvedTime));
```

This formula uses curvedTime to figure out what the sprite's position should be at the current frame. It expands the normalized (0 to 1) value back into real numbers that the sprite can use. If you constantly update curvedTime in a loop, the sprite will speed up and slow down to match the curve you've applied.

■ **Tip**   This basic technique will let you interpolate any two values; it's not just for sprite properties!

Easing in Action

All this code I've shown you happens inside a loop. It could be any kind of loop (like a for loop), but because we're making games, we'll use a game loop. So let's see exactly what your code needs to look like to tween the cat sprite from the left to the right side of the canvas to produce the effect shown in Figure 10-1.

First, in your game's setup function, create the variables you'll need:

```
totalFrames = 60;
frameCounter = 0;
startValue = cat.x;
endValue = 400;
smoothstep = x => x * x * (3 - 2 * x);
```

The totalFrames value is the entire duration of the animation. The frameCounter will be used to count the elapsed frames so that you can stop the animation when it has reached the totalFrames. The startValue and endValue define the start and end points of the animation.

The gameLoop counts the frames and runs the code we looked at in the first section:

```
function gameLoop() {
  requestAnimationFrame(gameLoop);

  //Run the animation while `frameCounter` is less than `totalFrames`
  if (frameCounter < totalFrames) {

    //Find the normalized time value
    let normalizedTime = frameCounter / totalFrames;

    //Apply the easing function
    let curvedTime = smoothstep(normalizedTime);

    //Interpolate the sprite's x position based on the curved time
    cat.x = (endValue * curvedTime) + (startValue * (1 - curvedTime));

    //Add 1 to the frame counter
    frameCounter += 1;
  }

  //Render the canvas
  render(canvas);
}
```

And that's all! You can use this same technique to tween *any* sprite property—alpha, width, height, whatever. What would happen if you tweened the cat's scaleX and scaleY properties? Let's find out.

First, set the tween's start and end values. We want the cat to scale from 1 (normal size) to 2 (double size.)

```
startValue = 1;
endValue = 2;
```

Then replace the interpolation code with these two new lines:

```
cat.scaleX = (endValue * curvedTime) + (startValue * (1 - curvedTime));
cat.scaleY = (endValue * curvedTime) + (startValue * (1 - curvedTime));
```

Figure 10-3 shows what happens. The cat smoothly inflates to double size over the period of one second. It looks like magic, but it's just simple math!

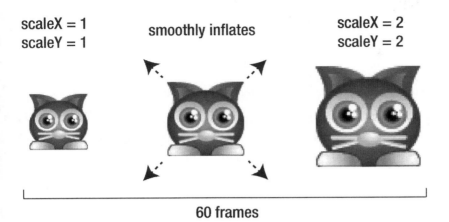

scaleX = 1
scaleY = 1

smoothly inflates

scaleX = 2
scaleY = 2

60 frames

Figure 10-3. *Smoothly inflate a sprite to double size by tweening its scale*

The Classic Easing Functions

You can completely change the style of the easing effect just by dropping in a different easing function. We used smoothstep in the first example, but there are plenty more formulas to choose from. Let's do a Greatest Hits tour of some of the most useful easing functions for making games.

Linear

The first stop on the tour is the simplest formula: **linear easing**. All it does is return the normalizedTime completely unchanged.

```
let linear = x => x;
```

It does nothing! It just returns the same value that you put in, unchanged. It's the same as if you didn't use an easing function at all; the result is just a straight line (Figure 10-4).

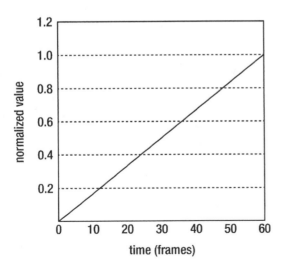

Figure 10-4. *Linear easing is just a straight line*

If you use linear easing to tween a sprite's position, the sprite will start moving at full speed, and then suddenly stop. There's no gradual speeding up or slowing down of the sprite. If that doesn't sound much fun, that's because it isn't! I've included linear easing here because it's the first step in learning to understand how these functions work, but my advice is not to use it in a real game. Nothing shouts "student game" louder than linear easing!

But luckily, linear easing has some siblings that are much more fun: **acceleration** and **deceleration**.

Acceleration

You can change boring linear easing into exciting acceleration by multiplying the `normalizedTime` value (x) by itself:

```
let acceleration = x => x * x;
```

This is an easing effect that starts slowly and then gradually speeds up, as shown by the graph in Figure 10-5.

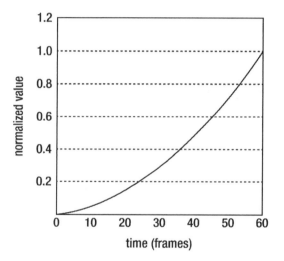

Figure 10-5. *Gradually speed up with acceleration*

When you multiply a value by itself, it's called a **squared** value. JavaScript has a convenient way to help you figure out squared values with the `Math.pow` function (pow stands for "power of"). `Math.pow` takes two arguments: the initial value, and the number of times you want to multiply the value by itself (the exponent).

```
Math.pow(initialValue, exponent);
```

That means you can alternatively write the `acceleration` function this way:

```
let acceleration = x => Math.pow(x, 2);
```

If you multiply the same value one more time, you get a **cubed** value. Here's the accelerationCubed function:

```
let accelerationCubed = x => Math.pow(x, 3);
```

The effect is similar to ordinary acceleration, but more extreme, as shown in Figure 10-6.

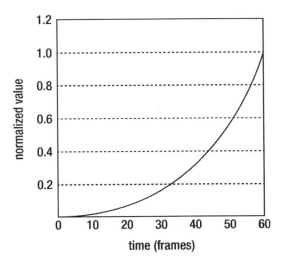

Figure 10-6. *Cubed acceleration is a more exaggerated effect*

Deceleration

Deceleration is the opposite of acceleration: it starts quickly and then gradually slows to a stop. The formula is just the reverse of the acceleration formula:

```
let deceleration = x => 1 - Math.pow(1 - x, 2);
```

And just as with acceleration, deceleration also has a cubed version, which exaggerates the effect:

```
let decelerationCubed = x => 1 - Math.pow(1 - x, 3);
```

Figure 10-7 is a graph comparing ordinary and cubed deceleration.

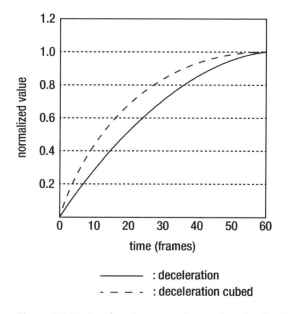

Figure 10-7. *Deceleration starts fast and gradually slows to a stop*

Smoothstep

The star of this whole show is the smoothstep formula. It's an extremely pleasing, natural-looking transition that works well with any kind of tweening. In addition to the standard formula you've already seen, smoothstep also has squared and cubed versions, which enhance the effect to additional degrees. Here are all three smoothstep functions, which you can see graphed in Figure 10-8.

```
let smoothstep = x => x * x * (3 - 2 * x);
let smoothstepSquared = x => Math.pow((x * x * (3 - 2 * x)), 2);
let smoothstepCubed = x => Math.pow((x * x * (3 - 2 * x)), 3);
```

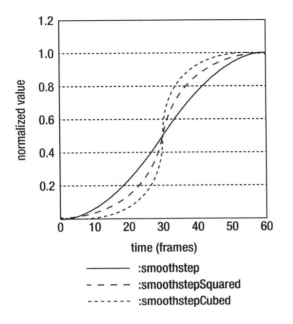

Figure 10-8. *Smoothstep produces an evenly balanced and natural-looking effect*

When in doubt, use smoothstepping! It can transform the appearance of any game from "student" to "professional."

Sine

A sine curve gives you a slightly more rounded deceleration effect. For a gentler acceleration, use an inverted sine.

```
let sine = x => Math.sin(x * Math.PI / 2);
let inverseSine = x => 1 - Math.sin((1 - x) * Math.PI / 2);
```

Figure 10-9 shows what these curves look like.

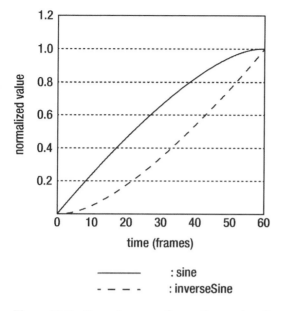

Figure 10-9. *Use a sine curve for gentler acceleration and deceleration*

There are also squared and cubed versions of both formulas, each of which exaggerates the curve proportionately:

```
let sineSquared = x => Math.pow(Math.sin(x * Math.PI / 2), 2);
let sineCubed = x => Math.pow(Math.sin(x * Math.PI / 2), 2);
let inverseSineSquared = x => 1 - Math.pow(Math.sin((1 - x) * Math.PI / 2), 2);
let inverseSineCubed = x => 1 - Math.pow(Math.sin((1 - x) * Math.PI / 2), 3);
```

All of these formulas actually just use half of the sine curve. If you use the full curve, you end up with a shape that's almost identical to smoothstep.

```
let sineComplete = x => 0.5 - Math.cos(-x * Math.PI) * 0.5;
```

However, this approach is much more computationally expensive than the smoothstep formula, so there's generally no need to use it.

Spline

So far all the formulas we've seen just tween a value between two points: 0 and 1. But sometimes it's useful to introduce two more points that extend just outside this range. This lets you create a tween that adds a little bounce or wobble before the value settles. You can do this with the help of a mathematical curve called a **spline**. You can think of a spline as a line which is curved along points that you define.

There are dozens of formulas you can use to generate splines, but an especially efficient one for games is the Catmull-Rom spline. Here's the formula:

```
let spline = (t, a, b, c, d) => {
  return 0.5 * (
    (2 * b) +
    (-a + c) * t +
    (2 * a - 5 * b + 4 * c - d) * t * t +
    (-a + 3 * b - 3 * c + d) * t * t * t
  );
}
```

Neither you nor I need to know why this formula works— we just need to send a big "Thank You!" to Catmull and Rom for figuring it out for us. All you really need to know is that the formula generates four points that you can control. The argument t is the normalizedTime, and a, b, c, and d are the spline's four points.

Here's how to use the spline with our current tweening setup:

```
let curvedTime = spline(normalizedTime, 10, 0, 1, -10);
```

The last four arguments represent the four points of the spline. The middle two, 0 and 1, represent the base tweening range:

```
10, 0, 1, -10
```

In general, don't change 0 and 1 to any other values, because our tweening system uses a normalized time value that's also between 0 and 1.

The numbers you should change are the first and last points, 10 and –10.

```
10, 0, 1, -10
```

Those are the **control points**. They determine how much the tween diverges outside the 0 to 1 range. The first number, 10, is the divergence at the beginning of the tween, and the last number, –10, is the divergence at the end. Giving them higher values makes the effect more dramatic, and giving them lower values makes it less dramatic.

Figure 10-10 shows what this spline looks like when it's graphed.

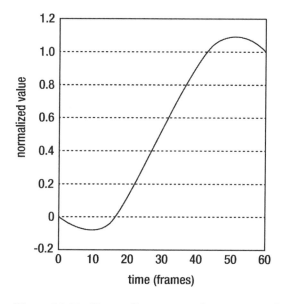

Figure 10-10. *Use a spline to tween the sprite outside the 0 to 1 range*

You can see on this graph that the curve starts at 0 and then moves to almost –0.1. It then curves up to about 1.1 before settling at 1.

What effect does this have when you tween a sprite? Figure 10-11 illustrates what happens when you use a spline to tween the cat's *x* position. It's a sort of elastic bounce effect. The sprite swings to the left, rebounds to the right, overshoots the end point by a bit, and then settles to its destination. This happens only on the *x* axis, so the cat moves back and forth along a straight line.

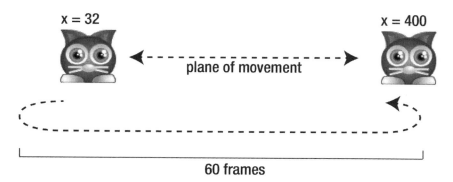

Figure 10-11. *Apply a spline to a sprite's position for an elastic bounce effect*

You can create a range of different effects by changing the values of the spline's control points: the first point value and the last point value. For example, if you change the first point to 0 and keep the last one at –10, the elastic bounce will happen only at the end of the cat's movement.

```
let curvedTime = spline(normalizedTime, 0, 0, 1, -10);
```

In your day-to-day game design, you're rarely going to need to use a spline for most of your tweening. But it's essential for some kinds of special effects. Later in this chapter you'll learn how to use a spline to produce a dramatic jelly-wobble effect.

Weighted Average

If your destination value is constantly changing each frame, consider using the `weightedAverage` function. Its effect is the same as the easing formula you learned in Chapter 6.

```
let weightedAverage = (p, d, w) => ((p * (w - 1)) + d) / w;
```

The argument p is the sprite property value, d is the destination value, and w is the amount of **weight** to add to the effect. The weight determines how slowly or quickly the easing happens. Weight values between 5 and 50 are a good place to start; you can then just tweak that number to fine-tune how the easing feels.

Unlike the other tweening functions in this chapter, `weightedAverage` doesn't require you to calculate the normalized time or apply any curve function to it. Just drop it anywhere inside your game loop.

```
function gameLoop() {
  requestAnimationFrame(gameLoop);
  cat.x = weightedAverage(cat.x, endValue, 30);
  render(canvas);
}
```

Yes, it's just another way of calculating simple easing.

Movement Along a Curve

So far the curves we've looked at have all helped modify how a sprite's property changes over time. But you can also use a curve to modify how a sprite moves through space. The Bezier curve is perfect for doing this. Here's the classic cubic Bezier formula:

```
function cubicBezier(t, a, b, c, d) {
    var t2 = t * t;
    var t3 = t2 * t;
    return a
      + (-a * 3 + t * (3 * a - a * t)) * t
      + (3 * b + t * (-6 * b + b * 3 * t)) * t
      + (c * 3 - c * 3 * t) * t2 + d * t3;
}
```

It's just a type of spline with four points that you can set. The argument t is the `normalizedTime`, and a, b, c, and d are the spline's four points.

You can think of a Bezier curve as a straight line that extends between its start and end points, a and d. Points b and c are control points that determine how much to bend the line. You can think of b and c as high-powered magnets that tug at the line to warp it. The shape of the Bezier curve depends on where you place the b and c points. Figure 10-12 illustrates how the b and c control points warp a line running between a and d.

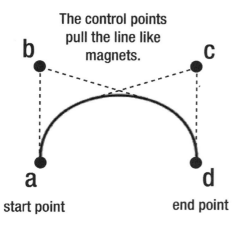

The control points pull the line like magnets.

b

c

a
start point

d
end point

Figure 10-12. *A Bezier curve*

With the tweening system we've set in place, you can easily make a sprite move along this curve. Just apply the return value of the cubicBezier function to the sprite's *x/y* position. And, as a bonus, you can optionally apply any of the easing functions to it as well. Here's how:

```
let curvedTime = smoothstep(normalizedTime);
cat.x = cubicBezier(curvedTime, startX, bX, cX, endX);
cat.y = cubicBezier(curvedTime, startY, bY, cY, endY);
```

If you run this code inside the tweening engine we wrote at the beginning of the chapter, the cat will smoothly arc from the start to the end point.

Here's the complete gameLoop that achieves this effect, and Figure 10-13 illustrates the result.

```
function gameLoop() {
  requestAnimationFrame(gameLoop);

  //Run the animation while `frameCounter` is less than `totalFrames`
  if (frameCounter < totalFrames) {

    //Find the normalized time value
    let normalizedTime = frameCounter / totalFrames;

    //Optionally apply an easing formula
    let curvedTime = smoothstep(normalizedTime);

    //Make the sprite follow a Bezier curve
    cat.x = cubicBezier(curvedTime, 25, 100, 175, 225);
    cat.y = cubicBezier(curvedTime, 250, 50, 0, 250);

    //Add 1 to the frame counter
    frameCounter += 1;
  }

  //Render the canvas
  render(canvas);
}
```

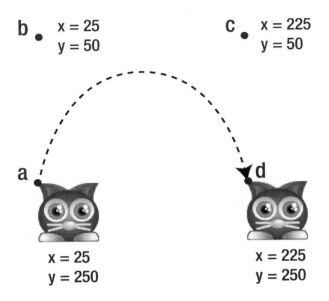

Figure 10-13. *Make a sprite follow a curve*

If you don't want to apply any easing, just supply the cubicBezier function with the raw normalizedTime instead of the curvedTime value as the first argument.

Building Tweening Components

You now know how the mechanics of tweening work, but how do you use it for games? That's a lot of code just to move a sprite between two points, and what if you want to move hundreds of them? You need a reusable system to create and manage tweens, so that's what we're going to create next.

You can think of tweens as game components that are somewhere between particle effects and keyframe animations. Like particles, they need to be updated by the game loop, and you could have dozens of tweens becoming active or inactive at any time. Like keyframe animations, tweens have duration, so they can be played, paused, and possibly reversed or looped over time. In this section we're going to build a set of low-level tools for building tweens so that you can easily build your own custom library of tween effects for games.

■ **Note** You'll find all the working code for this section in the library/tween.js file in the book's source files.

The tweens Array

Just as with particles and interactive buttons, your games will need an array that stores all the active tweens. Let's keep it simple and call it tweens.

```
export let tweens = [];
```

Then your game loop will need to loop through the tweens in the array and call an update method on each one:

```
if (tweens.length > 0) {
  for(let i = tweens.length - 1; i >= 0; i--) {
    let tween = tweens[i];
    if (tween) tween.update();
  }
}
```

This is the same system we used for our particle engine in Chapter 8. And, just as with particles, the code loops through the tweens in reverse order so that we can painlessly remove a tween from the array at any time without messing up the loop index counter.

You'll soon see what those tween objects are and what the update method does.

The Easing Library

In the first part of this chapter I showed you how to use 16 easing functions like smoothstep, linear, and spline. To make them easy to use, we're going add them as properties of an object called ease. That will let us use code that looks like this to access any of those functions:

```
ease.smoothstep(normalizedTime);
```

Or, because the function is a property of the ease object, we can optionally call the function by its string name:

```
ease["smoothstep"](normalizedTime);
```

That's a neat trick, which, as you'll see, will save us from having to write a lot of repetitive code later.

The ease object, which stores the easing functions, is just a plain old object literal with the functions as properties. Here's an abridged version of the ease object that shows how the first two functions are added as properties.

```
let ease = {
  linear(x) {return x;},
  smoothstep(x) {return x * x * (3 - 2 * x);},
  //... the rest of the easing functions follow the same pattern...
};
```

The rest of the code in the ease object follows exactly the same model for the remaining 14 functions. We now have a handy library of easing functions that will be easy to apply.

Creating Tween Objects

The next step is to build a flexible, low-level function called tweenProperty that we can use to tween any property of any sprite. I call it "low-level" because we're going to use it as a building block for creating easier-to-use, specialized tween effects.

Before I show you the code, here's how you'll be able to use the tweenProperty function:

```
tweenProperty(
  sprite,          //The sprite
  "x",             //The property you want to tween (a string)
  100,             //The start value
  200,             //the end value
  60,              //The tween duration, in frames
  ["smoothstep"],  //An array that defines the easing type (a string)
  true,            //Yoyo? True or false
  1000             //The delay, in milliseconds, before the tween yoyos
);
```

Notice that the easing type is listed as a string inside an array:

```
["smoothstep"]
```

All the easing types will use this same format, except for spline. If you want to use a spline, provide two additional values inside the array—the start magnitude and the end magnitude:

```
["spline" -10, 10]
```

Those two numbers refer to the spline control points that you can use to modify the elasticity. You'll see how they're used in the code ahead.

The seventh argument in the tweenProperty function is a Boolean value called yoyo. If yoyo is true, the tween will reverse its animation in a continuous loop—just like a yo-yo. The last argument is a number in milliseconds that determines how long the animation should pause before the yo-yo repeats.

The tweenProperty function returns a tween object.

```
let tween = tweenProperty(/*...arguments...*/);
```

The tween object has play and pause methods that you can use to control the tween, and a Boolean property called playing that tells you whether the tween is currently playing:

```
tween.play();
tween.pause();
tween.playing
```

You can optionally define the tween object's onComplete method with any code that should run when the tween is finished:

```
tween.onComplete = () => {
  //This code will run when the tween finishes
};
```

(If your tween is yo-yoing, onComplete will be called at the end of every yo-yo segment.)

The tween object also has an update function, which contains the code that should run inside the game loop. When the tweenProperty function creates the tween, it pushes the tween object into the global tweens array. The tween objects are made to animate by looping through the tweens array and calling the update method on every tween, in the code we looked at earlier.

The Complete tweenProperty Function

Here's the complete tweenProperty function to create and return tween objects. You'll see that most of the code is a hybrid between the addStatePlayer function we used to control sprite keyframe animations and the particleEffect function we used to make particles. The comments explain most of the details, but there are some new features that I'll explain in greater depth after the code listing.

```
export function tweenProperty(
  sprite,                       //The sprite object
  property,                     //The property to tween (a string)
  startValue,                   //Tween start value
  endValue,                     //Tween end value
  totalFrames,                  //Duration in frames
  type = ["smoothstep"],        //The easing type
  yoyo = false,                 //Yoyo?
  delayBeforeRepeat = 0         //Delay in milliseconds before repeating
) {

  //Create the tween object
  let o = {};

  //If the tween is a spline, set the
  //start and end magnitude values
  if(type[0] === "spline" ){
    o.startMagnitude = type[1];
    o.endMagnitude = type[2];
  }

  //Use `o.start` to make a new tween using the current
  //end point values
  o.start = (startValue, endValue) => {

    //Clone the start and end values so that any possible references to sprite
    //properties are converted to ordinary numbers
    o.startValue = JSON.parse(JSON.stringify(startValue));
    o.endValue = JSON.parse(JSON.stringify(endValue));
    o.playing = true;
    o.totalFrames = totalFrames;
    o.frameCounter = 0;

    //Add the tween to the global `tweens` array. The `tweens` array is
    //updated on each frame
    tweens.push(o);
  };

  //Call `o.start` to start the tween
  o.start(startValue, endValue);

  //The `update` method will be called on each frame by the game loop.
  //This is what makes the tween move
  o.update = () => {

    let time, curvedTime;
```

```
  if (o.playing) {

    //If the elapsed frames are less than the total frames,
    //use the tweening formulas to move the sprite
    if (o.frameCounter < o.totalFrames) {

      //Find the normalized value
      let normalizedTime = o.frameCounter / o.totalFrames;

      //Select the correct easing function from the
      //`ease` object's library of easing functions

      //If it's not a spline, use one of the ordinary easing functions
      if (type[0] !== "spline") {
        curvedTime = ease[type](normalizedTime);
      }

      //If it's a spline, use the `spline` function and apply the
      //two additional `type` array values as the spline's start and
      //end points
      else {
        curvedTime = ease.spline(normalizedTime, o.startMagnitude, 0, 1, o.endMagnitude);
      }

      //Interpolate the sprite's property based on the curve
      sprite[property] = (o.endValue * curvedTime) + (o.startValue * (1 - curvedTime));

      o.frameCounter += 1;
    }

    //When the tween has finished playing, run the end tasks
    else {
      o.end();
    }
  }
};

//The `end` method will be called when the tween is finished
o.end = () => {

  //Set `playing` to `false`
  o.playing = false;

  //Call the tween's `onComplete` method, if it's been assigned
  //by the user in the main program
  if (o.onComplete) o.onComplete();

  //Remove the tween from the `tweens` array
  tweens.splice(tweens.indexOf(o), 1);
```

```
  //If the tween's `yoyo` property is `true`, create a new tween
  //using the same values, but use the current tween's `startValue`
  //as the next tween's `endValue`
  if (yoyo) {
    wait(delayBeforeRepeat).then(() => {
      o.start(o.endValue, o.startValue);
    });
  }
};

  //Play and pause methods
  o.play = () => o.playing = true;
  o.pause = () => o.playing = false;

  //Return the tween object
  return o;
}
```

One important thing the tweenProperty does is convert the startValue and endValue into strings, and then back into numbers, before assigning them to the tween object:

```
o.startValue = JSON.parse(JSON.stringify(startValue));
o.endValue = JSON.parse(JSON.stringify(endValue));
```

This ensures that startValue and endValue are pure numbers, and not references that point back to properties on sprites. Sprite property values might change while a tween is animating, and if they do, they could mess up your tween. For example, let's imagine you initialize the tweenProperty function's start value (the third argument) with cat.x , as highlighted in the code below:

```
let tween = tweenProperty(cat, "x", cat.x ... )
```

cat.x is not a number! It's just a reference that points back to the value of x on the cat. If cat.x changes while the tween is animating (which it will), the tween object will read the cat's current *x* position and not its start position. For the tween to work properly, *you only want the start position value.*

Using the JSON.parse and JSON.stringify methods is a well-worn hack to help solve this problem. JSON.stringify converts any value into a string (a process called **serializing**). Then JSON.parse converts it back into a number (a process called **deserializing**). That conversion process obliterates any references, so you're left with just a pure number. This is an insurance policy that protects you against accidentally using references for the tween's start and end values.

■ **Note**   Making an exact duplicate of an object that doesn't contain reference pointers to values on the original object is called **cloning**. The current version of JavaScript (ES6) doesn't have a dedicated function to clone objects, although future versions might.

Now that we've written the tweenProperty function, how do we use it? The purpose of this function is not to use it directly in your game code. Instead, it's intended to be a low-level tool that you can use to build higher-level, useful tween functions for your sprites. Let's find out how to do that next.

Alpha Tweening

Now that we have a convenient way to tween single properties on sprites, there are three high-level functions that are easy for us to make right away: fadeIn, fadeOut, and pulse.

fadeIn

The fadeIn function lets you fade a sprite in by tweening its alpha property to 1:

```
export function fadeIn(sprite, frames = 60) {
  return tweenProperty(
    sprite, "alpha", sprite.alpha, 1, frames, ["sine"]
  );
}
```

Use it in your game code this way:

```
let fadeInTween = fadeIn(anySprite);
```

fadeOut

The opposite effect, fadeOut, tweens the sprite's alpha to 0:

```
export function fadeOut(sprite, frames = 60) {
  return tweenProperty(
    sprite, "alpha", sprite.alpha, 0, frames, ["sine"]
  );
}
```

Use it this way:

```
let fadeOutTween = fadeOut(anySprite);
```

These two effects are perfect for scene transitions or for making sprites appear or disappear.

pulse

The pulse function makes the sprite continually oscillate between low and high alpha values. This is a great effect to use to draw attention to a sprite.

```
export function pulse(sprite, frames = 60, minAlpha = 0) {
  return tweenProperty(
    sprite, "alpha", sprite.alpha, minAlpha, frames, ["smoothstep"], true
  );
}
```

The third argument, minAlpha, is the lowest alpha value to use before tweening back up to the original value. So if you just want the sprite to tween down to an alpha of 0.3, initialize the pulse function with this statement:

```
let pulseTween = pulse(anySprite, 120, 0.3);
```

If you set the frames argument to a low value, you can create a flashing effect.

All of these effects tween a single property, the sprite's alpha. But what if you want to create a more complex effect that requires multiple property tweens?

Tweening Multiple Properties

We need to build one more low-level component! We're going to build a new function called makeTween that will let you create complex effects by combining as many single-property tweens as you need. Here's how you'll be able to use it:

```
let complexTween = makeTween([
  [/* A property you want to tween */],
  [/* Another property you want to tween */],
  [/* Yet another property you want to tween */]
]);
```

makeTween accepts a single argument, which is an array containing subarrays of the properties you want to tween. The information you put in the subarrays is the same information you need to supply to the tweenProperty function we created earlier.

Here's how you could use makeTween to create a complex high-level function called slide, which will tween a sprite's *x/y* position to any other *x/y* position on the canvas.

```
export function slide(
  sprite,
  endX,
  endY,
  frames = 60,
  type = ["smoothstep"],
  yoyo = false,
  delayBeforeRepeat = 0
) {
  return makeTween([

    //The x axis tween
    [sprite, "x", sprite.x, endX, frames, type, yoyo, delayBeforeRepeat],

    //The y axis tween
    [sprite, "y", sprite.y, endY, frames, type, yoyo, delayBeforeRepeat]
  ]);
}
```

You can see that the data in the array is exactly the same as the arguments needed to initialize the tweenProperty function. You might use the slide function in your game code this way:

```
let catSlide = slide(cat, 400, 32, 60, ["smoothstep"], true, 0);
```

This will make the cat sprite smoothly slide back and forth from its current position to an *x/y* position of 400/30, over 60 frames.

All tweens have a user-definable onComplete method that will run when the tween is finished. Here's how you could use onComplete on the catSlide tween to write a message to the console when the tween is done:

```
catSlide.onComplete = () => console.log("Cat slide finished!");
```

The makeTween Function

The makeTween function will accept any number of tween arrays as arguments, so you can use it to build some really complex effects. It's essentially just a wrapper that uses tweenProperty to create each tween and keeps references to each tween object inside its own internal array. It also gives you higher-level play and pause methods that control all the tweens in the array, and it lets you assign an onComplete method that will run when all the tweens in the array have finished animating.

Here's the complete makeTween function that does all this.

```
function makeTween(tweensToAdd) {

  //Create an object to manage the tweens
  let o = {};

  //Create an internal `tweens` array to store the new tweens
  o.tweens = [];

  //Make a new tween for each array
  tweensToAdd.forEach(tweenPropertyArguments => {

    //Use the tween property arguments to make a new tween
    let newTween = tweenProperty(...tweenPropertyArguments);

    //Push the new tween into this object's internal `tweens` array
    o.tweens.push(newTween);
  });

  //Add a counter to keep track of the
  //number of tweens that have completed their actions
  let completionCounter = 0;

  //`o.completed` will be called each time one of the tweens finishes
  o.completed = () => {

    //Add 1 to the `completionCounter`
    completionCounter += 1;

    //If all tweens have finished, call the user-defined `onComplete`
    //method, if it's been assigned. Reset the `completionCounter`
    if (completionCounter === o.tweens.length) {
      if (o.onComplete) o.onComplete();
      completionCounter = 0;
    }
  };
```

391

```
//Add `onComplete` methods to all tweens
o.tweens.forEach(tween => {
  tween.onComplete = () => o.completed();
});

//Add pause and play methods to control all the tweens
o.pause = () => {
  o.tweens.forEach(tween => {
    tween.playing = false;
  });
};
o.play = () => {
  o.tweens.forEach(tween => {
    tween.playing = true;
  });
};

//Return the tween object
return o;
}
```

Because makeTween manages multiple tweens, it needs to know when all of them have finished their tasks. The code uses a counter variable called completionCounter to keep track of this, and initializes it to 0:

```
let completionCounter = 0;
```

After it has created the tweens, makeTween loops through all the tweens in its array and adds onComplete methods to them:

```
o.tweens.forEach(tween => {
  tween.onComplete = () => o.completed();
});
```

When they're done, the tweens will call a method called completed. The completed method adds 1 to the completionCounter. If the value of completionCounter matches the length of the internal tweens array, then you know all the tweens are finished. The code then runs an optional, user-defined onComplete method, if it exists.

```
o.completed = () => {

  //Add 1 to the `completionCounter`
  completionCounter += 1;

  //If all tweens have finished, call the user-defined `onComplete`
  //method, if it's been assigned in the main program.
  //Then reset the `completionCounter`
  if (completionCounter === o.tweens.length) {
    if (o.onComplete) o.onComplete();
    completionCounter = 0;
  }
};
```

The `removeTween` Function

Now that we have a way to make multiple tweens, we also need a way to remove them. The last bit of plumbing we need to add is a universal removeTween function:

```
export function removeTween(tweenObject) {

  //Remove the tween if `tweenObject` doesn't have any nested
  //tween objects
  if(!tweenObject.tweens) {
    tweenObject.pause();
    tweens.splice(tweens.indexOf(tweenObject), 1);

  //Otherwise, remove the nested tween objects
  } else {
    tweenObject.pause();
    tweenObject.tweens.forEach(element => {
      tweens.splice(tweens.indexOf(element), 1);
    });
  }
}
```

Use removeTween to remove any tween from a game, with this syntax:

```
removeTween(tween);
```

Finally, we can now start making some fun stuff!

Easy Easing!

We now have all the tools we need to create some easy-to-use high-level tweening functions that will work with any sprites. Here's a quick round-up of some of most useful functions for a wide variety of games. If you need anything more specialized, just use these functions as models for creating your own.

slide

If you need to make a sprite move between any two *x/y* points, use the slide function.

```
let slideTween = slide(
  anySprite,              //The sprite
  400,                    //Destination x
  32,                     //Destination y
  60,                     //Duration in frames
  ["smoothstep"],         //Easing type
  true,                   //yoyo?
  0                       //Delay, in milliseconds, before repeating
);
```

You saw the code for the slide function in the previous section, and Figure 10-14 illustrates what it does.

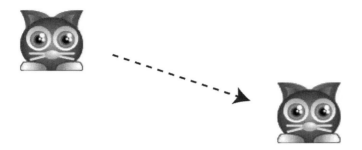

Figure 10-14. *Use* slide *to make a sprite move smoothly to any point*

breathe

By tweening the scaleX and scaleY properties back and forth in a yo-yo loop, you can make a sprite look like it's breathing (Figure 10-15).

Figure 10-15. *Tween the scaleX and scaleY properties to make a breathing sprite*

Here's the breathe function that does this.

```
export function breathe(
  sprite, endScaleX, endScaleY,
  frames, yoyo = true, delayBeforeRepeat = 0
) {
  return makeTween([

    //Create the scaleX tween
    [
      sprite, "scaleX", sprite.scaleX, endScaleX,
      frames, ["smoothstepSquared"], yoyo, delayBeforeRepeat
    ],
```

```
  //Create the scaleY tween
  [
    sprite, "scaleY", sprite.scaleY, endScaleY,
    frames, ["smoothstepSquared"], yoyo, delayBeforeRepeat
  ]
]);
}
```

Notice that breathe uses the smoothstepSquared function for a more pronounced effect: Use it in your game code to make a sprite breathe, as in this example:

```
let breathingTween = breathe(anySprite, 1.2, 1.2, 60);
```

scale

The breathe function scales the sprite up and down in a continuous yo-yo tween. But if you want the scaling effect to happen only once, use the scale function:

```
export function scale(sprite, endScaleX, endScaleY, frames = 60) {
  return makeTween([

    //Create the scaleX tween
    [
      sprite, "scaleX", sprite.scaleX, endScaleX,
      frames, ["smoothstep"], false
    ],

    //Create the scaleY tween
    [
      sprite, "scaleY", sprite.scaleY, endScaleY,
      frames, ["smoothstep"], false
    ]
  ]);
}
```

It's almost exactly the same as the breathe function, except that the yoyo argument is set to false. You can use scale to smoothly scale a sprite up or down, this way:

```
let scaleUpTween = scale(anySprite, 2, 2);
let scaleDownTween = scale(anySprite, 0.2, 0.2);
```

strobe

By rapidly yo-yoing the scale and using a spline, you can create a psychedelic strobe effect.

```
export function strobe(
  sprite, scaleFactor = 1.3, startMagnitude = 10, endMagnitude = 20,
  frames = 10, yoyo = true, delayBeforeRepeat = 0
) {
  return makeTween([
```

```
//Create the scaleX tween
[
  sprite, "scaleX", sprite.scaleX, scaleFactor, frames,
  ["spline", startMagnitude, endMagnitude],
  yoyo, delayBeforeRepeat
],

//Create the scaleY tween
[
  sprite, "scaleY", sprite.scaleY, scaleFactor, frames,
  ["spline", startMagnitude, endMagnitude],
  yoyo, delayBeforeRepeat
]
]);
}
```

You can see in this code how the "spline" easing type is set, along with its start and end magnitude values:

```
["spline", startMagnitude, endMagnitude]
```

Here's how to make a sprite strobe:

```
let strobeTween = strobe(anySprite, 1.3, 10, 20, 10);
```

It's a kind of flashing scaling effect that might give you a headache if you let it go on for too long. (You'll find a working example of the strobe function, as along with the rest of these effects, in the chapter's source files.)

wobble

Last but not least: the wobble function. Imagine a huge plate of the wobbliest jelly pudding you've ever seen in your life. Then, poke it with your finger. That's the effect of the wobble function. It works by scaling the sprite inversely on the *x* and *y* axes with the help of a spline. The sprite starts off extremely wobbly, and then gradually becomes less wobbly with each repetition until it settles back to normal. Figure 10-16 illustrates the effect.

Figure 10-16. *Make a sprite wobble like a plate of jelly*

wobble is the most complex of these tween functions because it does a little more work behind the scenes. It adds an onComplete method to both the *x* and *y* scale tweens so that a little bit of friction is added to the wobble each time it repeats. That's what gradually slows it down. Friction values between 0.96 (less wobbly) and 0.99 (more wobbly) are a good range to try. When the tweens' end values drop below 1, the effect is finished and the tweens are removed.

```
export function wobble(
  sprite,
  scaleFactorX = 1.2,
  scaleFactorY = 1.2,
  frames = 10,
  xStartMagnitude = 10,
  xEndMagnitude = 10,
  yStartMagnitude = -10,
  yEndMagnitude = -10,
  friction = 0.98,
  yoyo = true,
  delayBeforeRepeat = 0
) {

  let o = makeTween([

    //Create the scaleX tween
    [
      sprite, "scaleX", sprite.scaleX, scaleFactorX, frames,
      ["spline", xStartMagnitude, xEndMagnitude],
      yoyo, delayBeforeRepeat
    ],

    //Create the scaleY tween
    [
      sprite, "scaleY", sprite.scaleY, scaleFactorY, frames,
      ["spline", yStartMagnitude, yEndMagnitude],
      yoyo, delayBeforeRepeat
    ]
  ]);

  //Add some friction to the `endValue` at the end of each tween
  o.tweens.forEach(tween => {
    tween.onComplete = () => {

      //Add friction if the `endValue` is greater than 1
      if (tween.endValue > 1) {
        tween.endValue *= friction;
```

```
        //Set the `endValue` to 1 when the effect is finished and
        //remove the tween from the global `tweens` array
        if (tween.endValue <= 1) {
          tween.endValue = 1;
          removeTween(tween);
        }
      }
    };
  });

  return o;
}
```

Here's how to make a sprite wobble in your game:

```
let wobbleTween = wobble(anySprite, 1.2, 1.2);
```

Change the *x* and *y* scale factors (the second and third arguments) for a more dramatic effect.

I discovered the strobe and wobble effects completely by accident while playing around with different tween values. You can do the same! Use makeTween to compose multiple tweens that change different sprite properties in unexpected ways—you might surprise yourself with what you come up with!

Using Waypoints to Follow a Motion Path

In the previous section you learned how to use the slide function to make a sprite smoothly tween its position. But what if you want to make a sprite follow a route of connected paths? You can connect a series of slide functions together to make a sprite walk a path around the canvas.

To make this work you need to connect an array of *x/y* points; each point is called a **waypoint**. Each time the sprite reaches a waypoint, call the slide function and move the sprite to the next point. For example, imagine that you want a sprite to follow a rectangular path, as illustrated in Figure 10-17.

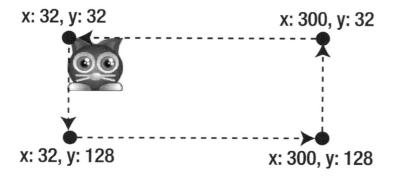

Figure 10-17. *Use waypoints to make a sprite follow a path*

You can define a 2D array of waypoints to describe the path this way:

```
[
  [32, 32],      //First x/y point
  [32, 128],     //Next x/y point
  [300, 128],    //Next x/y point
  [300, 32],     //Next x/y point
  [32, 32]       //Last x/y point
],
```

Because this is a closed path, the last point is the same as the first, but you can also keep the path open.

To make this work, you need to build a function that reads those waypoints and makes the sprite move between each adjacent point. When the movement between each point is finished, you need to make the sprite move between the next two points until it reaches the last one.

walkPath

You can use a new function called walkPath to help you do this. It does in code exactly what I've described in theory. Before we look at the details of how walkPath works, let's find out how to use it. Here's the code you'd need to use to make the cat sprite follow the rectangular path in Figure 10-17.

```
let catPath = walkPath(
  cat,                   //The sprite

  //An array of x/y waypoints to connect in sequence
  [
    [32, 32],            //First x/y point
    [32, 128],           //Next x/y point
    [300, 128],          //Next x/y point
    [300, 32],           //Next x/y point
    [32, 32]             //Last x/y point
  ],

  300,                   //Total duration in frames
  ["smoothstep"],        //Easing type
  true,                  //Should the path loop?
  true,                  //Should the path yoyo?
  1000                   //Delay in milliseconds between segments
);
```

You can see that the second argument is a 2D array that lists the path waypoints. If loop (the fifth argument) is true, the sprite will restart at the beginning of the path when it reaches the end. If yoyo (the sixth argument) is true, the sprite will walk the path in reverse when it reaches the end. (If you set yoyo to true and loop to false, the sprite will just go from the start to the end of the path and return, without repeating.) The final argument is the delay in milliseconds that the sprite should wait between each section of the path.

Here's the complete walkPath function that makes this work. It uses makeTween to create a tween between each waypoint in the 2D array. When the tween is finished a new tween is created between the last point in the previous array and the next point in the new array. When the last point is reached, the path is optionally looped and yo-yoed.

```
export function walkPath(
  sprite,                    //The sprite
  originalPathArray,         //A 2D array of waypoints
  totalFrames = 300,         //The duration, in frames
  type = ["smoothstep"],     //The easing type
  loop = false,              //Should the animation loop?
  yoyo = false,              //Should the direction reverse?
  delayBetweenSections = 0   //Delay, in milliseconds, between sections
) {

  //Clone the path array so that any possible references to sprite
  //properties are converted into ordinary numbers
  let pathArray = JSON.parse(JSON.stringify(originalPathArray));

  //Figure out the duration, in frames, of each path section by
  //dividing the `totalFrames` by the length of the `pathArray`
  let frames = totalFrames / pathArray.length;

  //Set the current point to 0, which will be the first waypoint
  let currentPoint = 0;

  //Make the first path using the internal `makePath` function (below)
  let tween = makePath(currentPoint);

  //The `makePath` function creates a single tween between two points and
  //then schedules the next path to be made after it

  function makePath(currentPoint) {

    //Use the `makeTween` function to tween the sprite's x and y position
    let tween = makeTween([

      //Create the x axis tween between the first x value in the
      //current point and the x value in the following point
      [
        sprite,
        "x",
        pathArray[currentPoint][0],
        pathArray[currentPoint + 1][0],
        frames,
        type
      ],

      //Create the y axis tween in the same way
      [
        sprite,
        "y",
        pathArray[currentPoint][1],
        pathArray[currentPoint + 1][1],
```

```
      frames,
      type
    ]
]);

//When the tween is complete, advance the `currentPoint` by 1.
//Add an optional delay between path segments, and then make the
//next connecting path
tween.onComplete = () => {

  //Advance to the next point
  currentPoint += 1;

  //If the sprite hasn't reached the end of the
  //path, tween the sprite to the next point
  if (currentPoint < pathArray.length - 1) {
    wait(delayBetweenSections).then(() => {
      tween = makePath(currentPoint);
    });
  }

  //If we've reached the end of the path, optionally
  //loop and yoyo it
  else {

    //Reverse the path if `loop` is `true`
    if (loop) {

      //Reverse the array if `yoyo` is `true`. Use JavaScript's built-in
      //array `reverse` method to do this
      if (yoyo) pathArray.reverse();

      //Optionally wait before restarting
      wait(delayBetweenSections).then(() => {

        //Reset the `currentPoint` to 0 so that we can
        //restart at the first point
        currentPoint = 0;

        //Set the sprite to the first point
        sprite.x = pathArray[0][0];
        sprite.y = pathArray[0][1];

        //Make the first new path
        tween = makePath(currentPoint);

        //... and so it continues!
      });
    }
  }
};
```

401

```
//Return the path tween to the main function
    return tween;
}

//Pass the tween back to the main program
    return tween;
}
```

By tweaking the parameters of the makePath function, you can achieve a versatile variety of motion path effects that will stand you well for all kinds of games. But makePath only moves a path made from straight line segments. What if you want a sprite to follow a curved path?

walkCurve

Instead of using an array of *x/y* waypoints, you can describe a sprite's path by using an array of Bezier curves. Figure 10-18 shows a sprite following a path made from two Bezier curves. The first curve makes the sprite arc toward the bottom of the canvas, and second curve makes it arc back to its starting point.

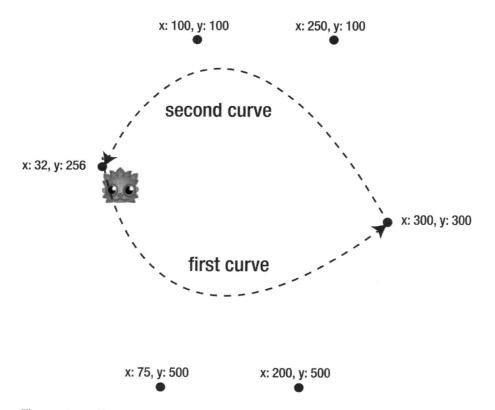

Figure 10-18. *Use Bezier curves to make a sprite follow a curved motion path*

Here's the array of two Bezier curves that describe the motion path shown in Figure 10-18:

```
[
  //Curve 1
  [[hedgehog.x, hedgehog.y],[75, 500],[200, 500],[300, 300]],

  //Curve 2
  [[300, 300],[250, 100],[100, 100],[hedgehog.x, hedgehog.y]]
]
```

The next step is to create a function called walkCurve that makes a sprite follow the path described by those Bezier curves. The walkCurve function is very similar to the walkPath function—the only real difference is that the waypoint data is replaced by curve data. Here's how you can use the walkCurve function to make a sprite follow the path in Figure 10-18:

```
let hedgehogPath = walkCurve(
  hedgehog,                 //The sprite

  //An array of Bezier curve points that
  //you want to connect in sequence
  [
    [[hedgehog.x, hedgehog.y],[75, 500],[200, 500],[300, 300]],
    [[300, 300],[250, 100],[100, 100],[hedgehog.x, hedgehog.y]]
  ],

  300,                      //Total duration, in frames
  ["smoothstep"],           //Easing type
  true,                     //Should the path loop?
  true,                     //Should the path yoyo?
  1000                      //Delay in milliseconds between segments
);
```

Here's the complete walkCurve function with comments that describe how it works.

```
export function walkCurve(
  sprite,                   //The sprite
  pathArray,                //2D array of Bezier curves
  totalFrames = 300,        //The duration, in frames
  type = ["smoothstep"],    //The easing type
  loop = false,             //Should the animation loop?
  yoyo = false,             //Should the direction reverse?
  delayBeforeContinue = 0   //Delay, in milliseconds, between sections
) {

  //Divide the `totalFrames` into sections for each part of the path
  let frames = totalFrames / pathArray.length;

  //Set the current curve to 0, which will be the first one
  let currentCurve = 0;
```

```
//Make the first path
let tween = makePath(currentCurve);

function makePath(currentCurve) {

  //Use the custom `followCurve` function (described earlier
  //in the chapter) to make a sprite follow a curve
  let tween = followCurve(
    sprite,
    pathArray[currentCurve],
    frames,
    type
  );

  //When the tween is complete, advance the `currentCurve` by one.
  //Add an optional delay between path segments, and then create the
  //next path
  tween.onComplete = () => {
    currentCurve += 1;
    if (currentCurve < pathArray.length) {
      wait(delayBeforeContinue).then(() => {
        tween = makePath(currentCurve);
      });
    }

    //If we've reached the end of the path, optionally
    //loop and reverse it
    else {
      if (loop) {
        if (yoyo) {

          //Reverse the order of the curves in the `pathArray`
          pathArray.reverse();

          //Reverse the order of the points in each curve
          pathArray.forEach(curveArray => curveArray.reverse());
        }

        //After an optional delay, reset the sprite to the
        //beginning of the path and create the next new path
        wait(delayBeforeContinue).then(() => {
          currentCurve = 0;
          sprite.x = pathArray[0][0];
          sprite.y = pathArray[0][1];
          tween = makePath(currentCurve);
        });
      }
    }
  };
```

```
//Return the path tween to the main function
  return tween;
}

//Pass the tween back to the main program
  return tween;
}
```

And with that, we're done! Tweening, solved!

Summary

You now have a useful set of tools to compose most kinds of animated tweening effects for all kinds of games. You've learned how all the classic easing functions work and how to use them to animate sprites. You also built a versatile and customizable tweening engine that you can use with any game project. Combined with the scripted motion and keyframe animation techniques that you learned in earlier chapters, you now have a dazzling palette of motion effects to choose from.

The most important thing about this chapter is that you know how to use the high-level tween functions like fadeIn, fadeOut, pulse, slide, strobe, breathe, followCurve, walkPath, and walkCurve. Don't let the technical details of how those tweening functions work bog you down. You can always study them more closely later if you ever want to try making your own custom tweens.

But how do you use these tweening functions in a game? In the next chapter you'll find out.

CHAPTER 11

■ ■ ■

Make Your Own Game Engine

So far in this book you've learned how to make a collection of flexible, low-level tools and use them to help build games. But one thing you'll notice after you've made a few games with those tools is that you end up writing a lot of repetitive code. This includes all the code to load your assets, import modules, run the game loop, create sprites, loop through sprites to check for collisions, move sprites, and countless other little uninspiring, tedious, but necessary tasks. All this is the **game engine** code, and it can end up being up to half of all the code you write.

The game engine code has nothing to do with the game logic code. The game logic is all the fun, imaginative code you write that is specific to each game. The game engine code is just the heavy lifting that makes the game logic work. It's good to expose all this code while you'll learning, because it's important to understand how all the bits and pieces of your game program fit together. But if you just want to get to the business of realizing your imagination clearly, without the clutter of all the technical stuff, you have to go a few steps further. That's what we'll do in this chapter. We're going to separate the game engine code from the game logic code so you're free to create games quickly without having to wade through the waist-deep mud of tedious mechanics. We're going to close the hood on the game engine and jump into the driver's seat of a super-charged, game-making sports car.

In this chapter I'll show you how to build your own easy-to-use game engine, as well as a few of the missing pieces you need to know to produce really polished games. You'll learn how to:

- Create and manage game states.
- Automatically scale and center games to fill the browser window.
- Create independent game scenes and levels, and animate transitions between them.
- Build a preloading screen with a loading progress bar.
- Create a fun new special effect: the screen shake!

At the end of this chapter you're going to learn how to take all these new skills and combine them with all the techniques you've learned in the book so far to build a Breakout-style game called Bloxyee (shown in Figure 11-1).

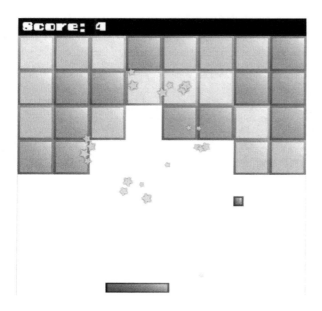

Figure 11-1. *The Bloxyee game you'll build in this chapter*

Using States to Structure a Game

In the previous chapters you learned how to create and use a set of tools to help you make games. But how can you organize that code to structure a game? The solution is to use **states**. A state is a function that contains code for each important section of your game. For example, in a basic game you might have these four states:

- **load**: What to do while the game assets are loading.

- **setup**: Code that should run after the assets have loaded. The setup state creates sprites and builds the game level.

- **play**: Your main game logic. This runs in a loop.

- **end**: Code that should run when the player has finished the game.

Figure 11-2 illustrates this basic model.

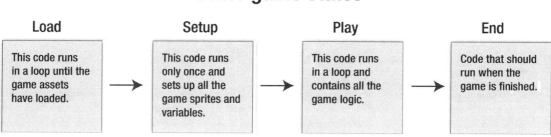

Figure 11-2. *Four basic game states*

Each of these states is just an ordinary function, containing ordinary game code:

```
function load() {/*What to do while loading assets*/}
function setup() {/*Create the sprites and game level*/}
function play() {/*The game code*/}
function end() {/*Code to run when the game finishes*/}
```

- Those functions should contain all the code you want to run for that state. But you need some way to switch between these states at any point in your game. Here's a simple way to do that:
- Create a single variable, called state:

```
let state;
```

Its job will be to hold a reference to the current game state function. For example, imagine that when your game starts, the first function you want to run is the load function. Set the value of state to load:

```
let state = load;
```

Now state has become an intermediate pointer to the load function.

Then all you need to do is call state within the game loop, like this:

```
function gameLoop() {
  requestAnimationFrame(gameLoop);
  state();
}
```

Because state has the value load, the load function will run in a loop.

The beauty of this system is that you can change the value of state to another function at any time in your code, and that function will then run in the game loop. You don't have to modify the game loop code at all. For example, if your code has finished loading the assets, and you want the main game to start playing, just redefine the value of state so that it points to the play function:

```
state = play;
```

Now whatever code you've written in the play function will run inside the gameLoop.

The loop will automatically run whatever function state happens to be referencing. If it's referencing the load function, all the code in the load function will run; if it's referencing play, all the code in the play function will run. Think of your game state functions (load, setup, play, end) as independent modules that you can trigger whenever you like just by assigning them to the state variable.

You can use as many states in your game as you need. If your states contain a lot of code, keep each state in a separate JS file. By using this one simple technique you can create really big, complex games, but because you've modularized the game into states, your game code will always be easy to manage.

A Template for Games

Before we move to the next step, let's look at how to use game states to build a simple template for making many kinds of games. The template imports useful code from the library, loads assets, and creates the canvas. It also sets up and manages the game state, runs the game loop, and renders the canvas.

```
//Import any useful code from the library
import {
  makeCanvas, sprite, group, particles, particleEffect,
  tilingSprite, emitter, stage, render
} from "../library/display";
import {assets, randomInt, contain, wait} from "../library/utilities";
import {makePointer} from "../library/interactive";
import {hit, hitTestRectangle} from "../library/collision";

//Load the assets
assets.load([
  "images/textureAtlas.json"
]).then(() => setup());

//Declare any variables shared between functions
let state, canvas;

function setup() {

  //Make the canvas and initialize the stage
  canvas = makeCanvas(512, 512);
  canvas.style.backgroundColor = "black";
  stage.width = canvas.width;
  stage.height = canvas.height;

  //...Create the game sprites and initialize variables...

  //Set the game state to the `play` function
  state = play;

  //Start the game loop
  gameLoop();
}

function gameLoop() {
  requestAnimationFrame(gameLoop);

  //Update all the particles in the game
  if (particles.length > 0) {
    for(let i = particles.length - 1; i >= 0; i--) {
      let particle = particles[i];
      particle.update();
    }
  }
```

```
  //Run the current game state
  state();
}

function play() {

  //...Add game logic...

  //Render the canvas
  render(canvas);
}
```

You can now start adding custom code to this template to build all kinds of games, like the Flappy Fairy game we developed in Chapter 7.

But wait—there's a better way! You can make all this much easier by creating a reusable **game engine**.

Start Your Engine!

The game template from the previous section is about 50 lines of code. That's not too bad, but you'll need to rewrite the same code for each game you make. And, if you want to make a game that uses tweening, sound, drag-and-drop, or other special features, you'll have to work that code into the template as well. That's a lot of boilerplate code you'll have to remember to include, and then test, tweak, and fine-tune for each game you make.

Why not just write all that boilerplate code once, bury it away in some kind of a reusable function, and call it up when you need it? That's precisely what we're going to do next: make a game engine.

Before I show you the code that makes the game engine work, let's find out how you'll be able to use it. The game engine is just an ordinary function called game that you'll find in the library/engine.js folder. So when you want to start making a new game, import it into your code with a statement like this:

```
import {game} from "../library/engine";
```

That's the *only* thing you need to import. As you'll see later, the game engine imports all the other dependencies automatically behind the scenes, so you don't have to worry about them.

Next, use the game function to create a new game object called g:

```
let g = game(512, 256, setup, ["images/textureAtlas.json"]);
```

The first two arguments are the width and height of the stage: 512 by 256. The third argument, setup, is the first function that should run when the game starts. The last argument is an array that lists all the assets you want to load. You can list as many assets as you need; here's how you could load a texture atlas, image, font, and sound:

```
let g = game(512, 256, setup, [
  "images/textureAtlas.json",
  "images/cat.png",
  "fonts/puzzler.otf",
  "sounds/bounce.wav"
]);
```

411

As soon as those assets have loaded, the game engine looks for and runs a function called setup, which is the third argument. (You don't have to give that function the name "setup"; you can call it any name you like.)

You can optionally add a final argument: the name of a function that should run while the assets are loading. For example, you might have a function called load that displays a loading progress bar while the assets load. You could tell the game engine that you want to add a load function, this way:

```
let g = game(512, 256, setup, ["images/textureAtlas.json"], load);
```

The game engine will look for and run a function called load while the assets are loading. You'll see a practical example of how to use this load state to create a loading progress bar later in this chapter.

Next, start the game engine by calling its start method:

```
g.start();
```

This is like turning on a car's ignition. The start method causes the assets to start loading.

When the assets have loaded, the engine automatically calls the setup state. The setup function will run only once, and you can use it to initialize your game sprites. When you're done setting up, change the game state to play. The game engine will automatically run the play function in a loop.

```
function setup() {

  //The setup function runs only once
  //Create your sprites like this:
  let cat = g.sprite(g.assets["cat.png"]);

  //When you're finished setting up, change the
  //game state to `play`
  g.state = play;
}

function play() {
  //...the game logic, which runs in a loop...
}
```

If you need to pause the game loop at any time, use the g.pause() method. To resume the game loop, use g.resume().

Notice that you need to prefix all the game engine code with g. Thus to make a sprite with the sprite function, use g.sprite. To access the game assets, use g.assets. All the functions and methods and utilities we've created in this book can all be accessed by prefixing their names with g (which stands for "game," if you haven't already guessed!).

Now let's look at all the code you need to write to start a new game, load a texture atlas, create a canvas, display a sprite, and make the sprite move.

```
import {game} from "../library/engine";

let g = game(512, 256, setup, ["images/animals.json"]);
g.start();

let cat;
```

```
function setup() {
  cat = g.sprite(g.assets["cat.png"]);
  g.state = play;
}

function play() {
  cat.x += 1;
}
```

Nice and easy! This is your most basic game engine framework, and you can use it to make any kind of game. By hiding away all the technical details, you've decluttered your code and freed your mind to work creatively.

But how does it work?

Making the Game Engine

You learned in the previous section that the game engine we're going to make will let you create a new game by calling the game function; the code looks like this:

```
let g = game(512, 256, setup, ["images/animals.json"]);
```

The game function creates and returns an instance of a class called Game, which does the following things:

- Imports all the object and methods from other modules and adds them as its own properties.

- Creates the canvas, initializes the stage, and creates the pointer.

- Sets the game's scale.

- Loads the assets and manages the game states.

- Runs the game loop and updates any tweens, buttons, particles, and drag-and-drop sprites. (It also updates any "shaking sprites"—which you'll learn about later.)

- Renders the canvas.

In short, it does all the tiresome management tasks you would have had to code manually.

None of the code in the Game class will be new to you. It's just the pure technical code you need to use to set up and run any game. In previous chapters, all this code was intermingled with the specific code of each game you've made. Now this code is completely abstracted.

Here's the complete Game class with comments that explain how each part works.

```
//Import the modules
module utilities from "../library/utilities";
module display from "../library/display";
module collision from "../library/collision";
module interactive from "../library/interactive";
module sound from "../library/sound";
module tween from "../library/tween";

export class Game {
  constructor(width = 256, height = 256, setup, assetsToLoad, load) {
```

```javascript
//Copy all the imported library code into
//properties on this class
Object.assign(this, utilities);
Object.assign(this, display);
Object.assign(this, collision);
Object.assign(this, interactive);
Object.assign(this, sound);
Object.assign(this, tween);

//Make the canvas and initialize the stage
this.canvas = this.makeCanvas(width, height, "none");
this.canvas.style.backgroundColor = "white";
this.stage.width = this.canvas.width;
this.stage.height = this.canvas.height;

//Make the pointer
this.pointer = this.makePointer(this.canvas);

//The game's scale
this.scale = 1;

//Set the game `state`
this.state = undefined;

//Set the user-defined `load` and `setup` states
this.load = load;
this.setup = setup;

//Get a reference to the `assetsToLoad` array
this.assetsToLoad = assetsToLoad;

//A Boolean to let us pause the game
this.paused = false;

//The `setup` function is required, so throw an error if it's
//missing
if (!setup) {
  throw new Error(
    "Please supply the setup function in the constructor"
  );
}
}

//The game loop
gameLoop() {
  requestAnimationFrame(this.gameLoop.bind(this));

  //Update all the buttons
  if (this.buttons.length > 0) {
    this.canvas.style.cursor = "auto";
    this.buttons.forEach(button => {
```

```
        button.update(this.pointer, this.canvas);
        if (button.state === "over" || button.state === "down") {
          if(button.parent !== undefined) {
            this.canvas.style.cursor = "pointer";
          }
        }
      }
    });
  }

  //Update all the particles
  if (this.particles.length > 0) {
    for(let i = this.particles.length - 1; i >= 0; i--) {
      let particle = this.particles[i];
      particle.update();
    }
  }

  //Update all the tweens
  if (this.tweens.length > 0) {
    for(let i = this.tweens.length - 1; i >= 0; i--) {
      let tween = this.tweens[i];
      if (tween) tween.update();
    }
  }

  //Update all the shaking sprites
  //(More about this later in the chapter!)
  if (this.shakingSprites.length > 0) {
    for(let i = this.shakingSprites.length - 1; i >= 0; i--) {
      let shakingSprite = this.shakingSprites[i];
        if (shakingSprite.updateShake) shakingSprite.updateShake();
    }
  }

  //Update the pointer for drag-and-drop
  if (this.draggableSprites.length > 0) {
    this.pointer.updateDragAndDrop(this.draggableSprites);
  }

  //Run the current game `state` function if it's been defined and
  //the game isn't `paused`
  if(this.state && !this.paused) {
    this.state();
  }

  //Render the canvas
  this.render(this.canvas);

}
```

```
//The `start` method that gets the whole engine going. This needs to
//be called by the user from the game application code, right after
//the engine is instantiated

start() {
  if (this.assetsToLoad) {

    //Use the supplied file paths to load the assets, and then run
    //the user-defined `setup` function
    this.assets.load(this.assetsToLoad).then(() => {

      //Clear the game `state` function for now to stop the loop
      this.state = undefined;

      //Call the `setup` function that was supplied by the user in
      //the Game class's constructor
      this.setup();
    });

    //While the assets are loading, set the user-defined `load`
    //function as the game state. That will make it run in a loop.
    //You can use the `load` state to create a loading progress bar
    if (this.load) {
      this.state = this.load;
    }
  }

  //If there aren't any assets to load,
  //just run the user-defined `setup` function
  else {
    this.setup();
  }

  //Start the game loop
  this.gameLoop();
}

//Pause and resume methods. These stop and start the
//game engine's game loop
pause() {
  this.paused = true;
}
resume() {
  this.paused = false;
}
}
```

To keep our API consistent with the rest of the code in this book, our interface for creating a Game instance is through a high-level wrapper function called game:

```
export function game(
  width = 256, height = 256, setup, assetsToLoad, load
) {
  return new Game(width, height, setup, assetsToLoad, load);
}
```

Now, just create a new game instance using the same code you saw earlier:

```
let g = game(512, 256, setup, ["images/textureAtlas.json"]);

g.start();
```

Take a look at the Game class's start method in the code just shown to see how it sets everything in motion. The start method loads the assets in the supplied array and then calls the user-defined setup function. (It will optionally call the user-defined load function while the assets are loading—but only if a load function has been supplied.) After the setup function runs, the start method calls the gameLoop. The gameLoop updates all the collections of game objects, like tweens and buttons, and then calls the current game state. The Game class's pause and resume methods let you start and stop the game loop whenever you need to.

You can now use this framework to start making any new game. Let's find out how.

Using the Game Engine

Let's look at a practical example to get you started: load three images from a texture atlas and make them draggable and droppable. Figure 11-3 shows what this simple example looks like running in a browser window. You can click on each sprite and drag it around.

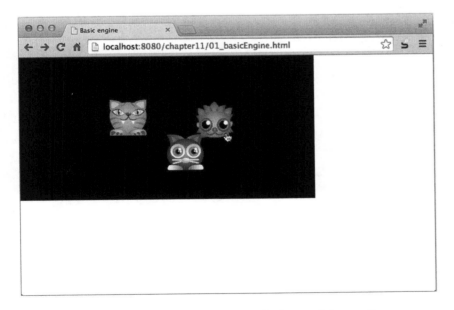

Figure 11-3. Use the game engine to make simple drag-and-drop sprites

417

Here's the code that does all this, using our new game engine.

```
//Create the engine
import {game} from "../library/engine";
let g = game(512, 256, setup, ["images/animals.json"]);
g.start();

//Give the canvas a black background
g.canvas.style.backgroundColor = "black";

//Declare any variables that should be used across functions
let cat, tiger, hedgehog;

function setup() {

  //Make three sprites and set their `draggable`
  //properties to `true`
  cat = g.sprite(g.assets["cat.png"]);
  g.stage.putCenter(cat, -32, -32);
  cat.draggable = true;

  tiger = g.sprite(g.assets["tiger.png"]);
  g.stage.putCenter(tiger);
  tiger.draggable = true;

  hedgehog = g.sprite(g.assets["hedgehog.png"]);
  g.stage.putCenter(hedgehog, 32, 32);
  hedgehog.draggable = true;

  //Optionally set the game state to `play`
  g.state = play;
}

function play() {
  //You don't actually need a `play` state in this example,
  //but if you did, all this code would run in a loop
}
```

All our hard work so far in this book is starting to pay off! You can see that our engine is doing an enormous amount of tedious automation behind the scenes to give us a usable drag-and-drop interface in just a few lines of code. Remember all that code we wrote earlier in the book to get our drag-and-drop interface working? You'll never have to look at it or think about it again!

■ **Tip** And remember, if you need to access any of the custom objects in methods we wrote in previous chapters, they're all there, ready for you to use—just prefix them with g.

Scaling Games to Fill Any Window Size

Let's add an advanced feature to our game engine: the ability to scale any game to the maximum width or height of the browser window. You can see in Figure 11-3 that the canvas is aligned to the top-left corner of the browser window. Wouldn't it be nice if the canvas could automatically scale and align itself to fill the maximum space available, as in Figure 11-4?

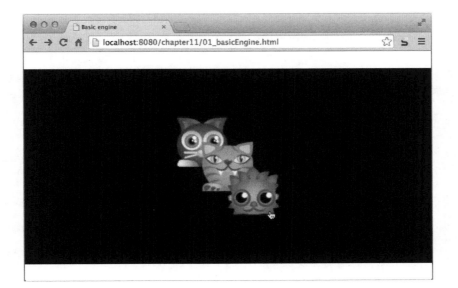

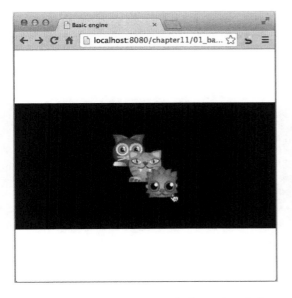

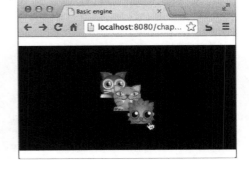

Figure 11-4. Scale the game to fit the entire window

The number of pixels on the canvas stays the same; they're just stretched or squashed proportionately depending on how much space they need to fill. This is a really useful feature because it means you can design a game to a single fixed canvas size and then scale it up or down for each screen size you need. Scaling the canvas like this is often preferable to running a game completely full-screen, using the Fullscreen API you learned about in Chapter 1. That's because your game doesn't risk alienating the player by taking over the entire browser UI, and it doesn't require a button-click to activate. It just naturally fills any browser window to its maximum size. This is not hard to do—let's find out how!

■ **Tip** It's usually a good idea to design your games for the smallest possible resolution you think you'll need and then scale up for the larger sizes. That's because fewer pixels mean better performance. What you lose when you scale up is definition on your graphics, but modern hardware handles this so elegantly that those blurry pixels are rarely noticeable. And players will definitely notice a janky, jittery game much more than they'll notice soft edges on your graphics.

Take a look at the Game class again, and you'll notice that it has a property called scale that's initialized to 1 in the constructor:

```
this.scale = 1;
```

Now think back to the makePointer function that we wrote in Chapter 6. Remember that the pointer has a property called scale, which can be initialized when the pointer is created:

```
export function makePointer(element, scale = 1) {

  let pointer = {
    element: element,
    scale: scale,
    _x: 0,
    _y: 0,
    get x() {
      return this._x / this.scale;
    },
    get y() {
      return this._y / this.scale;
    },
    //... the rest of the `makePointer` function...
```

The scale value is used to help convert the browser's mouse or touch *x/y* position to the equivalent position on the canvas. This is important because if the canvas is scaled to a larger or smaller size, the browser's *x/y* mouse position values will become misaligned. That means you won't be able to click on buttons or drag sprites. The browser will think those interactive elements are in a different place than they actually are. The pointer code fixes this problem by adjusting the mouse or touch *x/y* coordinates to the correct scale. You can set the pointer to a different scale value this way:

```
pointer.scale = anyScaleValue;
```

So far in this book we haven't needed to change the scale, but we're going to do that next.

The `scaleToWindow` Function

To make the canvas automatically scale to the maximum window size, we'll use a new method called scaleToWindow, which will be a property of the game object. So call it just after you create and start a new game engine, this way:

```
g.scaleToWindow("white");
```

Its single argument determines the background color of the HTML body that the canvas is floating inside.

Optionally, you might also want the canvas to rescale itself every time the size of the browser window is changed. If that's the case, call scaleToWindow inside a window event listener:

```
window.addEventListener("resize", event => {
  g.scaleToWindow("white");
});
```

scaleToWindow is a method that's directly on the Game class:

```
export class Game {
  //...
  scaleToWindow() {
    //... the method code...
  }
}
```

That's convenient because it means the code can directly access the canvas and pointer. Here's the complete scaleToWindow method. (Note that this in the code listing refers to the Game class, which the method belongs to.)

```
scaleToWindow(backgroundColor = "#2C3539") {

  let scaleX, scaleY, scale, center;

  //1. Scale the canvas to the correct size
  //Figure out the scale amount on each axis
  scaleX = window.innerWidth / this.canvas.width;
  scaleY = window.innerHeight / this.canvas.height;

  //Scale the canvas based on whichever value is less: `scaleX` or `scaleY`
  scale = Math.min(scaleX, scaleY);
  this.canvas.style.transformOrigin = "0 0";
  this.canvas.style.transform = "scale(" + scale + ")";

  //2. Center the canvas.
  //Decide whether to center the canvas vertically or horizontally.
  //Wide canvases should be centered vertically, and
  //square or tall canvases should be centered horizontally
```

```
  if (this.canvas.width > this.canvas.height) {
    center = "vertically";
  } else {
    center = "horizontally";
  }

  //Center horizontally (for square or tall canvases)
  if (center === "horizontally") {
    let margin = (window.innerWidth - this.canvas.width * scaleY) / 2;
    this.canvas.style.marginLeft = margin + "px";
    this.canvas.style.marginRight = margin + "px";
  }

  //Center vertically (for wide canvases)
  if (center === "vertically") {
    let margin = (window.innerHeight - this.canvas.height * scaleX) / 2;
    this.canvas.style.marginTop = margin + "px";
    this.canvas.style.marginBottom = margin + "px";
  }

  //3. Remove any padding from the canvas and set the canvas
  //display style to "block"
  this.canvas.style.paddingLeft = 0;
  this.canvas.style.paddingRight = 0;
  this.canvas.style.display = "block";

  //4. Set the color of the HTML body background
  document.body.style.backgroundColor = backgroundColor;

  //5. Set the game engine ("this") and the pointer to the correct scale.
  //This is important for correct hit testing between the pointer and sprites
  this.pointer.scale = scale;
  this.scale = scale;
}
```

There are some new things here that you haven't seen before, so let's walk through how this code works. The first thing the code does is figure out how many times larger the browser window is than the canvas:

```
scaleX = window.innerWidth  / this.canvas.width;
scaleY = window.innerHeight / this.canvas.height;
```

It then uses the smaller of those two values to set the canvas's scale:

```
scale = Math.min(scaleX, scaleY);
```

The resulting scale value is used with the CSS transformOrigin and transform methods to scale the canvas by that amount.

```
this.canvas.style.transformOrigin = "0 0";
this.canvas.style.transform = "scale(" + scale + ")";
```

(The transformOrigin method sets the canvas's *x/y* origin point to its top-left corner: "0 0".)

If the canvas is wider than it is tall, it should be centered vertically. If the canvas is taller than wide, or if it is square, it should be centered horizontally:

```
if (this.canvas.width > this.canvas.height) {
  center = "vertically";
} else {
  center = "horizontally";
}
```

To center the canvas, find the difference between the scaled canvas size and the size of the browser window. Then use half of that value to set either the left and right canvas margins (if the centering is vertical) or the top and bottom canvas margins (if the centering is horizontal).

```
//Center horizontally (for square or tall canvases)
if (center === "horizontally") {
  let margin = (window.innerWidth - this.canvas.width * scaleY) / 2;
  this.canvas.style.marginLeft = margin + "px";
  this.canvas.style.marginRight = margin + "px";
}
```

```
//Center vertically (for wide canvases)
if (center === "vertically") {
  let margin = (window.innerHeight - this.canvas.height * scaleX) / 2;
  this.canvas.style.marginTop = margin + "px";
  this.canvas.style.marginBottom = margin + "px";
}
```

Next, remove any possible padding on the canvas, set the canvas's display style to block, and set the HTML body element's backgroundColor to whatever color was supplied in the function arguments.

```
this.canvas.style.paddingLeft = 0;
this.canvas.style.paddingRight = 0;
this.canvas.style.display = "block";
document.body.style.backgroundColor = backgroundColor;
```

Finally, set the pointer and game engine's scale properties to the same value as the calculated scale.

```
this.pointer.scale = scale;
this.scale = scale;
```

This is what ensures that the browser's mouse and touch positions will correspond correctly to the points on the scaled canvas.

The very last thing you might want to do is remove any possible default padding from the HTML elements on the page where the game is running. Drop this CSS into your HTML document after the <title> tag:

```
<style> * {margin: 0; padding: 0;} </style>
```

The asterisk is CSS code for "everything." This statement sets the margins and padding for all HTML elements to 0.

Now we're ready to go! We've got a great little game engine full of bells and whistles. But how can we use it to make a real game?

423

Case Study: Bloxyee

In the chapter's source files you'll find a game prototype called Bloxyee that's been built using our new game engine. It's the most complete game prototype in this book and includes a number of features you'll want to use in professional standard games: a loading bar, animated scene transitions, tween and particle effects, and a simple user interface. Play Bloxyee a few times through to get a feel for it. Figure 11-5 illustrates the main features and flow of the game, based on the old Atari game Breakout.

Loading progress bar

Press the button to play

The title screen slides out to the right, the game screen slides in from the left

The main game

When the game is finished, it pauses for one second

The title screen slides in from the right, the game screen slides out to the left

Press the button to restart the game

Figure 11-5. *Bloxyee: a Breakout-style game*

When the ball hits the paddle, the paddle wobbles like jelly. When the ball hits one of the blocks, the block disappears in a shower of stars, and the player scores a point. If the ball hits the bottom of the screen, the screen shakes and the player loses a point. Music starts playing as soon as the play button is pressed, and the ball makes a bouncing sound whenever it hits one of the blocks or the paddle. When all the blocks have been broken, the title screen slides back in, displays the final score, and lets you click the play button to play again.

Most of the game code will be familiar to you from other examples in this book, but there are a few features like the screen shake effect and loading progress bar that are new. Let's first take a look at the fully commented code listing, and then a closer look at the game's special features in detail.

■ **Note** Why is the game called Bloxyee? Because it's a game about blocks. And after about 50 web searches and some wild experimentation with spellings, "Bloxyee" was the only name I could find that didn't match an already existing game about blocks. In fact, it seemed that no one in history had ever put those seven letters together in that exact order. Not for long, though—very soon after my web search, "bloxyee.com" was mysteriously registered by someone (or… *something*!).

The Complete Code Listing

Here's the complete Bloxyee code listing:

```
<!doctype html>
<meta charset="utf-8">
<title>Bloxyee</title>
<style> * {margin: 0; padding: 0;} </style>
<body>
<script type="module">

//Import the game engine
import {game} from "../../library/engine";

//Initialize the game engine and load all the assets
let g = game(
  512, 512, setup,
  [
    "images/bloxyee.json",
    "sounds/bounce.wav",
    "sounds/music.wav",
    "fonts/puzzler.otf"
  ],
  load
);

//Start the engine
g.start();

//Scale and center the game
g.scaleToWindow();

//Optionally rescale the canvas if the browser window is changed
window.addEventListener("resize", event => {
  g.scaleToWindow();
});

//Game variables
let paddle, ball, topBorder, blocks, blockFrames,
    music, bounceSound, message, titleMessage,
```

425

```
    //The size of the grid of blocks
    gridWidth = 8,
    gridHeight = 5,
    cellWidth = 64,
    cellHeight = 64,

    //title sprites
    title, playButton,

    //Groups
    titleScene, gameScene,

    //Score
    score = 0,

    //The paddle wobble tween
    paddleWobble;

function load() {

    //Display the loading progress bar while the game
    //assets load (you'll learn how asset loading works in later in this chapter)
    g.progressBar.create(g.canvas, g.assets);
    g.progressBar.update();
}

function setup() {

    //Remove the progress bar
    g.progressBar.remove();

    //Sound and music
    bounceSound = g.assets["sounds/bounce.wav"];
    music = g.assets["sounds/music.wav"];
    music.loop = true;

    //Create the sprites

    //1. The `titleScene` sprites

    //The `title`
    title = g.sprite(g.assets["title.png"]);

    //The play button
    playButton = g.button([
      g.assets["up.png"],
      g.assets["over.png"],
      g.assets["down.png"]
    ]);
```

```
//Set the `playButton`'s x property to 514 so that
//it's offscreen when the sprite is created
playButton.x = 514;
playButton.y = 350;

//Set the `titleMessage` x position to -200 so that it's offscreen
titleMessage = g.text("start game", "20px puzzler", "white", -200, 300);

//Make the `playButton` and `titleMessage` slide in from the
//edges of the screen using the `slide` function
g.slide(playButton, 250, 350, 30, ["decelerationCubed"]);
g.slide(titleMessage, 250, 300, 30, ["decelerationCubed"]);

//Create the `titleScene` group
titleScene = g.group(title, playButton, titleMessage);

//2. The `gameScene` sprites

//The paddle
paddle = g.sprite(g.assets["paddle.png"]);
g.stage.putBottom(paddle, 0, -24);

//The ball
ball = g.sprite(g.assets["ball.png"]);
g.stage.putBottom(ball, 0, -128);

//Set the ball's initial velocity
ball.vx = 12;
ball.vy = 8;

//Add a black border along the top of the screen
topBorder = g.rectangle(512, 32, "black");

//Plot the blocks
//First create an array that stores references to all the
//block frames in the texture atlas
blockFrames = [
  "blue.png",
  "green.png",
  "orange.png",
  "red.png",
  "violet.png"
];

//Use the `grid` function to randomly plot the
//blocks in a grid pattern
blocks = g.grid(
  gridWidth, gridHeight, 64, 64,
  false, 0, 0,
  () => {
```

427

```
    //Choose a random block from the tileset for each grid cell
    let randomBlock = g.randomInt(0, 4);
    return g.sprite(g.assets[blockFrames[randomBlock]]);
  }
);

//Position the blocks 32 pixels below the top of the canvas
blocks.y = 32;

//A text sprite for the score
message = g.text("test", "20px puzzler", "white");
message.x = 8;
message.y = 8;

//Add the game sprites to the `gameScene` group
gameScene = g.group(paddle, ball, topBorder, blocks, message);

//Position the `gameScene` offscreen at -514 so that it's
//not visible when the game starts
gameScene.x = -514;

//Program the play button's `press` function to start the game.
//Start the music, set the `state` to `play`
//make `titleScene` slide out to the right and
// `gameScene` slide in from the left
playButton.press = () => {
  if (!music.playing) music.play();
  g.state = play;
  g.slide(titleScene, 514, 0, 30, ["decelerationCubed"]);
  g.slide(gameScene, 0, 0, 30, ["decelerationCubed"]);
};
}

//The `play` function contains all the game logic and runs in a loop

function play() {

  //Move the paddle to the mouse position
  paddle.x = g.pointer.x - paddle.halfWidth;

  //Keep the paddle within the screen boundaries
  g.contain(paddle, g.stage.localBounds);

  //Move the ball using the `move` convenience function
  g.move(ball);

  //Bounce the ball off the screen edges. Use the `contain` method
  //with a custom `bounds` object (the second argument) that defines
  //the area in which the ball should bounce around.
  //Play the `bounceSound` when the ball hits one of these edges,
  //and reduce the score by 1 if it hits the ground
```

```
let ballHitsWall = g.contain(
  ball,
  {x: 0, y: 32, width: g.stage.width, height: g.stage.height},
  true,

  //what should happen when the ball hits the edges of the boundary?
  (collision) => {

    //Play the bounce sound
    bounceSound.play();

    //If the ball hits the bottom, perform these additional tasks:
    if (collision === "bottom") {

      //Subtract 1 from the score
      score -= 1;

      //Shake the screen (the `gameScene` sprite.)
      //(You'll learn how the `shake` method works later in this chapter)
      g.shake(gameScene, 0.05, true);
    }
  }
);

/*
Check for a collision between the ball and the paddle, and
bounce the ball off the paddle. Play the `bounceSound` when
the collision occurs.
You can use the universal `hit` collision function to do this.
`hit` arguments:
spriteA, spriteB, reactToCollision?, bounce?, useGlobalCoordinates?,
actionWhenCollisionOccurs
*/

let ballHitsPaddle = g.hit(
  ball, paddle, true, true, true,
  (collision) => {

    //1. Play the bounce sound
    bounceSound.play();

    //2. Make the paddle wobble when the ball hits it.
    //a. Remove any possible previous instances of the
    //`paddleWobble` tween, and reset the paddle's scale
    if (paddleWobble) {
      paddle.scaleX = 1;
      paddle.scaleY = 1;
      g.removeTween(paddleWobble);
    };
```

```
    //b. Create the wobble tween
    paddleWobble = g.wobble(
      paddle, 1.3, 1.2, 5, 10, 10, -10, -10, 0.96
    );
  }
);


/*
Check for a collision between the ball and all
the blocks in the grid.
You can use the universal `hit` collision function to do this. If one
of the first two arguments is an array, the `hit` function will loop
through all the sprites in that array and check it for a collision
with the other sprite.
`hit` arguments:
spriteA, spriteB, reactToCollision?, bounce?, useGlobalCoordinates?
actionWhenCollisionOccurs
*/

let ballHitsBlock = g.hit(
  ball, blocks.children, true, true, true,
  (collision, block) => {

    //Add 1 to the score, play the bounce sound
    //and remove the block that was hit
    score += 1;
    bounceSound.play();
    g.remove(block);

    //Create the particle effect
    //1. Find the `globalCenterX` and `globalCenterY`
    //position for the block that was hit
    let globalCenterX = block.gx + block.halfWidth,
        globalCenterY = block.gy + block.halfHeight;

    //2. Create the effect
    g.particleEffect(
      globalCenterX, globalCenterY,          //x and y position
      () => g.sprite(g.assets["star.png"]),  //Particle function
      20,                                    //Number of particles
      0.3,                                   //Gravity
      true,                                  //Random spacing
      0, 6.28,                               //Min/max angle
      12, 24,                                //Min/max size
      5, 10,                                 //Min/max speed
      0.005, 0.01,                           //Min/max scale speed
      0.005, 0.01,                           //Min/max alpha speed
      0.05, 0.1                              //Min/max rotation speed
    );
  }
);
```

```
//Display the current score
message.content = `Score: ${score}`;

//Check for the end of the game
if (blocks.empty) {

  //Pause the game, wait for 1 second, and then
  //call the `end` function
  g.pause();
  g.wait(1000).then(() => end());
}
}

function end() {

  //Display the `titleScene` and hide the `gameScene`
  g.slide(titleScene, 0, 0, 30, ["decelerationCubed"]);
  g.slide(gameScene, -514, 0, 30, ["decelerationCubed"]);

  //Display the final score
  titleMessage.content = `Score: ${score}`;

  //Lower the music volume
  music.volume = 0.3;

  //Assign a new button `press` action to
  //`restart` the game
  playButton.press = () => {
    restart();
  };
}

function restart() {

  //Remove any remaining blocks if there are any
  g.remove(blocks);

  //Plot a new grid of blocks
  blocks = g.grid(
    gridWidth, gridHeight, 64, 64,
    false, 0, 0,
    () => {
      //Choose a random block from the
      //`blockFrames` array for each grid cell
      let randomBlock = g.randomInt(0, 4);
      return g.sprite(g.assets[blockFrames[randomBlock]]);
    }
  );

  //Add the blocks to the `gameScene` and position it
  gameScene.addChild(blocks);
  blocks.y = 32;
  blocks.x = 0;
```

```
//Reset the ball and paddle positions
g.stage.putBottom(paddle, 0, -22);
g.stage.putBottom(ball, 0, -128);

//Reset the ball's velocity
ball.vx = 12;
ball.vy = 8;

//Reset the score
score = 0;

//Set the music volume to full
music.volume = 1;

//Hide the titleScene and reveal the gameScene
g.slide(titleScene, 514, 0, 30, ["decelerationCubed"]);
g.slide(gameScene, 0, 0, 30, ["decelerationCubed"]);

//Set the game state to `play` and `resume` the game
g.state = play;
g.resume();
}
</script>
</body>
```

Now let's find out how this all works.

The Loading Progress Bar

If you have lots of sounds or images in your game, it can take a few seconds or more to load them, especially if your game is running on the web. To keep your players informed, so that they don't think their devices have frozen while this is happening, it's important to display some kind of "Please wait while loading" message. It's common to show a loading bar, which scales to the percentage of game assets that have loaded. When it reaches 100%, the game runs.

Bloxyee displays just such a loading bar when it starts. In the second or two that it takes for the game to load, you'll see a blue bar over a gray background that increases in width as the game assets load. It also displays the percentage of assets that have loaded. The title screen appears when the percentage reaches 100%. Figure 11-6 shows what this loading progress bar looks like.

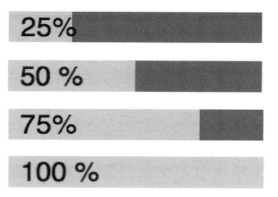

Figure 11-6. *A loading progress bar*

432

You'll find this progressBar object in the library/display folder. It's a composite object made from three sprites: a gray rectangle for the background, a blue rectangle for the foreground, and a text sprite to display the percentage. The progressBar has a reference to the canvas so that it can center itself vertically and horizontally. It also has a reference to the assets object so that it knows how many assets have currently loaded. The progressBar also needs an update method, which is called on each frame, so it can dynamically resize depending on the number of assets currently being loaded.

Here's the complete progressBar object.

```
export let progressBar = {
  maxWidth: 0,
  height: 0,
  backgroundColor: "gray",
  foregroundColor: "cyan",
  backBar: null,
  frontBar: null,
  percentage: null,
  assets: null,
  initialized: false,

  //Use the `create` method to create the progress bar
  create(canvas, assets) {
    if (!this.initialized) {

      //Store a reference to the `assets` object
      this.assets = assets;

      //Set the maximum width to half the width of the canvas
      this.maxWidth = canvas.width / 2;

      //Build the progress bar using two rectangle sprites and
      //one text sprite:

      //1. Create the background bar's gray background
      this.backBar = rectangle(this.maxWidth, 32, this.backgroundColor);
      this.backBar.x = (canvas.width / 2) - (this.maxWidth / 2);
      this.backBar.y = (canvas.height / 2) - 16;

      //2. Create the blue foreground bar. This is the element of the
      //progress bar that will increase in width as assets load
      this.frontBar = rectangle(this.maxWidth, 32, this.foregroundColor);
      this.frontBar.x = (canvas.width / 2) - (this.maxWidth / 2);
      this.frontBar.y = (canvas.height / 2) - 16;

      //3. A text sprite that will display the percentage
      //of assets that have loaded
      this.percentage = text("0%", "28px sans-serif", "black");
      this.percentage.x = (canvas.width / 2) - (this.maxWidth / 2) + 12;
      this.percentage.y = (canvas.height / 2) - 16;
```

```
            //Flag the `progressBar` as having been initialized
            this.initialized = true;
        }
    },

    //Use the `update` method to update the width of the bar and
    //percentage loaded each frame:

    update() {

        //Change the width of the blue `frontBar` to match the
        //ratio of assets that have loaded. Adding `+1` to
        //`assets.loaded` means that the loading bar will appear at 100%
        //when the last asset is being loaded, which is reassuring for the
        //player observing the load progress
        let ratio = (this.assets.loaded + 1) / this.assets.toLoad;
        this.frontBar.width = this.maxWidth * ratio;

        //Display the percentage
        this.percentage.content = `${Math.floor((ratio) * 100)} %`;
    },

    //Use the `remove` method to remove the progress bar when all the
    //game assets have finished loading
    remove() {

        //Remove the progress bar using the universal sprite `remove` function
        remove(this.frontBar);
        remove(this.backBar);
        remove(this.percentage);
    }
};
```

We create the progress bar by calling its create method. It needs access to the canvas and assets objects, so create should only be called after these objects exist in the game. The initialized property is used to make sure the code in the create method isn't run more than once.

```
initialized: false,
create(canvas, assets) {
    if (!this.initialized) {
        //...
        this.initialized = true;
    }
}
```

initialized is set to true as soon as the code in the create method has finished running.

You can see that the create method creates the rectangle and text sprites, and it centers and positions them inside the canvas. The update method is used to change the width of the blue frontBar and the percentage. It does this by figuring out the ratio between currently loaded assets and the total number of assets, and then uses that ratio to scale the width of the frontBar.

```
update() {
  let ratio = (this.assets.loaded + 1) / this.assets.toLoad;
  this.frontBar.width = this.maxWidth * ratio;
  this.percentage.content = `${Math.floor((ratio) * 100)} %`;
},
```

If this update method is called within a game loop, these sprites will display the current percentage loaded each frame:

```
function gameLoop {
  progressBar.update();
}
```

You also need a way to remove the progressBar's sprites from the game when we're done with them. The sprite remove method takes care of that:

```
remove() {
  remove(this.frontBar);
  remove(this.backBar);
  remove(this.percentage);
}
```

Implementing the Loading Progress Bar

Now that we've built the progressBar, how can we use it in a game like Bloxyee?

You'll remember that our game engine's game function has an optional final argument that determines the function that should run while the assets are loading. In Bloxyee this function is called load, as you can see in the following code:

```
let g = game(
  512, 512, setup,
  [
    "images/bloxyee.json",
    "sounds/bounce.wav",
    "sounds/music.wav",
    "fonts/puzzler.otf"
  ],
  load
);
g.start();
```

The game engine will call the load function in a loop while the assets are loading. Here's Bloxyee's load method. You can see that it first creates the progressBar and then updates it:

```
function load() {
  g.progressBar.create(g.canvas, g.assets);
  g.progressBar.update();
}
```

435

Although it's being called inside a loop, the create method will only run once, because progressBar. initialized will be false after the first time it's called. The update function is called continuously each frame, and that's what increases the width of the blue frontBar and updates the percentage number. Because the progressBar object is exported by the library/display module, and engine.js imports everything in the display module, progressBar is now a property of the game object: g. That's why we can access it as g.progressBar.

What happens when the assets are finished loading? The game engine runs the setup state. The first thing it does is remove the progressBar.

```
function setup() {
  g.progressBar.remove();
  //...create the game sprites...
```

And then the game sprites are created as usual.

This loading bar is just an example of one kind of information you could present to players while the game is loading. Maybe you want to use a spinning wheel or display some poetry instead? I've intentionally kept this example modular so that you can drop any kind of object that you like into the load state. Just follow the same general format to create your own unique loading object, and surprise me! You might also want to consider integrating the code for the progress bar deeper into the game engine or asset loader to declutter your game code even further.

Game Scenes and Transitions

There are two scenes in this game: the titleScene and the gameScene. These scenes are just groups that keep related sprites together.

```
titleScene = g.group(title, playButton, titleMessage);
gameScene = g.group(paddle, ball, topBorder, blocks, message);
```

Figure 11-7 shows what these scenes look like.

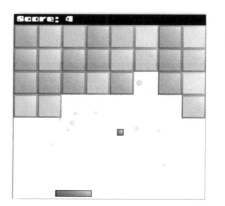 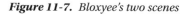 

gameScene   titleScene

Figure 11-7. *Bloxyee's two scenes*

When Bloxyee starts, the `titleScene` appears on the canvas but the gameScene is positioned off-screen to the left at an *x* position of –514.

```
gameScene.x = -514;
```

When the player clicks the play button, the `titleScene` slides away to the right, and the gameScene slides onto the canvas, as shown in Figure 11-8.

Figure 11-8. *Click the button to transition from the titleScene to the gameScene*

The effect works by using a `slide` tween to shift the scenes into position. It happens when the `playButton` is pressed.

```
playButton.press = () => {
  if (!music.playing) music.play();
  g.state = play;
  g.slide(titleScene, 514, 0, 30, ["decelerationCubed"]);
  g.slide(gameScene, 0, 0, 30, ["decelerationCubed"]);
};
```

The `titleScene` is tweened offscreen to an *x* position of 514, and the gameScene is tweened onscreen to an *x* position of 0.

It's no more complicated than that. You can use this basic system to create as many independent scenes or levels as you like in your games.

The Paddle and Block Collisions

Bloxyee's play function runs in a loop to handle all the game logic and check for collisions. The universal hit function from in Chapter 7 is used to check for a collision between the paddle and the ball. If the hit function detects a collision, it bounces the ball away, plays the bounceSound and makes the paddle wobble, as shown in Figure 11-9.

```
let ballHitsPaddle = g.hit(
  ball, paddle, true, true, true,
  (collision) => {

    //1. Play the bounce sound
    bounceSound.play();

    //2. Make the paddle wobble

    //Remove any possible previous instances of the
    //`paddleWobble` tween, and reset the paddle's scale
    if (paddleWobble) {
      paddle.scaleX = 1;
      paddle.scaleY = 1;
      g.removeTween(paddleWobble);
    };

    //Create the wobble tween
    paddleWobble = g.wobble(
      paddle, 1.3, 1.2, 5, 10, 10, -10, -10, 0.96
    );
  }
);
```

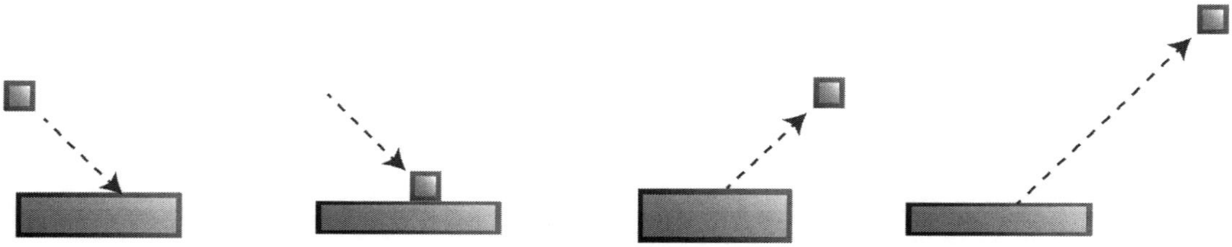

Figure 11-9. *The paddle wobbles when the ball hits it*

If the paddle is hit more than once in rapid succession, the collision code might try to create a new paddleWobble tween before the first one has finished. If it does, the paddle's scale could become distorted because the two tweens will be acting upon it simultaneously. The code just shown prevents this from happening by resetting the paddle's scale and removing any current paddleWobble tweens before creating a new one.

If the ball hits one of the blocks, the block disappears in a cascade of stars, the score is increased by 1, a bouncing sound plays, and the ball bounces away, as shown in Figure 11-10. Here's the code that accomplishes that:

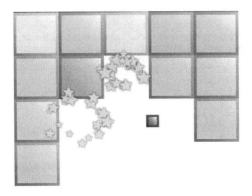

Figure 11-10. *Star particles fly in all directions when a block is hit*

```
let ballHitsBlock = g.hit(
  ball, blocks.children, true, true, true,
  (collision, block) => {

    //Add 1 to the score, play the bounce sound
    //and remove the block that was hit
    score += 1;
    bounceSound.play();
    g.remove(block);

    //Create the particle effect

    //1. Find the globalCenterX and globalCenterY
    //position for the block that was hit
    let globalCenterX = block.gx + block.halfWidth,
        globalCenterY = block.gy + block.halfHeight;

    //2. Create the effect
    g.particleEffect(
      globalCenterX, globalCenterY,          //x and y position
      () => g.sprite(g.assets["star.png"]),  //Particle function
      20,                                    //Number of particles
      0.3,                                   //Gravity
      true,                                  //Random spacing
      0, 6.28,                               //Min/max angle
      12, 24,                                //Min/max size
      5, 10,                                 //Min/max speed
      0.005, 0.01,                           //Min/max scale speed
```

```
      0.005, 0.01,                      //Min/max alpha speed
      0.05, 0.1                         //Min/max rotation speed
    );
  }
);
```

There's an important detail to be aware of in the way the particle effects are positioned. The star particle explosions start from the center *x/y* points of each block. However, all the blocks are in a single group called blocks. When the blocks group is created by the setup function, its *y* position is set to 32:

```
blocks.y = 32;
```

This places the grid of blocks 32 pixels below the top of the canvas, as shown in Figure 11-11.

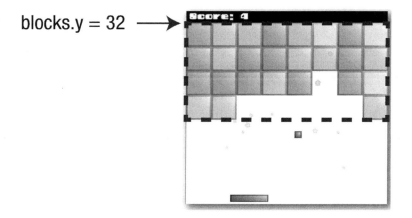

Figure 11-11. *All the blocks are a in a single group, positioned 32 pixels below the top of the canvas*

Why is that positioning important? Remember that groups have their own local coordinates. Because the blocks group is offset by 32 pixels from the top of the canvas, the local *y* position of each sprite inside that group will be 32 pixels less than its *y* global position. You know that you can access a sprite's global position by using its gx and gy properties. However, sprites don't have any built-in properties that give you their **global center** positions. If you need global center positions, you have to calculate them manually. Here's how the preceding code does that:

```
let globalCenterX = block.gx + block.halfWidth,
    globalCenterY = block.gy + block.halfHeight;
```

You can now use globalCenterX and globalCenterY to set the particle effects' start points at the center of the block, with this code:

```
g.particleEffect(globalCenterX, globalCenterY, //...
```

When you start making games as relatively complex as Bloxyee, little details like these will be important to keep an eye on.

■ **Note**   If you find yourself making games that frequently require you to access sprites' global center points, just go ahead and add global center properties to the `DisplayObject` class; you might call them gcx and gcy.

Shaking the Screen

Bloxyee introduces a new special effect: the screen shake. If the paddle misses and the ball hits the bottom of the canvas, the screen shakes violently around its axis, as shown in Figure 11-12.

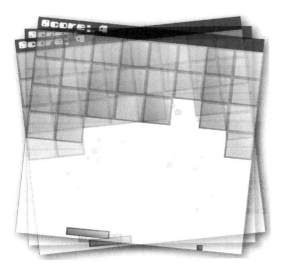

Figure 11-12.   *The screen shakes if the ball hits the bottom of the canvas*

It's a powerful, visceral effect that gives the player a deep sense of immersion in the game.

■ **Caution**   However, screen shake is also the most over-used effect in recent video game history. Please use it sparingly!

Of course, it's not the screen that's shaking—It's just the gameScene group that's being rapidly tilted left and right around its center point. The effect is created with the help of a new function called shake:

```
shake(gameScene, 0.05, true);
```

The shake function's first argument is the sprite, and the second is the shake magnitude in radians. The third argument is a Boolean that when `true` means the shaking should be angular around the sprite's center point.

You can alternatively make the shaking happen up and down on the *x*/*y* plane, as illustrated in Figure 11-13.

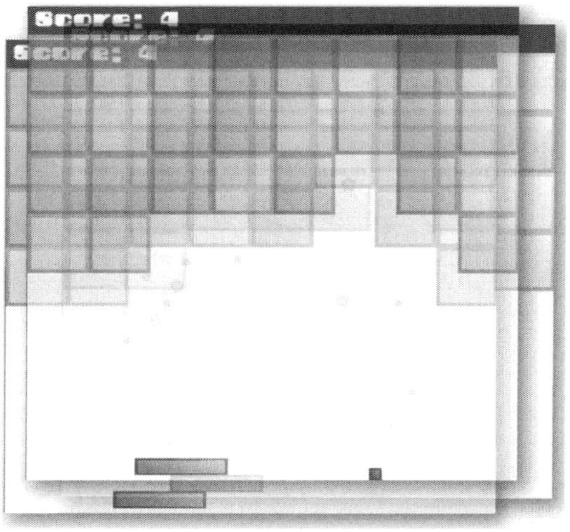

Figure 11-13. *Make the screen shake up and down*

Just set the second argument to a number, in pixels, that determines the maximum amount by which the sprite should shake. Then set the third argument to `false`, to disable angular shaking.

```
shake(gameScene, 16, false);
```

Which shaking style you prefer is entirely up to you.

The shake function works in a similar way to the particle effect and tween functions you learned to use in earlier chapters. All the shaking sprites in a game are stored in an array called `shakingSprites`.

```
export let shakingSprites = [];
```

Then all the sprites in that array have their shaking updated each frame by the game loop:

```
if (shakingSprites.length > 0) {
  for(let i = shakingSprites.length - 1; i >= 0; i--) {
    let shakingSprite = shakingSprites[i];
      if (shakingSprite.updateShake) shakingSprite.updateShake();
  }
}
```

This is same technique we used to update tweens, particles, and buttons.

The `shake` function works by adding an `updateShake` method to the supplied sprite and deciding whether the effect should be angular or up and down. If the effect is angular, the sprite is rapidly rotated alternately to the left and right. If the effect is up and down, the sprite is rapidly moved by a random amount within the range of the supplied shake magnitude. In both cases the magnitude is reduced by 10 percent on each shake, so that the shaking gradually stabilizes. Here's the complete shake function that does all this work. (You'll find it in the `library/display` file.)

```
export function shake(sprite, magnitude = 16, angular = false) {

  //A counter to count the number of shakes
  let counter = 1;

  //The total number of shakes (there will be 1 shake per frame)
  let numberOfShakes = 10;

  //Capture the sprite's position and angle so you can
  //restore them after the shaking has finished
  let startX = sprite.x,
      startY = sprite.y,
      startAngle = sprite.rotation;

  //Divide the magnitude into 10 units so that you can
  //reduce the amount of shake by 10 percent each frame
  let magnitudeUnit = magnitude / numberOfShakes;

  //The `randomInt` helper function
  let randomInt = (min, max) => {
    return Math.floor(Math.random() * (max - min + 1)) + min;
  };

  //Add the sprite to the `shakingSprites` array if it
  //isn't already there
  if(shakingSprites.indexOf(sprite) === -1) {
    shakingSprites.push(sprite);

    //Add an `updateShake` method to the sprite.
    //The `updateShake` method will be called each frame
    //in the game loop. The shake effect type can be either
    //up and down (x/y shaking) or angular (rotational shaking)
    sprite.updateShake = () => {
      if(angular) {
        angularShake();
      } else {
        upAndDownShake();
      }
    };
  }

  //The `upAndDownShake` function
  function upAndDownShake() {

    //Shake the sprite while the `counter` is less than
    //the `numberOfShakes`
    if (counter < numberOfShakes) {

      //Reset the sprite's position at the start of each shake
      sprite.x = startX;
      sprite.y = startY;
```

443

```
    //Reduce the magnitude
    magnitude -= magnitudeUnit;

    //Randomly change the sprite's position
    sprite.x += randomInt(-magnitude, magnitude);
    sprite.y += randomInt(-magnitude, magnitude);

    //Add 1 to the counter
    counter += 1;
  }

  //When the shaking is finished, restore the sprite to its original
  //position and remove it from the `shakingSprites` array
  if (counter >= numberOfShakes) {
    sprite.x = startX;
    sprite.y = startY;
    shakingSprites.splice(shakingSprites.indexOf(sprite), 1);
  }
}

//The `angularShake` function
//First set the initial tilt angle to the right (+1)
let tiltAngle = 1;

function angularShake() {
  if (counter < numberOfShakes) {

    //Reset the sprite's rotation
    sprite.rotation = startAngle;

    //Reduce the magnitude
    magnitude -= magnitudeUnit;

    //Rotate the sprite left or right, depending on the direction,
    //by an amount in radians that matches the magnitude
    sprite.rotation = magnitude * tiltAngle;
    counter += 1;

    //Reverse the tilt angle so that the sprite is tilted
    //in the opposite direction for the next shake
    tiltAngle *= -1;
  }

  //When the shaking is finished, reset the sprite's angle and
  //remove it from the `shakingSprites` array
  if (counter >= numberOfShakes) {
    sprite.rotation = startAngle;
    shakingSprites.splice(shakingSprites.indexOf(sprite), 1);
  }
 }
}
```

Bloxyee uses the shake function when the ball hits bottom of the canvas. The game code uses our custom contain function to bounce the ball off the canvas edges. You'll recall that the contain function returns a collision object that tells you which side of the container the ball has hit. If it hits the "bottom," a point is subtracted from the score and the gameScene shakes. Here's the code from Bloxyee's play function that does this:

```
let ballHitsWall = g.contain(
  ball,
  {x: 0, y: 32, width: g.stage.width, height: g.stage.height},
  true,

  //what should happen when the ball hits the edges of the boundary?
  (collision) => {

    //Play the bounce sound
    bounceSound.play();

    //If the ball hits the bottom, perform these additional tasks:
    if (collision === "bottom") {

      //Subtract 1 from the score
      score -= 1;

      //Shake the screen (the `gameScene` sprite)
      g.shake(gameScene, 0.05, true);
    }
  }
);
```

This shake function isn't just for creating a screen shake effect. Because you can use it to shake *any* sprite, you could use it as a general special effect—for example, if a game object is hit by a missile.

Ending the Game

Bloxyee ends when there are no more blocks left. Because each block is a child of the parent blocks group, you can use the empty property to check whether blocks contains any children. You'll recall from Chapter 4 that we created the empty property on the DisplayObject class, which is inherited by all the sprite types. All empty does is return true if a sprite or group has no children. Here' the code from the DisplayObject class that creates the empty property:

```
get empty() {
  if (this.children.length === 0) {
    return true;
  } else {
    return false;
  }
}
```

It's really just a convenience property to help us write more readable code.

If `blocks.empty` is `true`, you know there are no more blocks left. When that happens, the game is paused and, after a 1 second delay, the end function is called. Here's the code from Bloxyee's `play` function that checks for the end of the game:

```
if (blocks.empty) {
  g.pause();
  g.wait(1000).then(() => end());
}
```

The pause method tells the game engine not to run the `state` function in the game loop. This essentially freezes all the action on the screen, except for the special effects, like particles or tweens.

The end function slides the gameScene away to the left and slides the `titleScene` back into view from the right. It displays the score and lowers the music volume. It then reprograms the `playButton`'s `press` method so that pressing the play button will call the `restart` function to restart the game.

```
function end() {

  //Display the `titleScene` and hide the `gameScene`
  g.slide(titleScene, 0, 0, 30, ["decelerationCubed"]);
  g.slide(gameScene, -514, 0, 30, ["decelerationCubed"]);

  //Display the final score
  titleMessage.content = `Score: ${score}`;

  //Lower the music volume
  music.volume = 0.3;

  //Assign a new button `press` action to
  //`restart` the game
  playButton.press = () => {
    restart();
  };
}
```

If the button is pressed, the `restart` function resets all the game's initial conditions and rebuilds the grid of blocks. It resets the score, sets the music back to full volume, and slides the gameScene back in again. The final, most important things the `restart` function does are to set the game `state` back to `play` and call the game engine's resume method:

```
g.state = play;
g.resume();
```

The `resume` function tells the engine to run the current `state` function in the game loop. That's what starts the whole game going again.

You can play Bloxyee over and over again like this, forever, if you want to. It's just a simple prototype to get you started, but why not spend a bit of time and turn it into a real game? For example, you could modify the game to increase the difficulty with each level, increase the number of blocks, add power-ups and falling objects to collect or avoid, and increase the number of blocks in the grid.

Your Next Steps

We've reached the end of the book! Where do you go from here? There's a lot more that you can learn about the craft of videogame design in the Appendix the follows, but you've now got all the skills you need to start making games.

Bloxyee is a fundamental video game prototype. That means that if you understand how a game like Bloxyee works, you can make almost any game. Between Bloxyee, Flappy Fairy, Treasure Hunter, and all the other game prototypes and techniques you've studied in this book, you have the tools and skills to make a whole universe of 2D action games. So go ahead and do it! Think about the kind of game you want to make, decide which of the prototypes and techniques in this book will be the most help to you, and then use them as a model to start building your game. With a bit of imagination, you'll be amazed at what you can create.

But, of course, this is not the end. It's nowhere near the end! There's much more you can learn to deepen and improve your skills. Here are a few technologies and special interests that you might want to explore further:

- **WebGL**: A lower-level alternative rendering system to the Canvas API, it can give you improved performance for 2D games and is fast enough to render complex 3D graphics. Although WebGL is used as an under-the-hood rendering engine by many popular rendering engines like PixiJS, BabylonJS and ThreeJS, it's worth spending the time to learn how the core API works in detail. A good place to start learning WebGL is Brian Danchilla's *Beginning WebGL for HTML 5* (Apress, 2012).

- **Physics**: Although this book covers most of the physics you need to know for 2D action games, if you want to do any detailed, accurate physics simulations, you'll need to delve further. An excellent book on the subject is Dev Ramtal and Adrian Dobre's *Physics for JavaScript, Games, Animation and Simulations"* (Apress, 2014).

- **Animation and Motion Graphics**: You know the basics of scripted animation and how to do tweening and create motion paths. But what if you want to make something really complex, like a fully interactive, articulated robotic arm? It would help to learn about inverse kinematics. What if you want to create a simulated 3D environment? Some 3D matrix math will help you there. You can learn all these topics and more in Billy Lamberta and Keith Peter's book, *Foundation HTML5 Animation with JavaScript* (Apress, 2011). It's a classic!

- **Collision detection**: The appendix that follows this chapter will give show you how to do accurate collision detection for 2D games, and it will cover almost everything you need to know. But if you want to take those skills to the next level, Christer Ericson's classic book Real-Time Collision Detection (Morgan Kaufmann, 2005) is the place to start. Although the code examples are in written C++ (which is in the same family of languages as JavaScript), the vector math and algorithms are universal and it is not difficult to translate the concepts to JavaScript. Real-Time Collision Detection also covers everything you need to know about collision detection for 3D games, so, when you're ready to take that step, you'll be well prepared.

This book has been all about learning how to make your own games, by yourself, from scratch. As you've seen, you don't need to use commercial game engines, frameworks, third-party libraries, or expensive software. You can make and publish games for free, using just a text editor, a browser, and any old computer. And because all the code in this book uses bedrock technologies, plain-vanilla JavaScript, and open-source standardized APIs (like Canvas and the WebAudio API), you can be certain that the code you write will stand the test of time for years or decades to come. Your code base and all the time and effort you've put into learning aren't at the mercy or whims of some big corporation that might go out of business, sell out, or decide to change its API completely overnight. All your code belongs to you, and always will. You know how to make great games with only a few hundred lines of code, and you understand how every iota of that code works and how to change and fine-tune it to achieve just the effect you need. Congratulations, you're now a video game designer!

So, where do you go from here?

Isn't it obvious?

Just go start making some great games!

■ ■ ■

Vectors for Movement and Collision Detection

You may not know it, but there's an unseen world of invisible forces at work in your games, called **vectors**. They're what make your objects move and detect collisions, and they help you create simulations of real-world physical objects. Vectors are like the atoms and molecules of the game universe—everything depends on them, but they're very hard to see with the naked eye.

In this appendix, we're going to peel away the veil of this mysterious realm to examine these smallest but most important components of the video game universe. With the help of a bit of easy math, vectors are the key to decoding the entire geometry of your game environment space. Learning how to work with them gives you unlimited control over your games.

How would you feel if you could control gravity, wind, the trajectory of bullets, and the laws of physics and thermodynamics at will? Like a character from *The Matrix*, you will have that kind of power in your own game world.

What Are Vectors?

Vectors are lines. They have a starting point and an ending point. Figure A-1 shows an example of a vector called *v1*. The vector starts at point A and ends at point B.

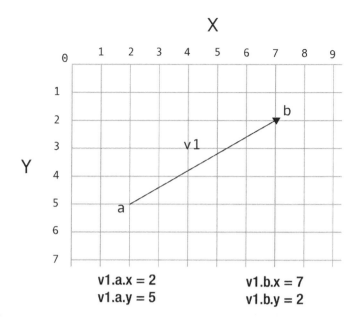

v1.a.x = 2   v1.b.x = 7
v1.a.y = 5   v1.b.y = 2

Figure A-1. *A vector called v1 (shorthand for vector 1) with starting and ending points*

▓ **Note**   In this appendix, I'll use a simple naming convention for describing vectors. Vector names will start with *v* plus the number of the vector, such as *v1*, *v2*, and *v3*. This will help to keep the code compact.

What can two points that define a line tell us? As you can see in Figure A-1, the vector tells you where it starts, where it ends, and the direction it's pointing toward. These are the two defining characteristics of vectors:

- Length (often referred to by the more technical term **magnitude**)

- Direction

Does that sound like information that might be of use in a game? Well, you are already using this information. It's called *velocity*!

The *x* and *y* Components

Whenever a sprite moves, it creates a vector. The vector is created by the sprite's vertical and horizontal velocity, better known as our dear friends, **vx** and **vy**, as illustrated in Figure A-2.

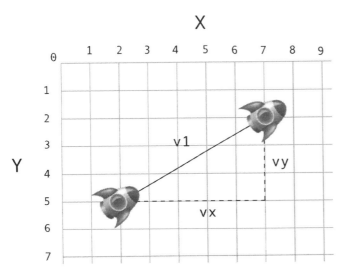

Figure A-2. *When game objects move, their vx and vy properties describe a vector*

Any moving sprite has horizontal velocity (*vx*) and vertical velocity (*vy*). When these velocities are combined, the sprite moves in some direction. If the sprite has a *vx* of 5 and *vy* of –5, it will appear to move diagonally toward the top right. And when that happens, the sprite invisibly creates a vector between its previous position and its new position.

This kind of vector, which is created by an object's movement, is called a **motion vector**. So you've been creating and using vectors all this time without even knowing it!

The value *vx* is known as the vector's **x component**., and *vy* is the vector's **y component**. Figure A-3 shows how *vx* and *vy* fit into the big picture.

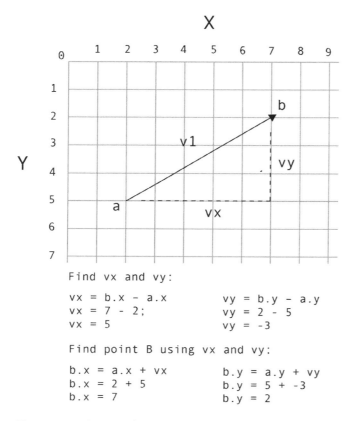

```
Find vx and vy:

vx = b.x - a.x          vy = b.y - a.y
vx = 7 - 2;             vy = 2 - 5
vx = 5                  vy = -3

Find point B using vx and vy:

b.x = a.x + vx          b.y = a.y + vy
b.x = 2 + 5            b.y = 5 + -3
b.x = 7               b.y = 2
```

Figure A-3. *The vector's x and y components: vx and vy*

You can describe any vector using *vx* and *vy* values. In fact, *vx* and *vy* values *are* vectors. You don't need any more information than that to use vectors effectively.

If you know where the vector starts and where it ends, you can find a vector's *vx* and *vy* values using these simple formulas:

```
vx = b.x - a.x;
vy = b.y - a.y;
```

Just subtract the starting *x* and *y* points from the ending *x* and *y* points.

If you know only the vector's *vx* and *vy* properties and where the vector starts, you can figure out the end point using these formulas:

```
b.x = a.x + vx;
b.y = a.y + vy;
```

Take a look at Figure A-3 and see if you can work out how the values were found. It's pretty easy if you just take it one small step at a time. In plain English, it says:

The new position (point B) is the same as the old position (point A), plus velocity (vx and vy).

There's a shorthand way to write this formula. Does this look familiar?

```
x += vx;
y += vy;
```

That's what we've used to move all the sprites in this book!
Do you see how easy all these concepts are to grasp? It's just basic math.
A very important thing to remember is that *if you have vx and vy properties, you have a vector.*

Vector Magnitude

Every vector has a length. In geometry, a vector's length is referred to as its **magnitude**. It's important to know what a vector's magnitude is so that you can figure out how far away things are or how fast they're moving. If a spaceship sprite's motion vector has a magnitude of 3, then you know what its velocity is. And you can also use that information to anticipate or resolve a collision with another object, as you'll soon learn.

So how can we find out what a vector's magnitude is? It's the distance between point A and point B. You can easily calculate this with the help of the game designer's reliable old standby, the Pythagorean theorem:

```
m = Math.sqrt(vx * vx + vy * vy);
```

I'm using the variable name m to refer to magnitude. Figure A-4 illustrates how the vector's magnitude is found.

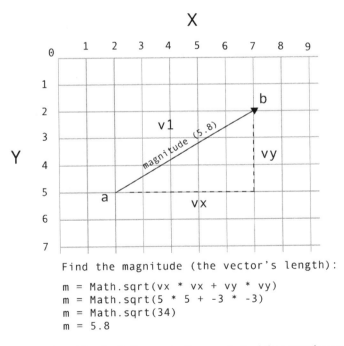

```
Find the magnitude (the vector's length):
m = Math.sqrt(vx * vx + vy * vy)
m = Math.sqrt(5 * 5 + -3 * -3)
m = Math.sqrt(34)
m = 5.8
```

Figure A-4. *Use the Pythagorean theorem to find the vector's magnitude. Values have been rounded*

In a game, a magnitude of 5.8 could tell you how fast a spaceship is moving. Point A would be the ship's start position, Point B would be its end position, and the magnitude would be its speed. In this example, 5.8 could mean that the spaceship has travelled 5.8 pixels during one frame of movement (1/60th of a second.)

Or you could use the magnitude to find out how far away the ship is from an enemy. In that case Point A would be the ship, Point B would be the enemy, and the magnitude would represent the distance between them.

Calculating the Angle

It's often useful to know a vector's angle. A bit of simple trigonometry will find it for you:

```
angle = Math.atan2(vy, vx);
```

■ **Note**   With the `Math.atan2` method, the y property is the first argument and the x property is the second.

This formula gives you a value in radians. To find the angle in degrees, multiply the result by 180 divided by PI (3.14), as follows:

```
angle = Math.atan2(vy, vx) * 180 / Math.PI;
```

There's an interesting flip side to this. How can you find a vector if you have only its angle and magnitude (its length)? A little more trigonometry will help here as well:

```
vx = m * Math.cos(angle);
vy = m * Math.sin(angle);
```

And remember, all you need are the *vx* and *vy* properties to calculate any vector. So with these results, you're all set. With vx and vy, you still have a vector, even though it may not have a specific starting or ending point yet.

These formulas are the keys to being able to switch between vectors and angles, and, as you will see in this appendix, they have endless utility. Figure A-5 shows how they're used.

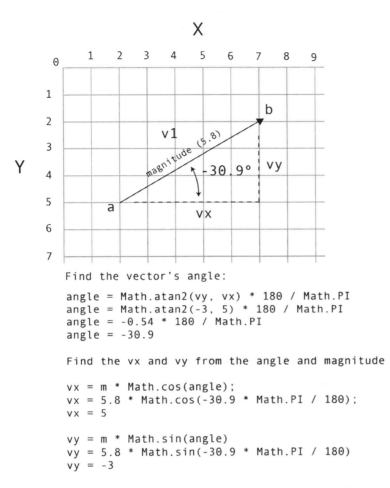

```
Find the vector's angle:

angle = Math.atan2(vy, vx) * 180 / Math.PI
angle = Math.atan2(-3, 5) * 180 / Math.PI
angle = -0.54 * 180 / Math.PI
angle = -30.9

Find the vx and vy from the angle and magnitude

vx = m * Math.cos(angle);
vx = 5.8 * Math.cos(-30.9 * Math.PI / 180);
vx = 5

vy = m * Math.sin(angle)
vy = 5.8 * Math.sin(-30.9 * Math.PI / 180)
vy = -3
```

Figure A-5. *Finding a vector's angle and finding the vx and vy values*

Vector Normals

Vectors hide a deep, dark secret. Clinging to the base of each vector are two invisible and somewhat shadowy additional vectors called **normals**.

One of these normals runs to the left of the vector, and the other runs to its right. They are exactly perpendicular (at 90 degrees) to the main vector. Together, they form a base on which the vector stands. Figure A-6 illustrates how the left and right normals connect with the main vector. The normals define the "normal" orientation of the vector. They define the ground that the vector stands on, so you always know which way is "up" in the vector's coordinate system.

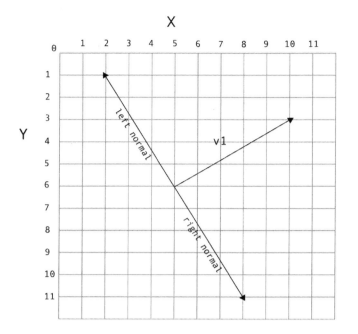

Figure A-6. *The left and right normals are perpendicular to the main vector and help define the vector's coordinate space*

Both the left and right normals are also vectors. The left normal is a vector that points to the left, and the right normal points to the right. Whether you want to or not, every time you create a vector, you're actually creating three vectors: the main vector and its two normals. The normals have the same magnitude as the main vector. They help to define what's known as the vector's coordinate space.

The left normal is represented by the variables lx and ly. They're very easy to calculate:

```
lx = vy;
ly = -vx;
```

As you can see, it's just a 90-degree twist on the main vector's *vx* and *vy* properties. The right normal is found this way:

```
rx = -vy;
ry = vx;
```

Once you've found the left and right normals' lx, ly, rx, and ry values, you can easily figure out the rest of the vector information. Their starting point (a) will always be the same as the main vector, so you can calculate their ending points (b) this way:

```
leftNormal.b.x = v1.a.x + lx;
leftNormal.b.y = v1.a.y + ly;
rightNormal.b.x = v1.a.x + rx;
rightNormal.b.y = v1.a.y + ry;
```

And now you have two completely new vectors if you need them. You can apply any of the other vector calculations in this appendix to these new vectors.

It's much easier to understand all this visually, so Figure A-7 shows how all these values are found. Keep this information close at hand, because you'll need to use it soon.

Why is important to be able to calculate a vector's normals? They're essential for working out how to bounce objects off of other objects, as you'll soon see.

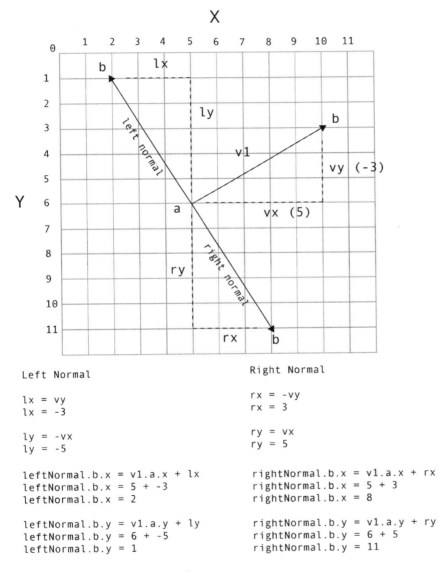

Left Normal

```
lx = vy
lx = -3

ly = -vx
ly = -5

leftNormal.b.x = v1.a.x + lx
leftNormal.b.x = 5 + -3
leftNormal.b.x = 2

leftNormal.b.y = v1.a.y + ly
leftNormal.b.y = 6 + -5
leftNormal.b.y = 1
```

Right Normal

```
rx = -vy
rx = 3

ry = vx
ry = 5

rightNormal.b.x = v1.a.x + rx
rightNormal.b.x = 5 + 3
rightNormal.b.x = 8

rightNormal.b.y = v1.a.y + ry
rightNormal.b.y = 6 + 5
rightNormal.b.y = 11
```

Figure A-7. *Calculate the normals*

Normalizing Vectors

Sometimes you need to know the direction that a vector is pointing. Where is an object going? And, more important, can you use that information to orient other objects in the same direction?

This is where the technique of **normalizing** a vector becomes important. Normalized vectors have a definite direction, but have their magnitude scaled to 1, which is the smallest size that a vector can be. If you first make the vector as small as possible, you can easily scale it up to any size and keep it perfectly proportioned.

Normalized vectors are represented by the variable names dx and dy, and they are found this way:

```
dx = vx / m;
dy = vy / m;
```

You just divide the *vx* and *vy* by the vector's magnitude. The result is a really tiny vector with a length of 1. In a game, it will be the size of a single pixel. Figure A-8 illustrates how this works.

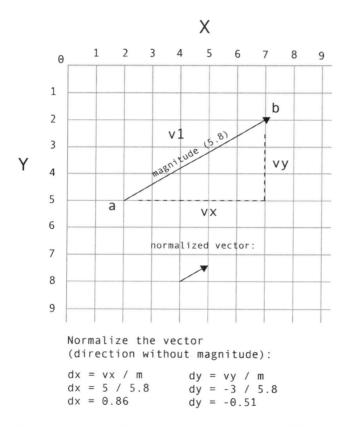

Normalize the vector
(direction without magnitude):

```
dx = vx / m        dy = vy / m
dx = 5 / 5.8       dy = -3 / 5.8
dx = 0.86          dy = -0.51
```

Figure A-8. *Normalize the vector to help scale it to a different magnitude*

▧ **Caution**   Don't confuse **normalizing** with **vector normals**. Very confusingly (and it is confusing!), they are two completely separate things. Normals are the vectors perpendicular to the main vector. Normalizing is a technique used to scale a vector.

Normalized vectors are also called **unit vectors** because their size is 1, which is the smallest possible whole unit that the vector can be. You can use unit vectors to scale a vector to any size, either larger or smaller. Have you ever wondered what the magic ingredient was in that bottle that Alice drank? It was a unit vector!

The normalized vector doesn't have any starting or ending points, so you can think of it as just hanging in space, waiting for someone to tell it what to do. But most important, the *dx* and *dy* values that result from normalizing are useful for figuring out the vector's direction.

■ **Tip** What does the *d* in *dx* and *dy* mean? It stands for delta, which in mathematics is often used to show that there has been a change in a value. It's usually used to indicate that a large value has been reduced to a smaller one. By convention, *dx* and *dy* are used to represent normalized *vx* and *vy* values.

There's a small detail you need to be conscious of when calculating unit vectors. If there's a chance that the magnitude, *vx,* or *vy* values could ever be zero, the formula will return NaN (Not a Number.) To avoid that, give dx and dy default values of 0, just in case:

```
dx = vx / m || 0;
dy = vy / m || 0;
```

Division by zero is *always* a bad thing in computer programming—it can lead to all kinds of hard-to-find bugs.

Adding and Subtracting Vectors

You can think of vectors as forces. A vector with a magnitude of 5 is a force that makes your spaceship move 5 pixels each frame. Sometimes in a game, you'll have more than one force acting on an object. Maybe the force of gravity is pulling your spaceship down, and wind is pushing it to the right. You can create vectors for gravity and wind, and then add or subtract those vectors to your ship's motion vector to find the ship's new direction.

Let's take gravity as an example. Imagine that you have a spaceship sprite that has a motion vector with a magnitude of 5. Then imagine that in your game you have a gravity vector with a magnitude of 2. If gravity is acting on your spaceship, you want to subtract 2 from 5 to find the ship's new motion vector, which will be 3.

Subtracting the magnitudes of vectors isn't useful in most cases, because the magnitude alone doesn't tell you the vector's direction. Instead, you need to subtract the vector's *vx* and *vy* values in two separate calculations. This is incredibly easy to do.

As an example, imagine that you have a spaceship hovering above a flat planet surface. The force of gravity on the *y* axis is pulling the ship down. If the force of gravity is 2, you can describe gravity's *vx* and *vy* properties this way:

```
gravityVx = 0;
gravityVy = 2;
```

Remember: *if you have a vx and a vy value, you have a vector*. It might not have starting or ending points, but it's still a vector. In this case, the gravity acts only on the *y* axis, so you don't need a value for *vx*.

Here's how you can add the force of gravity to the ship's motion vector:

```
ship.vy += gravityVy;
```

If the ship started with a *vy* of –5, its new value would now be –3. This would pull the ship down in the next frame. Figures A-9 and A-10 illustrate how this vector addition works.

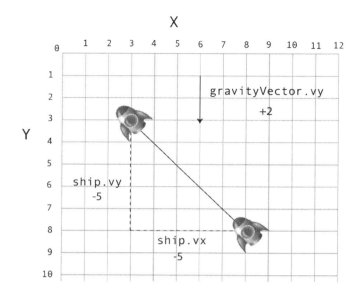

Figure A-9. *What happens when you combine a gravity vector and the ship's motion vector? In this example, the ship's vy value is -5, and the gravity vector is +2*

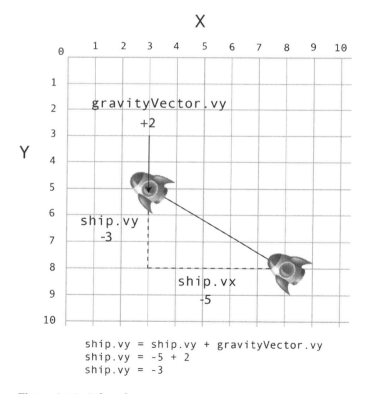

```
ship.vy = ship.vy + gravityVector.vy
ship.vy = -5 + 2
ship.vy = -3
```

Figure A-10. *When the two vectors are added together, a new vector results, which combines their forces. This pulls the ship down toward the planet surface*

When you add vectors together this way, the result is a new vector. It's a combination of the downward pull of gravity and the upward push of the ship. As you can see, the math is amazingly simple, but it's a very accurate description of what happens in the real world.

Scaling Vectors

In our simple gravity example, the ship was pulled down on the *y* axis. This is fine in a platform or pinball game, where "down" is the bottom of the screen. But suppose your spaceship is circling a planet? Which way is down? Look at Figure A-11 and see if you can figure it out.

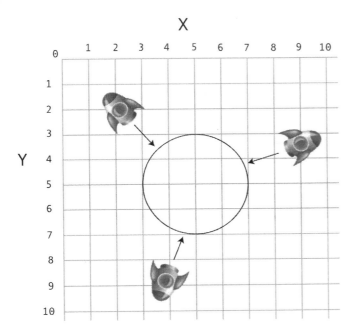

Figure A-11. *To pull a spaceship toward a round planet, gravity must act on both the x and y axes*

Looking at that diagram, two things should come to mind:

- The ship needs to know where the center of the planet is.

- To move the ship toward the planet's center, gravity must act on the both the *x* and *y* axes.

Let's put together everything we know about vectors so far to solve this problem. Run gravity.html in the chapter's source files for a working example of a spaceship orbiting a planet using gravity, as shown in Figure A-12.

Figure A-12. *Use vectors to simulate gravity*

Use the left and right keyboard keys to rotate the ship, and use the up-arrow key to make the ship move forward (you learned how to do that in Chapter 6). Here's the code that pulls the ship toward the planet in a very realistic simulation of gravity. You can see that it uses most of the vector math you've learned so far:

```
//1. Create a vector between the planet and the ship
let vx = planet.x - ship.x,
    vy = planet.y - ship.y;

//2. Find the vector's magnitude
let m = Math.sqrt(vx * vx + vy * vy);

//3. Normalize the vector
let dx = vx / m,
    dy = vy / m;

//4. Create the gravity vector. Do this by scaling the vector
//between the planet and the ship to a tiny
//fraction of its original size
let gravityVx = dx * 0.05,
    gravityVy = dy * 0.05;
```

//5. Apply the new gravity vector to the ship's motion vector
```
ship.vx += gravityVx,
ship.vy += gravityVy;
```

//6. Apply the ship's velocity to its position to make the ship move
```
ship.x += ship.vx;
ship.y += ship.vy;
```

Let's find out how this works.

The code first calculates the vector between the ship and the planet (vx and vy). It then figures out the magnitude (m) and works out the unit vector (dx and dy.) Figure A-13 shows how to calculate dx and dy from the original ship-to-planet vector.

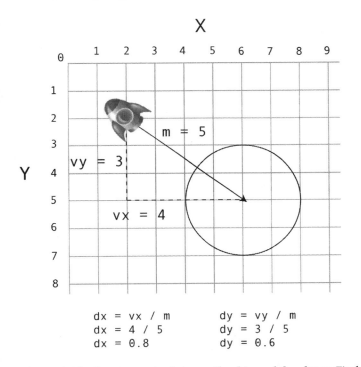

```
dx = vx / m        dy = vy / m
dx = 4 / 5         dy = 3 / 5
dx = 0.8           dy = 0.6
```

Figure A-13. *Create a vector between the ship and the planet. Find its dx and dy values, which tell you the vector's direction*

The gravity vector is calculated by scaling the unit vector (dx and dy) down to a twentieth of its original size:

```
let gravityVx = dx * 0.05,
    gravityVy = dy * 0.05;
```

This creates a vector that's extremely small, but precisely equivalent in scale to the original vector between planet and the ship. It points from the center of the ship directly toward the center of the planet.

Finally, apply this gravity vector to the ship's motion vector:

```
ship.x += ship.vx;
ship.y += ship.vy;
```

The ship will very náturally be drawn toward the center of the planet, no matter which side of the planet it's on. Figure A-14 shows how the position of the ship is influenced by this new gravity vector. Compare it to Figure A-13 to see the difference.

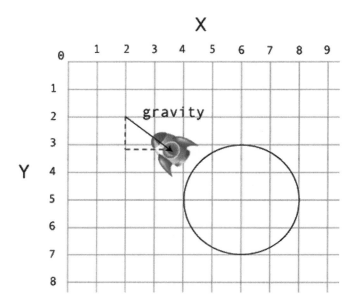

Figure A-14. *Adding gravity to the ship's motion vector pushes it toward the planet*

Real Gravity

There's one small problem with our spaceship example that you may have noticed. The force of gravity is the same no matter how far away the ship is from the planet. In space, the force of gravity between objects weakens as they move further apart. Also, large objects with a lot of mass will have a greater gravitational attraction than smaller objects. We can implement a more realistic gravitational system with just a bit more tweaking.

First, create some values that represent the mass of the planet and the spaceship. The values you use will depend on trial and error, but the following values work well in this example:

```
ship.mass = 1;
planet.mass = 10;
```

Then calculate the gravity vector using this formula:

```
let gravityVx = dx * (planet.mass * ship.mass) / m,
    gravityVy = dy * (planet.mass * ship.mass) / m;
```

If you add a few more planets with different masses and initial velocities, you could use this technique to create a complex, gravity-based space exploration game with realistic physics. Start building your own universe!

The Dot Product

A value that's useful when working with vectors is the **dot product**. The dot product tells you whether two vectors are pointing in the same direction or in opposite directions.

Imagine you have the two vectors v1 and v2. You can find their dot product with this syntax:

```
dotProduct = v1.vx * v2.dx + v1.vy * v2.dy
```

If the dot product is positive, the vectors point in the same direction. If the dot product is negative, the vectors point away from each other. This apparently useless bit of information can actually give you a powerful description of where your game objects are in relation to each other, and it forms the basis for sophisticated collision and boundary detection.

Run the boundary.html file for a working example of how you can use a dot product to create an environmental boundary. Fly the spaceship through the diagonal line. If the center of the ship is on the left side of the line, the line color is yellow. If the ship is on the right side of the line, the line becomes red. A text sprite displays the current value of the dot product at the top of the screen. You'll notice that the line color changes as soon as the dot product changes from a positive to a negative number. Figure A-15 shows what you'll see.

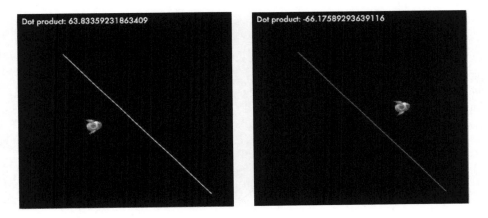

Figure A-15. *The dot product changes from positive to negative when the spaceship crosses the line*

Another significant feature you can see in this example is that the dot product also tells you exactly how many pixels the center of the ship is away from the line. As you'll see later in this appendix, that number will prove to be extremely useful for doing collision detection and reaction.

Here's the code from the game loop that creates this effect:

```
//1. Get a vector between the center of the ship and the start point of the line
let v1 = {};
v1.vx = boundary.ax - ship.centerX;
v1.vy = boundary.ay - ship.centerY;

//2. Get the boundary line's vector and magnitude
let v2 = {};
v2.vx = boundary.bx - boundary.ax;
v2.vy = boundary.by - boundary.ay;
v2.m = Math.sqrt(v2.vx * v2.vx + v2.vy * v2.vy);
```

//3. Figure out the line vector's left normal
```
v2.ln = {};
v2.ln.vx = v2.vy;
v2.ln.vy = -v2.vx;
```

//4. Get the left normal's unit vector (dx and dy)
```
v2.ln.dx = v2.ln.vx / v2.m;
v2.ln.dy = v2.ln.vy / v2.m;
```

//5. Get the dot product between v1 and v2's left normal
```
let dotProduct = v1.vx * v2.ln.dx + v1.vy * v2.ln.dy;
```

//If the dot product is positive, make the line yellow,
//if it's negative, make the line red
```
if (dotProduct > 0) {
  boundary.strokeStyle = "yellow";
} else {
  boundary.strokeStyle = "red";
}
```

//Display the value of the dot product
```
message.content = `Dot product: ${dotProduct}`;
```

The first thing the code does is create a vector named v1, between the center point of the ship and the start point of the line. It then creates another vector, named v2, between the starting and ending points of the line. Figure A-16 illustrates these two vectors.

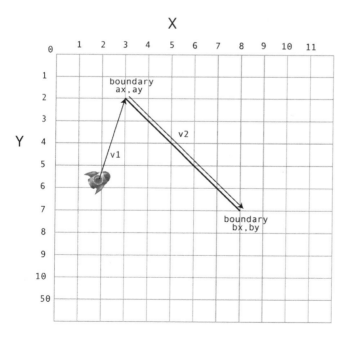

Figure A-16. *Create two vectors*

The code then calculates v2's left normal, as shown in Figure A-17.

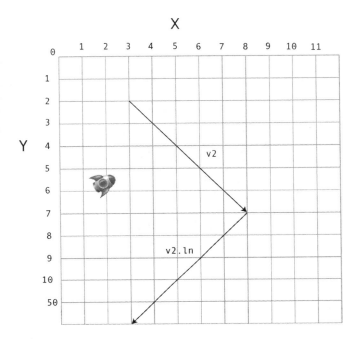

Figure A-17. *The line's left normal*

The code then shrinks the left normal down by converting it to a unit vector:

```
v2.ln.dx = v2.ln.vx / v2.m;
v2.ln.dy = v2.ln.vy / v2.m;
```

Finally, the code finds the dot product between v1 and the left normal's unit vector:

```
let dotProduct = v1.vx * v2.ln.dx + v1.vy * v2.ln.dy;
```

That's the magic number we need. If the dot product is positive, the ship is on the left side of the line; if it's negative, the ship is on the right side.

The Perpendicular Dot Product

Another fun value you can use is the **perpendicular dot product**. It's exactly the same as an ordinary dot product, except that instead of using v1 in the equation, you use v1's normal: the *perpendicular* vector. (You can use either the left or the right normal; it doesn't matter which) The perpendicular dot product is sometimes called the **perp product** or **perp-dot product**. Here's how to find it.

```
perpProduct = v1.ln.vx * v2.dx + v1.ln.vy * v2.dy;
```

Let's find out how to use this to figure out the point where two vectors intersect. Run the `intersection.html` file for a working example. Aim the spaceship at the line and fly toward it. You'll notice that a white circular target appears on the line at *exactly* the point at which the ship will intersect the line. Figure A-18 illustrates what you'll see. It's kind of spooky when you see it in action, but it's just math!

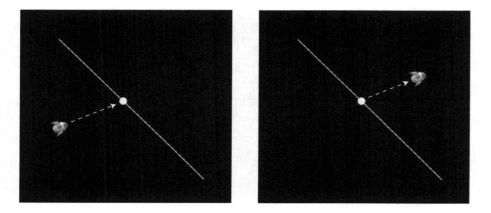

Figure A-18. *The circular target anticipates where the ship will hit the line*

Here's the code from the game loop that does all this.

```
//1. Get the ship's motion vector and left normal
let v1 = {};
v1.vx = ship.vx;
v1.vy = ship.vy;
v1.ln = {};
v1.ln.vx = v1.vy;
v1.ln.vy = -v1.vx;

//2.Figure out the motion vector's start and end points
v1.ax = ship.centerX;
v1.ay = ship.centerY;
v1.bx = v1.ax + v1.vx;
v1.by = v1.ay + v1.vy;

//3. Get the boundary line's vector, magnitude, and unit vector
let v2 = {};
v2.vx = boundary.bx - boundary.ax;
v2.vy = boundary.by - boundary.ay;
v2.m = Math.sqrt(v2.vx * v2.vx + v2.vy * v2.vy);
v2.dx = v2.vx / v2.m;
v2.dy = v2.vy / v2.m;
```

```
//4. Get a vector between v1 (the ship's motion vector)
//and the start point of the line. Get its left normal
let v3 = {};
v3.vx = boundary.ax - v1.ax;
v3.vy = boundary.ay - v1.ay;
v3.ln = {};
v3.ln.vx = v3.vy;
v3.ln.vy = -v3.vx;

//5. Find the perpendicular dot product of v3 and v2
let perpProduct1 = v3.ln.vx * v2.dx + v3.ln.vy * v2.dy;

//6. Find the perpendicular dot product of v1 and v2
let perpProduct2 = v1.ln.vx * v2.dx + v1.ln.vy * v2.dy;

//7. Find the ratio between perpProduct1 and perpProduct2
let t = perpProduct1 / perpProduct2;

//8. Find the intersection point on the boundary line
let intersectionX = v1.ax + v1.vx * t,
    intersectionY = v1.ay + v1.vy * t;

//9. Set the circular target sprite to the intersection point
//(You only want to do this if the intersection point falls
//between the starting and ending points of the line)
if (intersectionX > boundary.ax
    && intersectionX < boundary.by
    && intersectionY > boundary.ay
    && intersectionY < boundary.by
) {
  target.x = intersectionX - target.halfWidth;
  target.y = intersectionY - target.halfWidth;
}
```

The code calculates three vectors: the ship's motion vector, the boundary line's vector, and a vector between the ship's motion vector and the boundary line. Figure A-19 illustrates where these vectors are.

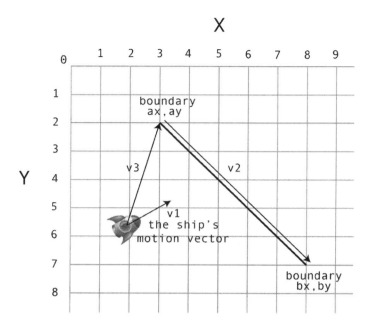

Figure A-19. *Use three vectors to help find the intersection point*

The code then figures out the intersection point by calculating the perpendicular dot products between v2 and the other two vectors, and then gets the ratio between them:

```
let perpProduct1 = v3.ln.vx * v2.dx + v3.ln.vy * v2.dy;
let perpProduct2 = v1.ln.vx * v2.dx + v1.ln.vy * v2.dy;
let t = perpProduct1 / perpProduct2;
```

(Note that t stands for *tangent*—the point of intersection.)

That ratio, t, is then used to find the intersection point's pixel position on the line. That point is found by multiplying the ship's motion vector by the ratio:

```
let intersectionX = v1.ax + v1.vx * t,
    intersectionY = v1.ay + v1.vy * t;
```

The code essentially draws a line from the center of the ship to the point on the line that the ship will cross.

intersectionX and intersectionY now tell you the pixel position value of the intersection point on the canvas. You can use those values to position any other sprite at that point. In this example a circle sprite called target is moved to that position. However, you only need to move the target if the intersection happens to fall on the line itself, and not beyond its starting and ending points. An if statement checks for that before positioning the target sprite.

```
if (intersectionX > boundary.ax
    && intersectionX < boundary.by
    && intersectionY > boundary.ay
    && intersectionY < boundary.by
) {
  target.x = intersectionX - target.halfWidth;
  target.y = intersectionY - target.halfWidth;
}
```

■ **Note**   All vectors will eventually intersect, unless they're parallel. Two vectors are parallel if their dx and dy values are exactly the same.

Now that you know how to use vectors to create an environmental boundary, let's find out how you can prevent a sprite from crossing it.

Collision with a Line

Run the lineCollision.html file for a working example of how to use a line as a collision boundary. Fly the spaceship into the line from left to right—you'll see that you can't fly through it, no matter how hard you try. The line is a solid collision boundary, as shown in Figure A-20.

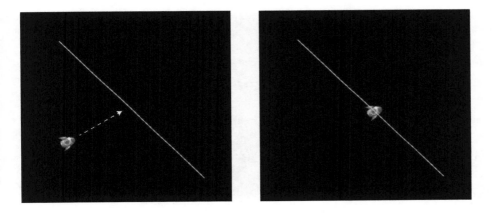

Figure A-20. *You can't fly through the line*

Here's all the code from the game loop that makes this work—I'll explain exactly what it does after the listing.

```
//1. Get the ship's motion vector and magnitude
let v1 = {};
v1.vx = ship.vx;
v1.vy = ship.vy;
v1.m = Math.sqrt(v1.vx * v1.vx + v1.vy * v1.vy);

//2. Find the unit vector
v1.dx = v1.vx / v1.m || 0;
v1.dy = v1.vy / v1.m || 0;

//3. Get the boundary line's vector, unit vector, left normal,
//and left normal unit vector
let v2 = {};
v2.ax = boundary.ax;
v2.ay = boundary.ay;
v2.bx = boundary.bx;
v2.by = boundary.by;
v2.vx = v2.bx - v2.ax;
```

471

```
v2.vy = v2.by - v2.ay;
v2.m = Math.sqrt(v2.vx * v2.vx + v2.vy * v2.vy);
v2.dx = v2.vx / v2.m || 0;
v2.dy = v2.vy / v2.m || 0;
v2.ln = {};
v2.ln.vx = v2.vy;
v2.ln.vy = -v2.vx;
v2.ln.dx = v2.ln.vx / v2.m || 0;
v2.ln.dy = v2.ln.vy / v2.m || 0;

//4. Get a vector between the starting point of
//the ship's motion vector and the starting point of the line
let v3 = {};
v3.vx = v2.ax - ship.centerX;
v3.vy = v2.ay - ship.centerY;

//5. You need two dot products.
//The first tells you whether the ship is
//between the starting and ending points of the line
let dp1 = v3.vx * v2.dx + v3.vy * v2.dy;

//The second dot product tells you if the ship has crossed the line
let dp2 = v3.vx * v2.ln.dx + v3.vy * v2.ln.dy;

//6. Check to see if the ship is within the vector's scope
if(dp1 > -v2.m && dp1 < 0) {

    //7. Check if the ship's motion vector has crossed the line from right to left
    if(dp2 <= 0) {

        //8. Find the collision vector
        let collisionVx = v1.dx * Math.abs(dp2),
            collisionVy = v1.dy * Math.abs(dp2);

        //9. Move the ship out of the collision
        ship.x -= collisionVx;
        ship.y -= collisionVy;

        //10. Set the ship's velocity to zero
        ship.vx = 0;
        ship.vy = 0;
    }
}
```

The code first creates three vectors: the ship's motion vector, a vector to represent the line, and a third vector between the center of the ship and the start point of the line. It then calculates two dot products. The first dot product tells you if the ship is between the starting and ending points of the line. If dp1 is greater than the negative magnitude of v2, and less than 0, then you know the ship is between the line's points and the code should check for a collision.

```
let dp1 = v3.vx * v2.dx + v3.vy * v2.dy;
if(dp1 > -v2.m && dp1 < 0) {
    //The ship is within the start and end points of the line
}
```

The second dot product is used to check whether the ship has crossed the line from left to right. You know this is true if the dot product becomes negative:

```
let dp2 = v3.vx * v2.ln.dx + v3.vy * v2.ln.dy;
if(dp2 <= 0) {
  //The ship has crossed the line from left to right
}
```

When the ship crosses the line, calculate the **collision vector**. The collision vector tells you by how many pixels the ship has gone over the line:

```
let collisionVx = v1.dx * Math.abs(dp2),
    collisionVy = v1.dy * Math.abs(dp2);
```

For example, if the ship crosses the line by 4 pixels, the dot product will be –4. If you multiply that number by the dx and dy of the ship's motion vector, you end up with a tiny vector that describes by how much the ship has overshot the line. That's the collision vector.

You can resolve the collision by moving the ship back onto the line. You can do that by subtracting the collision vector from the ship's position.

```
ship.x -= collisionVx;
ship.y -= collisionVy;
```

This sets the ship exactly on the line.

▧ **Tip** For a more robust solution in complex physics situations, calculate the intersection point between the sprite and the line (as in the previous example), and position the sprite on that point.

Finally, set the ship's velocity to 0:

```
ship.vx = 0;
ship.vy = 0;
```

This makes the collision look more precise by preventing the ship from continuously trying to cross the line after the collision has been resolved.

The Other Side of the Line

The example code you've just seen works only if the ship is flying through the line from left to right. If you want to check for a collision from right to left, reverse v2's starting and ending points:

```
v2.ax = boundary.bx;
v2.ay = boundary.by;
v2.bx = boundary.ax;
v2.by = boundary.ay;
```

You also know that if dp2 is positive, the ship is on the right side of the line, and if it's negative, the ship is on the left side. If your game needs to, you can use this information to create a more sophisticated line collision system that would let the ship fly around the line and collide on both sides.

Bounce

In the previous example the spaceship came to a dead standstill when it hit the line. But in most games you'll probably want the ship to bounce away at an angle. We can easy add a bounce effect with the help of a technique called **projection**.

Projection occurs when you overlay a vector onto another vector's coordinate system. Imagine that you're standing on the sidewalk. It's a sunny day, and the sun is behind you casting your shadow on the concrete. Your shadow is the *projection* of you onto the sidewalk. If you think of yourself as a vector, and the sidewalk as another vector, your shadow is a third vector. It has a lot of your qualities, but conforms to the sidewalk's coordinate system.

That's all a projection is: *the vector's shadow on another vector*. Figure A-21 shows two examples of v1 projected onto v2. The projection itself becomes a new vector.

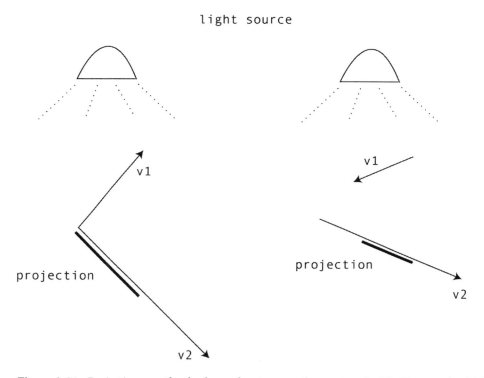

Figure A-21. *Projections are the shadows of vectors on other vectors. In this diagram the thick black lines are the projections of v1 onto v2*

The math to project v1 onto v2 in this example is pretty simple. First, find the dot product of v1 and v2:

```
dotProduct = v1.vx * v2.dx + v1.vy * v2.dy
```

Then multiply the dot product by v2's dx and dy to find the projected vector:

```
projectionVx = dotProduct * v2.dx;
projectionVy = dotProduct * v2.dy;
```

And that's it; you have your projected vector! But how is projection useful?

Bouncing! When a sprite hits an angled line, it needs to bounce away at the correct angle. That's where the technique of projection saves the day. Let's look at the general procedure for making an object bounce.

First, we need to combine the sprite's motion vector with the angle of the line with which it's colliding. The first step is to project v1 onto v2 and v2's normal. Figure A-22 illustrates this. (The projected vectors are called p1 and p2 in this example.)

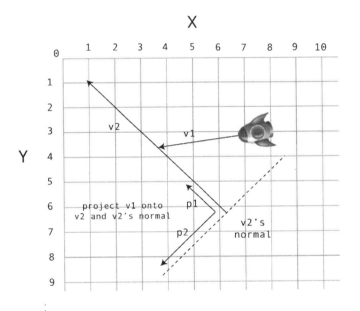

Figure A-22. *Project v1 onto v2 and v2's normal*

Next, *reverse* the p2 vector. We want our collision object to bounce, so reversing this projection will create a force directly opposite to the collision force. To reverse a vector, simply multiply its vx and vy values by –1. Then add the vx and vy values of both projected vectors together. This gives you a new **bounce vector**. Figure A-23 illustrates this.

X

Y

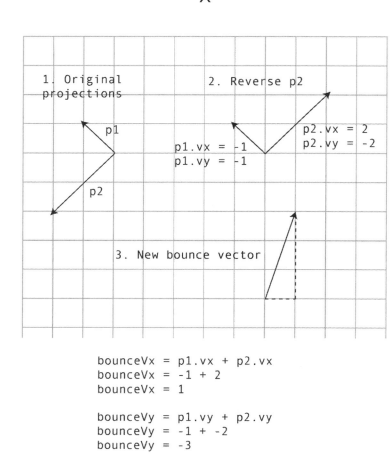

```
bounceVx = p1.vx + p2.vx
bounceVx = -1 + 2
bounceVx = 1

bounceVy = p1.vy + p2.vy
bounceVy = -1 + -2
bounceVy = -3
```

Figure A-23. *Reverse p2 and add the projections together to create a new bounce vector*

The last step is to apply this new bounce vector to the collision sprite's velocity (v1). The sprite will bounce away at exactly the right angle, no matter what the angle of the line is. Compare the bounce vector in Figure A-23 with the way that it has been applied in Figure A-24, and you'll see that it's exactly the same vector. It makes the sprite bounce correctly!

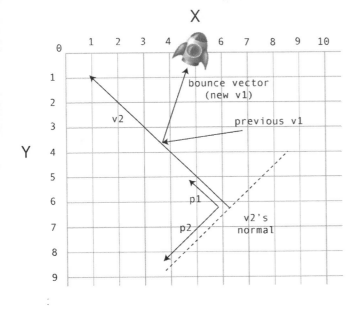

Figure A-24. *Assign the new bounce vector to the object's velocity*

Now let's turn all this theory into code. Run the `lineBounce.html` file to see this in action. Fly the spaceship into the line, and it will bounce away at the correct angle, as shown in Figure A-25.

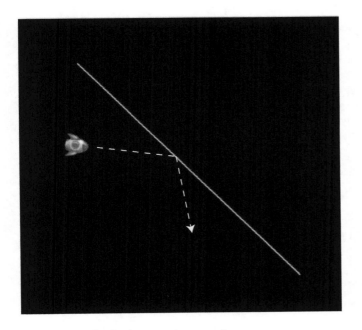

Figure A-25. *Perfect bounce at any angle*

Most of the code is the same as the previous example. The only additions are the following lines from the inner nested `if` statement. They figure out the projections, create the bounce vector, and add the bounce vector to the ship's velocity:

```
//Find the dot product of v1 and v2
let dp3 = v1.vx * v2.dx + v1.vy * v2.dy;

//Find the projection of v1 onto v2
let p1Vx = dp3 * v2.dx,
    p1Vy = dp3 * v2.dy;

//Find the dot product of v1 and v2's normal (v2.ln)
let dp4 = v1.vx * v2.ln.dx + v1.vy * v2.ln.dy;

//Find the projection of v1 onto v2's normal (v2.ln)
let p2Vx = dp4 * v2.ln.dx,
    p2Vy = dp4 * v2.ln.dy;

//Reverse the projection on v2's normal by multiplying it by -1.
//This is what creates the bounce effect
p2Vx *= -1;
p2Vy *= -1;

//Add up the projected vectors' vx and vy values
//to create a new bounce vector
let bounceVx = p1Vx + p2Vx,
    bounceVy = p1Vy + p2Vy;

//Finally, assign the bounce vector to the spaceship's velocity.
//Add an optional damping value
ship.vx = bounceVx * 0.8;
ship.vy = bounceVy * 0.8;
```

And that makes the ship bounce!

You can see in the last line that the bounce vector is multiplied by 0.8. That reduces the bounce force by 20%, which simulates loss of energy when the ship hits the line. Optionally, you can multiply the bounce vector by another number to exaggerate or dampen the bounce effect. A number greater than 1 will make the bounce force more powerful than the original collision force, which creates a trampoline effect. 0 means that there's no bounce at all.

Bounce solved!

Circle Collisions

Congratulations, you've just graduated from vector math boot camp! Now let's find out how to use our new vector skills to solve some really interesting collision problems. First up: collisions between circles. Circle collisions fall into three categories:

- General circle collision detection.

- Reactive collisions between moving circles and stationary circles.

- Reactive collisions between moving circles.

Let's first consider the easiest problem to solve: detecting a collision between any two circles.

General Circle Collision Detection

In this book we've been using a function called hitTestCircle to find out whether two circular sprites are touching:

```
hitTestCircle(sprite1, sprite2)
```

Use it with any sprite that has a radius property. It returns true if the circles are touching.

Here's the hitTestCircle function from the library/collision.js file that does this work. It first plots a vector between the center points of each circular sprite (c1 and c2). If the magnitude of that vector is less than the combined radii of both circles, then you know the circles are touching.

```
export function hitTestCircle(c1, c2, global = false) {

  let vx, vy, magnitude, combinedRadii, hit;

  //Calculate the vector between the circles' center points
  if(global) {

    //Use global coordinates
    vx = (c2.gx + c2.radius) - (c1.gx + c1.radius);
    vy = (c2.gy + c2.radius) - (c1.gy + c1.radius);
  } else {

    //Use local coordinates
    vx = c2.centerX - c1.centerX;
    vy = c2.centerY - c1.centerY;
  }

  //Find the distance between the circles by calculating
  //the vector's magnitude
  magnitude = Math.sqrt(vx * vx + vy * vy);

  //Add together the circles' combined radii
  combinedRadii = c1.radius + c2.radius;

  //Set `hit` to `true` if the distance between the circles is
  //less than their ` combinedRadii `
  hit = magnitude < combinedRadii;

  //`hit` will be either `true` or `false`
  return hit;
};
```

Figure A-26 shows how this works.

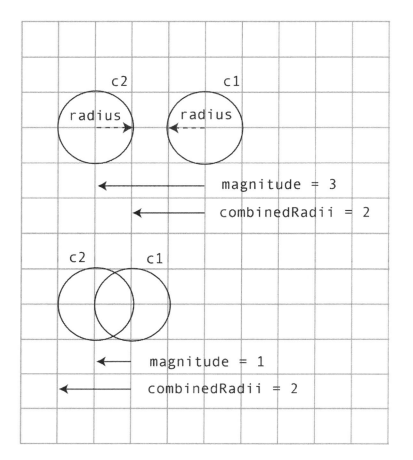

Figure A-26. *A collision occurs when the magnitude of the vector between the circles is less than their combined radii*

The next step is to create a collision reaction by separating the circles when they touch.

Reactive Collision between a Moving and a Stationary Circle

How do you separate circles when they collide? The code you use is slightly different depending on whether one or both of the circles in the collision are moving. Let's first find out how to handle a collision between a moving circle (c1) and stationary circle (c2).

First, find out by how much the circles are overlapping. Subtract the magnitude of the distance vector between the circles from the circles' combined radii to figure this out.

```
overlap = combinedRadii - magnitude;
```

Figure A-27 illustrates how this overlap value is found.

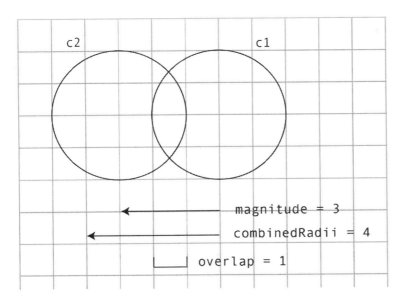

```
overlap = combinedRadii - magnitude
overlap = 4 - 3
overlap = 1
```

Figure A-27. *Find the amount of overlap*

Next, normalize the distance vector to find its dx and dy values:

```
dx = vx / magnitude;
dy = vy / magnitude;
```

Multiply the dx and dy values by the overlap value, and subtract those new values from the moving circle's x and y position.

```
c1.x -= overlap * dx;
c1.y -= overlap * dy;
```

That gives you a perfectly clean separation between the circles. Figure A-28 illustrates how this code works.

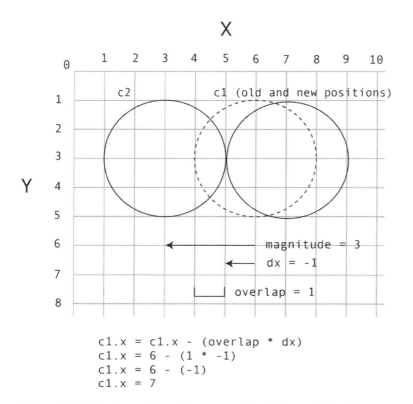

```
c1.x = c1.x - (overlap * dx)
c1.x = 6 - (1 * -1)
c1.x = 6 - (-1)
c1.x = 7
```

Figure A-28. *Use the overlap value to move the circle out of the collision*

Quantum Padding

This math works fine in a perfect, laboratory situation. Think clean rooms, white lab coats and Bunsen burners. But unfortunately, the world of a video game programing is a lot messier. Think pajamas, pizza, and hangovers. Our programming world is full of floating-point rounding errors, velocity spikes, complex collision environments, lots of colliding objects jostling around, and sprite positions that are being updated in different orders. In some extreme situations this accurate math doesn't always translate into seamless collisions on screen. To smooth out any potential mathematical spikes, I like to add a bit of what I call **quantum padding** around colliding circles. Quantum padding is just an extra, tiny, value that's added to the overlap value so that the colliding sprites separate just slightly more than the pure math says they should.

To implement quantum padding, add an arbitrary small number to the overlap value. 0.3 generally works well:

```
let quantumPadding = 0.3;
overlap += quantumPadding;
```

The padding adds a tiny amount of space between the circles to reduce their surface tension and make them more slippery. A value of 0.3 is a good place to start, but you might need to modify it slightly depending on the exact behavior you want. Too little padding and the colliding circles will feel sticky; too much and they could start to jitter if they're jammed together.

Quantum padding is purely my own invention. I started adding it after years of experimentation to improve the aesthetic appearance of certain kinds of collisions. In the real world, atomic particles and surfaces never actually touch each other; all particles are separated by quantum forces that push each other away before they come into physical contact. Quantum padding simulates these forces, and it seems to work well with circle collisions.

The `circleCollision` Function

In this book we've been using the `circleCollision` function to make a moving circle bounce off a stationary circle. Here's the complete `circleCollision` function that implements all this theory. You'll notice that if the bounce parameter is `true`, another function called bounceOffSurface is called. I'll explain how that works in the next section.

```
export function circleCollision(c1, c2, bounce = false, global = false) {

  let magnitude, combinedRadii, overlap,
      vx, vy, dx, dy, s = {},
      hit = false;

  //Calculate the vector between the circles' center points

  if(global) {

    //Use global coordinates
    vx = (c2.gx + c2.radius) - (c1.gx + c1.radius);
    vy = (c2.gy + c2.radius) - (c1.gy + c1.radius);
  } else {

    //Use local coordinates
    vx = c2.centerX - c1.centerX;
    vy = c2.centerY - c1.centerY;
  }

  //Find the distance between the circles by calculating
  //the vector's magnitude
  magnitude = Math.sqrt(vx * vx + vy * vy);

  //Add together the circles' combined half-widths
  combinedRadii = c1.radius + c2.radius;

  //Figure out if there's a collision
  if (magnitude < combinedRadii) {

    //Yes, a collision is happening
    hit = true;

    //Find the amount of overlap between the circles
    overlap = combinedRadii - magnitude;
```

```
//Add some "quantum padding"
let quantumPadding = 0.3;
overlap += quantumPadding;

//Normalize the vector
//These numbers tell us the direction of the collision
dx = vx / magnitude;
dy = vy / magnitude;

//Move circle 1 out of the collision by multiplying
//the overlap with the normalized vector and subtract it from
//circle 1's position
c1.x -= overlap * dx;
c1.y -= overlap * dy;

//Bounce
if (bounce) {

    //Create a collision vector object, `s`, to represent the bounce "surface".
    //Find the bounce surface's x and y properties
    //(This represents the normal of the distance vector between the circles)
    s.x = vy;
    s.y = -vx;

    //Bounce c1 off the surface
    //(I'll explain this ahead)
    bounceOffSurface(c1, s);
  }
}
return hit;
}
```

Bouncing Circles

There's a trick to making circles bounce away at the correct angle. Pretend that the circle is hitting an imaginary wall created by the normal of the distance vector between them. All you need to do is bounce c1's motion vector against this imaginary wall. It's the same solution to the problem of bouncing the spaceship against the line that we looked at earlier in this appendix. The only difference is that we can't "see" the line that the circle is bouncing against; it just exists mathematically. Figure A-29 shows what this imaginary wall created by the distance vector's normal would look like if it were visible (it's the dotted line in the diagram).

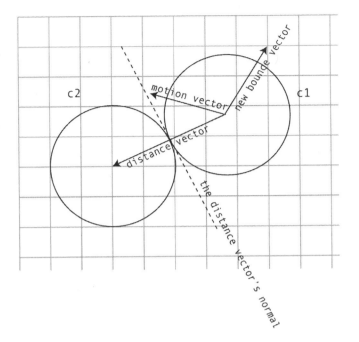

Figure A-29. Bounce the circle against an imaginary wall (the dotted line) created by the distance vector's normal

If you can bounce a point off a line, you can bounce anything off anything else—it's all the same problem. That means it makes sense to create a generic bounce function that you can use with points, lines, circles and rectangles. That same bounce function can work for all of those elements. In the library/collision.js file you'll find a function called bounceOffSurface that does this. Here's how the code from the circleCollision function uses bounceOffSurface to bounce the circles apart.

//Create a vector to represent the bounce surface
```
let s = {};
```

//Set the surface vector's x and y properties to the
//distance vector's left normal
```
s.x = vy;
s.y = -vx;
```

//Bounce c1 (the moving circle) off the surface
```
bounceOffSurface(c1, s);
```

Here's the complete bounceOffSurface function that creates the bounce effect. You'll see that the code uses all the same vector techniques to make an object bounce that we looked at earlier in this appendix. If the sprite in the collision has a mass property, that value will be used to dampen the bounce effect. (In this code, the variable o stands for "object". It can be any object, such as a sprite, with x, y, vx and vy properties.)

```javascript
function bounceOffSurface(o, s) {
  let dp1, dp2,
      p1 = {},
      p2 = {},
      bounce = {},
      mass = o.mass || 1;

  //1. Calculate the collision surface's properties

  //Find the surface vector's left normal
  s.lx = s.y;
  s.ly = -s.x;

  //Find its magnitude
  s.magnitude = Math.sqrt(s.x * s.x + s.y * s.y);

  //Find its normalized values
  s.dx = s.x / s.magnitude;
  s.dy = s.y / s.magnitude;

  //2. Bounce the object (o) off the surface (s)

  //Find the dot product between the object and the surface
  dp1 = o.vx * s.dx + o.vy * s.dy;

  //Project the object's velocity onto the collision surface
  p1.vx = dp1 * s.dx;
  p1.vy = dp1 * s.dy;

  //Find the dot product of the object and the surface's left normal (s.lx and s.ly)
  dp2 = o.vx * (s.lx / s.magnitude) + o.vy * (s.ly / s.magnitude);

  //Project the object's velocity onto the surface's left normal
  p2.vx = dp2 * (s.lx / s.magnitude);
  p2.vy = dp2 * (s.ly / s.magnitude);

  //Reverse the projection on the surface's left normal
  p2.vx *= -1;
  p2.vy *= -1;

  //Add up the projections to create a new bounce vector
  bounce.x = p1.vx + p2.vx;
  bounce.y = p1.vy + p2.vy;

  //Assign the bounce vector to the object's velocity
  //with optional mass to dampen the effect
  o.vx = bounce.x / mass;
  o.vy = bounce.y / mass;
}
```

You can use bounceOffSurface to bounce any sprite off any surface. Just identify or create a surface vector, and then find a sprite with *x*, *y*, *vx* and *vy* properties that you can use to bounce against it.

Reactive Collisions between Moving Circles

In games like billiards or marbles, you'll need both circles in a collision to react. When the circles collide, each circle transfers its motion force to the other circle.

When the collision occurs, you need to separate the circles and then figure out their new bounce velocities. These are the same concepts we looked at in earlier examples. However, when both circles are in motion, there are some important differences:

- **Separation**: If one circle is moving and the other isn't, it's easy to separate them in a collision. We did this in the first example in this chapter by simply positioning the moving circle at the boundary of the stationary circle. But when both circles are moving, where is that boundary? You need to find a compromise position: separate each by a proportional amount. Luckily, a very simple formula can help us do that.

- **Bounce**: When moving circles collide, their new bounce vectors are not only determined by the angle of collision, but also by the force with which the other circle is hitting it. The circles need to transfer their motion vectors to each other. Again, there are no big surprises here, and you already have the tools you need for the solution.

First, figure out by how much the circles are overlapping.

```
overlap = combinedRadii - magnitude;
```

Next, create a collision vector. This will give us the vx and vy values we need to separate the circles. This vector must be divided in half so that we can share it between the two circles. One half will go to circle 1, and the other half will go to circle 2.

```
dx = vx / magnitude;
dy = vy / magnitude;

vxHalf = Math.abs(dx * overlap / 2);
vyHalf = Math.abs(dy * overlap / 2);
```

The vx and vy values need to be absolute (without a plus or minus sign). We need these values to be neutral because we want the flexibility to decide whether to add or subtract this vector to each circle's position (you'll see how in the next step). Figure A-30 illustrates how these calculations are found.

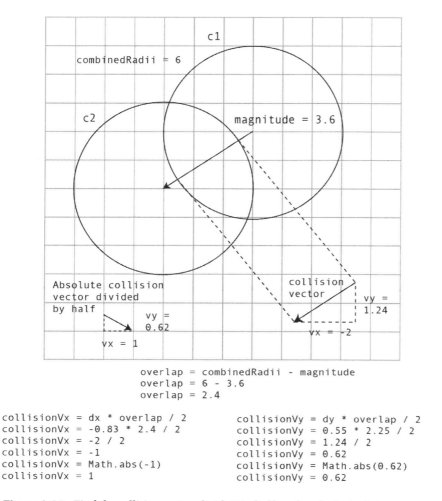

```
overlap = combinedRadii - magnitude
overlap = 6 - 3.6
overlap = 2.4
```

```
collisionVx = dx * overlap / 2
collisionVx = -0.83 * 2.4 / 2
collisionVx = -2 / 2
collisionVx = -1
collisionVx = Math.abs(-1)
collisionVx = 1
```

```
collisionVy = dy * overlap / 2
collisionVy = 0.55 * 2.25 / 2
collisionVy = 1.24 / 2
collisionVy = 0.62
collisionVy = Math.abs(0.62)
collisionVy = 0.62
```

Figure A-30. *Find the collision vector, divide it in half, and make it absolute*

The next question to ask: Is the first circle above, below, to the right of, or to the left of the second circle? We need to know this so that we can correctly add or subtract the overlap vector to or from each circle's position. The easiest way to track it is by creating variables that are assigned 1 or –1, depending on where the circles are in relation to each other. Here's some terse JavaScript syntax that will find this value for you:

```
(c1.x > c2.x) ? xSide = 1 : xSide = -1;
(c1.y > c2.y) ? ySide = 1 : ySide = -1;
```

We need to push the circles apart to resolve the collision. For example, on the *x* axis, we'll need to push one circle to the left and the other to the right. The collision vector will be the correct direction for one of the circles, but not the other. However, we know that the directions the circles need to move in will be the polar opposites of each other. That means we can use the xSide and ySide variables (which will be 1 or –1) to correctly invert one of the vectors:

```
//Move c1 out of the collision
c1.x = c1.x + (vxHalf * xSide);
c1.y = c1.y + (vyHalf * ySide);
```

```
//Move c2 out of the collision
c2.x = c2.x + (vxHalf * -xSide);
c2.y = c2.y + (vyHalf * -ySide);
```

The orientation of the circles will always be changing, so we can never know which circle's overlap vector to invert. Luckily, the xSide and ySide variables keep track of that for us automatically. Figure A-31 shows how the circles' new positions are found.

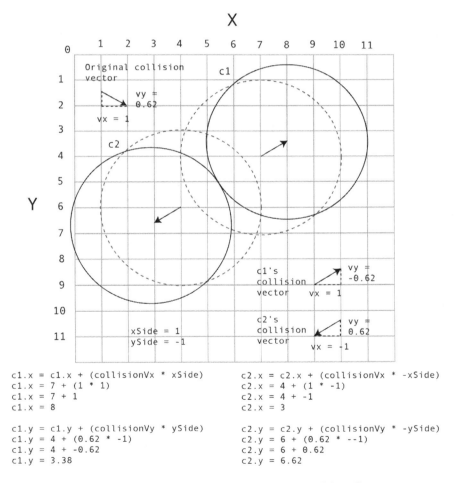

```
c1.x = c1.x + (collisionVx * xSide)        c2.x = c2.x + (collisionVx * -xSide)
c1.x = 7 + (1 * 1)                         c2.x = 4 + (1 * -1)
c1.x = 7 + 1                               c2.x = 4 + -1
c1.x = 8                                   c2.x = 3

c1.y = c1.y + (collisionVy * ySide)        c2.y = c2.y + (collisionVy * -ySide)
c1.y = 4 + (0.62 * -1)                     c2.y = 6 + (0.62 * --1)
c1.y = 4 + -0.62                           c2.y = 6 + 0.62
c1.y = 3.38                                c2.y = 6.62
```

Figure A-31. *Use the collision vector to move the circles out of the collision*

After you've separated the circles this way, you can bounce them apart using the same techniques we've used in the other examples.

In this book I've used the movingCircleCollision function to make moving circles bounce apart. Here's the complete code for the movingCircleCollision function that implements all these techniques, including the bounce code. (In this code, s represents the distance vector between the two circles.)

```
export function movingCircleCollision(c1, c2, global = false) {

  let combinedRadii, overlap, xSide, ySide,
      //`s` refers to the distance vector between the circles
      s = {},
      p1A = {}, p1B = {}, p2A = {}, p2B = {},
      hit = false;

  //Apply mass, if the circles have mass properties
  c1.mass = c1.mass || 1;
  c2.mass = c2.mass || 1;

  //Calculate the vector between the circles' center points
  if(global) {

    //Use global coordinates
    s.vx = (c2.gx + c2.radius) - (c1.gx + c1.radius);
    s.vy = (c2.gy + c2.radius) - (c1.gy + c1.radius);
  } else {

    //Use local coordinates
    s.vx = c2.centerX - c1.centerX;
    s.vy = c2.centerY - c1.centerY;
  }

  //Find the distance between the circles by calculating
  //the vector's magnitude
  s.magnitude = Math.sqrt(s.vx * s.vx + s.vy * s.vy);

  //Add together the circles' combined half-widths
  combinedRadii = c1.radius + c2.radius;

  //Figure out if there's a collision
  if (s.magnitude < combinedRadii) {

    //Yes, a collision is happening
    hit = true;

    //Find the amount of overlap between the circles
    overlap = combinedRadii - s.magnitude;

    //Add some "quantum padding" to the overlap
    overlap += 0.3;
```

```
//Normalize the vector.
//These numbers tell us the direction of the collision
s.dx = s.vx / s.magnitude;
s.dy = s.vy / s.magnitude;

//Find the collision vector.
//Divide it in half to share between the circles, and make it absolute
s.vxHalf = Math.abs(s.dx * overlap / 2);
s.vyHalf = Math.abs(s.dy * overlap / 2);

//Find the side on which the collision is occurring
(c1.x > c2.x) ? xSide = 1 : xSide = -1;
(c1.y > c2.y) ? ySide = 1 : ySide = -1;

//Move c1 out of the collision by multiplying
//the overlap with the normalized vector and adding it to
//the circles' positions
c1.x = c1.x + (s.vxHalf * xSide);
c1.y = c1.y + (s.vyHalf * ySide);

//Move c2 out of the collision
c2.x = c2.x + (s.vxHalf * -xSide);
c2.y = c2.y + (s.vyHalf * -ySide);

//Now that the circles have been separated, you can bounce
//them apart. The code below does this in 4 major, numbered steps:

//1. Calculate the collision surface's properties

//Find the surface vector's left normal
s.lx = s.vy;
s.ly = -s.vx;

//2. Bounce c1 off the surface (s)

//Find the dot product between c1 and the surface
let dp1 = c1.vx * s.dx + c1.vy * s.dy;

//Project c1's velocity onto the collision surface
p1A.x = dp1 * s.dx;
p1A.y = dp1 * s.dy;

//Find the dot product of c1 and the surface's left normal (s.lx and s.ly)
let dp2 = c1.vx * (s.lx / s.magnitude) + c1.vy * (s.ly / s.magnitude);

//Project c1's velocity onto the surface's left normal
p1B.x = dp2 * (s.lx / s.magnitude);
p1B.y = dp2 * (s.ly / s.magnitude);
```

```
//3. Bounce c2 off the surface (s)

//Find the dot product between c2 and the surface
let dp3 = c2.vx * s.dx + c2.vy * s.dy;

//Project c2's velocity onto the collision surface
p2A.x = dp3 * s.dx;
p2A.y = dp3 * s.dy;

//Find the dot product of c2 and the surface's left normal (s.lx and s.ly)
let dp4 = c2.vx * (s.lx / s.magnitude) + c2.vy * (s.ly / s.magnitude);

//Project c2's velocity onto the surface's left normal
p2B.x = dp4 * (s.lx / s.magnitude);
p2B.y = dp4 * (s.ly / s.magnitude);

//4. Calculate the bounce vectors

//Bounce c1 using p1B and p2A
c1.bounce = {};
c1.bounce.x = p1B.x + p2A.x;
c1.bounce.y = p1B.y + p2A.y;

//Bounce c2 using p1A and p2B
c2.bounce = {};
c2.bounce.x = p1A.x + p2B.x;
c2.bounce.y = p1A.y + p2B.y;

//Add the bounce vector to the circles' velocity
//and add mass if the circle has a mass property
c1.vx = c1.bounce.x / c1.mass;
c1.vy = c1.bounce.y / c1.mass;
c2.vx = c2.bounce.x / c2.mass;
c2.vy = c2.bounce.y / c2.mass;
  }
  return hit;
}
```

And, with that, we're done with circles!

Rectangle Collisions

Rectangle collisions are probably the most common kinds of collision you'll need to detect in games. There are two basic types of detection required:

- General rectangle collision detection

- Calculating reactive collisions between a stationary and a moving rectangle

Both techniques rely on a widely used and reliable collision detection technique for polygons called the separating axis theorem (SAT).

The Separating Axis Theorem

The separating axis theorem, first formulated by legendary computer scientist Stefan Gottschalk, is widely regarded as the most efficient way to check whether polygons are colliding. It's also pretty easy to understand:

- If there is any axis (*x* or *y*) on which any two objects *don't* overlap, then there's no collision between the objects. In the case of two rectangles, this means that if the rectangles overlap on the *x* axis but not the *y* axis, they're not colliding. The axis on which they don't intersect is the **separating axis** that gives the theorem its name.

- If the objects overlap on all their axes (both *x* and *y*), then a collision has occurred.

- The axis with the least amount of overlap is the axis on which the collision is occurring.

In any game, the chance that two objects are *not* colliding is far greater than that they are colliding. The SAT capitalizes on this fact. It's very efficient because you can find out immediately whether two objects are overlapping just by testing one axis. If there's no overlap on that axis, you have your answer: there's no collision. It's a quick escape, and you've just saved yourself some processing power. You don't need to bother testing any of the other axes.

In the case of rectangles, this means you can reduce collision checks by up to half. In the case of a complex polygon, such as a hexagon, it means only a third as many collision checks are needed.

However, if you find that two objects are overlapping on one axis, it doesn't mean that the objects are actually colliding. It means that they *could be*, but you don't know yet. So you next need to check another axis to be sure. In the case of rectangles, if you find an overlap on both the *x* and *y* axes, then the rectangles are definitely overlapping and you have a collision. If you find any axis without an overlap, then there's no collision, and you can stop further checking.

Imagine that you need to check for a collision between two squares on the stage. In pseudo code, a basic SAT algorithm for squares looks like this:

```
if(the squares overlap on the x axis) {

  //There might be a collision! Let's check:

  if(the squares overlap on the y axis){

    //The squares overlap on both axes, so there's definitely a collision
    //The collision is occurring on the axis with the smallest amount of overlap

  } else {

    //There's no overlap on the y axis, so there's no collision

  }
} else {

  //There's no overlap on the x axis, so there's no collision

}
```

What do I mean by "if the squares overlap on the *x* or *y* axis"?

Figure A-32 depicts two squares on the screen. We can see that they're obviously not intersecting. But we need to find a way to describe their status in programming code.

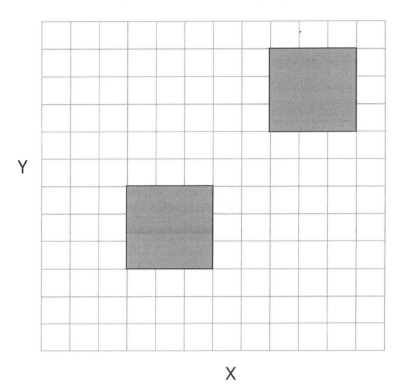

Y

X

Figure A-32. *Two squares that are not intersecting. How can we describe this in code?*

To check whether the squares are intersecting, we don't need to check all four sides of each square against all four sides of the other square. We just need to check whether the sides of the squares are intersecting on the two axes: *x* and *y*. To do this, we need to use projection. We must project each square onto the *x* and *y* axes. You'll recall that the projection of a shape is the shadow it casts if you were standing behind it shining a light. In this case, each square needs to cast two shadows: one shadow onto the *x* axis and another onto the *y* axis. Figure A-33 illustrates this.

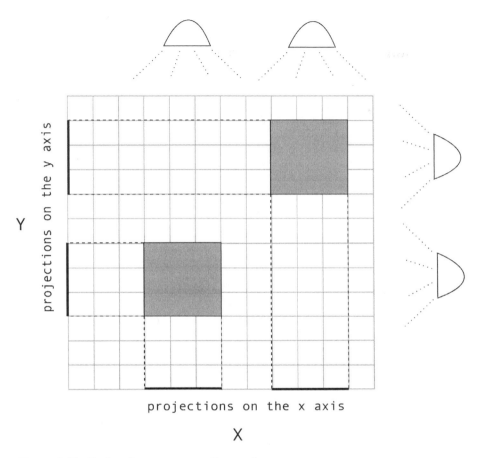

Figure A-33. *Project the squares onto the x and y axes*

Because the rectangle is aligned to the stage's *x* and *y* axes, its height and width equal its projections. This means we don't have to do any math to work out the projection values—we can just use a rectangle's height and width as is.

■ **Note**   In technical collision detection literature, squares or rectangles whose sides are aligned to the *x* and *y* axes are called **axis-aligned bounding boxes**, or **AABBs**. In other words, the game world is rectangular, and the squares are rectangular. Nothing is rotated. This is the simplest collision scenario you can have. Game designers will often wrap odd-shaped, nonrectangular objects in AABBs because using them for collision detection is extremely fast.

What happens if the squares overlap on the *x* axis? Let's find out.

In Figure A-34, you can see that the top square has moved to the left. The projections of both squares are now overlapping on the *x* axis.

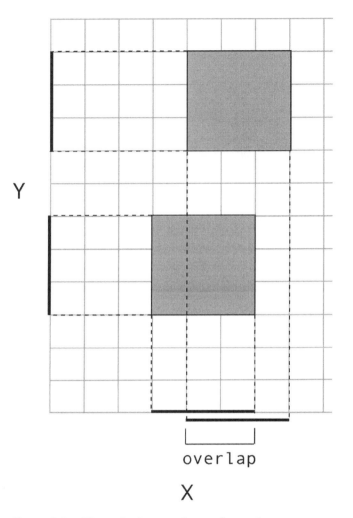

overlap

X

Figure A-34. *The projections overlap on the x axis*

Of course, you can see that even though they overlap on the *x* axis, the squares still don't intersect—so there's no collision. Now let's push the example further and see what happens when the squares overlap on the *y* axis as well, as in Figure A-35.

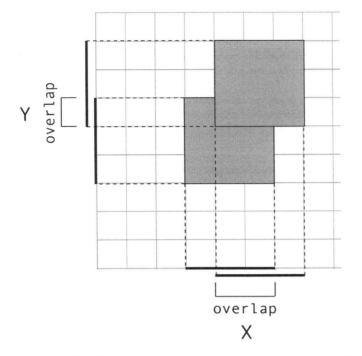

Figure A-35. *The squares overlap on both axes, so we have a collision. The collision occurs on the y axis, which has the least overlap*

The squares are now clearly intersecting. You can also tell that the collision is happening on the y axis, because that's the axis with the smallest amount of overlap.

The next step is to figure out by how much the squares are overlapping. We need a distance vector that runs between the centers of both squares. The distance vector also needs to be projected onto each axis, as shown in Figure A-36.

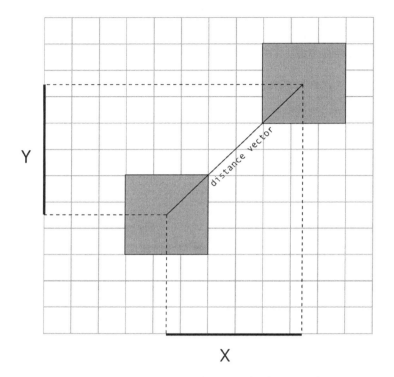

Figure A-36. *Plot a distance vector between the shapes and project it onto the x and y axes*

Use the distance vector's projections to measure the distance between the centers of the projections of the squares on each axis, as illustrated in Figure A-37.

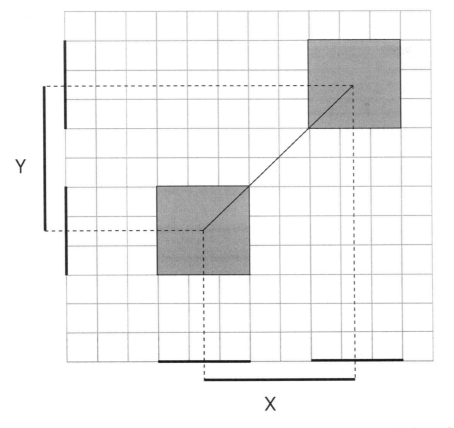

Figure A-37. *Measure the distance between the projections of the shapes to find out whether they overlap*

Add the projections of the shapes together and divide that number in half. If the magnitude of the projected distance vector is less than that value, then the shapes overlap on that axis.

This is much easier to see in pictures than it is to read, so take a good look at Figure A-38. (The convention I'm using is that variable names that start with p refer to projection vectors.)

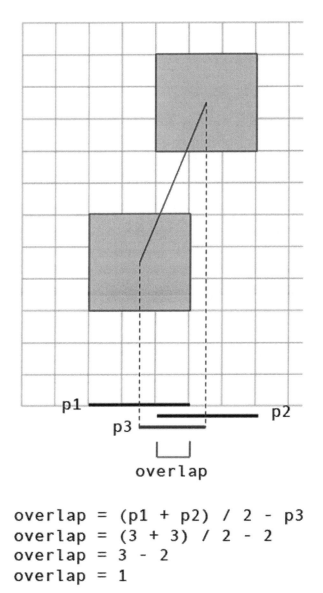

```
overlap = (p1 + p2) / 2 - p3
overlap = (3 + 3) / 2 - 2
overlap = 3 - 2
overlap = 1
```

Figure A-38. *Calculate the overlap*

If you know the overlap, you can resolve the collision; just move one of the squares out of the collision area by the same amount.

Now that we know on which axis the collision is happening, we need to find on which side of the square it's taking place. This is easy to figure out by checking whether the distance vector's vx and vy are greater or less than zero.

- If the collision is happening on the *x* axis, is it happening on the right or left side of the square? Find the distance vector's vx. If it's greater than zero, the collision is happening on the right. If it's less than zero, the collision is on the left.

- If the collision is happening on the *y* axis, is it happening on the top or bottom side of the square? Find the distance vector's vy. If it's greater than zero, the collision is happening on the top. If it's less than zero, the collision is on the bottom.

Figure A-39 shows how to find the collision side.

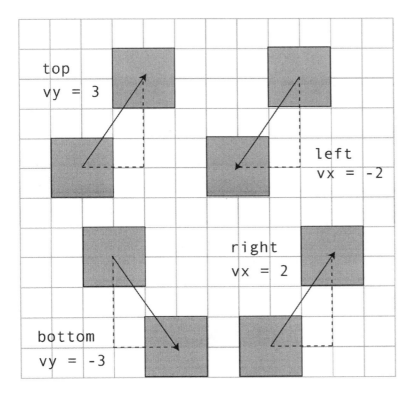

```
Y Axis

if(vy > 0){
    side = top
}
else{
    side = bottom
}
```

```
X Axis

if(vx > 0){
    side = right
}
else{
    side = left
}
```

Figure A-39. *Find the collision side*

These are the general fundamentals of a SAT-based collision detection system. This basic theory applies to all shapes, no matter how complex. I've used squares in these examples to keep things simple, but you can apply the same techniques to rotated rectangles or polygons with any number of sides. When you're ready to start doing more complex collision detection that goes beyond what we've done in this book, this is the theory that you can use as the foundation for your collision system.

But, as you'll see next, it's very easy to apply this theory to nonrotated rectangles.

■ **Caution**   There's one limitation of using an SAT-based collision system that you need to be aware of. If objects are moving very quickly, the axis with the least overlap might not be the one on which the collision is occurring. In that case, use a different collision technique. Plot a vector from the center of your fast-moving object in the direction of its motion vector. Test points along the vector at fixed intervals to see if they're intersecting any shapes. If any of them are, you have a collision and you can decide how to resolve that collision. (You'll find out how to test for a collision between a point and shape in the pages ahead).

General Rectangle Collision Testing

In this book I've used a function called `hitTestRectangle` to tell you whether two rectangular sprites are colliding. It simply returns `true` or `false`, depending on whether or not there's a collision. It implements the basic SAT theory. But because a nonrotated rectangle's width and height are equivalent to its x and y projections, we can skip the projection calculations and just use the existing width and height values in their place. Here's the complete `hitTestRectangle` function:

```
export function hitTestRectangle(r1, r2, global = false) {

  let hit, combinedHalfWidths, combinedHalfHeights, vx, vy;

  //A variable to determine whether there's a collision
  hit = false;

  //Calculate the distance vector
  if(global) {
    vx = (r1.gx + r1.halfWidth) - (r2.gx + r2.halfWidth);
    vy = (r1.gy + r1.halfHeight) - (r2.gy + r2.halfHeight);
  } else {
    vx = r1.centerX - r2.centerX;
    vy = r1.centerY - r2.centerY;
  }

  //Figure out the combined half-widths and half-heights
  combinedHalfWidths = r1.halfWidth + r2.halfWidth;
  combinedHalfHeights = r1.halfHeight + r2.halfHeight;

  //Check for a collision on the x axis
  if (Math.abs(vx) < combinedHalfWidths) {
```

```
//A collision might be occurring. Check for a collision on the y axis
if (Math.abs(vy) < combinedHalfHeights) {

  //There's definitely a collision happening
  hit = true;
} else {

  //There's no collision on the y axis
  hit = false;
}
} else {

  //There's no collision on the x axis
  hit = false;
}

//`hit` will be either `true` or `false`
return hit;
}
```

The hitTestRectangle function doesn't resolve the collision; it just returns true or false. To make rectangles react to a collision, let's use another function, called rectangleCollision.

Reactive Rectangle Collisions

The rectangleCollision function tests for a collision, pushes the colliding sprites apart, and optionally bounces the first sprite off the second sprite. It also checks on which side the first rectangle hit the second rectangle and returns a string that tells you: top, bottom, left or right. It implements a very simple bounce system, but if you prefer, you could optionally use the bounceOffSurface function to bounce the rectangles apart. Here's the complete rectangleCollision function:

```
export function  rectangleCollision(
  r1, r2, bounce = false, global = true
) {

  let collision, combinedHalfWidths, combinedHalfHeights,
      overlapX, overlapY, vx, vy;

  //Calculate the distance vector
  if(global) {
    vx = (r1.gx + r1.halfWidth) - (r2.gx + r2.halfWidth);
    vy = (r1.gy + r1.halfHeight) - (r2.gy + r2.halfHeight);
  } else {
    vx = r1.centerX - r2.centerX;
    vy = r1.centerY - r2.centerY;
  }

  //Figure out the combined half-widths and half-heights
  combinedHalfWidths = r1.halfWidth + r2.halfWidth;
  combinedHalfHeights = r1.halfHeight + r2.halfHeight;
```

```
//Check whether vx is less than the combined half widths
if (Math.abs(vx) < combinedHalfWidths) {

  //A collision might be occurring!
  //Check whether vy is less than the combined half heights
  if (Math.abs(vy) < combinedHalfHeights) {

    //A collision has occurred! This is good!
    //Find out the size of the overlap on both the X and Y axes
    overlapX = combinedHalfWidths - Math.abs(vx);
    overlapY = combinedHalfHeights - Math.abs(vy);

    //The collision has occurred on the axis with the
    //*smallest* amount of overlap. Let's figure out which
    //axis that is

    if (overlapX >= overlapY) {

      //The collision is happening on the X axis
      //But on which side? vy can tell us

      if (vy > 0) {
        collision = "top";

        //Move the rectangle out of the collision
        r1.y = r1.y + overlapY;
      } else {
        collision = "bottom";

        //Move the rectangle out of the collision
        r1.y = r1.y - overlapY;
      }

      //Bounce
      if (bounce) {
        r1.vy *= -1;

        /*Alternative
        //Find the bounce surface's vx and vy properties
        let s = {};
        s.vx = r2.x - r2.x + r2.width;
        s.vy = 0;

        //Bounce r1 off the surface
        bounceOffSurface(r1, s);
        */

      }
    } else {
```

```
    //The collision is happening on the Y axis
    //But on which side? vx can tell us

    if (vx > 0) {
      collision = "left";

      //Move the rectangle out of the collision
      r1.x = r1.x + overlapX;
    } else {
      collision = "right";

      //Move the rectangle out of the collision
      r1.x = r1.x - overlapX;
    }

    //Bounce
    if (bounce) {
      r1.vx *= -1;

      /*Alternative
      //Find the bounce surface's vx and vy properties
      let s = {};
      s.vx = 0;
      s.vy = r2.y - r2.y + r2.height;

      //Bounce r1 off the surface
      bounceOffSurface(r1, s);
      */

    }
  }
} else {

  //No collision
  }
} else {

  //No collision
}

//Return the collision string. It will be either "top", "right",
//"bottom", or "left" depending on which side of r1 is touching r2.
return collision;
}
```

You can see in this code that the bounce effect is created by simply multiplying the first rectangle's velocity by –1.

```
r1.vy *= -1;
r1.vx *= -1;
```

That's all we need to do. Because the rectangles aren't rotated, we don't have to work out any complicated projections or bounce vectors off angles as we did with circles.

Collisions between Circles and Rectangles

You now know how to code collisions between circles and between rectangles. But how do you code a collision between a circle and rectangle? You need to break it into two parts:

- When the circle is closer to the sides of the square than it is to the square's corners, it becomes a rectangle-vs.-rectangle collision problem.

- When the circle is closer to any of the corners than it is to the sides, it becomes a circle-vs.-point collision problem. You'll see how to do a circle-vs.-point collision check in the pages ahead.

To know when to use which collision strategy is just a matter of logic, and it is not hard to work out. You just need to find out which region of space (called the **Voronoi region**) the circle occupies, and apply the correct collision strategy for that region. Figure A-40 illustrates where these regions are and which strategy to use for each.

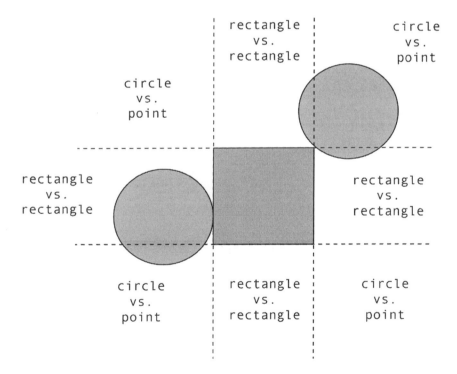

Figure A-40. *Choose the collision strategy based on which region the circle occupies*

You can figure out which region the circle is in by comparing its center position to the square's position, plus its half-height and half-width.

When the circle is in a rectangle-vs.-rectangle region, it literally *becomes* a square for collision purposes, as shown in Figure A-41. It might look like a circle on the screen, but the collision code interprets it as a square.

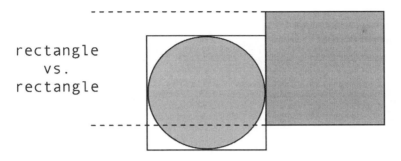

Figure A-41. *The collision code treats the circle as a square when it's in a rectangle-vs.-rectangle region*

When the circle is in a circle-vs.-point region, it completely ignores the square shape and just checks for a collision with the square's closest corner point, as shown in Figure A-42.

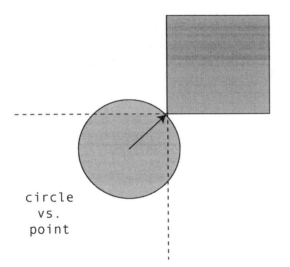

Figure A-42. *The circle checks for a collision with the corner point and ignores the square's sides completely*

Once you know this, all you have to do is write some logic code that figures out which region the circle is in, and apply the appropriate collision strategy.

In the library/collision.js file you'll find the hitTestCircleRectangle function that implements this technique. It first does a simple conditional check to find out where the circle is. If the circle is in a circle-v.-rectangle region, it calls the hitTestRectangle function. If the circle is in the circle-vs.-point region, it calls a function named hitTestCirclePoint (a new function that you'll learn about shortly).

hitTestCircleRectangle returns a value that tells you which region the circle is in. If the return value is undefined, you know that there's been no collision. Here's the complete hitTestCircleRectangle function:

```
export function hitTestCircleRectangle(c1, r1, global = false) {

  let region, collision, c1x, c1y, r1x, r1y;

  //Use either global or local coordinates
  if (global) {
    c1x = c1.gx;
    c1y = c1.gy
    r1x = r1.gx;
    r1y = r1.gy;
  } else {
    c1x = c1.x;
    c1y = c1.y
    r1x = r1.x;
    r1y = r1.y;
  }

  //Is the circle above the rectangle's top edge?
  if(c1y < r1y - r1.halfHeight) {

    //If it is, we need to check whether it's in the
    //top left, top center, or top right.
    //(Increasing the size of the region by 2 pixels slightly weights
    //the text in favor of a rectangle vs. rectangle collision test.
    //This gives a more natural-looking result with corner collisions
    //when physics calculations are added)
    if(c1x < r1x - 1 - r1.halfWidth) {
      region = "topLeft";
    }
    else if (c1x > r1x + 1 + r1.halfWidth) {
      region = "topRight";
    }
    else {
      region = "topMiddle";
    }
  }

  //The circle isn't above the top edge, so it might be
  //below the bottom edge
  else if (c1y > r1y + r1.halfHeight) {

    //If it is, we need to check whether it's in the bottom left,
    //bottom center, or bottom right
    if (c1x < r1x - 1 - r1.halfWidth) {
      region = "bottomLeft";
    }
    else if (c1x > r1x + 1 + r1.halfWidth) {
      region = "bottomRight";
    }
```

```
  else {
    region = "bottomMiddle";
  }
}

//The circle isn't above the top edge or below the bottom edge,
//so it must be on the left or right side
else {
  if (c1x < r1x - r1.halfWidth) {
    region = "leftMiddle";
  }
  else {
    region = "rightMiddle";
  }
}

//Is the circle touching the flat sides
//of the rectangle?
if (region === "topMiddle"
|| region === "bottomMiddle"
|| region === "leftMiddle"
|| region === "rightMiddle") {

  //Yes, it is, so do a standard rectangle vs. rectangle collision test
  collision = hitTestRectangle(c1, r1, global);
}

//The circle is touching one of the corners, so do a
//circle vs. point collision test
else {
  let point = {};

  switch (region) {
    case "topLeft":
      point.x = r1x;
      point.y = r1y;
      break;

    case "topRight":
      point.x = r1x + r1.width;
      point.y = r1y;
      break;

    case "bottomLeft":
      point.x = r1x;
      point.y = r1y + r1.height;
      break;
```

```
    case "bottomRight":
      point.x = r1x + r1.width;
      point.y = r1y + r1.height;
  }

  //Check for a collision between the circle and the point
  collision = hitTestCirclePoint(c1, point, global);
}

//Return the result of the collision.
//The return value will be `undefined` if there's no collision
if (collision) {
  return region;
} else {
  return collision;
}
}
```

You can see that if the circle is in a circle-vs.-point region, the code calls a function named hitTestCirclePoint:

```
collision = hitTestCirclePoint(c1, point, global);
```

But how do you check for a collision between a circle and a point? It's easy: a point is just a very small circle with a diameter of one pixel. So all you need to do is create a point object with a diameter of 1 and a radius of 0.5, and use an ordinary circle-vs.-circle collision test to see if it's touching a circle.

You can create a point object this way:

```
let point = {}
point.x = anyXPosition;
point.y = anyYPosition;
```

Then run it through the hitTestCirclePoint function, which just adds some properties to the point, such as diameter and radius, and then calls and returns an ordinary hitTestCircle function against the supplied circular sprite. If it returns true, you know the point is intersecting the circle:

```
export function hitTestCirclePoint(c1, point, global = false) {
  point.diameter = 1;
  point.radius = 0.5;
  point.centerX = point.x;
  point.centerY = point.y;
  point.gx = point.x;
  point.gy = point.y;
  return hitTestCircle(c1, point, global);
}
```

All of these functions just return true or false if there's a collision between a circle and rectangle. But what if you want to bounce the circle off the edges of the rectangle?

Bouncing Circles Off Rectangles

The `library/collision.js` file contains a function called `circleRectangleCollision`, which makes a circle bounce off a rectangle. The code is identical to `hitTestCircleRectangle` except for two lines. If it detects a collision it calls the `rectangleCollision` or `circlePointCollision` functions to bounce the circle away, depending on which region the circle is in.

```
collision = rectangleCollision(c1, r1, bounce, global);
collision = circlePointCollision(c1, point, bounce, global);
```

We've seen the `rectangleCollision` function earlier in this appendix. The `circlePointCollision` function is almost identical to the `hitTestCirclePoint` function, except that in its final line it calls and returns a `circleCollision` function:

```
export function circlePointCollision(c1, point, bounce = false, global = false) {
  //...the code is the same as hitTestCircleRectangle...
  return circleCollision(c1, point, bounce, global);
}
```

And that's all!

Collision between a Single Point and a Sprite

The `library/collision.js` file contains another useful function, called `hitTestPoint`. Its job is to return `true` or `false` depending on whether a single point (such as the mouse pointer) is intersecting a rectangular or circular sprite. `hitTestPoint` takes two arguments: a point object (with *x* and *y* values) and a sprite. If the sprite is rectangular, the code checks to see if the point is inside the area of the rectangle. If the sprite is circular, it measures the distance between the point and the center of the circle. If that distance is less than the circle's radius, it knows that the point must be intersecting the circle. Here's the complete `hitTestPoint` function that does all this.

```
export function hitTestPoint(point, sprite) {

  let shape, left, right, top, bottom, vx, vy, magnitude, hit;

  //Find out if the sprite is rectangular or circular depending
  //on whether it has a `radius` property
  if (sprite.radius) {
    shape = "circle";
  } else {
    shape = "rectangle";
  }

  //Rectangle
  if (shape === "rectangle") {

    //Get the position of the sprite's edges
    left = sprite.x;
    right = sprite.x + sprite.width;
    top = sprite.y;
    bottom = sprite.y + sprite.height;
```

```
    //Find out if the point is intersecting the rectangle
    hit = point.x > left && point.x < right && point.y > top && point.y < bottom;
  }

  //Circle
  if (shape === "circle") {

    //Find the distance between the point and the
    //center of the circle
    vx = point.x - sprite.centerX,
    vy = point.y - sprite.centerY,
    magnitude = Math.sqrt(vx * vx + vy * vy);

    //The point is intersecting the circle if the magnitude
    //(distance) is less than the circle's radius
    hit = magnitude < sprite.radius;
  }

  //`hit` will be either `true` or `false`
  return hit;
}
```

This is a useful little utility that implements many of the concepts in this appendix.

The Universal `hit` Function

The last collision function we will look at is the universal `hit` function. It automatically detects the kinds of sprites that are being used in the collision and chooses the appropriate collision function for you:

```
hit(spriteOne, spriteTwo, react, bounce, global, extra)
```

(The last argument, `extra`, is an optional callback function you can include with code you want to run if a collision takes place.)

If you want to check a point object for a collision against a sprite, use the point as the first argument, this way:

```
hit({x: 145, y:65}, sprite)
```

The `hit` function also lets you check for a collision between a sprite and an array of sprites. Just include the array as the second argument:

```
hit(ball, bricks.children, true, true, true);
```

`hit` automatically loops through all the sprites in the array for you and checks them against the first sprite. This means you don't have to write your own loop code.

The `hit` function also returns a `collision` object, with a return value that matches the kinds of sprites you're checking.

The `hit` function is convenient because it means you only need to use one function for every game collision problem you need to solve. But it's really just a luxury wrapper for the low-level collision functions you already know, with a bit of logic to figure out which of those collision functions to use. If your game depends on the highest performance possible, just use the lower-level collision functions directly so you don't incur the slight processing debt. It's very little overhead, but it's still overhead.

Here's the complete hit function. The code isn't pretty—it's mostly just a tangle of gnarly conditional checks to find out which collision function to implement. I'm listing it just as reference, in case you need to write a similar universal function of your own. An especially convenient feature is that the hit function will automatically loop through arrays of sprites, which saves you from the extra clutter of filter, for, or forEach loops in your game code—I'll explain in closer detail how that feature works after the code listing.

```
export function hit(
  a, b, react = false, bounce = false, global, extra = undefined
) {

  let collision,
      aIsASprite = a.parent !== undefined,
      bIsASprite = b.parent !== undefined;

  //Check to make sure one of the arguments isn't an array
  if (aIsASprite && b instanceof Array
  || bIsASprite  && a instanceof Array) {

    //If it is, check for a collision between a sprite and an array
    spriteVsArray();
  } else {

    //If one of the arguments isn't an array, find out what type of
    //collision check to run
    collision = findCollisionType(a, b);
    if (collision && extra) extra(collision);
  }

  //Return the result of the collision.
  //It will be `undefined` if there's no collision and `true` if
  //there is a collision. `rectangleCollision` sets `collision` to
  //"top", "bottom", "left" or "right" depending on which side the
  //collision is occurring on
  return collision;

  function findCollisionType(a, b) {

    //Are `a` and `b` both sprites?
    //(We have to check again if this function was called from
    //`spriteVsArray`)
    let aIsASprite = a.parent !== undefined;
    let bIsASprite = b.parent !== undefined;

    if (aIsASprite && bIsASprite) {

      //Yes, but what kind of sprites?
      if(a.diameter && b.diameter) {
```

```
      //They're circles
      return circleVsCircle(a, b);
    }
    else if (a.diameter && !b.diameter) {

      //The first one is a circle and the second is a rectangle
      return circleVsRectangle(a, b);
    }
    else {

      //They're rectangles
      return rectangleVsRectangle(a, b);
    }
  }

  //They're not both sprites, so what are they?
  //Is `a` not a sprite and does it have x and y properties?
  else if (bIsASprite && !(a.x === undefined) && !(a.y === undefined)) {

    //Yes, so this is a point vs. sprite collision test
    return hitTestPoint(a, b);
  }
  else {

    //The user is trying to test some incompatible objects
    throw new Error(
      `I'm sorry, ${a} and ${b} cannot be used together in a collision test.'
    `);
  }
}

function spriteVsArray() {

  //If `a` happens to be the array, flip it around so that it becomes `b`
  if (a instanceof Array) {
    let [a, b] = [b, a];
  }

  //Loop through the array in reverse
  for (let i = b.length - 1; i >= 0; i--) {
    let sprite = b[i];
    collision = findCollisionType(a, sprite);
    if (collision && extra) extra(collision, sprite);
  }
}
```

```
function circleVsCircle(a, b) {

  //If the circles shouldn't react to the collision,
  //just test to see if they're touching
  if(!react) {
    return hitTestCircle(a, b);
  }

  //Yes, the circles should react to the collision
  else {

    //Are they both moving?
    if (a.vx + a.vy !== 0 && b.vx + b.vy !== 0) {

      //Yes, they are both moving
      //(moving circle collisions always bounce apart so there's
      //no need for the third, `bounce`, argument)
      return movingCircleCollision(a, b, global);
    }
    else {

      //No, they're not both moving
      return circleCollision(a, b, bounce, global);
    }
  }
}

function rectangleVsRectangle(a, b) {

  //If the rectangles shouldn't react to the collision, just
  //test to see if they're touching
  if(!react) {
    return hitTestRectangle(a, b, global);
  }
  else {
    return rectangleCollision(a, b, bounce, global);
  }
}

function circleVsRectangle(a, b) {

  //If the rectangles shouldn't react to the collision, just
  //test to see if they're touching
  if(!react) {
    return hitTestCircleRectangle(a, b, global);
  }
  else {
    return circleRectangleCollision(a, b, bounce, global);
  }
}
```

How the hit Function Loops through Arrays

Let's see how the hit function handles arrays of sprites. It first checks to see if either the first or second argument is an array. If either of them is, it calls the spriteVsArray function.

```
if (aIsASprite && b instanceof Array || bIsASprite  && a instanceof Array) {
  spriteVsArray();
}
```

spriteVsArray does the job of looping through the array of sprites.

```
function spriteVsArray() {

  //If `a` happens to be the array, flip it around so that it becomes `b`
  if (a instanceof Array) {
    let [a, b] = [b, a];
  }

  //Loop through the array in reverse
  for (let i = b.length - 1; i >= 0; i--) {
    let sprite = b[i];
    collision = findCollisionType(a, sprite);
    if (collision && extra) extra(collision, sprite);
  }
}
```

The spriteVsArray function expects the array to be the second argument: b. If it isn't—if the first argument, a, happens to be the array—the code flips these values around so that a becomes b. It does this with the help of the JavaScript ES6 destructuring assignment:

```
let [a, b] = [b, a];
```

This is a neat trick that copies the value of b into a and the value of a into b. It saves you from having to use a third, temporary variable to help exchange the values.

Next, the code loops through the array in reverse. (It loops in reverse so that if you remove a sprite from the array during the loop, the removal won't create a hole in the array.) It runs the appropriate collision function and then, if there's a collision, runs an extra callback function that you define:

```
if (collision && extra) extra(collision, sprite);
```

Here's an example of how you could define this extra callback function in your game code. The extra function uses two arguments: the return value of the collision check, and the sprite from the array that was involved in the collision.

```
let playerVsPlatforms = hit(
  gameCharacter, world.platforms, true, false, false,
```

```
//The `extra` function
(collision, platform) => {

    //`collision` tells you the side of the `gameCharacter` sprite
    //on which the collision occurred.
    //`platform` is the sprite from the `world.platforms` array
    //that the player is colliding with

  }
);
```

This is a compact way of doing complex collision checks that gives you a lot of information and low-level control, but it also saves you from having to loop manually through all the sprites in the array.

Summary

This appendix was a deep dive into the world of vector math that gave you all the tools you need to take complete control over the geometry of your game world. You now know what vectors are, and the basic math and concepts you need to know to use them in a wide variety of game scenarios. You've learned not just some useful functions for working with vectors, but also all the low-level skills you need to create your own custom effects. You've also learned how to apply vector math skills to create some useful collision functions that will hold you well for most kinds of 2D action games, and you've learned the basics of the separating axis theorem, which you can use to build custom collision systems if you need to.

Index

Get the eBook for only $5!

Why limit yourself?

Now you can take the weightless companion with you wherever you go and access your content on your PC, phone, tablet, or reader.

Since you've purchased this print book, we're happy to offer you the eBook in all 3 formats for just $5.

Convenient and fully searchable, the PDF version enables you to easily find and copy code—or perform examples by quickly toggling between instructions and applications. The MOBI format is ideal for your Kindle, while the ePUB can be utilized on a variety of mobile devices.

To learn more, go to https://www.apress.com/index.php/companion or contact support@apress.com.